St. Peter Port – July 10th 2002.

St. Peter Port – July 10th 2002.

North Brittany &
the Channel Islands

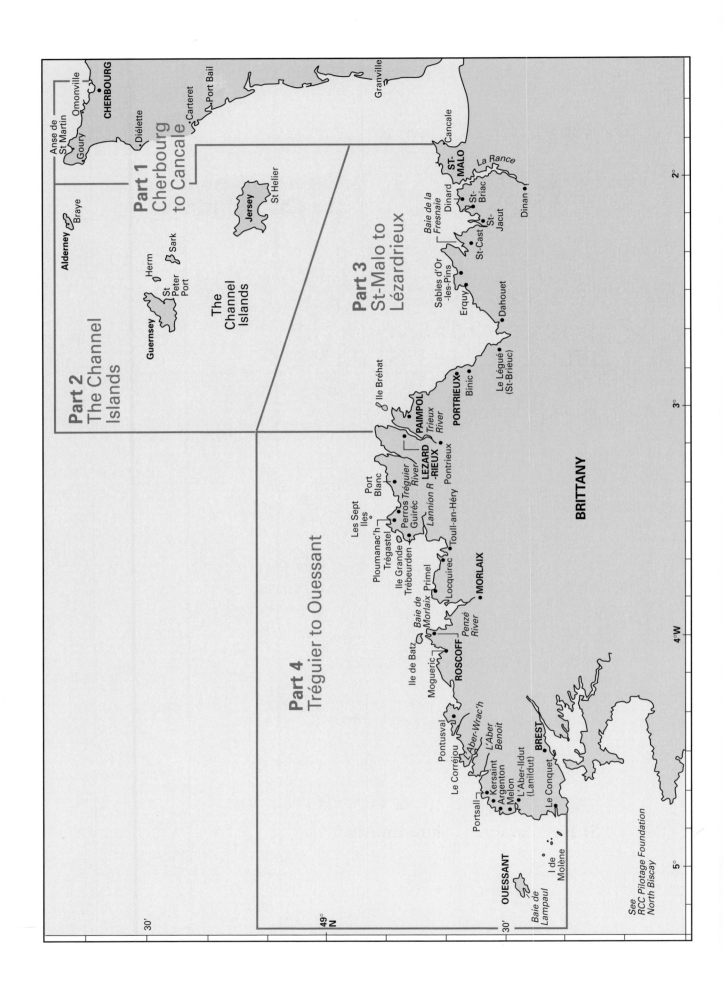

Part 2
The Channel Islands

Part 1
Cherbourg to Cancale

Part 3
St-Malo to
Lézardrieux

Part 4
Tréguier to Ouessant

CHERBOURG

Omonville
Anse de
St Martin
Goury
Diélette
Carteret
Port Bail
Granville

Alderney
Braye

Guernsey
St
Peter
Port
Herm
Sark

Jersey
St Helier

The
Channel
Islands

Cancale

ST-
MALO
La Rance
Dinard
St-
Briac
St-
Jacut
Dinan
St-Cast
Baie de la
Fresnaie

Sables d'Or
-les-Pins
Erquy
Dahouet

Ile Bréhat

PAIMPOL
Trieux
River
PORTRIEUX
Binic
Le Légué
(St-Brieuc)

LEZARD
-RIEUX
Pontrieux

Port
Blanc
Perros Tréguier
Guirec River
Lannion R
Toull-an-Héry

Les Sept
Iles
Ploumanac'h
Trégastel
Ile Grande
Trébeurden Primel
Locquirec MORLAIX

Ile de Batz
Baie de
Morlaix
Mogueric Penzé
ROSCOFF River

BRITTANY

Pontusval
Le Corréjou
Aber-Wrac'h
L'Aber
Benoit
Kersaint
Argenton L'Aber-Ildut
Melon (Lanildut)
BREST
Portsall
Le Conquet

OUESSANT
I de
Molène
Baie de
Lampaul

30'

2°

3°

4°W

5°

49°
N

30'

30'

North Brittany & the Channel Islands

Cherbourg to Ouessant

ROYAL CRUISING CLUB
PILOTAGE FOUNDATION

JOHN LAWSON

Imray Laurie Norie & Wilson Ltd
St Ives Cambridgeshire England

Published by
Imray Laurie Norie & Wilson Ltd
Wych House St Ives Cambridgeshire PE27 5BT
England
☎ +44 (0)1480 462114, *Fax* +44 (0)1480 496109
E-mail ilnw@imray.com
www.imray.com
2001

© Text and photographs Royal Cruising Club
 Pilotage Foundation 2001
© Plans Imray Laurie Norie & Wilson Ltd 2001

ISBN 0 85288 483 4

British Library Cataloguing in Publication Data.
A catalogue record for this book is available from the
British Library.

The last input of technical information was March
2001.

CAUTION

Every effort has been made to ensure the accuracy of
this book. It contains selected information and thus
is not definitive and does not include all known
information on the subject in hand; this is
particularly relevant to the plans, which should not
be used for navigation. The Pilotage Foundation
believes that its selection is a useful aid to prudent
navigation, but the safety of a vessel depends
ultimately on the judgement of the navigator, who
should assess all information, published or
unpublished.

CORRECTIONS

The editor would be glad to receive any corrections,
information or suggestions which would improve
the book. Letters should be addressed to the Editor,
North Brittany and the Channel Islands, care of the
publishers. The more precise the information the
better, but even partial or doubtful information is
helpful, if it is made clear what the doubts are.

CORRECTIONAL SUPPLEMENTS

This pilot book will be amended at intervals by the
issue of correctional supplements which will be
published on our website www.imray.com and may
be downloaded free of charge. Printed copies are
also available on request from the publishers at the
above address.

PLANS

The plans in this guide are not to be used for
navigation – they are designed to support the text
and should always be used together with
navigational charts. Every effort has been made to
align the harbour and anchorage plans to European
Datum 1950 but they are not suitable for plotting of
accurate positions from electronic systems such as
GPS. See also page 3 – Horizontal Chart Datum.

It should be borne in mind that the characteristics
of lights may be changed during the life of the book,
and that in any case notification of such changes is
unlikely to be reported immediately. When the book
is no longer new, light characteristics, both in the
text and on the plans, may be updated from the
current edition of the *Admiralty List of Lights*.

All bearings are given from seaward and refer to
true north. Scales may be taken from the scales in
metres or from the latitude scale. Symbols are based
on those used by the British Admiralty – users are
referred to *Symbols and Abbreviations (NP 5011)*.

Printed in Great Britain at
Butler and Tanner Ltd, Frome, Somerset

Contents

Appendices

Foreword and preface

FOREWORD

Although the origins of this pilot can be traced back for almost 50 years, much of the present work is new. The scope has been enlarged to include the west coast of the Cherbourg peninsula and the main harbours of the Channel Islands so that in one volume the yachtsman has information on the whole fascinating cruising area from Cherbourg to Ushant. Since the last edition was published in 1992 so much has changed – not only in harbour facilities which are detailed here but in the capabilities of the cruising yacht and in particular the excellence of the latest navigation equipment. However this continues to be a challenging coastline with large tides, fast tidal streams and many unmarked rocks: great care is still needed to cruise safely.

The Pilotage Foundation is indebted to John Lawson for his painstaking work in visiting all the harbours, often in very poor weather conditions. He has also covered the area by land and in the air to collect all the latest data and take the photographs needed for a pilot of this type.

Updating corrections to this pilot will be published from time to time on the Imray website and may be downloaded from there. For those who prefer printed corrections, these will be available by post on request to Imray.

Francis Walker
Director
March 2001

PREFACE

The *North Brittany Pilot* was first produced in 1952 by Blondie Hasler, taken over by Adlard Coles in 1965 and finally by the RCC Pilotage Foundation in 1980. Nick Heath wrote the 6th and most recent edition in 1992 on which this new pilot is based. There have, however been many changes and this book has been virtually rewritten to include the Channel Islands and the Normandy coast west of Cherbourg to accommodate the large numbers of yachts following this route from the Solent and up-channel. Alderney, Guernsey, Herm, Sark and Jersey have all been covered but those wishing to visit Les Écrehous, Les Minquiers and Ile Chausey or indulge in serious rock-dodging outside the main ports, harbours and anchorages in the Channel Islands should consult the latest (2000) edition of the *The Channel Islands* by the RCC Pilotage Foundation.

All the harbours and most of the coast have been covered by sea, land and air in 1999 and 2000. I am most grateful for the splendid aerial photographs by Peter Carnegie who overflew most of North Brittany in 2000 and supplemented Patrick Roach's excellent earlier work in the area. A number of Nick Heath's photographs from the 6th edition have been retained which is a tribute to their quality. I have been much assisted by amendments and suggestions from members of the Royal Cruising Club and in particular from David Pentreath and Geoffrey Dunster. Finally my thanks to the hard-working team at Imray, Laurie, Norie and Wilson who have transformed the original work to the standard and practical format of this pilot.

John Lawson
Newton Ferrers
March 2001

Royal Cruising Club Pilotage Foundation

In 1976 an American member of the Royal Cruising Club, Dr Fred Ellis, indicated that he wished to make a gift to the Club in memory of his father, the late Robert E. Ellis, of his friends Peter Pye and John Ives and as a mark of esteem for Roger Pinkney. An independent charity known as the RCC Pilotage Foundation was formed and Dr Ellis added his house to his already generous gift of money to form the Foundation's permanent endowment. The Foundation's charitable objective is 'to advance the education of the public in the science and practice of navigation' which is at present achieved through the writing and updating of pilot books covering many different parts of the world.

The Foundation is extremely grateful and privileged to have been given the copyrights to books written by a number of distinguished authors and yachtsmen including the late Adlard Coles, Robin Brandon and Malcolm Robson. In return the Foundation has willingly accepted the task of keeping the original books up to date and many yachtsmen and women have helped (and are helping) the Foundation fulfill this commitment. In addition to the titles donated to the Foundation, several new books have been created and developed under the auspices of the Foundation. The Foundation works in close collaboration with two publishers – Imray Laurie Norie and Wilson, and Adlard Coles Nautical – and in addition publishes in its own name short run guides and pilot books for areas where limited demand does not justify large print runs. Several of the Foundation's books have been translated into French, German and Italian.

The overall management of the Foundation is entrusted to Trustees appointed by the Royal Cruising Club, with day to day operations being controlled by the Director. All these appointments are unpaid.

In line with its charitable status, the Foundation distributes no profits, which are used to finance new books and developments and to subsidise those covering areas of low demand.

Royal Cruising Club Pilotage Foundation Pilots and Cruising Guides

Published by Imray Laurie Norie & Wilson Ltd
Faroe, Iceland & Greenland
The Baltic Sea
Channel Islands
North Brittany & the Channel Islands
North Biscay
South Biscay
Atlantic Spain and Portugal
Atlantic Islands
Islas Baleares
Mediterranean Spain – Costas del Sol & Blanca
– Costas del Azahar, Dorada & Brava
Corsica and Northeast Sardinia
North Africa
Chile

Published by A & C Black Ltd
Atlantic Crossing Guide
Pacific Crossing Guide

Published by RCC Pilotage Foundation
South Atlantic Coast of South America
Cruising Guide to West Africa
Supplement to Falkland Island Shores
Guide to the Pembrokeshire Coast
(in collaboration with Pembrokeshire Afloat)

Cruising in Normandy and Brittany

The cruising conditions vary appreciably if not dramatically between the sandy and low-lying shores of the Cotentin peninsula in the east, to the rock-strewn and iron-bound coasts of Ouessant. The whole area is subject to strong tidal streams and a great range of tide in the southeast and Channel Islands, which gradually decreases as westing is made. The likelihood of swell and fog increases at the western end and accurate navigation is always of importance in the whole area where mistakes in narrow channels and rocky areas can have severe consequences.

GPS, now without Selective Availability, can be a great comfort but it must be remembered that all the charts are not yet on the same datum in this area and allowance must be made for any differences. However while GPS allows for accurate navigation to the outer end of a narrow channel or entrance, leading marks or lines are then more accurate and essential for safe navigation. These are given for each port or anchorage where they exist. A well operated radar set can also be a very useful navigational aid especially in poor visibility. Having said that, the coast is well endowed with lights, beacons and buoys and there are many harbours, some quite insignificant, with their well lit and marked leading lines.

A successful and quick passage will often depend on timing to make the tidal streams work in one's favour. While this is relatively easy when going east or west along the north coast of Brittany, it can be confusing in the Channel Islands. In this section will be found recommendations on optimum departure times to proceed in any direction from each port.

Marinas or harbours specifically for yachts are spaced at convenient distances and for those unwilling to pay for their facilities, there are hundreds of anchorages in sheltered or not so sheltered surroundings many of which have been included.

The Bretons and the Channel Islanders may have their occasional differences over fishing rights but they are both friendly and helpful to visiting yachtsmen. The Celtic ties between the Welsh, Cornish and Bretons precede Roman times and are maintained today in many exchange visits and folk festivals. The Channel Islands have been part of the United Kingdom since William the Conqueror brought them as part of the Kingdom of Normandy in 1066, the only break being during the German occupation during the Second World War.

TIDES AND TIDAL STREAMS

The range of tides is the highest in European waters in the Baie de Mont St-Michel where the highest spring tide can reach 13m with a range of 12m. These decrease at the W and E ends of the areas (around 6m range at Cherbourg and Ouessant) but the tidal streams increase dramatically especially in the choke points of Passage du Fromveur inside Ouessant (9 knots) and the Alderney Race (10 knots by Cap de la Hague). Tides and their streams are always a factor on these coasts even at neaps.

SWELL AND VISIBILITY

Swell (*la houle*) and fog (*la brume*) become more prevalent to the W and are included in the French weather forecasts. Swell at the western end combined with the strong streams can produce steep and dangerous overfalls. Fog in the islands around Ouessant is more frequent than on the mainland and further E.

TYPE OF YACHT

Yachts with a draught of over 3m will be confined to the major ports (Cherbourg, Alderney, Guernsey, Jersey, St-Malo, Le Légué, St-Quay-Portrieux, Paimpol, Bloscon) and the deeper anchorages. Yachts of 2m draught have fewer restrictions and can use nearly all the ports at the appropriate state of tide, although there will be many more sheltered anchorages available at neaps. For bilge-keelers, multihulls and yachts able to dry out alongside, the coast and islands offer myriad opportunities for exploration and many anchorages not available to the deep-keeled.

PROVISIONS AND SHOPPING

Most villages now have their small *supermarché* but there are a number of harbours where these are some distance from the landing and all that can be obtained within a short walk are bread and milk. Details are noted for each place; generally shopping for food and drink becomes more of an exercise the further W one gets and a bicycle becomes more necessary for the less energetic. Shops selling bread open early and most close mid-morning. French bread does not keep but may be revived by a short spell in the oven after 24 hours. Ask for *pain complet* for longer lasting and wholemeal bread. Fish and crustaceans can be found readily along the coast and it is often possible to buy direct from the fishing facility in the fishing ports.

Yacht chandlers will only be found in the major marinas (Cherbourg, St-Malo, St-Quay-Portrieux and the Channel Islands) but ironmongers selling some chandlery and fishing or commercial chandlers can be found elsewhere.

WATER

Nearly all water near harbours now is piped, clean and drinkable. It is a requirement in France for any water that is NOT drinkable to be labelled *non potable*. Marinas are well provided with taps but not hoses. At least 20m of hose and a variety of end fittings are a necessity.

FUEL

The use of low tax red diesel – known as *Fuel Oil Domestique* or FOD in France – is officially permitted in yachts for use with generators or heater units provided they are supplied from a different tank to the main engine. Difficulty may be found convincing a supplier that this is the case for bulk deliveries but there should be no objection from the customs or suppliers in securing a limited amount in cans.

Recent receipts for red diesel obtained in the UK or Channel Islands should be retained and produced if needed. A 'reasonable quantity' of such fuel carried in vessels tanks can be imported into France without further formality or payment of tax.

FOD, however is rarely available at marinas and only from fishing ports. Marinas supply fully taxed diesel from pumps which are increasingly operated by a credit card which must have a microchip incorporated. There are still some cards issued in the UK without these and in this event ask at the harbour office and pay cash.

Petrol is often provided by pump from marinas otherwise recourse must be made to the nearest garage.

TELEPHONES

Nearly all French telephones accept only cards and not cash. They may be obtained from post offices, tobacconists, newsagents and some cafés/bars. Mobile telephone coverage along the coast is good.

MONEY

Cash machines can be found in unexpected places and are not confined to banks. All but the smallest post offices will advance cash against a *Visa* card. There is a growing reluctance to take eurocheques although travellers' cheques are negotiable.

FORMALITIES

It is essential that a Certificate of Registry, or for British yachts the Small Ships Registry document is carried on board and produced on demand to the authorities. Photocopies are NOT acceptable and failure to produce the originals is likely to lead to a fine on the spot.

The following documents should also be carried
a. RYA Certificate of Competence at least for the skipper.
b. Evidence of insurance for the yacht. This is not a legal requirement but some marinas may refuse access to a non-insured boat.
c. Passports for all on board. These are likely to be demanded if boarded by the customs, will be needed for return to the UK by other means and are useful as a means of identification if cashing cheques etc.

Yachts registered in an EU country arriving in French waters need not complete any formalities (and should not fly a Q flag) unless they are carrying goods dutiable in France or have non-EU residents on board. In these cases entry should be made at a port with a customs office (noted in the text) and a Q flag flown until cleared.

Customs officers may board at any time while in French waters. On the first occasion ask for *une fiche* which will be issued if the officers are satisfied and may be produced to prevent subsequent boarding.

VALUE ADDED TAX (TVA)

The RYA issues a guide on VAT for yachts and this should be consulted if in doubt. In general, EU yachts must be able to demonstrate that they have paid VAT in order to enjoy freedom of movement within the EU. A VAT receipt issued by the builder should satisfy French Customs, and a Bill of Sale and Registration Document issued in the UK may do so particularly for an older yacht. A yacht built, or first registered before the introduction of VAT in the UK and which cannot produce a VAT receipt may have a problem. UK Customs and Excise may be able to issue such an exemption and they should be consulted. Failure to carry the correct documentation may result in a non-negotiable demand for the tax to be paid immediately at the French rate which is currently above the UK one of 17½%.

Yachts registered outside the EU, on which VAT has not been paid, may be temporarily imported into the Union tax free. At present the time limit for importation is for 6 months but this may be increased. In the past it has been sometimes possible to obtain an extension to the permitted length of stay if a yacht has been laid up in the EU whilst her owners return to their home countries.

New yachts, exported VAT-free from the UK and calling in France en route to a non-EU destination are a special case on which early advice should be obtained regarding the current time limits that apply to them.

INLAND WATERWAYS

The only inland waterway in this book runs from La Rance and all details will be found in that section.

YACHT CLUBS

There are yacht clubs and sailing schools in most French harbours; they are invariably hospitable to visitors. Assistance or advice is readily given and there are often showers available.

LAYING UP

There are many ports and marinas where yachts may be hauled out and/or laid up and where the prices are cheaper than in the UK. Details and suitability are noted in the text for each port.

TRAVEL AND CREW CHANGES

Road, rail and air communications are good all along the coast to the rest of France and to the UK, mostly via the Channel Islands but direct and frequent ferries run to England from Cherbourg, St-Malo and Roscoff. The various small airfields connect with Paris but Dinard connects with the Channel Islands, and Cherbourg connects with the UK and Channel Islands. Details may be found under each port.

FISHING

Nearly every port or harbour in this book has its fishing fleet from a few inshore open boats to sea-going fleets that are often away for weeks at a time. There are only a few ports where yachts and fishing boats are not mutually catered for and the French usually manage to accommodate the needs of both users in the one port. The fishermen are friendly to yachtsmen but berths alongside fishing boats should always be sought rather than taken.

There is a lot of lobster and crab-potting along the coast and a sharp lookout should be kept for their markers which are often awash or just under the surface in the strong streams.

Many of the estuaries and rivers have oyster and shellfish beds, and fish farms continue to appear in the bays. Anchoring is prohibited in these areas.

SEARCH AND RESCUE

The Centres Régionaux Opérationels de Surveillance et de Sauvetage (CROSS) are Maritime Rescue Co-ordination Centres (MRCCS). CROSS Joburg (near Cap de la Hague) covers the area from Cherbourg to Granville with substations at Granville and Roches Douvres. CROSS Corsen (near Le Conquet) covers the area from Cancale to Ile d'Ouessant with substations at Cap Fréhel, Bodic (near Lézardrieux), Ile de Batz and Le Stiff (Ouessant). They will respond to COSPAS/ SARSAT emergency transmissions from EPIRBS, to DSC activation of Ch 70 or to emergency calls on Ch 16. VHF coverage of the whole coast is total. Medical advice can be given from both MRCCs.

See below for details of weather forecasts and in each of the larger ports.

Technical and navigational information

Chart datum and tidal heights

Chart datum (CD) is fixed at a level below which the sea level will not fall in normal circumstances, but it may do so under extreme meteorological conditions. The chart datum of French charts is the same as Admiralty charts. The figures on the charts of soundings and drying heights are both related directly to CD.

Predicted heights of tides have been taken from *Admiralty Tide Tables Vol 1* and are related to CD and to times of HW and LW at Cherbourg, St Helier, St-Malo or Brest. Simplified conversion figures for times and heights in relation to these standard ports are shown for most of the minor ports; these figures are within 15 minutes and 0·2m of the given figures.

Heights of tide at any given time and place can be calculated by the 'Twelfth Rule', by straight interpolation or by constructing a tidal curve for the day.

A continual awareness of the tidal height above CD in this rocky area is of vital importance when entering or leaving most harbours or navigating in the channels.

Heights

On Admiralty charts this is above MHWS and applies to air clearances under bridges or overhead obstructions.

Horizontal chart datum – satellite derived positions.

Positions derived from satellite systems such as GPS are usually expressed in terms of World Geodetic System 1984 (WGS 84). Admiralty and French charts in this area are at the moment (2000) to European Datum 1950 (EU 50) but this is in the course of change to WGS 84 equivalent. In order to use the high accuracy that DGPS, or GPS without Selective Availability both now give, note must be taken of the datum that the chart in use is constructed to. The GPS should then be set to this datum or the correction given on the chart applied. This caution applies to ARCS as well as paper charts.

Caution should be exercised if using pre-metric or old French or private charts which do not show any correction. There may be significant discrepancies between the latitude and longitude on the chart and that shown by GPS set to any datum.

Bearings

Bearings are given in degrees True from seaward. Magnetic variation is about 4°W throughout the area (2000) decreasing about 8' annually. Magnetic bearings in compass points are generally given for the photographic views and sometimes in the text to indicate a general direction.

Lights

The description of all lights are shown for each port and follow the conventions in *Admiralty List of Lights*. Details of buoys and their lights are shown where appropriate. This section of the French coast is covered by light numbers 1469 to 1524 and from 1632 to 1886 covered by *Volume A NP74*.

The French make widespread use of leading lights and marks or of sectored lights at entrances to harbours and estuaries.

Harbour plans

While every effort has been made to align them to European Datum 1950, the harbour plans should be used with caution for navigation and pilotage especially when using GPS. The scales are indicated by latitude.

Beacon towers and beacons

Beacons usually consist of a single, spindly post with or without a topmark. Beacon towers are substantial towers usually of masonry which may or may not have a light.

Charts

Details of Admiralty and Imray charts for the area are shown in Appendix 1 on page 219. They are also shown in the text for each port or feature. Admiralty charts may be obtained from any chart agent and are corrected up to the date of purchase. They can be kept corrected from the free (but not post free) *Admiralty Notices to Mariners* or from the quarterly small craft summaries. They may also be found on website www.ukho.gov.uk. In addition to supplying these Imray Norie Laurie and Wilson Ltd, Wych House, The Broadway, St Ives, Cambridgeshire PE27 5BT ☎ 01480 462114 *Fax* 01480 496109 www.imray.com can obtain French charts but it takes some time. It may be quicker to order direct from Librairie Maritime et d'Outremer, 17 rue Jacob, 75006 Paris, ☎ 01 46 33 47 48 *Fax* 01 43 29 96 77, www.librairie-outremer.com or from the chart agents in the principal ports. Some chandlers will hold a limited stock of local charts. These are not kept corrected after receipt. French SHOM charts with the suffix P are printed on waterproof paper and folded like a map for small craft.

The French also produce the Navicarte series of charts to a scale of 1:50,000 with large-scale inserts specifically for yachtsmen. These may be obtained from Imray, Laurie, Norie and Wilson or direct from Librairie Maritime et d'Outremer.

In general Admiralty charts give an excellent coverage of the area and are increasingly convergent in coverage, scales, datums and styles with the French charts but with slightly different symbols and conventions. French SHOM chart numbers are only given in the text where the scale is substantially larger for a particular port or area. A case in point is above La Rance barrage where only two SHOM charts provide coverage. Where Admiralty Small Craft (SC) or Admiralty Raster Chart (ARCS) editions are also available this is indicated in the listing.

Radio services

In common with other European countries French coastal radio stations have ceased operation. Port radios are shown for each harbour. Only aero radiobeacons still transmit.

CROSS Jobourg and Corsen emergency services provide a full VHF coverage of the area. They will also provide navigational assistance on VHF in an emergency. This is particularly relevant in the Chenal du Four area where fogs are more prevalent.

Weather forecasts

CROSS Jobourg on Ch 80 at 0710, 0733, 1545, 1603, 1910, 1933 LT in French and English.
Granville on Ch 80 at 0703, 1533, 1903 LT in French and English.
Cap Fréhel on Ch 79 at 0545, 0803, 1203, 1633, 2003 LT in French and English.
Bodic on Ch 79 at 0533, 0745, 1145, 1615, 1945 LT in French and English.
Ile de Batz on Ch 79 at 0515, 0733, 1133, 1603, 1933 LT in French and English.
CROSS Corsen on Ch 79 at 0150, 0450, 0750, 1050, 1350, 1650, 1950, 2250 LT in French and English.
Le Stiff on Ch 79 at 0503, 0715, 1115, 1545, 1915 LT in French and English.

Navtex Corsen (A) or Niton (S) or (K)

The forecast areas are Manche Ouest from the Cotentin peninsula to about 3°30'W, thence Ouest Bretagne.

Météo France broadcast bulletins for coastal areas up to 20M off in French by telephone. The following numbers are relevant to the indicated areas:

08 36 68 08 50   Cherbourg to Granville.
08 36 68 08 35   Cancale to Ile de Bréhat including St-Malo tides.
08 36 68 08 22   Ile de Bréhat.
08 36 68 08 29   Ile de Batz to Ile d'Ouessant including Brest and Roscoff tides.

In addition there is a high seas forecast for the Atlantic including a 5-day forecast available on 08 36 68 08 08.

1. Cherbourg to Cancale

Introduction

This section of the Normandy coast is included so that those sailing from the Solent or further E can visit ports in France en route, as well as the Channnel Islands. However, apart from Cherbourg, entry and exit to all the harbours is tide limited to deep draught vessels between some 2 hours either side of HW. Including Cherbourg, there are four marinas, one drying yacht harbour and four open anchorages which partly dry.

The coast is sandy and low-lying and is divided by the tidal gate at Cap de la Hague off the Alderney Race. Here the streams can run up to 10 knots at springs and overfalls are dangerous and extensive in wind over tide conditions. Creeping close round Cap de la Hague to avoid an adverse tide is dangerous amongst the off-lying rocks, and will only partly reduce the strength of the stream against.

Better to wait at Omonville or Anse de St-Martin until slack water with the stream turning in favour.

Cherbourg

General

A huge commercial and naval harbour with a very large marina, Port Chantereyne, accessible at all times and in all weathers. English yachtsmen have been coming here since the last century. A natural first or last visit across the channel only 60 miles from the Solent. Everything possible that a sailor needs can be found here except solitude.

Regular ferries from Poole and Portsmouth, a nearby airport and good marina security make it a useful place to change crews or leave the boat.

Data

Charts

Admiralty *1106* (SC) (ARCS), *2602* (ARCS) (plan)
Imray *C32* (plan), *C33A*

Tides

Cherbourg is a Standard Port

MHWS	MHWN	MLWN	MLWS	MTL
6·4m	5·0m	2·5m	1·1	3·8m

Spring range 5·3m. Neap range 2·5m
HW Cherbourg is 0410 BEFORE HW Dover, allowing for the time difference between UK and France as shown in *Admiralty Tide Tables*.

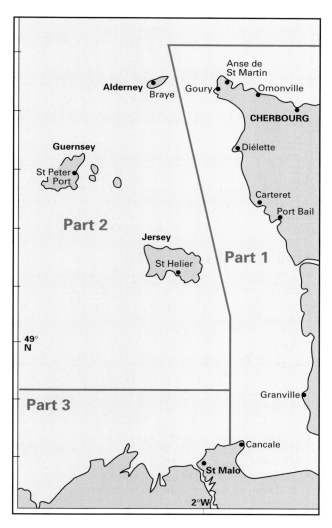

Tidal streams

3M N of the breakwater the streams start as follows

HW Cherbourg −0330 E-going
HW Cherbourg +0215 W-going

The maximum spring rates are 3 knots. The rate lessens as the coast is approached and a counter-eddy starts close to the coast at up to 1 hour before slack water. This is particularly noticeable and useful when proceeding W from Cherbourg.

The tidal streams inside the breakwater and in the two main entrances are slack at around the times of HW and LW. The E and W-going streams start to run inside and through the entrances at about 1½ hours before the times above.

Planning guide
Cherbourg – Channel Islands – Tréguier

	Cherbourg	A de St-Martin	Goury	Alderney	Diélette	Guernsey	Carteret	Port Bail	Jersey (St H)	Granville	Is Chausey	Cancale	St-Malo	St-Briac	St-Jacut	St-Cast	B de Fresnaie	Erquy	Dahouet	St-Brieuc	Binic	St-Q/Portrieux	Paimpol	Ile Bréhat	Lézardrieux	Pontrieux	Tréguier
Cherbourg		12	16	24	26	42	37	41	57	69	69	86	89	89	89	89	90	92	97	103	105	104	87	82	87	93	93
A de St-Martin	12		4	12	14	30	25	29	45	57	57	74	77	77	77	77	78	80	85	91	93	92	75	70	75	81	81
Goury	16	4		10	10	27	22	26	42	54	43	71	74	74	74	74	75	77	82	88	90	89	72	67	72	78	78
Alderney	24	12	10		17	22	28	32	40	60	58	71	72	72	73	73	73	76	80	85	81	79	67	64	69	75	75
Diélette	26	14	10	17		28	13	17	33	48	48	61	64	67	69	72	74	68	83	90	83	85	68	63	68	74	74
Guernsey	42	30	27	22	28		30	32	28	54	47	58	54	52	52	52	51	50	54	57	54	51	44	43	48	54	50
Carteret	37	25	22	28	13	30		4	22	35	35	43	44	46	48	51	53	63	68	73	73	73	62	63	67	73	73
Port Bail	41	29	26	32	17	32	4		21	31	31	44	42	44	46	49	51	61	66	73	73	73	62	60	65	71	71
Jersey (St H)	57	45	42	40	33	28	22	21		30	25	34	35	35	35	35	35	37	43	48	48	45	44	42	47	53	60
Granville	69	73	70	62	48	54	35	31	30		10	13	22	26	28	31	33	43	48	55	65	65	74	77	82	88	91
Is Chausey	69	73	70	62	48	47	35	31	25	10		13	14	18	20	23	25	35	40	47	57	58	67	70	75	81	84
Cancale	86	74	71	71	61	58	43	39	34	13	13		17	21	23	26	28	38	43	50	60	61	70	70	75	81	84
St-Malo	89	77	74	72	64	54	44	42	35	22	14	17		7	9	12	14	24	29	36	36	37	46	46	51	57	60
St-Briac	89	77	74	72	67	52	46	44	35	26	18	21	7		2	5	7	17	22	29	29	29	39	39	44	50	53
St-Jacut	89	77	74	73	69	52	48	46	35	28	20	23	9	2		3	5	15	20	27	27	27	28	37	42	48	51
St-Cast	89	77	74	73	72	52	51	49	35	31	23	26	12	5	3		2	12	17	24	24	25	34	34	39	45	48
B de Fresnaie	90	78	75	73	74	51	53	51	35	33	25	28	14	7	5	2		10	15	22	22	23	32	32	37	43	46
Erquy	92	80	77	76	68	50	63	61	37	43	35	38	24	17	15	12	10		5	12	14	14	25	25	30	36	40
Dahouet	97	85	82	80	73	54	68	66	43	48	40	43	29	22	20	17	15	5		7	10	11	25	25	28	34	39
St-Brieuc	103	91	88	85	80	57	73	73	48	55	47	50	36	29	27	24	22	12	7		6	9	24	24	29	35	42
Binic	105	93	90	81	83	54	73	73	48	65	57	60	36	39	27	24	22	14	10	6		3	18	17	22	28	31
St-Q/Portrieux	104	92	89	79	85	51	72	73	45	65	58	61	37	29	27	25	23	14	11	9	3		15	14	19	25	28
Paimpol	87	75	72	67	68	44	63	62	44	74	67	70	46	39	37	34	32	25	25	24	18	15		8	13	19	22
Ile Bréhat	82	70	67	64	63	43	62	60	42	77	70	70	46	39	37	34	32	25	25	23	17	14	8		5	11	18
Lézardrieux	87	75	72	69	68	48	67	65	47	82	75	75	51	44	42	39	37	30	28	29	22	19	13	5		6	18
Pontrieux	93	81	78	75	74	54	73	71	53	88	81	81	57	50	48	45	43	36	34	35	28	25	19	11	6		24
Tréguier	93	81	78	75	74	50	73	71	60	91	84	84	60	53	51	48	46	40	39	42	31	28	22	18	18	24	

Distances are given over the shortest navigable route and are measured to and from inner harbour or anchorage

Lights

Only the major lights covering the two outer entrances, the inner harbour entrance and the entrance to the marina at Port Chantereyne are given below.

Fort d'Ile Pelée E side of E entrance
Oc(2)WR.6s19m10/7M White and red pedestal on fort 055°-W-120°-R-055°

Jetée des Flamands E Ldg Lts 189°
Front Q.9m13M White metal pylon on hut
Rear (Terre-plein des Mielles) Q.16m13M White column, black bands, white top

Fort de l'Est W side of E entrance Iso.G.4s19m9M White pylon, green top

Fort de l'Ouest E side of W entrance
Fl(3)WR.15s19m24/20M Horn(3)60s Grey tower, red top, on fort 122°-W-355°-R-122°

Digue de Querqueville W side of W entrance.
Fl(4)WG.15s8m6/4M White column, green top 120°-W-290°-G-120°

Digue de Homet Ldg line through W entrance 141°
Front Dir2Q(hor)5m17M White triangle on parapet at root of jetty, lights 63m apart 137°-intens-143°, 139°-intens-145°
Rear **Gare Maritime** DirQ.35m19M Lattice structure on SE tower of building 140°-intens-143°

Digue de Homet head W side of inner entrance
F.G.10m.8M White pylon, green top, on blockhouse 114°-intens-134° Horn(2+1)60s

Gare Maritime E side of marina entrance
Oc(2)R.6s3m3M

Marina môle head W side of Marina entrance
Oc(2)G.6s7m6M Green pylon

Wavescreen pontoon end inside entrance
Fl.G.2·5s4m2M White post, green top. S end of this pontoon has a F.Vi light marking it

Buoys

CH1 3M N of breakwater Fl.10s89m4M Whis Ball on red buoy, white stripes RaRefl

Fort de l'Ouest Oc.R.4s port, marking rocks close W of fort

Digue de Homet La Ténarde N cardinal VQ, on N side of jetty

Jetée des Flamands Fl.R.2·5s Ra Refl On E side of entrance

Search and rescue

Cherbourg is in the CROSS Jobourg region. Jobourg is 12M to the W and will respond to distress calls on Ch 16 or activation of GMDSS on Ch 70.

The nearest all-weather lifeboats are at Goury and Barfleur.

There are several hospitals in the town.

Weather forecasts

CROSS Jobourg on Ch 80 at 0710. 0733,1545, 1603, 1910, 1933 LT in French and English.

Port Chantereyne

Cherbourg looking NW   *SHOM*

Daily weather map at the marina office renewed at 0800.
Météo France ☎ 08 36 68 08 50.
Navtex Corsen (A), Niton (S) and (K).

Communications

Port Chantereyne Ch 9 (0600–2300).

Customs

There is an office in Cherbourg ☎ 02 33 23 34 02 or
ask at the marina office.

Consular office

There is an Honorary British Consul at P & O European
Ferries, Gare Maritime Sud, 50104 Cherbourg.

Approaches

By day from the N There are no dangers or
difficulties in approaching the port from the N
except to calculate the tidal streams, especially at
springs so that one is not set past the intended
entrance. Various towers, TV masts and forts are
conspicuous on the skyline above the town as is the
breakwater with Fort Central in the middle of it.
CH1 buoy gives an indication of distance off. Both
entrances are clear of dangers and commercial
shipping should not be impeded in or near them.

From the E The banks and shoals extend up to 3
miles off the coast between Cap Barfleur and Cap
Levi. While sufficient water may be found further
inshore up to 1 mile off, if the tide so serves, the
tidal streams run hard and overfalls are frequent
over the uneven bottom inside the Haute Fond des
Equets, Basse du Nord Ouest and the Tête
Septentrionale buoys although the corner may be
cut inside the latter to make the E entrance. A red
and white, and a red beacon tower mark the N
extent of the rocks to the N and NE of Fort Pelée
and should be left to port before turning in to the
entrance.

From the W After rounding Cap de la Hague, leave
Basse Bréfort buoy to starboard, Raz de Bannes N
cardinal beacon tower 3M to the E, 500m to
starboard and head for the W entrance keeping
outside the 5m line unless of deeper draught.

Cherbourg. Port Chantereyne and Avant Port looking
south   *SHOM*

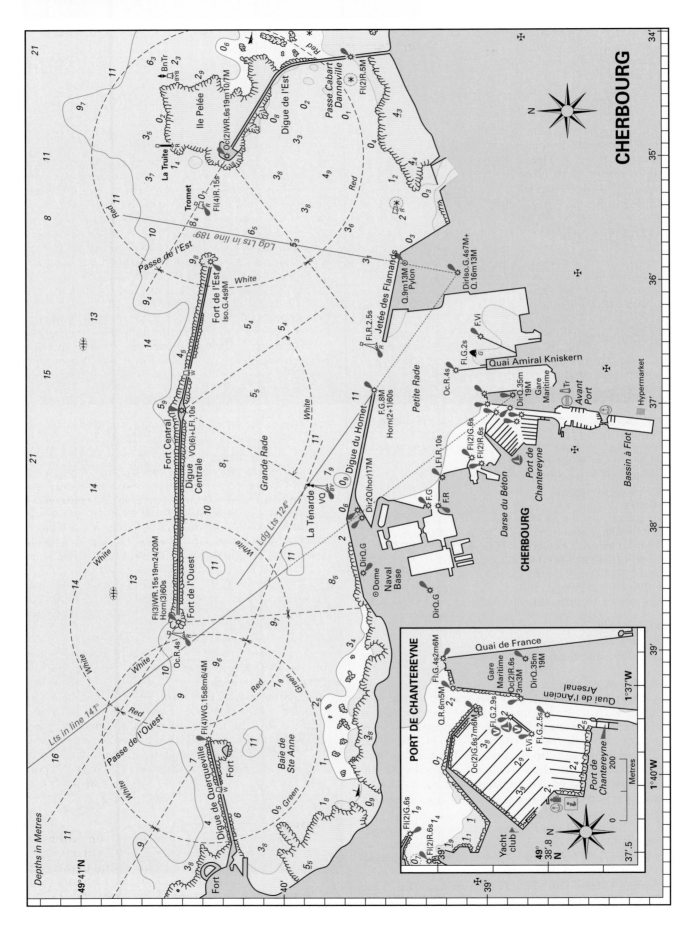

CHERBOURG

Depths in Metres

49°41'N

Lts in line 141°

Passe de l'Ouest

Baie de
Ste Anne

Digue de Querqueville

Fort

Fort

White
Red
Green
Red
White
White

Fl(4)WG.15s8m6/4M
Fl(4)WG.15s19m24/20M
Horn(3)60s

Fort de l'Ouest

Oc.R.4s

Fl(3)WR.15s19m24/20M
Horn(3)60s

Fort Central

Digue
Centrale

Digue VQ(6)+LFl.10s

Fort de l'Est
Iso.G.4s9M

Passe de l'Est

Ldg Lts in line 189°

Red

Tromet
Fl(4)R.15s

La Truite
Oc(2)WR.6s19m10/7M

Ile Pelée

BnTr
BYB 2₃

Digue de l'Est

Passe Cabart
Danneville
Fl(2)R.5M

White

Grande Rade

La Ténarde
VQ
B

Dir2Q(hor)17M
Dir Q.G
© Dome
Naval
Base

Digue du Homet
F.G.8M
Horn(2+1)60s

Petite Rade

Dir Q.G

Ldg Lts 124°

White

F.G
F.R
LFl.R.10s

Fl(2)G.6s
Fl(2)R.6s

Oc.R.4s

Jetée des Flamands
Fl.R.2.5s

Q.9m13M Pylon

DirIso.G.4s7M+
Q.16m13M

F.Vi

Fl.G.2s
Quai Amiral Kniskern

Gare
Maritime
DirQ.35m
19M

Avant
Port

Darse du Béton

Port de
Chantereyne

CHERBOURG

Bassin à Flot

Hypermarket

N

PORT DE CHANTEREYNE

Quai de France

Fl.G.4s2m6M
Fl.G.4s2m6M

Gare
Maritime
Oc(2)R.6s
3m3M

DirQ.35m
19M

Quai de l'Ancien
Arsenal

Q.R.6m5M
2₂

Fl.G.2.9s

Fl.G.2.5s
F.Vi

Oc(2)G.6s7m6M

Oc(2)G.6s

Port de
Chantereyne

Fl(2)G.6s
Fl(2)R.6s

Fl(2)G.6s
Fl(2)R.6s

Yacht
club

49°
38'.8 N
N

1°40'W   1°37'W

Metres
0   200

37'.5

By night The principal entrance is the western one where the leading lights (front Dir2Q(hor) and rear DirQ) on 141° lead through. The E entrance is equally well lit with leading lights on the Jetée des Flamands (front Q.9m13M and rear Q.16m13M) bearing 189°.

Entrance

The least depth in the approaches up to the marina entrance is 6·3m. The marina is dredged to 3m but there is more at its N end.

From E entrance A south westerly track will lead through the inner entrance leaving the head of Digue du Homet (white pylon, green top on blockhouse F.G) to starboard and taking care to leave the VQ.R buoy marking the W extent of the Jetée des Flamands to port; the outer end of this jetty covers at HW. From here the entrance to Port Chantereyne will be seen just to the W of the conspicuous Gare Maritime. The N mole head is marked by a green pylon (Oc(2)G.6s) and 100m SE of this lies a wave screen marked at its N end by a white post with a green top (Fl.G.2·5s) and its S end with a post (F.Vi); this may be passed on either side to reach the visitors' pontoons to the S of it.

From the W entrance When past the Fort de l'Ouest and its off-lying port buoy, move off the leading line to the NE to pass La Ténarde N cardinal buoy to starboard and round the end of Digue du Homet (white pylon, green top on blockhouse F.G) turning S towards the marina entrance. Proceed then as from the E entrance.

Berths

There are nearly 1300 berths in Port Chantereyne, 300 for visitors, maximum length 15m but up to 25m length can be accommodated at the N end on moorings and/or pontoons where up to 4·5m may be found. Call on Ch 9 if over 15m before entering.

The Avant Port, to the S of Port Chantereyne now has no berths or facilities for visiting yachts.

Moorings

None for yachts except for the larger ones at the N end of the marina.

Anchorage

Anchorage is prohibited in the vicinity of the two outer and the inner entrances and discouraged in the Petite Rade where there is much traffic.

Anchorage may be found in westerlies in the Baie de Sainte-Anne in 3m or more at the W end of the outer harbour but there is a prohibited area in the NW corner. In easterlies there is a less sheltered anchorage under the jetty running SE to the shore from Ile Pelee in 4m or more.

Facilities

Cherbourg can provide all the facilities of a large naval and commercial port.
Water and electricity On the pontoons.
Fuel Diesel and petrol at the fuel berth by the harbour office (open 0800–1145, 1400–1645).
Travel-lift 30 tons.
Cranes Up to 600kg for masts, mobile crane on request.
Slip In SE corner of marina.
Showers and heads 24 by the harbour office.
Chandlers By the harbour office.
Yacht club By the harbour office, visitors welcome.
Ice A machine by the harbour office.
Shops and banks Within 200m of the Marina shore entrance. There is large *supermarché* to the S of the Avant Port. Market days Tuesdays and Thursdays, in the vicinity of rue des Halles.
Restaurants and hotels Many of all qualities; few of the hotels in Cherbourg have restaurants.
Travel The railway station is 15 minutes' walk from the marina near the town centre where there are regular and direct connections to Paris and the rest of France. The bus station is close by and buses run to St-Lô, Valognes and Barfleur. The airport is above the town at Maupertois; flights to Jersey, Guernsey, Alderney, Bournemouth, Bristol and Exeter as well as French internal flights. Ferries run daily to Poole and Portsmouth (high speed); also up to 4 times weekly to Rosslare. Taxis ☎ 02 33 53 36 38.

Historical

Napoleon inaugurated Cherbourg as a major port with the building of the massive breakwaters and the start of its fortifications. The defences around the harbour were extended in the middle of the 19th century to protect the growing naval base during a period of French maritime and colonial expansion.

During the American Civil War in 1864 the Confederate raider *Alabama* fought the Unionist ship *Kearsarge* 7M off the town in view of a large crowd ashore. The *Alabama* sunk after nearly an hour's battle and many of the survivors were picked up by an English yacht *Deerhound* who was spectating. The wreck of the *Alabama* was not rediscovered until 1984 and there are recovery operations in train.

The town and base were surrendered to the Germans with little fight in 1940 but were defended vigorously by them before being retaken by the Allies in 1944 with the harbour blocked by wrecks and all the installations destroyed.

Before and after the war Cherbourg was the terminal for the major transatlantic liners – *Queen Mary*, *France*, *Liberté*, *Bremen* of the last generation, which berthed at the Gare Maritime – and continued as a major commercial and container port when this trade declined; to this was added a growing ferry trade with England.

Leisure

There is much to see in the town although surprisingly for a major naval port, not much of maritime interest except a small maritime museum at Port des Flamands to the E of the container port. The theatre in the centre of the town and Trinity Church are worth a visit, as is the Thomas Henry

Fine Art Museum with many of Millet's portraits. There is also a natural history museum and several fine parks and gardens. Perhaps the best visit is to climb or take a bus up Montagne du Roule behind the town to visit the Liberation Museum in the old Fort du Roule whence there are splendid views over the harbour.

Omonville-la-Rogue

General

A small harbour 5M to the E of Cap de la Hague and W of Cherbourg protected by a breakwater and providing shelter from the S through W to NW. Accessible by day or night although the moorings now extend into the sheltered anchorage area; there are drying berths alongside the wall. Few facilities

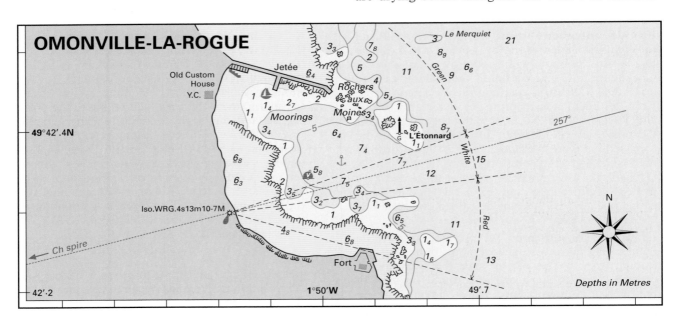

Front leading mark & light
(white with red top)

L'Etonnard
beacon tower

Omonville-la-Rogue looking SW

ashore but a useful harbour to await the stream round Cap de la Hague in westerly weather.

Data

Charts

Admiralty *1106* (SC) (ARCS)
SHOM *5636* (plan)
Imray *C32, C33A* (plan)

Tides

Times of HW and LW are about 10 minutes before those at Cherbourg at the same heights.

Tidal streams

2M N of the port the E-going stream starts at −0215 HW Cherbourg and the W-going at +0120 attaining 4 and 5 knots respectively at springs.

Lights

Omonville Iso.WRG.4s13m10-7M White pylon, red top 180°-G-252°-W-262°-R-287°
Basse Bréfort buoy N cardinal VQ.8m4M Whis

Approaches

The only off-lying dangers in the approaches are Les Tataquets rocks (drying 2·6m) 800m N of the breakwater end. Navigate to a position 1M ENE of the breakwater end and align the white pylon with red top with the church spire on 257°. At night get into the white sector of the light (green to the N, red to the S) on the same middle bearing. This leads S of L'Etonnard starboard beacon tower marking the end of the rocks extending 200m ESE from the breakwater end. An unlit buoy with an × topmark is in the red sector ½M to the E of the breakwater end. Steer for the centre of the harbour after passing L'Etonnard beacon tower.

Entrance and anchorage

The best part of the harbour is taken up by some 60 moorings of which there are four for visitors. Either pick one up or anchor clear on patchy sand.

Berths

There is a clean, sandy bottom at the inner end of the breakwater beyond a spur halfway along it where it dries 1m and where an alongside berth may be found. Do not go alongside the breakwater to the E of the spur where there are rocks.

Facilities

A small café/restaurant and a sailing school by the harbour. There is a small shop on the main road.

Anse de St-Martin (Port Racine)

General

An open bay 2M E of Cap de la Hague and to the W of Omonville accessible only by day and sheltered from W through S to ESE. It would be safer as a tide-waiting anchorage in easterly weather when Omonville would not.

Data

As for Omonville-la-Rogue. There is no plan on any chart of which SHOM *5636* is the largest scale. Admiralty *1106*

Anse de St-Martin. Port Racine from SE near HW

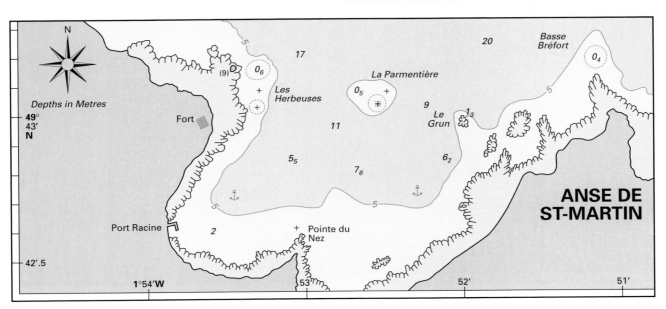

and *3653* show the dangers clearly but on smaller scales. Tide times will be earlier than for Omonville and the heights of HW and LW greater.

Approaches

Identify Pointe du Nez, a low bluff at the W end of the sandy beach at the head of the bay and approach this on a track of 187° making allowance for any cross stream, which can be strong in the offing. This will pass 300m to the W of La Parmetière, a shoal patch drying at CD and 400m to the E of Les Herbeuses rocks (drying 9m but with rocks awash at CD off them). Port Racine, a small, drying boat harbour will soon appear in the SW corner of the bay.

Anchorage

There are a few small boat moorings off Port Racine. Anchor clear of them in 2–3m, sand. Tuck into the E corner of the bay in easterly weather.

Facilities

None, except for a small restaurant up the hill above Port Racine. Port Racine claims, without much foundation to be the smallest port in France.

Goury

General

A small, drying harbour in the rocks ¾M SSW of Cap de la Hague. Accessible on the tide in fine weather by day or night. The harbour, sheltered by

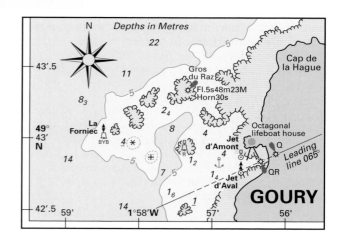

a breakwater dries between 3·8m and 4·5m, sand and mud. There is a least depth of 1·2m in the approach but drying rocks are close to the leading line. There is little shelter from the SW and the surf can be violent in the harbour. In the summer it is used by *vedettes* to Alderney.

Data

Charts

SHOM *7133* has a plan of the harbour and approaches, otherwise Admiralty *3653* gives a general indication of the immediate area. Plan on Imray C33A.

Tides

HW and LW are approximately 1 hour before the same times at Cherbourg. Add 1·7m to the heights of HW at Cherbourg for those at Goury: add 1m to the height of LW neaps and 0·3m to the height of LW springs at Cherbourg for the heights at Goury.

Tidal streams

The Alderney Race attains its greatest rates 1M W of La Foraine buoy in the approaches to Goury, up to 9¾ knots N-going and up to 6½ knots S-going. However these rates fall off appreciably as the harbour is approached and may be replaced by an opposite eddy close inshore. 1M to the W of La Foraine buoy the stream turns to the NNW at −0200 HW St Helier (−0245 HW St-Malo) and to the S at +0150 HW St Helier (+0235 HW St-Malo).

Lights

Cap de la Hague Fl.5s48m23M Horn 30s Grey tower, white top
La Platte Fl(2+1)WR.10s11m9/6M N cardinal octagonal tower 115°-W-272°-R-115°
Goury Ldg Lts 065° *Front* Q.R.5m7M Red square on a white square on breakwater end
Rear Q.11m7M White pylon on masonry hut

Buoys

La Foraine is an unlit W cardinal 1½M W of Goury

Search and rescue

An all-weather lifeboat is maintained in the building with the octagonal grey roof at the N end of the harbour.

Approach

Navigate to a position ½M S of La Foraine buoy and pick up the leading line 065°, the front mark a

Lifeboat house — Rear leading mark & light (white lattice pylon) — Front leading mark & light (end of breakwater) — Jet d'Amont beacon

Goury looking ESE

red square within a white square, and the rear a white pylon on a masonry hut, both to the S of the conspicuous lifeboat building. This will leave La Forniec E cardinal beacon tower some 500m to the N and the following beacons marking rocks on the sides indicated – Ban Charlain to starboard, Petit Grois to port, Grois to starboard, Hervieu to starboard, Jet d'Aval to starboard and Jet d'Amont to port. The harbour will then be open.

Anchorage
Close W of the lifeboat slip in 3m, patchy sand but only in settled or easterly weather.

Berths
Dry out alongside the inner breakwater or in the harbour clear of the small boat moorings, sand and mud but only if no weather threatens from the W.

Facilities
None apart from a tourist information office and small restaurant. The latter has a good reputation and is often crowded at lunchtime. The nearest shop is ¾M at Auderville.

There is a memorial to a shipwreck in 1912 to the N of the car park.

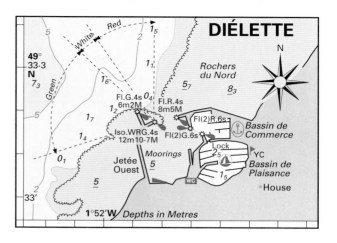

Diélette

General
Diélette is a small port which has recently been much enlarged to cater for yachts. It lies 10M S of Cap de la Hague and just N of Cap Flamanville which is surmounted by the conspicuous nuclear power station. The least depth in the approach is 0·5m and there is between 1·5 and 2·5m in the

Diélette outer entrance bearing 140°

Diélette looking ESE

Entrance over sill. Tide gauge on right

basins. There is a small fishing fleet and *vedette* traffic with the Channel Islands in the summer. Apart from the breakwaters, there is no protection from strong W or NW winds and entry in these conditions should not be contemplated; if already inside in these conditions, it will be uncomfortable even in the inner Bassin de Plaisance around HW. As yet (2001) there are few facilities ashore.

Data

Charts

Admiralty *3653* (SC) (ARCS)
SHOM *7133* (plan)
Imray *C33A* (plan)

Tides

HW is 40 minutes after HW St-Malo and LW 30 minutes after LW St-Malo. At springs subtract 2·5m from the heights of HW St-Malo and 1·9m at neaps; subtract 0·5m from the heights of LW at St-Malo for the heights at Diélette.

Tidal streams

The streams outside Diélette start at the following times
-0325 HW St Helier (-0410 HW St-Malo) NE
+0220 HW St Helier (+0135 HW St-Malo) SW
The maximum spring rate in each direction is 1¾ knots

Lights

Diélette W breakwater Iso.WRG.4s12m10-7M White tower, green top 070°-G-135°-W-145°-R-180°
W breakwater head Fl.G.4s6m2M 115°-vis-358°
N head Fl.R.4s8m5M White mast, red top
Basin corner Fl(2)R.6s6m1M Metal post
Basin corner Fl(2)G.6s 6m2M Metal post

Buoys

Cap Flamanville W cardinal buoy Q(9)15s lies 1½M WSW of Diélette just outside the green sector of the leading light

Weather forecasts

A daily weather map is available from the harbour office on request.

Communications

Bureau du Port on Ch 9 (0800–2000 in the summer).

Approaches

There are no off-lying dangers within 5M of the port which may be readily identified below the hill just to the N of the conspicuous nuclear power station on Cap Flamanville. The W cardinal buoy to the W of the Cape will also assist. Navigate to a position ½M to the NW and align the sectored light structure with a conspicuous house above the port bearing 140°. At night this will be in the centre of the white sector (10°) with the red sector to the NE and the green to the SW. The Cap Flamanville W cardinal buoy Q(9)15s is just outside the green sector. There is reported to be 0·5m least depth on this line which shallows to drying 1m just to the NW of the outer entrance.

Entrance

Turn to port once through the outer entrance into the Bassin de Commerce. The arrival pontoon is the middle one to the N of the harbour office. Berth here and seek a berth in the Bassin de Plaisance from the office. There may be room to stay here if a berth inside the sill is not wanted. There is 2m in the Bassin du Commerce.

Alternatively proceed straight to Bassin de Plaisance turning to starboard round the S mole. The entrance is at the W end of the submerged wall and is marked by a red post to be left to port, past the fuel berth. The sill dries 5m and will be opened when there is 1·5m over it which is approximately HW±3 hours 15 minutes. There is 2·5m at the N end of the basin, shallowing to 1·5m at the S end.

Gate signals are as follows:
3 vertical red lights   Gate closed
2 green over 1 white light Gate open

Berths

There are over 400 berths, maximum 20m with 70 for visitors. The pontoons have fingers. There are drying visitors' berths in the Avant Port but these will be exposed in NW winds and the bottom is hard sand. The W wall can be dried out against; it dries 4m–5m, hard sand.

Facilities

Water and electricity On the pontoons.
Fuel Petrol and diesel at fuel berth outside Bassin de Plaisance.
Showers and heads 12 of each in the block at the S end of the S mole; also in the yacht club.
Washing machines In the shower block.
Slip and travel-lift 30 tons, two slips in the Avant Port.
Restaurants There is a café by the harbour office and a restaurant near the S end of the harbour; small hotel up the hill.
Yacht club On the E side of the port with a good restaurant.
Sailing school By the shower block.
Shops Remarkable by their absence.
Travel Nearest railway station and airport is at Cherbourg 15M; local taxi ☎ 02 33 52 53 53.

Carteret

General

A small fishing and yachting port which dries 4·5m in the approaches and river, lies close to the SE of Cap de Carteret. The marina basin can be entered 2½ hours either side of HW. Carteret, and Barneville on the other side of the estuary are mainly holiday towns with excellent beaches. There are reasonable facilities at Carteret. The entrance should not be attempted in strong westerly winds and the best time to enter is between HW −1 and HW.

Data

Charts

Admiralty *3655* (SC) (ARCS)
SHOM *7133* (plan)
Imray *C33A* (plan)

Fishing quay — Jetée Ouest head — Marina — Training wall head

Carteret looking E

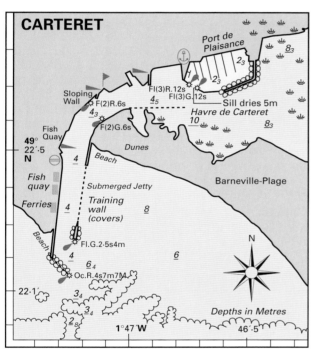

Tides

Add 25 minutes to the times of HW and LW St-Malo for the times of HW and LW Carteret; subtract 1·4m from the heights of HW St-Malo and 0·3m from the heights of LW St-Malo for the heights at Carteret.

Tidal streams

The streams start at the following times off the entrance
−0105 HW St Helier (−0150 HW St-Malo) NW
+0315 HW St Helier (+0400 HW St-Malo) SE
The maximum spring rate is 3¾knots.

Lights

Cap de Carteret Fl(2+1)15s81m26M Grey tower, green top
Jetée Ouest head Oc.R.4s7m7M White column, red top
Training wall head Fl.G.2·5s4m2M White mast, green top
At first bend to starboard Fl(2)G/Fl(2)R.6s on each side of channel
Marina entrance Fl(3)G/Fl(3)R.12s on each side of gate

Carteret. Approach to marina, looking upstream

Weir up river

Carteret marina entrance looking outwards

Search and rescue

An inshore lifeboat is maintained here.

Weather forecasts

From the *capitainerie* and the yacht club daily in the
season.

Communications

Bureau du Port on Ch 9 from 0900 to 1200, 1400–1800
☎ 02 33 04 70 84.

Customs

There is a customs office at Carteret.

Approaches

The only danger in the approaches is Plateau des
Trois Grunes 5M to the W with a least depth of
drying 1·6m which is marked by a W cardinal buoy
Q(9)15s. Approach with Cap de Carteret lighthouse
(grey tower, green top 81m, Fl(2+1)15s) bearing
approximately 040° until the Jetée Ouest head
(white column, red top, Oc.R.4s) ¾M to the E can
be identified and leave this 100m to port. Note that
the outer part of this jetty submerges near HW.
When approaching the entrance before HW, the
stream will be setting strongly to the NW outside.

The least depth in the approaches to the
breakwater end is drying 4m.

Entrance

Once the Jetée Ouest head has been rounded, the
stream will set strongly up the channel until HW.
Allow for this to leave the training wall head (white
mast, green top, Fl.G.2·5s) 50m to starboard and
then regain the centre of the channel to leave the
fishing quays 50m to port. Note that the training
wall to the N of its outer end will be submerged near
HW. Turn to starboard between the green and red
metal columns with Fl(2)G or R.6s and head for the
marina gate marked by red and green pylons Fl(3)R
or G.12s. There is a depth gauge by the port beacon.

The traffic signals on the *capitainerie* just to the
NW of the gate are:

3 red vertical	Gate closed
2 green over 1 white	Gate open

Beware of an easterly set across the gate if entering
before HW.

The sill dries 5m and opens or closes when there
is 1·3m over it which is ±HW 2½ hours.

Berths

There are over 300 berths in the marina, 60 for
visitors. There appears to be no length limit but any
vessel over 15m might have difficulty manoeuvring
inside. The basin is dredged to 2·3m. The waiting
pontoon is just inside the entrance below the
capitainerie and the visitors' pontoon is the last one
(F) at the E end of the basin.

It would be possible to dry out in the estuary
above the marina but it is crossed by a weir about
¼M further up.

Fishing boats dry out alongside the fishing quay in
the entrance channel but the quay is high and a
ladder would be needed unless a berth could be

found by one. The outer end of this quay is used by
the *vedettes*.

Facilities

Water and electricity On the pontoons.
Fuel On the reception pontoon.
Showers and heads Next to the *capitainerie*.
Slip and travel-lift 35 tons; in NE corner of basin.
Shops and restaurants A selection of good quality
shops and restaurants in the town which is a short
walk from the marina; also a chandler. There are
more restaurants/cafés towards the harbour
entrance.
Yacht club Yacht Club Barneville-Carteret is on the
N side of the marina; ice may be obtained here.
Leisure Walks and beaches.
Travel The railway to Carteret no longer runs.
Nearest station Valognes (15M) or Cherbourg
(25M) where there is also an airport. There may
be a bus, otherwise taxi Côte des Isles ☎ 02 33
04 61 02. There is a tourist information office in
Carteret in the season ☎ 02 33 04 94 54.

Port Bail

General

A drying and sheltered harbour lying 4M SE of Cap
de Carteret which is used by *vedettes* running to
Jersey. The approach channel dries 5·2m and the
marina basin dries 7m. There are some facilities in
the small town of Port Bail ½M across the bridge.

Data

Charts

Admiralty *3655* (SC) (ARCS)
SHOM *7133* (plan)
Imray *C33A* (plan)

Tides

Add 30 minutes to the times of HW and LW St-Malo to
find those times at Port Bail; subtract 0·7m from the

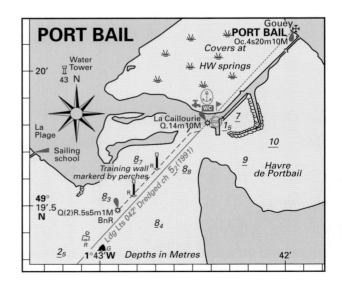

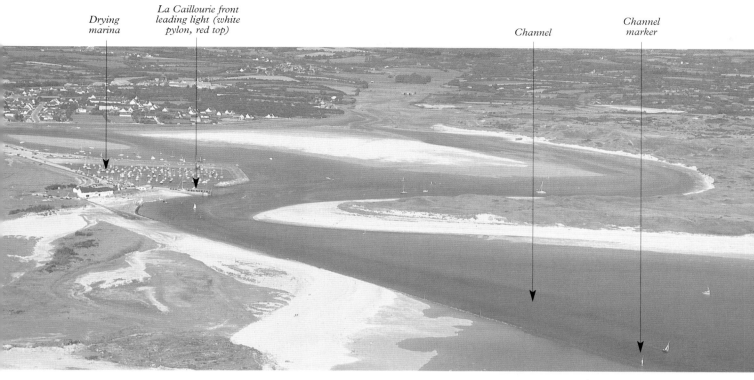

Port Bail looking SE at half-tide

heights of HW St-Malo and 0·2m from the heights of LW St-Malo for those at Port Bail.

Tidal streams

The tidal streams off Port Bail start at the following times:

–0130 HW St Helier (–0215 HW St-Malo) N
+0425 HW St Helier (+0340 HW St-Malo) S

The maximum spring rate is 3 knots.

Lights

La Caillourie Ldg Lt 042° *Front* Q.14m10M White pylon, red top
Rear Oc.4s20m10M in church belfry
Training wall head Q(2)R.5s5m1M White mast, red top

Buoys

Landfall Unlit RW ball topmark 1½M SW of entrance, just NW of leading line.

Communications

Bureau du port Ch 9 around HW during the season.
☎ 02 33 04 83 48.

Approaches

Reference should be made to charts *3665*, *2669* or SHOM *7133* for the approach. There are drying patches and shallows to the NW of the approach line and a prohibited anchorage to the SE where cables run to Jersey. The best time to enter is 1 hour before HW.

Port Bail. The drying yacht basin, jetty and entrance. Pontoon along the N side

Port Bail. The drying yacht basin from the jetty and entrance

Approach the landfall buoy from the SW provided there is enough water to cross the 0·7m patch just to the SW of it, and identify the leading line which is front La Caillourie beacon white pylon, red top (Q), and rear Port Bail church belfry (Oc.4s) 042°. A conspicuous water tower ½M to the W helps the identification. There is one set of port and starboard buoys before the outer end of the training wall (white beacon, red top Q(2)R.5s) is reached. Thence the channel is bounded to the NW by the training wall marked by beacons, and unlit buoys to the SW. It is dredged to drying 5·2m.

La Caillourie beacon lies just to the W of the jetty/slip which forms the W entrance to the drying basin.

Entrance and berths

Turn to port close round the end of the jetty into the basin where there is a pontoon on the W and along the N sides. The stream sets strongly across the entrance except at HW. The rest of the basin is occupied by head and stern moorings with a bottom of mud and sand which dries 7m. There is a drying pontoon along the NW side.

It may be possible to dry out alongside the jetty but ask first at the *capitainerie* as it is used by the *vedettes*.

Facilities

Water There are 4 water points, one by the *capitainerie* at the root of the jetty.
Showers and heads 4 near the *capitainerie*.
Slip In the NE corner of the basin.
Yacht club By the *capitainerie*; there is also a sailing school which operates from a slip on the W side of the peninsula to the W of the basin.
Shops Modest shops across the bridge to the E. Market day Tuesday.
Hotels and restaurants A small hotel and two restaurants near the end of the bridge.
Visits The small Romanesque church of Notre Dame with its 6th-century baptistry is worth a visit; guided tours 1000–1130, 1500–1630.

Granville

General

Granville is the principal port on the W side of the Cotentin peninsula and consists of the commercial part with a drying Avant Port and Bassin à Flot, and Port de Hérel, the newer marina adjoining it to the SE. The least depth in the approaches to Port de Hérel dries 2m and the gate to the marina opens ±3 hours HW. Granville has an exceptional range of tide, equinoctial springs can be over 13m and neaps over 10m. It is a large town with most facilities.

Data

Charts

Admiralty *3656, 3659, 3672* (plan) (SC) (ARCS)
Imray *C33B* (plan)

Tides

Times of HW are within 5 minutes of the times at St-Malo and the times of LW within 20 minutes. The heights at springs are 0·6m greater and 0·2m at neaps than at St-Malo.

Le Loup beacon tower   Entrance to Avant Port   Entrance to Port de Hérel

Granville, looking N

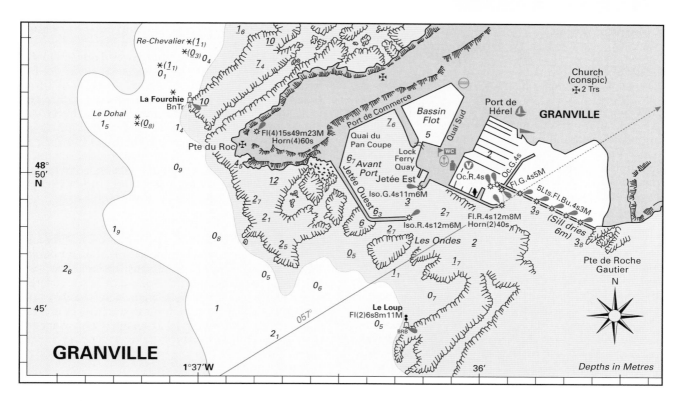

Tidal streams

The streams start at the following times off the port:

  −0145 HW St Helier (−0230 HW St-Malo) N
  +0255 HW St Helier (+0210 HW St-Malo) S

The maximum rate is 2 knots in either direction.

Lights

Pointe du Roc Fl(4)15s49m23M Horn(4)60s Grey
  tower, red top
Jetée Ouest head Iso.R.4s12m6M Red pylon
Jetée Est head Iso.G.4s11m6M White pylon, green top
  on hut
Le Loup Fl(2)6s8m11M White tower, red band
Hérel Marina Digue Principale head Fl.R.4s12m8M
  Horn(2)40s White round tower, red top
Hérel Marina Secondary mole head Fl.G.4s4m5M
  Green structure

Gate to marina Marked by red and green pylons with
  Oc.R or G.4s lights

Buoys

Le Videcoq W cardinal VQ(9)10s Whis marks a shoal
  drying 0·8m 3M W of the port.

Search and rescue

Granville is in the CROSS Jobourg region which will
  respond to emergency calls on Ch 16 or activation of
  GMDSS on Ch 70, as will Jersey Radio.
An all-weather lifeboat is maintained at Granville.

Weather forecasts

Granville (originated by CROSS Jobourg) at 0703,
  1533, 1903 LT in French on Ch 80.
Méteo France 08 36 68 08 50
Navtex Niton (S) and (K), Corsen (A)
Daily weather map in *bureau du port*.

Granville, looking NE. Church conspic over Port de Hérel

Granville. Port de Hérel. Marina entrance and sill from inside

Communications

Bureau du port de Plaisance Ch 9 (0800–2200)

Customs

There is an office in the N corner of the Bassin à Flot.

Approaches

Apart from the Iles Chausey 6M to the WNW, there are no off-lying dangers in the approaches.

Le Videcoq buoy, W cardinal Q(9)10s Whis, marking a drying 0·8m patch lies nearly 4M W of the port and from here the town may be identified by its buildings up the hill, the Pointe du Roc and the conspicuous twin towers of the church. Make the latter bear about 045° and approach on this line to leave Le Loup distant water beacon tower Fl(2)6s to starboard. At night run in on 057° on the outer marina breakwater end light Fl.R.4s which will be just to the right of the Avant Port outer breakwater end light Iso.R.4s.

Entrance to Le Hérel Marina

The least depth from Le Loup inwards is drying 2m. To the NE of the breakwater is a submerged wall running ESE/WNW marked by posts with fixed blue lights. Give the head of Le Hérel breakwater a good 50m clearance in case of any leavers cutting it fine. Once between the breakwater heads, turn to starboard through the gate marked by red and green beacons Fl.R or G.4s. The sill dries 4·5m and opens when there is 1·2m over it. There is a depth gauge by the entrance.

Berths

The visitors' pontoon is the first one (G) immediately inside the gate where there is 2·5m. Maximum length is 15m and there are short fingers on the pontoons to berth on. There are over 1,000 berths with 150 for visitors.

Port de Commerce

Yachts are not welcomed in the Avant Port which dries about 6·7m nor expected in the Bassin à Flot whose gates open from HW Granville −1½ hours to +1 hour and has a depth over the sill of drying 3·9m. The basin is used by commercial and fishing vessels and ferries.

Anchorage

An anchorage may be found in settled or offshore weather to the W of Le Loup beacon in 2m or more.

Facilities

Water and electricity On the pontoons.
Fuel Fuel berth at the base of the visitors' pontoon.
Showers and heads 18 near the *bureau du port*.
Chandlers To the N of the *bureau du port*.
Shops and supermarkets A number of all qualities a short walk away in the town.
Restaurants and cafés Many in the vicinity of the marina.
Hotels A number of all qualities; there is one on the marina.

Yacht club Next to the *bureau du port* which welcomes visitors. There is a nationally famous sailing school in the NE corner of Port de Hérel.
Travel-lift and cranes Cranes available, travel-lift up to 30 tons.
Repairs Engineers, electricians and shipwrights are available for repairs; ask at the *bureau du port*.
Travel The railway station is ½M to the WNW of the marina and connects to the main network at Argentan. The nearest airport is at Dinard which connects with the Channel Islands. There are ferries to Jersey, Guernsey, Sark, Iles Chausey and St-Malo. Taxi ☎ 02 33 50 50 06.

Historical

Granville, like St-Malo has a long history of piracy; also a rather uninteresting citadel at the top of the town built to defend the approaches to Mont St-Michel. There was a bizarre incident in early 1945 when German commandos from Jersey landed and took over the town for an hour and a half, long after it had been recaptured by the Allies who were by then well in to Germany.

Leisure

Granville is endowed with a number of museums – Musée de Granville (historical), Musée d'Art Moderne Richard-Anacréon, Historial Granvillais (historical with wax models), a butterfly museum near Pointe du Roc and even a museum to Christian Dior. There is also an aquarium, a shell exhibition and mineral stones exhibition near Point du Roc.

Cancale

General

Cancale lies at the NW corner of the large and shallow bay of Mont Saint-Michel, the spire of whose abbey in the SE corner dominates the area. The whole bay is given over to the cultivation of oysters, mussels and other shellfish and there are no deep water harbours. The word 'Cancale' to most Frenchmen suggests 'oysters' as 'Colchester' does to the English. Cancale has a large breakwater drying 6m alongside, and there are some deep water anchorages to the N of the town sheltered from the W, but only two where the holding is reasonable in the strong streams.

A place for bilge keelers or for those able to dry alongside the wall. Otherwise there is a sheltered anchorage in westerly weather in Port Mer 2M to the N where there are some facilities.

Data

Charts

Admiralty *3659* (SC) (ARCS)
Imray *C33B*
There are no larger-scale plans of the area.

Tides

The times are virtually the same as for St-Malo; add 0·7m

Port Mer   Ile des Landes   Herpin   Ile des Rimains

Cancale. Bay to N, looking NW

to the heights of HW St-Malo and 0·2m to the heights of LW for the heights at Cancale.

Tidal streams

Off Cancale the streams start at the following times

−0015 HW St Helier (−0030 HW St-Malo) N
+0430 HW St Helier (+0515 HW St-Malo) S

Off Port Mer the N-going stream starts earlier and the S-going later.

In both places the maximum rate does not exceed 3 knots.

Lights

La Pierre de Herpin 3M to the NE Oc(2)6s20m17M White tower, black top and base Siren Mo(N)60s

Cancale Jetty head Oc(3)G.12s12m7M White pylon, green top on green hut Obscd when bearing less than 223°

Buoys

There are three unlit cardinal buoys to the N and NW of Pointe de Grouin

La Fille N cardinal with whis marking a drying 3·8m rock close to the NW of Le Pierre de Herpin

Ruet W cardinal with bell close WNW of Herpin Rock (21m)

Grande Bunouse N cardinal close N of a drying 1·6m patch.

Approaches

From the N and W A night approach from these directions is not recommended unless the visibility is such as to be able to see the unlit buoys at a reasonable distance.

Identify Pointe du Grouin with its conspicuous semaphore building on the end, Ile des Landes close to the E of it, Herpin rock (21m) and Le Pierre de Herpin light tower. When the buoys Ruet W cardinal and Grande Bunouse N cardinal have been identified, pass between them to go through narrow (150m) but deep (5m) Chenal de la Veille Rivière between Ponte du Grouin and Ile des Landes to leave Barbe Brulée E cardinal beacon tower to starboard. The stream runs fast but true through this channel.

Port Mer.
Moorings and
anchorage

Pointe du
Grouin and
Sémaphore

Ile des
Landes

Cancale. Port Mer, looking NW

Cancale looking SW near HW

If this passage does not appeal, leave Ruet W cardinal buoy and Herpin Rock close to starboard before turning S in to Grande Rade.

Cancale may now be reached by passing through the narrow channel (0m) close to the E of the starboard beacon tower marking the extremity of dangers off Pointe de la Chaine and the small island to the SW of Ile des Rimains. Otherwise pass to the E of Ile des Rimains with its fort before turning SW to close Cancale breakwater end on a course of at least 240°.

From the E or NE There are no dangers on the approaches from these directions provided La Pierre de Herpin and its NW off-lier, and Ile des Rimains and its SW out-lier are all left to the W to approach Cancale breakwater end on a track of at least 240°, or Port Mer on a westerly course.

Anchorages

Port Mer as far W as depths and moorings allow to avoid the stream, on sand.

Close SE of Ile des Rimains in 2m, sand and mud.

Other areas that may attract as anchorages should be treated with caution as there may be only a shallow layer of mud over rock which may not hold in the strong streams.

Berths

The inner side of the breakwater is much used by *vedettes* at the outer end, and by fishing boats along the length of it. If seeking a berth on it, ask at the *bureau du port* before settling down; a ladder may be needed to get ashore.

The bay is mostly flat sand and suitable for grounding with bilge keels in westerly weather.

Facilities
Cancale

The town is a bustling seaside resort devoted also to the cultivation and consumption of shellfish. It offers few concessions to yachtsmen except for a water tap on the quay and many restaurants and cafés plus quite adequate shops.

Port Mer

No shops in the vicinity but a restaurant, café, bars and a sailing school by the beach.

Historical

Cancale is the most easterly Breton port of any substance and is steeped in the Breton sea-going traditions. During the 18th century Cancalese were famous all over the world as daring seamen and in the navy of Louis XIV entire ships' companies came from this port. Like so many ports along this coast they contributed to the corsair and privateer traditions of robbing the trade passing through the Channel and many ended up in English prisons during the Napoleonic Wars.

Three manifestations today recall the past of Cancale:

The *bisquines* were the beautiful local design of fishing boat unique to this area with straight stems, long overhanging counters, two masts setting lugsails with topsails above them and a huge jib set on a long bowsprit. Thankfully, a few have been restored to their former glory and ply for pleasure between the port and Iles Chausey.

Strong Roman Catholic beliefs have been maintained, unlike further west in Brittany where communism between the wars eroded the old faith in an increasing materialistic age. Their devotion to Notre Dame du Verger whose shrine stands above Pointe du Grouin, remains steadfast.

The Fishery School founded in the 19th century by one of the local priests became nationally famous and did much to raise the standards and education of the fishermen.

2. The Channel Islands

Introduction

The main ports and anchorages in Alderney, Guernsey, Herm, Sark and Jersey are included in this Pilot for the benefit of those on passage to and from North Brittany. It does not include the minor islands of Les Écrehous, Les Minquiers and Ile Chausey for which the *Channel Islands Pilot* by the RCC Pilotage Foundation should be consulted. Each island section contains advice on the optimum time to leave each port in any direction to make the best use of the tidal streams and there is also a Planning Guide giving distances between them and ports in France.

The Channel Islands have been part of Britain since 1066 with a brief interlude under German

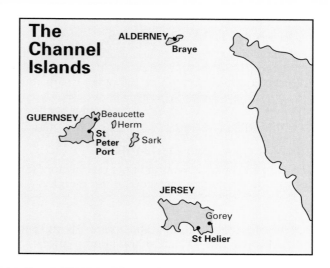

Planning guide
Cherbourg – Channel Islands – Tréguier

	Cherbourg	A de St-Martin	Goury	Alderney	Diélette	Guernsey	Carteret	Port Bail	Jersey (St H)	Granville	Is Chausey	Cancale	St-Malo	St-Briac	St-Jacut	St-Cast	B de Fresnaie	Erquy	Dahouet	St-Brieuc	Binic	St-Q/Portrieux	Paimpol	Ile Bréhat	Lézardrieux	Pontrieux	Tréguier
Cherbourg		12	16	24	26	42	37	41	57	69	69	86	89	89	89	89	90	92	97	103	105	104	87	82	87	93	93
A de St-Martin	12		4	12	14	30	25	29	45	57	57	74	77	77	77	77	78	80	85	91	93	92	75	70	75	81	81
Goury	16	4		10	10	27	22	26	42	54	43	71	74	74	74	74	75	77	82	88	90	89	72	67	72	78	78
Alderney	24	12	10		17	22	28	32	40	60	58	71	72	72	73	73	73	76	80	85	81	79	67	64	69	75	75
Diélette	26	14	10	17		28	13	17	33	48	48	61	64	67	69	72	74	68	73	80	83	85	68	63	68	74	74
Guernsey	42	30	27	22	28		30	32	28	54	47	58	54	52	52	52	51	50	54	57	54	51	44	43	48	54	50
Carteret	37	25	22	28	13	30		4	22	35	35	47	44	46	48	51	53	63	68	73	73	72	63	62	67	73	73
Port Bail	41	29	26	32	17	32	4		21	31	31	44	42	44	46	49	51	61	66	73	73	73	62	60	65	71	71
Jersey (St H)	57	45	42	40	33	28	22	21		30	25	34	35	35	35	35	35	37	43	48	48	45	44	42	47	53	60
Granville	69	73	70	62	48	54	35	31	30		10	13	22	26	28	31	33	43	48	55	65	65	74	77	82	88	91
Is Chausey	69	73	70	62	48	47	35	31	25	10		13	14	18	20	23	25	35	40	47	57	58	67	70	75	81	84
Cancale	86	74	71	71	61	58	47	44	34	13	13		17	21	23	26	28	38	43	50	60	61	70	70	75	81	84
St-Malo	89	77	74	72	64	54	44	42	35	22	14	17		7	9	12	14	24	29	36	36	37	46	46	51	57	60
St-Briac	89	77	74	72	67	52	46	44	35	26	18	21	7		2	5	7	17	22	29	29	29	39	39	44	50	53
St-Jacut	89	77	74	73	69	52	48	46	35	28	20	23	9	2		3	5	15	20	27	27	27	28	37	42	48	51
St-Cast	89	77	74	73	72	52	51	49	35	31	23	26	12	5	3		2	12	17	24	24	25	34	34	39	45	48
B de Fresnaie	90	78	75	73	74	51	53	51	35	33	35	28	14	7	5	2		10	15	22	22	23	32	32	37	43	46
Erquy	92	80	77	76	68	50	63	61	37	43	35	38	24	17	15	12	10		5	12	14	14	25	25	30	36	40
Dahouet	97	85	82	80	73	54	68	66	43	48	40	43	29	22	20	17	15	5		7	10	11	25	25	28	34	39
St-Brieuc	103	91	88	85	80	57	73	73	48	55	47	50	36	29	27	24	22	12	7		6	9	24	24	29	35	42
Binic	105	93	90	81	83	54	73	73	48	65	57	60	36	39	27	24	22	14	10	6		3	18	17	22	28	31
St-Q/Portrieux	104	92	89	79	85	51	72	73	45	65	58	61	37	30	28	25	23	14	11	9	3		15	14	19	25	28
Paimpol	87	75	72	67	68	44	63	62	44	74	67	70	46	39	37	34	32	25	25	24	18	15		8	13	19	22
Ile Bréhat	82	70	67	64	63	43	62	60	42	77	70	70	46	39	37	34	32	25	23	24	17	14	8		5	11	18
Lézardrieux	87	75	72	69	68	48	67	65	47	82	75	75	51	44	42	39	37	30	28	29	22	19	13	5		6	18
Pontrieux	93	81	78	75	74	54	73	71	53	88	81	81	57	50	48	45	43	36	34	35	28	25	19	11	6		24
Tréguier	93	81	78	75	74	50	73	71	60	91	84	84	60	53	51	48	46	40	39	42	31	28	22	18	18	24	

Distances are given over the shortest navigable route and are measured to and from inner harbour or anchorage

occupation during the Second World War. They have their own governments and Jersey and Guernsey both have Lieutenant Governors appointed by the Crown. They are not part of the EU and VAT is not imposed. Each island has its own characteristics and a short summary will be found at the beginning of each island section. In general the differences between the UK/France and the islands are:

TIDES AND TIDAL STREAMS

The streams run extremely fast round Alderney but the range is moderate. Perversely, this is reversed towards Jersey in the S where the range is large and the streams less swift. Wherever in the islands and whatever the stage of the lunar cycle, they are to be reckoned with.

PROVISIONS AND SHOPPING

The advantages of a favourable tax regime are often negated by the cost of transport to the islands.

FUEL

Red diesel prices are comparable to the UK and very much cheaper than French marina pump prices.

MONEY

The islands have their own currency in notes and coins. UK money is accepted readily but there may be difficulty getting Channel Islands money accepted in the UK except in banks.

FORMALITIES

As the islands are not in the EU, a Q flag must be flown and a written declaration made when stopping at any of the islands on the way from UK or France. Forms are usually supplied without demand on arrival at Alderney, St Peter Port and St Helier.

YACHT CLUBS

Visitors are welcome at Alderney, St Peter Port and St Helier provided the usual courtesies are observed.

LAYING UP

Facilities are available at Alderney (limited), St Peter Port, Beaucette and St Helier but not usually at such advantageous rates as in France.

SEARCH AND RESCUE

There is no coastguard in the islands and this function is carried out by Jersey and St Peter Port Radios who will respond to emergency calls on Ch 16 or the activation of Ch 70 on GMDSS. All the islands are also in the area of responsibility of CROSS Jobourg. There are all-weather lifeboats at Alderney, St Peter Port and St Helier. There are hospitals at St Peter Port and St Helier.

Technical and navigational information

The data and information shown under Cruising in France on page 1 apply with the following exceptions.

Radio services

St Peter Port and Jersey Radios still offer a public service facility (link calls). The VHF frequencies are shown under St Peter Port and St Helier. There is no longer an MF link.

Weather forecasts

Jersey Radio only provides weather forecasts on Channels 25 and 82 at 0645, 0745, 0845 (all 1 hour earlier during DST), 1245,1845 and 2245 UTC.
BBC Radio Guernsey on 1116kHz and 93·2mHz broadcast weather bulletins at 0807, 1235, 1710 LT Mon–Fri, 0810 Sat and Sun, all LT.
Island FM on 93·7mHz for Alderney broadcast a synopsis and forecast every H+30.
BBC Radio Jersey on 1026kHz and 88·8mHz broadcast weather bulletins at 0635, 0810 and 1835 Mon–Fri, 0735 Sat and Sun, all LT.
See also under Cruising in Normany and Brittany on page 4 for details of further weather services in the vicinity.

Alderney

General

An attractive and unspoilt island which is part of the Bailiwick of Guernsey but autonomous with its own President and local government. There is a good harbour at Braye and a few open, fine weather anchorages which may be suitable to wait out a tide. Ashore the leisure facilities should satisfy for a day or two. The capital, St Anne lies on the hill above Braye.

The name Alderney is derived from the Scandinavian. Aurigny is the modern French name and the local patois is based on Norman French. To the Romans it was Ridunia and the natives to this day are known as Ridunians.

Warning

The island is beset with the strongest tidal streams in the area and are not to be trifled with. The Alderney Race to the east of the island and The Swinge to the north should only be navigated in good weather and favourable tidal conditions. In heavy weather and at springs the overfalls in both areas can be lethal to small vessels. The tidal flow can reverse in a short distance in some places near the shores.

The areas of the worst overfalls are shown on Admiralty chart *60* and in wind over tide conditions should be given a wide berth. They are in The Swinge, and to the east of Quenard Point in the vicinity of Blanchard, Inner and Outer Race Rocks.

Braye Harbour

General

A well protected and organised harbour except in winds from the north east when it offers little shelter. There are over 80 mooring buoys for visitors but the holding is indifferent with many rock patches. The pier is in continual use by ferries, commercial craft and fishing boats; the inner harbour dries out. All normal facilities needed by yachts can be found in Braye or up the hill at St Anne.

Warning

The breakwater extends underwater from its apparent end for a further 600 metres. It has a least depth of 1·2 metres over the remains. The tidal stream inshore sets westward on to it for 9½ out of the 12 hours and the leading marks to clear the end of the underwater section are very difficult to see in daylight and unlit.

Data

Charts

Admiralty *3653, 2845, 2669, 60* (SC and ARCS)
  SC Folio *5604* (10 charts)
Imray *C33A*

Tidal information

Time differences			Height differences			
HW		LW	MHWS	MHWN	MLWN	MLWS
St Helier						
0300	0900	0200 0900				
and	and	and and	11·0	8·1	4.0	1·4
1500	2100	1400 2100				
Braye Harbour						
+0050	+0040	+0025 +0105	−4·8	−3·4	−1·5	−0·5

Tidal streams

The tidal streams round the island are shown in diagrams on Admiralty chart *60*, and more generally in *Admiralty Tidal Stream Atlas – Channel Islands NP264*.

In the Swinge slack water is at 2½ hours before and 3½ after HW St Helier. In the Alderney Race, about 1 mile to the east of the island the SW/NE-going stream is slack at 2 hours before and 4½ hours after HW St Helier. It should be noted that the periods of slack water do not coincide with the times of HW and LW at Braye. In both areas the flood stream sets NE and the ebb SW but there are two inshore anomalies:

a. Along the SE coast of the island the set is always to the NE except between 5 and 6 hours after HW St Helier when it is slack.

b. Along the N corner of the island between Gros Nez Point at the root of the breakwater and The Grois Rocks off Château à l'Etoc the inshore stream sets SW except between 2 hours before and HW St Helier. This counter current runs at up to 4 knots at springs and is separated only by a narrow band of water from the main flood stream setting NE at the same rate.

Both these anomalies can be made use of when approaching Braye from the S through the Alderney Race or entering the harbour from the NE during the flood. They are of only limited use when coming through The Swinge.

Lights

Casquets Fl(5)30s37m24M Horn(2)60s Racon White tower, highest and NW of three
Quenard Point LtHo Fl(4)15s37m23M Horn(1)30s White tower, black band 027°-obscd-085°
Château à L'Etoc Iso.WR.4s20m10/7M 071°-R-111°-W-151° R sector covers Burhou
Braye Harbour breakwater LFl.10s.7m5M
Braye Harbour Ldg Lts 215°
  Front Q.8m17M 210°-vis-220° Synchronised with rear White column with yellow triangle on concrete base on elbow of old harbour pier
  Rear 335m from front Q.17m18M 210°-vis-220° white column with yellow base
Braye Pier head 2F.R(vert)8m5M

Buoys

There are three port and starboard-hand buoys with Q.R and Q.G lights which indicate the channel clear of moorings.

Weather forecasts

Jobourg CROSS on Ch 80 at 0710, 0733, 1545, 1603, 1910, 1933 local French time in French and English.
Island FM on 93·7MHz; synopsis and forecast every H+30.
Daily weather map at harbour office.

Communications

Braye harbour office Ch 74 and 16. Call sign *Alderney Radio* 0800–1800.
Water taxi (Mainbrayce Chandlers) Ch 37.
Emergency ☎ 112 or 999. Harbour office, coastguard ☎ 01481 822620. Mainbrayce ☎ 01481 822772. Doctor ☎ 01481 822077.

Customs

A Q flag must be flown and a written customs declaration made if the last port was any other than Guernsey.

Approaches

From the north and east Navigate to a position 1½ miles N of the conspicuous Quenard Point Lighthouse when the harbour entrance will be open. Care must be taken on the ebb not to be set S into the race off the E end of the island. From this position the leading lights will be visible at night but the beacons are difficult to see by day particularly in the afternoon sun. There are plans (2001) to increase this visibility. If in doubt St Anne's church spire is conspicuous on the skyline; keep this bearing 215° until the leading marks can be identified and proceed down them into the harbour.

From the north and west If passing S of Burhou through the Swinge, see Warning and Tidal Stream information above. It is preferable to pass through The Swinge either at slack water or between 2½ hours before to 2½ hours after HW St Helier. If passing N of Burhou navigate to a position ½ mile N of the visible end of the Breakwater and endeavour to pick out the two spindly and inconspicuous beacons which lead clear of the submerged breakwater. If they cannot be picked out keep the lighthouses of Quenard Point and Château à L'Etoc open or bearing more than 112° until St

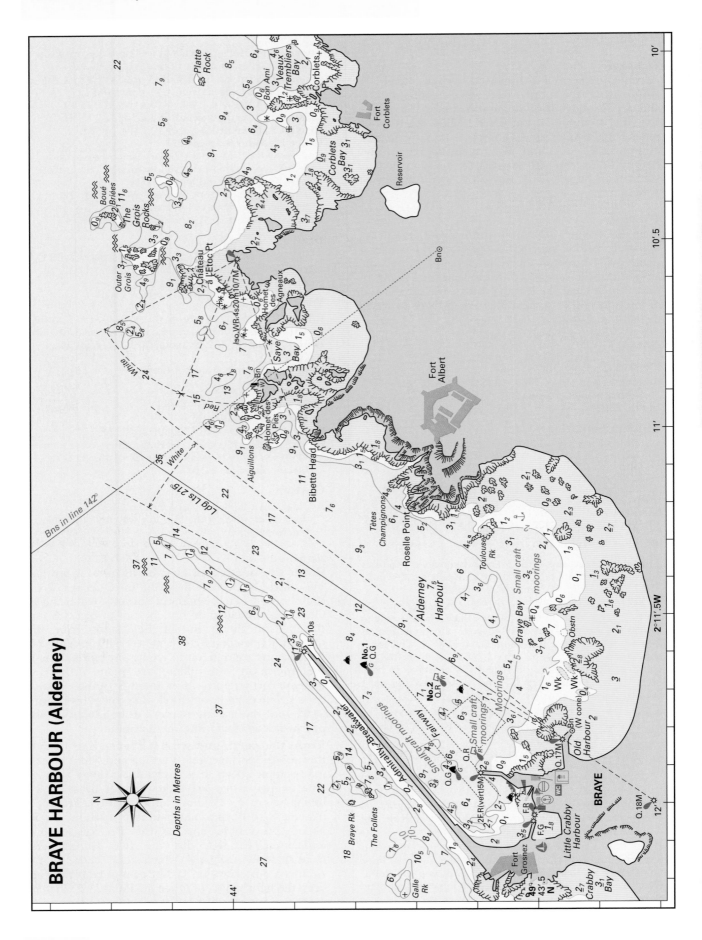

BRAYE HARBOUR (Alderney)

Alderney. Braye, looking SSW. In the summer the moorings extend half the length of the breakwater

Anne's spire bears 215° and the leading line can be identified. At night keep in the white sector of Château à L'Etoc until the leading lights are seen.

From the south through the Swinge The only off-lying danger is Pierre au Vraic with 1·2m over it lying some 2 miles S of Ortac. Time arrival at the SW end of The Swinge either at slack water or between 2½ hours before to 2½ hours after HW St Helier. See Warnings above when using this passage.

From the south passing E of island Advantage may be made of the almost permanent set NE along the SE coast of the island. Aim to arrive off Raz Island between 2 hours before and 4 hours after HW St Helier to make the most of the favourable inshore eddies round to Braye. There is a clearing transit of more than 240° of Etac de la Quoire and Coque Lihou which leads clear of the rocks S of Brinchetais Ledge; otherwise keep outside the 20m line until Quenard Point bears 310° or less when course may be altered to the N to pass round Quenard Point with its off-liers of Sauquet Rock and The Grois Rocks. Keep outside the 15m line until St Anne's spire bears 215° and/or the harbour leading line is identified.

Entrance

Once past the breakwater head, the straight channel clear of moorings is marked by red and green lit buoys and leads up to the pier and the inner harbour.

Moorings

There are at least 80 visitors' moorings in rows parallel to the breakwater and more in the SE corner of Braye Bay. They have a small ring on the top and unless a patent pick-up device is used will need to be lassoed initially in any wind. Yachts longer than about 15m may find some of the spaces between some moorings too small.

Anchoring

There are many rocky patches in the bay which should be avoided if possible. In northeasterly winds some shelter may be found in the southeastern part of Braye Bay SW of Toulouse Rock and clear of the moorings.

Berths

Berths alongside the pier are very unlikely to be available. Ask the harbour office on Ch 74 before proceeding there.

Facilities

Water and fuel From Mainbrayce chandlers inside the inner harbour. There is a drying berth alongside just to port inside the entrance. A tide gauge at the entrance shows the depth at this berth. Call on Ch 80.

Water taxi Call on Ch 37.

Dinghy landing At the slip at all stages of the tide.

Showers and heads By the harbour office.

Yacht club On the quay, welcomes visitors.

Shops Supermarket and shops in Braye village. There is also a duty-free alcohol and tobacco outlet here which delivers on board.

Restaurant, cafés and pubs In Braye village with more ¾M up the hill in St Anne.

Bicycle hire Available in Braye.

Post office and banks In St Anne.

Leisure There are pleasant walks and rides round the island.

Travel A high speed passenger ferry operates several times weekly from March to October from Portsmouth, Poole and Weymouth via Jersey and Guernsey. There is a direct ferry service from Southampton and Torquay. Aurigny Air Services have regular flights to Guernsey, Jersey and Southampton. Jersey and Guernsey have international airports.

Other anchorages

The Lug of Burhou A bay opening to the S between Burhou and Little Burhou. It can be approached from the SW avoiding the overfalls in The Swinge if they are active. A stern transit that leads in is Coupé Rock just open of the Garden Rocks on 154°. This anchorage has a very strong tidal flow NE through it near HW springs but is otherwise sheltered.

Hannaine Bay At the W end of the island and suitable to wait for the tide in The Swinge if it is foul. The transit of the white pyramid beacon S of Roque Tourgis Fort open to the right of Fort Clonque on 055° should be carefully held as the passage in is only 200m wide. Anchor in 3m sand 100m or more S of Fort Clonque.

Longy Bay A bay on the SE shore S of Quenard Point and just W of Raz Island. Useful to await the tide round the E end of the island. Enter leaving Queslingue (14m) 100m to port and the rock drying 0·6m clear to starboard. See chart *60*.

Departures

To the north and east 2½ hours before HW St Helier will find slack water outside Braye Harbour and turning to the NE.

To the north and west 4 hours after HW St Helier will find the inshore stream starting to the SW and the best time to pass N of Burhou. If going through the Swinge 3–3½ hours after HW St Helier will find slack water there, turning to the SW.

To the south As above if going through The Swinge. If passing round Quenard Point before turning S, 4 hours after HW St Helier will find a counter current against inshore until clear of Branchetais Ledge when at 5 hours after HW St Helier the SW stream will be away.

Guernsey

The Bailiwick of Guernsey is the most western of the Channel Islands; it is a well-developed and prosperous island although not as commercialised as Jersey. It has two busy ports and four marinas and is a popular stopping off point for yachts bound to and from Brittany. Visitors are welcomed, well catered for and there are all the facilities a yachtsman needs at hand. A longer stay to explore the island or to make day trips to Herm and Sark is well worthwhile.

There are two marinas readily available to visitors – Victoria Marina in St Peter Port and Beaucette on the NE corner of the island. There are also moorings in St Peter Port and several anchorages round the island. St Sampsons is a commercial port, partially dries out and is not for yachtsmen.

Warnings

Tidal streams, while not so fierce as further north are strong and should always be considered. The tidal range is up to 10 metres. In thick weather and bad visibility navigation becomes difficult in the vicinity of the islands even with radar and GPS.

St Peter Port

General

A busy port with all facilities for yachtsmen. Victoria Marina can be entered up to 2½ hours either side of local HW depending on draught and there are numbers of buoys or pontoons in the outer harbour. The commercial part of the port caters for ferries and containers; this traffic must not be impeded and the traffic signals or instructions from port control followed when entering or leaving.

Albert Marina in the SW corner of St Peter Port, and Queen Elizabeth II Marina just to the north can only be used by prior arrangement. The latter can accommodate rather deeper draught yachts than Victoria.

Warning

The port is well sheltered from the west, Herm and Sark give some protection from the east but easterly gales make the outer harbour uncomfortable for yachts and there can be a considerable surge in Victoria Marina near HW. This marina is dredged to 2m although most of the bottom is soft.

Data

Charts

Admiralty *807, 808, 2669, 3140, 3654* (SC and ARCS) SC Folio *5604* (10 charts)

Imray *C33A*

Tidal information

	Time differences			Height differences			
	HW		LW	MHWS	MHWN	MLWN	MLWS
St Helier							
	0300	0900	0200 0900				
	and	and	and and	11·0	8·1	4·0	1·4
	1500	2100	1400 2100				

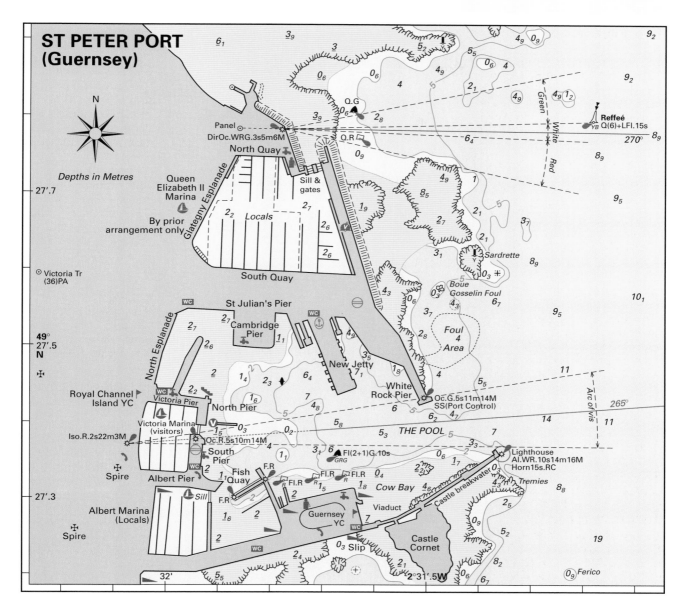

ST PETER PORT (Guernsey)

St Peter Port
This is a Standard Port with its own predictions
The mean of differences
is within 10 minutes
of St Helier   −2·2   −1·1   −0·4   0

Lights

Hanois Fl(2)13s33m20M Tyfon(2)60s
Big Russel
Noire Pute Fl(2)WR.15s8m6M 220°-W-040°-R-220°
   On rock
Fourquies Q N cardinal buoy
Little Russel
From the north
Platte Fougère Fl.WR.10s15m16M Horn 45s 155°-W-
   085° White octagonal tower, black band Racon (P)
Tautenay Q(3)WR.6m7/6M 050°-W-215° Black and
   white beacon tower
Petite Canupe Q(6)+Fl.15s S cardinal beacon
Roustel Q.10m7M Lattice structure
Platte Fl.WR3s6m7/5M 024°-R-219°-W-024° Green
   conical tower
Brehon Iso.4s19m9M Beacon on squat round tower

St Martin's Point Fl(3)WR.10s15m14M Horn(3)30s
   185°-R-191°-W-011°-R-081°
Buoys
Reffée (off entrance to QE II Marina)VQ(6)+Fl.10s S
   cardinal.
Lower Heads Q(6)+Fl.15s Bell S cardinal
St Peter Port
Castle Breakwater head Ldg Lts 220°
   Front Al.WR.10s14m16M Horn15s synchronised with
   lights 187°-vis-007° Dark tower, white on NE side
   Rear **Belvedere** Oc.10s61m14M 179°-vis-269° White
   square with orange stripe 217°-intens-223°
White Rock (north) pierhead Oc.G.5s11m14M Stone
   tower, white lantern Traffic signals
Victoria Marina Ldg Ls 265°
   Front on S pierhead Oc.R.5s10m14M White
   framework tower, red top
   Rear 160m from front Iso.R.2s22m3M 260°-vis-270°

Search and rescue

Call St Peter Port Radio on Ch 16 or activate GMDSS
   on Ch 70 to which Guernsey is fully converted.

*(1₈)Platte Boue

*(3₉) **Grande Amfroque** Bn Trs (17)

*(0₃)

*(1₂)

(3₁)

(9) Cul de l'Autel

(2₇) Longue Pierre

Gran Hayes Channel

Noire Pute (2) Fl(2)WR.15s8m6M

(1₆)

38

38

44

20

Le Boursée

The Humps

5₉

(4₆)

Tautenay Bn Tr Q(3)WR.6s7m7/6M

1₅

(1₅)

(2₁)

Cavale

6₇ *(1₂)

Obelisk (13)

HERM

White drums

Pte Sauzebourge

Fourquies Q BY

Fourquies of Big Russel (2₃)

21

30

0₂

(0₈)

Jethou

(3)

(2₇)

(8)

(2)

(5₁) Rocquerie

(0₃)

Vermerette Fl(2)Y.5s

Gate Rock Fl(9)15s

Percée Passage

63

Tobar's Passage

(7₉)

(1)

(4)

Little Russel

Roustel à Brehon 198

Beaucette Ldg Line 267°

30

4

Roustel Q.8m7M

Rousse Bn

Grosse Pierre (9)

Fondu(8)

(0₃)

Bn

(1₂)

(0₁)

(7₃) (1₆)

(1₈)

Pt Creux Bn Q.R

Corbette Pass

Fl.G.3s

3₉

(32)

Alligande Bn Fl(3)G.5s

15

Brehon Iso.4s19m9M

2

(5₉)

See plan

14

Platte Fougère Fl.WR.10s15m16M Horn 45s (4)

Petite Canupe Q(6)+LFl.15s

(0₈)

Les Fourquies 18

(3)

(7) (1₈)

(7₆)

Tasse

Corbette d'Amont (0₉)

(5₅)

0₆ 0₉

8₈

Bectondu (4)

Platte Fl.WR.3s6m7/5M

0₃

(0₆)

*(1₅)

(3₇)

Grandes Braves

R Vieille

(0.5)

Doyle Passage

5₂

Bn Tr

6₇

Belvidere House 265°

(3₁)

7₆

Castle Breakwater à

(5₉)

18

Doyle Passage 149°

2

19

Fort Doyle

I Grune Pierre

(2₁)

4₉

Britt Sauvary Pass

(2₁)

1₂

(2₇)

1₅

Boue Agenor

Houmet Paradis

Bordeaux Hbr

Bequets

Wh Patch

(2₁)

4₁

(1₅) Fourquies Belle Grève

Victoria Marina Ldg line265°

24

L'Ancresse

(4₆)

Vale Mill Tr (55)

Vale Cas (31)

FR

F.G

Mt Cevlet Tr

Shed

4₅

(0.3)

Bn (4₁)

Refée VQ(6)+ Fl.10s YB

Al.WR. 10s16M Castle Horn 15s

See plan

Ferico

Martello Tr No.7

7

St Sampson

DirOc.WRG. 3s5m6M

Victoria Tr

Oc.G.5s

Oyster, Ferico

(0₉)

Roque au Nord (0.5)

5₆ 5₉

Mt Chouet Martello Tr No.10 (0₂)

Vale Spire

Tel Tr

Tr 265°

Corget

St Peters

Havelet

(1₁)

(1₅)

(1)

7

GUERNSEY

ST PETER PORT

G Spire

(1₄)

Rousse de Mer (6₈)

Silleuse (1)

(3₁)

Rousse Pt Martello Tr

Grand Havre

Bn

49° 29' N

28'

21

31'

15

20

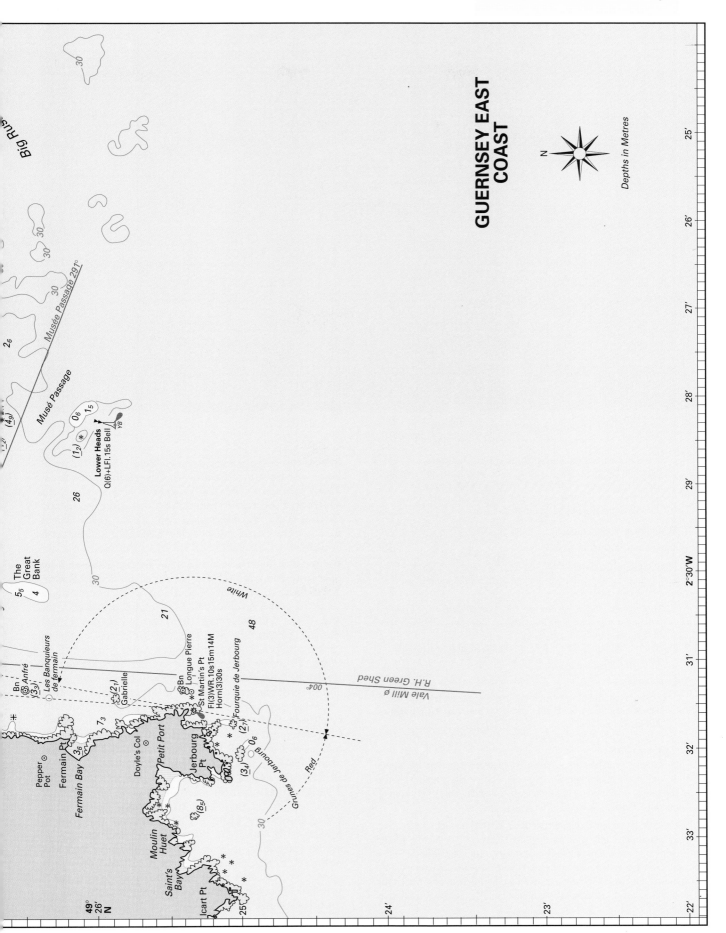

Big Russel

30

30

30

30

Musée Passage 291°

30

2₆

Musé Passage

(4₉)

0₆ 1₅

(1₂) (*)

Lower Heads
Q(6)+LFl.15s Bell

Y8

26

The
Great
Bank

5₅
4

30

30

White

21

48

Les Banquieurs
de fermain

Bn
⊙ Anfré

(3₁)
⊙ Les Banquieurs
de fermain

(3₁)
⊙ Gabrielle

Longue Pierre

Bn
* St Martin's Pt
Fl(3)WR.10s15m14M
Horn(3)30s

Fourquie de Jerbourg

(2₁)

Vale Mill ø
R.H. Green Shed

004°

⊞

7₃

Pepper
Pot ⊙

Fermain Pt

3₆

Doyle's Col

Petit Port

Jerbourg
Pt

(3₁)

0₆

Gnumes de Jerbourg

Red

Fermain Bay

(8₅)

30

Moulin
Huet

Saint's
Bay

Icart Pt

**49°
26'
N**

25'

**GUERNSEY EAST
COAST**

N

Depths in Metres

25'   26'   27'   28'   29'   **2°30'W**   31'   32'   33'

24'

23'

22'

Havelet Bay   *Castle Cornet*   *Port control*

Guernsey. St Peter Port looking W

Entrance track to Victoria Marina

Search and rescue operations are co-ordinated through St Peter Port Radio who will usually handle any emergencies within 12 miles of Guernsey or Alderney under the aegis of CROSS Jobourg.
A lifeboat is maintained at St Peter Port.

Weather forecasts

See Introduction above.

Communications

St Peter Port Control Ch 12; Victoria Marina Ch 80; Water taxi Ch 10.

St Peter Port Radio listens on Ch 16, 20 and 62. They will accept public service (link) calls for which Ch 62 is the principal channel.

Harbour authority ☎ 01481 720229, signal station ☎ 720085.

Customs

A Q flag must be flown and customs cleared by making a written declaration if the last port was any other than Alderney.

Approaches

In thick weather when leading lines cannot be seen at a distance, navigation in the Big and Little Russels and along the S coast lends itself to using parallel index if radar is fitted.

From the northeast via the Big Russel Leave the Grande Amfroque and its off-liers, the Noire Pute beacon and the Fourquies buoy to starboard. The best time to arrive off the Lower Heads buoy is 3½ hours before HW St PeterPort/St Helier to carry the last of the S-going stream in the Big Russel and the

first of the N-going across to St Peter Port. This will also be at the time of minimum overfalls in this area. The corner may be cut at Lower Heads provided Victoria Tower and the right-hand edge of Castle Cornet can be identified on 291°. This leads through the Musé passage leaving the Musé beacon (yellow with M topmark) 300m to the N.

From the northeast via the Little Russel The best time to arrive off the N end of the Little Russel is 3½ hours before HW St Peter Port when only a weak N-going stream will be met for another hour and there will be water over the sill into Victoria Marina (4·2m above CD) and Beaucette Marina (2·4m above CD). Navigate to a point 1 mile NE of Platte Fougère light to pick up the first transit of Roustel (lattice structure with low black and white chequered base and square solid top) and Brehon (small beacon on squat round tower) 198°. Continue down it leaving Petite Canupe beacon to starboard and Tautenay light well to port until 300 metres to the N of Roustel. Alter then to 220° on the main leading line and leading lights of Castle Breakwater light (white tower) and Belvedere light. The latter light is intensified on the line but not very conspicuous by day. It is to the right of the large white Belvedere House. Platte beacon (G conical tower) with Vale Mill tower behind will shortly be left to starboard, followed by the chimneys and fuel tanks of St Sampsons. Brehon is left to port. This approach has the most latitude and is the most suitable from the N in poor visibility; others may be found on chart *807*.

Guernsey. Les Hanois lighthouse looking NW

From the northwest via the Little Russel Either pass N of the Grandes Brayes, Petites Brayes and Platte Fougère Rocks to pick up the first transit as above or use the Doyle Passage. Whichever is used 3 hours before HW St Peter Port is a good time as the stream will be still setting E along the N coast.

Doyle Passage Useful if going to Beaucette or as a short cut inside Platte Fougère. Navigate to a position 2 miles NW of Platte Fougère and pick up the transit Roustel (lattice tower with square solid top) in the centre of the gap between Herm and Jethou 149°; on this line the islet of Fondu may be visible just to left of Roustel. Continue until Fort Doyle is abeam to starboard when course may be altered for the waiting buoys outside Beaucette. If continuing in to the Little Russel, turn to port off the 149° line on to the leading line for Beaucette 096° and DO NOT overshoot it (see inset on chart *807*). Continue closely on this line along the Beaucette buoyed channel until Petite Canupe beacon (S cardinal) is abeam to port when course may be altered to 170° on Roustel when the final leading line may be picked up.

From the northwest via Les Hanois and St Martins There is more latitude tidewise in using this southern route and it is probably just as quick as approaching St Peter Port from the N as from 5 hours before to HW St Peter Port the stream is fair along the S coast and up the Little Russel. It is a preferable route to the N entrance in poor visibility.

Navigate to be within 2 miles of Les Hanois light between these times and keep 1 mile off the S coast or outside the 30m line until St Martin's light bears 000°. Identify Longue Pierre beacon (black pole with basket) and Brehon Tower (squat and round) and when the latter is well open to the right, alter N. The next transit is Vale Mill Tower over the right-hand green-roofed shed at St Sampsons with the three conspicuous chimneys to the left of it on 005°. At night or if these cannot be seen, keep the breakwater light bearing less than 355° and outside the 30m line until the harbour entrance is opened.

From the south The stream sets N in the S part of the Little Russel from 3 hours before to 3 hours after HW St Peter Port. The strongest flow is in the middle to E side. It reverses ½ hour after HW inshore on the Guernsey side while the N-going flow continues on the Herm side until 3 hours after HW. The Little Russel is clear of all dangers between Longue Pierre off St Martin's Point and Lower Heads S of Jethou provided the breakwater head lighthouse is kept between 310° and 355°. The transit of Vale Mill Tower and the right-hand green roofed shed at St Sampson on 004° is useful if needing to keep close to the Guernsey shore to avoid a foul stream, as is the 20m line. There are always some overfalls close to St Martin's on the S-going stream and/or wind over tide conditions. They are not so severe as those at the S end of the Great Russel.

Entrance
Listen out on Ch 12 especially if a red light is exhibited on the pierhead which prohibits entry to

all vessels except those under 15m and under power. The entrance is wide and hazard free except for other vessels entering or leaving. The Victoria Marina leading line and lights will give a good indication of the cross stream outside the entrance. Contrary to usual convention keep to the port (south) side on entering when the yacht approach channel marked by a green conical buoy (Fl(2+1)G.10s) and three red can buoys with Fl.R will be seen parallel to Castle Cornet Pier. When the last port-hand buoy is reached and just past the fuel jetty, turn hard to starboard towards the waiting and visitors' pontoons and moorings. Visitors are usually met by the marina staff in a dory and directed but if not call on Ch 80.

Moorings

There are head and stern visitors' moorings in the NW corner of the harbour lying E/W, also berths on pontoons where yachts can double up.

Anchoring

It would be unwise to anchor in the harbour except in an emergency. There are many old chains and mooring blocks on the bottom making it impossible to find swinging room that would not foul moorings or encroach on fairways or manoeuvring areas.

Berths

Alongside pontoons in Victoria Marina which is dredged to 2m (sill depth 4·2m above CD) for up to 14m length although longer can be accepted if space is available.

Facilities

For further details see *A Handbook for Visiting Yachtsmen* which is in the package given to visiting yachts by the marina staff.

Water and electricity On the pontoons.

Fuel Diesel and petrol from fuel berth on S side of harbour at duty-free prices.

Dinghy landing At steps outside Victoria Marina.

Showers and heads On the E pier of Victoria Marina.

Yacht clubs The Guernsey Yacht Club and the Royal Channel Islands Yacht Club welcome visitors. The former is on the S pier leading to Castle Cornet. The latter is opposite the root of Victoria Pier at the N side of the marina but is seeking to move to a position near the marina entrance (2001).

Shops, restaurants, pubs, chandlers Many of all qualities within short walking distance of the harbour. Although VAT-free, prices are comparable to the mainland because of transportation costs.

Car and bicycle hire Readily available.

Travel There are daily passenger/RoRo ferries to Portsmouth and fast ferries to Poole and Weymouth although the latter are more weather dependent. There are fast ferries to Herm, Sark Jersey and St-Malo. There are daily or more frequent flights to Gatwick, Stansted, Manchester, Exeter, Southampton, Jersey and Dinard.

Beaucette Marina

General

This small marina at the NE corner of the island was made by breaking through into an abandoned quarry. It is quieter and more intimate than St Peter Port, has a lower sill (2·4m above CD) which allows passage over it earlier than the St Peter Port Marinas, and customs can be cleared here as well as at St Peter Port. It has facilities for yachts like cranes, slips, hoists and fuel but shops within walking distance are limited to basic provisions although cars can be hired and there is a restaurant on site during the season.

Warning

Do not attempt to enter in strong NE or E winds. There is considerable movement inside during strong easterlies and the top half of the tide. Buoys to haul off the pontoons are provided in the outer part of the harbour.

Data

Charts and tidal information

As for St Peter Port.

Lights

Petite Canupe beacon Q(6)+Fl.15s S cardinal
Ldg Lts *Front* F.R on N side of entrance
    Rear F.R on top of marina building bearing 276°

Communications

Call Beaucette Marina on Ch 80 before entering the buoyed channel. ☎ 01481 245000.

Approaches
See St Peter Port

Doyle Passage is not advised in the dark and a safe approach from the Little Russel at night is dependent on seeing the two leading lights before Petite Canupe is reached.

Entrance

From Little Russel leave Petite Canupe S cardinal beacon to starboard and head for the red and white buoy which marks the end of the buoyed channel. Thereafter there are 4 port and 4 starboard-hand buoys on either side of the leading line. The latter may be difficult to see with the evening sun behind it. From the Doyle Passage enter this buoyed channel before the final buoys and be careful not to stray out of it to the S (see inset on chart *807*). The rocks on either side of the entrance are painted white and there is a gauge on the N side showing depth over the sill. Boats LEAVING have priority. When through the entrance turn hard to port before the first wall and G pontoon will be seen ahead with its yellow hauling-off buoys. If not allocated a berth here turn back to starboard for the rest of the marina. The fuel berth will be on the port bow at this stage.

There are 8 yellow waiting buoys to the N of the entrance if there is not enough water over the sill.

Guernsey. Beaucette Marina looking NW

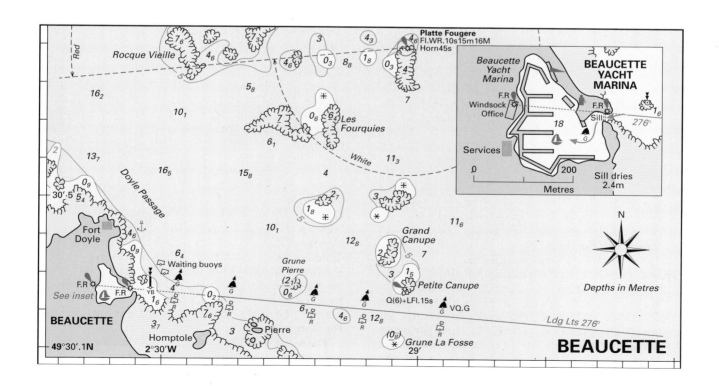

Apart from the hauling-off buoys just inside there are no moorings and no room to anchor.

Facilities
Water and electricity On the pontoons.
Fuel From the fuel barge at any time; Calor Gas from office.
Shower, heads and launderette In the office block.
Travel-lift and *crane* Travel-lift to 16 tons, crane to 12 tons.
Shop One for basic necessities in the marina, another 10 minutes' walk outside.
Car and bicycle hire Through the office.
Restaurant One at the marina during the season, otherwise in St Sampsons.
Travel An occasional bus, otherwise taxi.

Other anchorages

Havelet Bay Lies on the S side of Castle Cornet and is a convenient anchorage for those not caring for the hurly-burly of St Peter Port. Enter between Oyster Bn (yellow spindle with O topmark) and Moulinet Bn (yellow spindle with M topmark) and anchor as convenient in between 1·1m and 7m avoiding the rocky patches towards the edges. The entrance is also marked by port and starboard-hand buoys Fl.R and Fl.G. The moorings on the N side are private. Subject to swell near HW and on the N-going stream. A landing slip lies just to the W of Castle Cornet and close to the Guernsey YC.

Icart Bay On the S side of the island, it is over ½ mile wide with Fourquie de la Moye (drying 3·3m) in its middle. Locate the Martello tower at the head of Petit Bôt Bay and approach it on a bearing of between 350° and 005° or with the tower just over the point to the SW of it. Anchorage in 3m may be found 100m S of the point in relative shelter from W through N to E.

Bay between Icart Point and Jerbourg Point See chart *807*. There are three small bays within this large one – Saints Bay, Moulin Huet and Petit Port. Avoiding Moulière (dries 8·5m) anchor in a suitable depth between Moulin Huet and Petit Port. Saints Bay has a fibre optic cable running through it which is marked by a beacon.

Departures
To the north and west southabout The optimum time to leave St Peter Port is 3 hours after HW which carries the first of the S-going stream to St Martins and a fair stream along the S coast with a further 1 or 2 hours W-going stream to clear the island. This means leaving Victoria Marina early to clear the sill. Leaving 2 hours after HW will find a foul stream to St Martin's but turning fair along the S coast.

To the north and west northabout Leave 2 hours after HW to carry the last of the N-going stream up the Little Russel and benefit from 6 hours of W and SW-going stream in the Channel.

To the northeast 2½ hours before HW or as soon as the sill can be cleared will take the first of the N-going stream out of the Little Russel and then carry nearly 7 hours fair stream to Alderney or the race.

To the southwest Leave at 3½ hours after HW to catch the first of the S-going stream and carry 3 hours of fair stream thereafter.

To the southeast Leave at 3½ hours after to carry 6 hours of fair stream. Jersey can then be reached at a reasonable state of the flood and the lock at St-Malo may just be open.

Jethou *Herm*

Herm and Jethou looking N

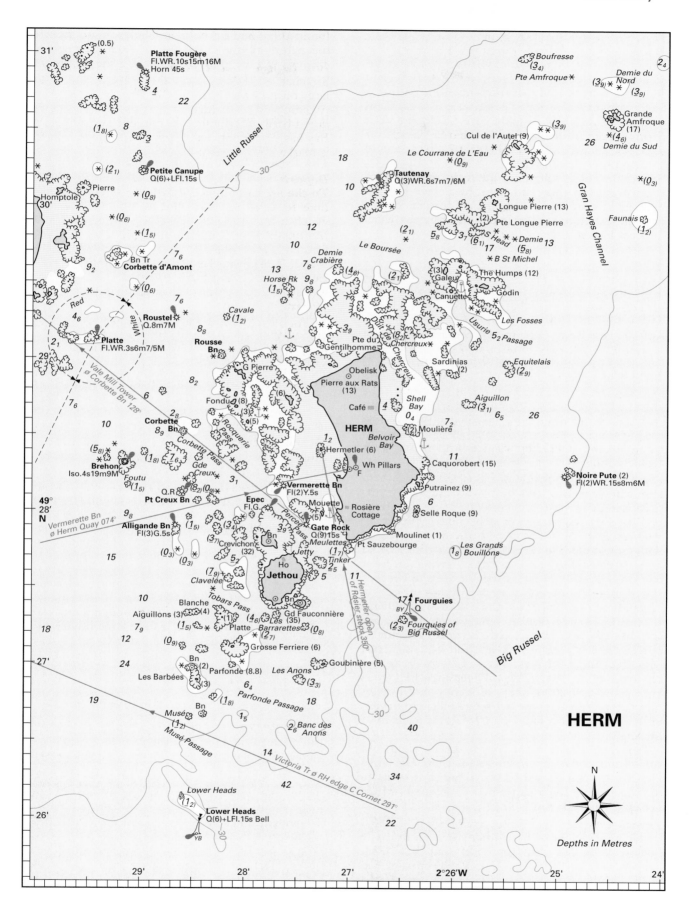

HERM

Depths in Metres

Herm and Jethou

These islands lie 3 miles E of Guernsey. The States of Guernsey purchased Herm after the Second World War from HM Government and lease it to a family who have developed it and keep it in excellent condition. Visiting yachts are welcome but permission must be obtained before remaining over night at anchor. Jethou is privately owned and landing is not permitted.

Brief directions follow for the main passage in to Herm from Guernsey and for The Percée Passage between Herm and Jethou. For further details consult *The Channel Islands* produced by the RCC Pilotage Foundation.

Data

Charts

Admiralty *808* is the largest scale available.

Tidal information

As for St Peter Port. Tidal streams in the Percée Passage run SE for 9 hours commencing at about LW St Peter Port. After a period of slack they then run NW from HW +3 for three hours.

Lights

Apart from house lights on the island, F lights are positioned on the two white columns N of the quay. Lit beacons in the approaches may be identified on chart *808* but night navigation is not recommended for visitors. An additional Fl.R light has been established on Petit Creux beacon (008°, 500m from Alligande Beacon).

Communications

Island ☎ 01481 722377.

Approaches

Alligande Passage This is the most direct route from St Peter Port and is useable drawing 2m from half tide onwards as far as the Vermerette beacon. When the Vermerette's rock (drying 4·3m) is covered there will be 1m at the end of Herm Quay.

Leave Alligande beacon (green with A topmark and lit) 200m to the S and identify Vermerette beacon (yellow with V topmark and lit). Align this with the white patch on the end of Herm Quay (see photograph) on 074°. This will lead into the Percée Passage. When 200m short of Vermerette beacon turn to port and align the two white pillars to the left of the end of Herm Quay on 078°. This leads in to the anchorage and quay.

The drying area N of Vermerette is sand and stones and not rocky as shown on chart *808*. Also the drying 4·3m should be bracketed as it refers to the Vermerette Rock and not the surrounds which dry approximately 2m.

Perceé Passage While proceeding along the first transit above identify the Corbette beacon to the N (yellow with red disc topmark) and Vale Mill Tower. Turn to 128° when Vale Mill is open by two of its widths to the LEFT of Corbette beacon and hold this alignment to leave Epec beacon (green with E topmark and lit) to starboard, Perceé beacon

(W cardinal and lit) to port and continue through the gap until the 20m line is reached when all dangers will be passed except for the Fourquies whose N cardinal buoy should be left to starboard.

Anchorages

It may just be possible to lie afloat to the E of Vermerette beacon if drawing 2m over the slackest neaps. Otherwise legs or bilge keels will be needed. The deeper water anchorage is off Rosière Steps just to the S. This may be approached from the Perceé Passage by keeping Hermétier well open of Rosière Steps to avoid Meulettes and anchoring as the depth dictates to the E of Mouette. The stream runs strongly to the S through this anchorage until half tide when the sands to the N start to uncover, and dinghy work can be dangerous especially in south westerlies.

Facilities

Water Tap near the quay.
Showers and heads Near the quay.
Shop Supplying basic needs near the quay.
Rubbish bins and telephone Near the quay.
Travel Frequent ferries run from St Peter Port and this may be a preferable way to visit the island if in a deep draught boat.

Sark

Sark lies 3 miles to the SE of Herm and Jethou and is 6 miles from Guernsey. It has been self governing with its own constitution since 1565 but sadly this is changing with the pressures of the 21st century and from the EU. It is a beautiful and still unspoilt island with no cars and the minimum trappings of civilisation. There is one landing pier at La Maseline, a very small harbour at Creux and several anchorages. Sark Mill and St Peter's Tower marked as conspicuous on the chart are no longer so.

Brecqhou is private, has a very large building on its summit and landing is not allowed.

Data

Charts

Admiralty *808* is the largest scale chart of the island.

Tidal information

The mean of the time differences on St Helier is +10 minutes; HW is on average 1·7m less, LW 0·5m less than St Helier.

Admiralty Tidal Stream Atlas NP264 only gives a general picture of the tidal flow round the island which becomes more complex with many eddies and reversals in places close inshore. For a full description see the RCC Pilotage Foundation's *The Channel Islands*.

Lights

Point Robert Fl.15s65m20M Horn(2)30s 138°-vis-353° White octagonal tower

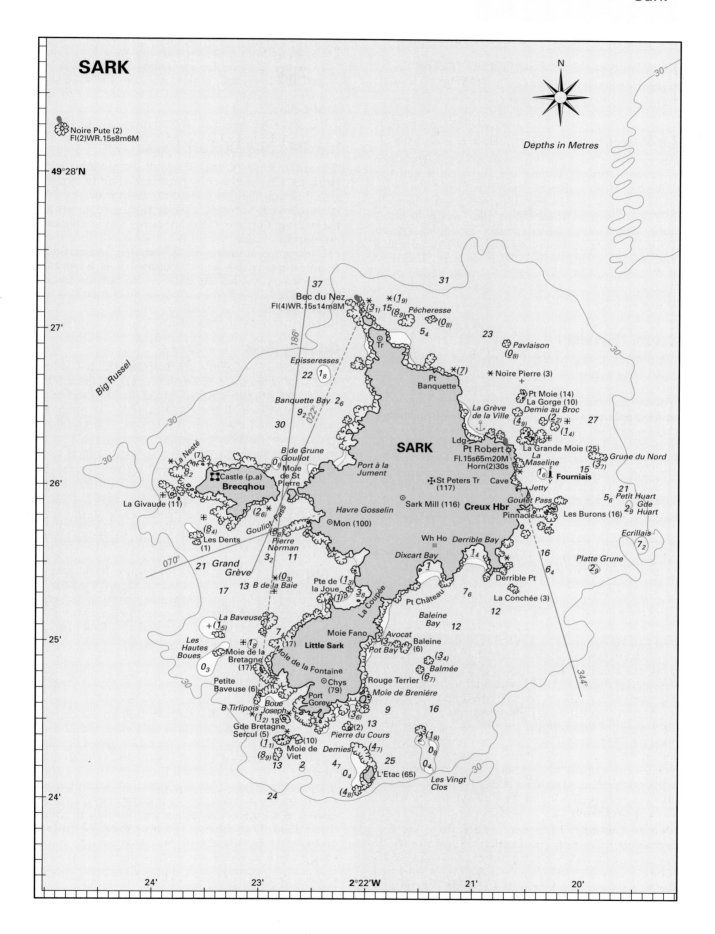

SARK

N

Depths in Metres

Noire Pute (2)
Fl(2)WR.15s8m6M

49°28′N

27'

Big Russel

Bec du Nez
Fl(4)WR.15s14m8M

37   31

*(1₉)
(3₁) 15 (8₉)   Pécheresse
                        (0₈)
                  5₄
Tr
                              23   Pavlaison
Episseresses   (0₈)
22 1₈   *(7)   * Noire Pierre (3)
                                            +
Banquette Bay 2₆   Pt Moie (14)
    9₂ 022°   La Gorge (10)
30   La Grève   Demie au Broc
                          de la Ville   (4₉) (2₂) ⁑
                                                    (1₄)   27
                          Ldg   La Grande Moie (25)
B de Grune   SARK   (3₇) Grune du Nord
La Nesté (7) Goullot   Pt Robert ⁑
        8₂   0₈ Moie   Fl.15s65m20M La Maseline 15
Castle (p.a) de St   Horn(2)30s   1₆ Fourniais
Brecqhou   Pierre   Port à la   21
                        Jument   St Peters Tr Cave Jetty
La Givaude (11)   (117)   Goulet Pass 5₆ Petit Huart
        (2₆)   Pinnacle Les Burons (16) 2₉ Gde
                  Havre Gosselin Sark Mill (116) Creux Hbr   Huart
(8₄)   ⊙ Mon (100)   Ecrillais
Les Dents Goullot Pass   7₂
(1)   (8₆) Wh Ho Derrible Bay   16
070° Pierre   16   Platte Grune
      Norman 3₂ 11   1₄   6₄   2₉
21 Grand   1   Derrible Pt
    Grève   La Conchée (3)
17 13 B de la Baie *(0₃) Pte de (1₃) 7₆ 12
                      (1) la Joue 3₈ Pt Château
La Baveuse   Baleine
+(1₅)   La Coupée Bay   12
Les   Moie Fano Avocat Baleine
Hautes ⁑(1₈) 7₄   (17) (3₄) Pot Bay (6)
Boues Moie de la   Little Sark   (3₄) Balmée
0₃   Bretagne   (6₇)
Petite (17)   Moie de la Fontaine Rouge Terrier
Baveuse (6)   ⊙ Chys   Moie de Breniére
B Tirlipois Boue (79) Port   9   16
        Joseph (1₂) 18 Gorey (3₆) 13
Gde Bretagne   (2)   2 (1₉)
Sercul (5)   Pierre du Cours   0₈
      (1₁) (10) Demies (4₇)   0₄
(8₉) Moie de 13 2 4₇ 25 L'Etac (65) Les Vingt
      Viet 0₄   Clos
24   (4₈)

25'

24'

24'   23'   2°22′W   21'   20'

344°

186°

Les Vingt Clos

Bec du Nez Fl(4)WR.15s14m8M 057°-W-230°-R-057°
White wood structure
Basse Blanchard buoy E cardinal Q(3)10s Bell

Communications

Harbourmaster ☎ 01481 832323.

La Maseline

Approaching from the NE Point Robert Lighthouse is easily identified. Round the Petite Moie and the Grande Moie outside the 20m line until La Maseline jetty is seen and approach it on a bearing of 220° between Grande Moie and Grune du Nord over which the stream runs strongly. Leave Fourniais beacon (yellow with letter F) to port and anchor clear of and to the NW of the jetty. This jetty is for commercial use only, has 4m alongside most of it and may be used briefly to land or take off crew provided it is clear.

Creux Harbour

This small drying harbour to the S of La Maseline also offers access via a tunnel to the track up to the village. The only approach is from the SSE with Point Robert Lighthouse in transit with the white arched entrance to the Creux tunnel over the centre of the harbour wall bearing 344°. Proceed up this transit until a convenient depth for anchoring is found clear of any mooring buoys. It is possible to dry out alongside in the harbour but permission should be sought and a prior reconnaissance is advisable.

Facilities

Water From taps on the quays.
Fuel Diesel might be available from the power station in an emergency.
Bank In the village. Open Mon–Fri 1000–1200, 1400–1500.
Shops and post office In the village.

Sark. Creux (below) and La Maseline harbours looking NNW

Hotels, pubs and restaurants Several round the island.
Travel Bicycles may be hired or rides in horse-drawn carriages. Transport by tractor and trailer is available up and down the hill for the less energetic. The ferries from Guernsey run to La Maseline.

Derrible and Dixcart bays

These two bays on the SE coast are popular with visiting yachts. They are separated by Point Château and although sheltered to some extent from the SW are sometimes subject to swell. Both give access to the village but the climb is easier from Dixcart, through the valley.

The approach transit of 337° shown on chart *808* is no longer visible but the approach is wide and danger free provided the Balmeé and Baleine Rocks are avoided. Anchor as close-in in either bay as depths and other yachts allow, on sand.

Gouliot Pass

This passage between Sark and Brecqhou is 80m wide with clean sides and a least depth of 2·6m. The tidal stream through it generally follows the direction of that in the Big Russel but it tends to turn earlier in the passage. Slack water is at half tide. Spring rates can reach 7 knots.

Passage N Keep the Bec du Nez bearing 022° well open of Moie St Pierre to clear Pierre Norman to the S and a rock drying 2·6m to the S of Brecqhou. When through continue on the stern transit 186°/006° of Moie de la Bretagne open of Moie St Pierre and in the centre of the passage to clear Boue de Grune Gouliot to the W and the Episseresses to the E.

Passage S Pick up the transit of Moie de la Bretagne open of Moie St Pierre and in the centre of the passage 186° when to the W of Bec du Nez and continue through. Turn to port in to Havre Gosselin when clear of Moie St Pierre and its off-lier, or to the SW when clear of the rock drying 2·6m.

Havre Gosselin

Another popular anchorage sheltered all round except from the SW. A swell can build up at certain states of the tide. Sark Mill is no longer visible and the approach transit shown on chart *808* is invalid. Leave Les Dents (1m) S of Brecqhou 200m to port steering 070° and identify Pierre Norman (dries 8·8m) and leave it to starboard. A conspicuous fissure on the N inner side of the Havre may help to lead in. A number of moorings put down by the Sark Yacht Club now take up the best space to anchor and there appears to be no objection to their temporary use. Otherwise anchor where depths and space allow, mostly sand. There is a good dinghy landing and 299 steps up the cliff to a pub.

Jersey

Jersey is the largest, most commercial and populated island with a greater influx of visitors in the season than all the other Channel Islands. It has a large, busy commercial and passenger port at St Helier with three marinas (two for visitors) and a smaller drying port at Gorey. There are many anchorages round the island. Granville lies 30 miles to the SE, St-Malo 35 miles to the S and Guernsey 20 miles to the NW.

Warnings

The tidal range is over 11 metres at springs and while not as large as at St-Malo and Granville is the highest in the Channel Islands. The tidal streams are not as strong as further N but need careful notice taken of them.

Data

Charts

Admiralty *1136* (ARCS), *1137* (SC), *1138* (ARCS), *2669* (ARCS), *3278*, *3655* (SC) SC Folio *5604* (10 charts)
Imray *C33A*, *C33B*

Tidal information

St Helier is a Standard Port and has its own predictions.

MHWS	MHWN	MLWN	MLWS	MTL
11·0	8·1	4·1	1·4	6·1

St Helier is on average 45 minutes earlier than St-Malo for times of HW and LW. Tidal differences around the coast of Jersey are within 10 minutes and 0·3m of those at St Helier.

Lights

Grosnez Point (NW corner) Fl(2)WR.15s50m19/17M 081°-W-188°-R-241° White hut
St Helier approaches
La Corbière (SW corner) Iso.WR.10s36m18/16M Horn Mo(C)60s synchronised with light for distance off Stone tower shore-W-294°-R-328°-W-148°-R-shore **Noirmont Point** Fl(4)12s18m13M Black tower white bands
Demi de Pas Mo(D)WR.12s11m14/10M Horn(3)60s 303°-W-130°-R-303° Black tower yellow top Racon
Platte Rock Fl.R.1·5s6m5M Red column
Western Passage Lights 082° Front Oc.5s23m14M 034°-129° White column red rectangle
Rear **Mont Ubé** 1M to rear Oc.R.5s46m12M 250°-095° White framework tower Racon
Red and Green Passage Lights 023°
Front Oc.G.5s10m11M
Rear 230m from front Oc.R.5s18m12M Synchronised with front Two thin metal columns, the rear on land and the front on white painted caisson with a vertical red stripe on the right-hand side of the RoRo berth
St Helier Inner Harbour Ldg Lts 078° *Front* F.G
Rear F.G White column

Buoys

Passage Rock N cardinal VQ
Les Fours N cardinal Q
Ruardière Rock Starboard Fl.G.3s Bell
Diamond Rock Port Fl(2)R.6s
East Rock (just to W of Dog's Nest) Starboard Q.G
Hinguette Port Fl(4)R.15s
Small Road Port Q.R

Search and rescue

Call *Jersey Radio* on Ch 16 or use GMDSS on Ch 70 to which Jersey Radio will respond. Search and rescue operations are conducted through Jersey Radio.
A lifeboat is maintained at St Helier.

Weather forecasts

Jersey Radio on Ch 25 and 82 at 0645, 0745, 0845 (all 1 hour earlier during DST), 1245, 1845 and 2245 UTC.
BBC Radio Jersey on 88·8MHz broadcasts weather bulletins at 0635, 0810 and 1835 Mon–Fri, 0735 Sat and Sun, all LT.
Daily weather charts at the harbour and marina offices.
An automatic broadcast of wind direction and strength at St Helier pierheads is made every 2 minutes on Ch 18.

Communications

Port control Ch 14.
Jersey radio listens on Ch 16, 25, 67, 82 and 2182kHz.
Telephones: Emergency ☎ 999; harbour office ☎ 01534 885588; La Collette ☎ 01534 79549.

Customs

A customs declaration must be made if coming from any port outside the Channel Islands.

St Helier

General

A busy commercial port with three marinas for yachtsmen. La Collette Yacht Basin to starboard and S of the entrance is usable at all states of the tide and is dredged to 1·8m below CD. The St Helier Marina in the upper harbour has a sill and is accessible for some 3 hours either side of HW; Elizabeth Marina to the N of the RoRo berth and W of St Helier Marina requires pre-booking and a minimum stay of 1 month. St Helier Marina is near the town centre and all facilities. La Collette has Marina facilities but is a fair walk to the shops.

Approaches

From the NW and N The S-going stream along the W coast runs from 5 hours after HW to 3 hours before; the E-going stream along the S coast starts at LW and continues to 1 hour before HW. An arrival off Grosnez Point 4 hours before HW will carry a fair stream for another 3 hours to find plenty of water in to La Collette and over the sill into St Helier Marina.

From the N, the Swashway Channel can be used in daylight provided the Great Rock on the Paternosters can be identified to keep open of Grosnez Point on a back bearing of 045° to keep clear of Moulière Rock (see chart *1136*).

At night or coming from the NW, keep in the white sector of Corbière light and navigate to a position 1 mile to the SW of it remaining outside the 20m line. From here Noirmont Point and light will be visible (Fl(4)12s). Keep the lighthouse well open of Le Fret Point and at night the light bearing 095°

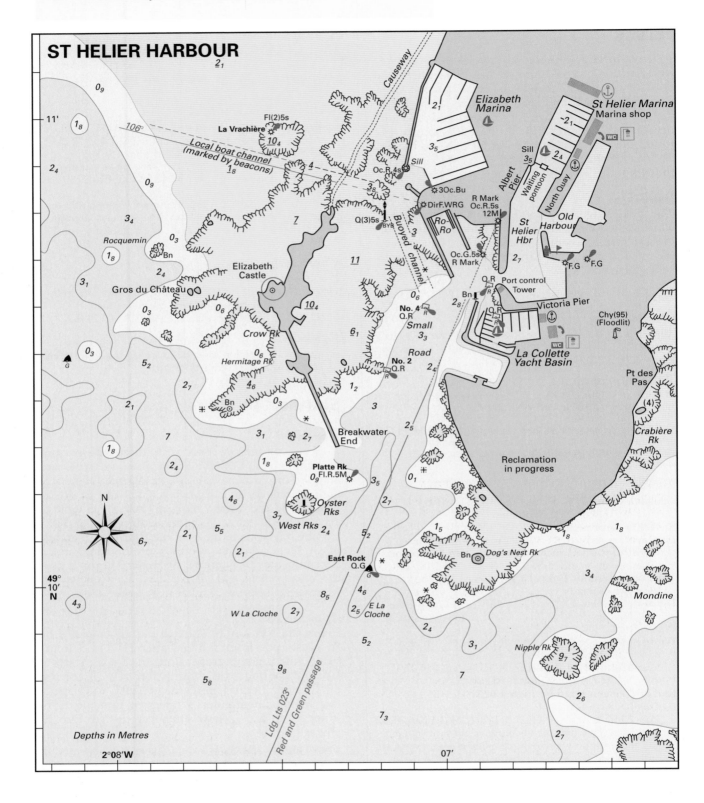

ST HELIER HARBOUR

2₁

0₉

11' 1₈

106°

La Vrachière Fl(2)5s
10₄

2₄

Local boat channel
(marked by beacons)
1₈ 4

0₉

3₈

3₄ 0₃

Rocquemin
1₈ Bn
2₄

3₁

7

11

Elizabeth Castle
Gros du Château

10₄

0₃ 0₆

G 0₃

5₂

Crow Rk

0₆

Hermitage Rk

6₁

Small
3₃

2₇ 4₆ 0₃

Bn

No. 4
Q.R

No. 2
Q.R

Road
2₄

2₁

7 3₁ 2₇

Breakwater End

1₈

3 2₅

1₂

1₈

N

4₆

2₁ 5₅

Platte Rk
0₉ Fl.R.5M 3₅

Oyster Rks

3₇ West Rks 2₄

2₇

0₁

6₇

1₈

2₄

2₁ 5₂

East Rock
Q.G
G

8₅ 4₆

W La Cloche 2₇ 2₅ E La Cloche

49° 10' N

4₃

5₂

9₈

5₈

7₃

Red and Green passage

Ldg Lts 023°

Depths in Metres

2°08'W 07'

Causeway

Elizabeth Marina
2₁
3₅

Oc.R.4s Sill

3Oc.Bu

DirF.WRG

Q(3)5s
BYB

Buoyed channel

Ro Ro

R Mark
Oc.R.5s
12M

Oc.G.5s
R Mark

Q.R
R

Bn
R

Q.R
R

Albert Pier

Waiting pontoon

North Quay

Sill
3₅

St Helier Marina
Marina shop
2₁
WC
2₄

St Helier Hbr

Old Harbour
2₇

F.G F.G

Port control Tower

Victoria Pier

Chy(95)
(Floodlit)

Pt des Pas

(4)

Crabière Rk

La Collette Yacht Basin
WC

Reclamation in progress

1₅

Bn Dog's Nest Rk

1₈

3₄

Mondine

2₄ 3₁

Nipple Rk 9₇

2₆

2₇

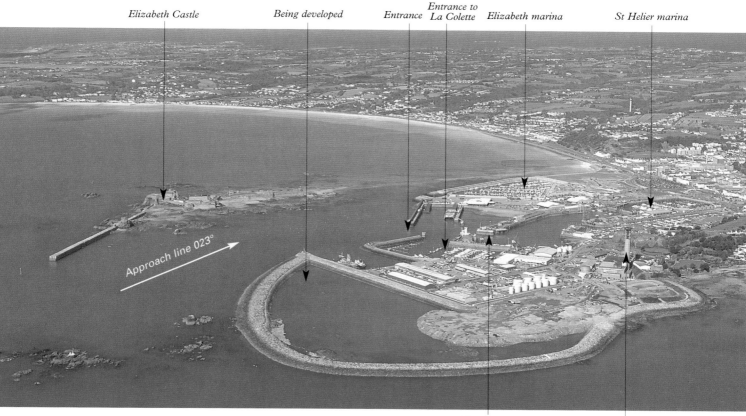

Elizabeth Castle   Being developed   Entrance   Entrance to La Colette   Elizabeth marina   St Helier marina

Approach line 023°

Entrance to main harbour   Chimney (conspic.)

Jersey. St Helier looking NNW

or less to close Noirmont Point. Shortly before Passage Rock buoy (VQ N cardinal) comes abeam alter course to 110° on the stern transit of La Corbière lighthouse just open to the left of the white patch on Le Jument Rock 290° or at night the junction of the red and white sectors of La Corbière light is on the same bearing. If neither are visible, keep Noirmont Point bearing more than 095° and pass to the N of Les Fours buoy (Q N cardinal) until the Western Passage Leading Line 082° is picked up. By day only Dog's Nest on this line is conspicuous but the lights at night are easily identifiable. Leave Ruardière Rock buoy (starboard Fl.G.3s) to starboard and turn short of E Rock buoy (starboard Q.G) on to the Red and Green Passage line 023° (Oc.G and Oc.R.5s) which leads in to the harbour.

If joining Western Passage transit further to the W, note that Passage Rock buoy is to the N of the transit and that Passage Rock to the S of it carries 4m. The least depth in this area on the transit is 2·7m but shallower dangers exist further to the S both here and in the vicinity of Les Fours.

From the SW and S There are three alternative approaches:

a. Join the Western passage transit in the vicinity of Passage Rock buoy and proceed as above.

b. Use Red and Green passage by day or night. This passes over a 1·2m patch and within 200m of rocks drying 1·5m so there must be enough water

and/or the transit held exactly. Approaching from the SSW in deep water navigate to identify the marks well inside the harbour entrance bearing 023°. They are two thin metal columns the rear on land and the front on a white painted caisson with a vertical red stripe; the lights are synchronised, the front Oc.G.5s and the rear Oc.R.5s. This line leads right up to the inner harbour entrances (see photograph).

If this line cannot be picked out by the time the 20m line is crossed, consider using the south, eastern or Electric passages instead. See chart *1137*.

c. The south, eastern and Electric passages are all approaches using the same stretch of hazard-free water between Demi de Pas light and Hinguette buoy (least depth 2·1m). A day or night transit of Demi de Pas and the illuminated power station chimney (95m conspicuous) 350° may help otherwise approach Demi de Pas between 330° and 050° until 400m from it when turn to the NW to leave Hinguette buoy to port until the Red and Green passage line is picked up and so into the harbour.

From the SE Identify Demi de Pas and approach on a bearing of 315° or more to pass S of Plateau de la Frouquie buoy (S cardinal Q(6)+Fl.15s) and then proceed via the south, Electric or eastern passages. The tidal stream along the SE coast is slack or sets to the NW from HW St Helier to LW.

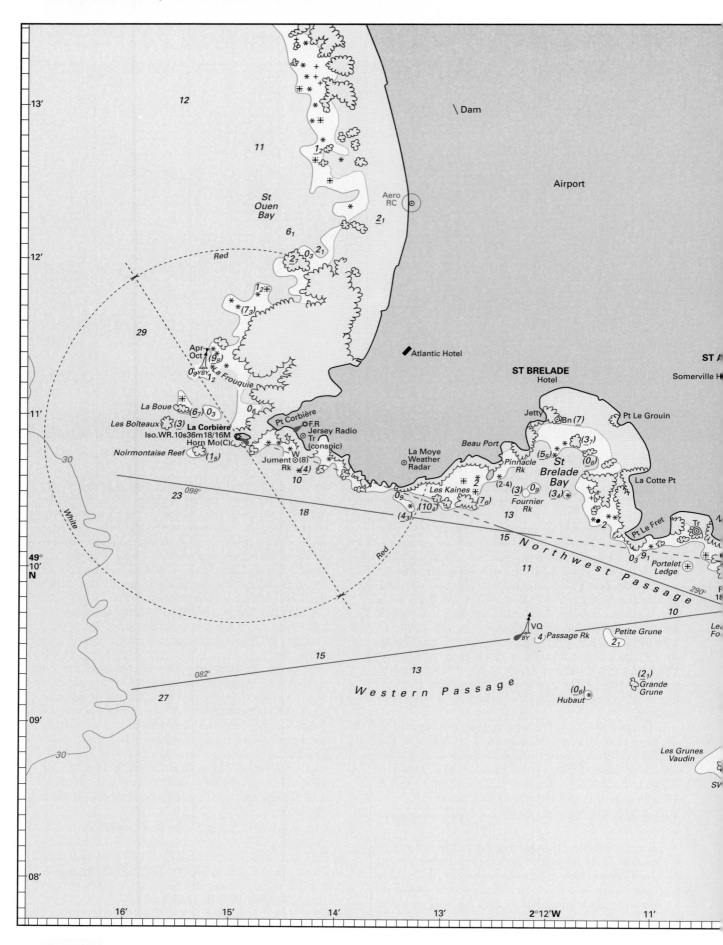

13′

12

11

St Ouen Bay

Dam

Airport

Aero RC

1_2

2_1

12′

Red

6_1

2_1

2_7 0_3

29

1_2

(7_3)

Apr-Oct (9_8)

0_9 YBY 1_2 *La Frouquie*

Atlantic Hotel

ST BRELADE
Hotel

ST A

Somerville H

La Boue (6_7) 0_3

11′

0_6

Jetty

Bn (7)

Pt Le Grouin

Les Boîteaux (3) **La Corbière**

Iso.WR.10s36m18/16M
Horn Mo(C)

Pt Corbière

⚓F.R
Jersey Radio
Tr
(conspic)

Beau Port

(3_7)

(5_5)

(0_6)

La Cotte Pt

Noirmontaise Reef (1_5)

Jument
Rk
⊙(8)
W (4)

10

La Moye
Weather
Radar

Pinnacle
Rk

St Brelade Bay

(3) 0_9
Fournier
Rk

(3_4) *

23 098°

18

0_9 *Les Kaines*
(7_6)

2

(2.4)

13

Pt Le Fret

Tr

$*$ (10_4)

(4_3)

15 *Northwest Passage*

2

0_3 9_1

Portelet
Ledge

290°

White

49°
10′
N

30

Red

11

10

15

VQ
BY 4 Passage Rk

Petite Grune
2_1

Le
Fo

15

13

(2_1)
Grande
Grune

082°

27

Western Passage

(0_6)
Hubaut

09′

30

Les Grunes
Vaudin

SV

08′

16′   15′   14′   13′   2°12′W   11′

JERSEY SOUTH COAST

N

Depths in Metres

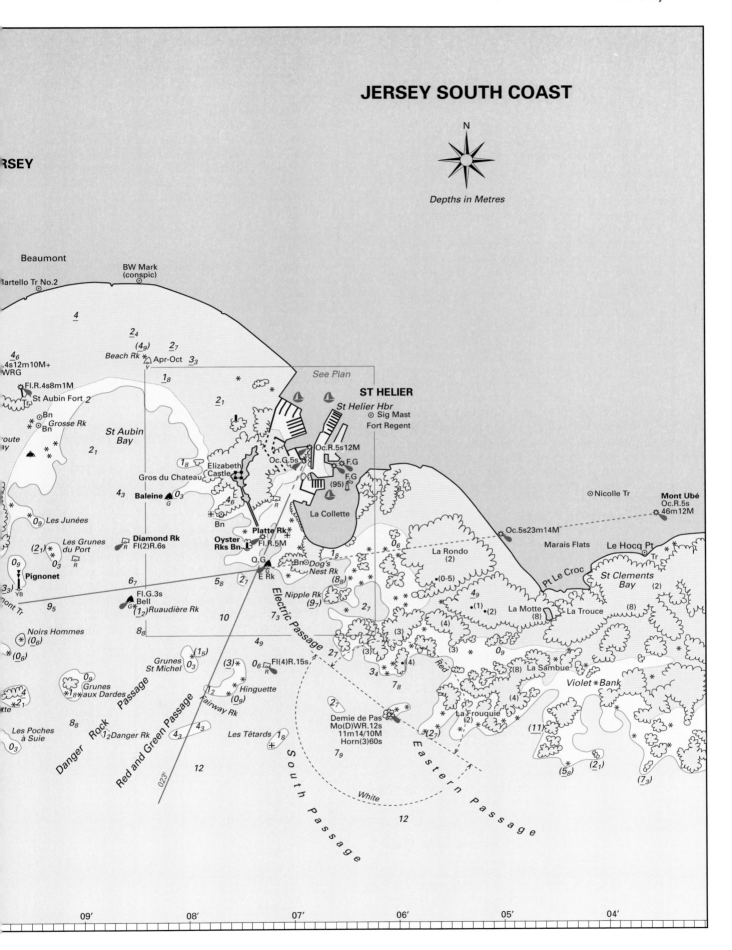

RSEY

Beaumont

BW Mark (conspic)

Martello Tr No.2

4

2₄

(4₉)   2₇

Beach Rk ✳ Apr-Oct   3₃

4₆
.4s12m10M+
WRG

1₈

Fl.R.4s8m1M
St Aubin Fort 2

Bn
Grosse Rk
Bn

2₁

St Aubin Bay

See Plan

ST HELIER

St Helier Hbr
Sig Mast
Fort Regent

oute
ay

2₁

0₉ Les Junées

Gros du Chateau

Elizabeth Castle

Oc.R.5s12M
Oc.G.5s
F.G
F.G
(95)

La Collette

Nicolle Tr

Mont Ubé
Oc.R.5s
46m12M

4₃   **Baleine** ▲ 0₃
G

4₆

Bn

Oc.5s23m14M

Marais Flats   Le Hocq Pt
Tr

(2₁) ✳
Les Grunes du Port
R

Diamond Rk
Fl(2)R.6s
R

Oyster Rks Bn

Platte Rk ✳
Fl.R.5M

0₆

La Rondo
(2)

Pt Le Croc   St Clements Bay   (2)

0₉

Q.G
G
E Rk

Bn Dog's Nest Rk
(8₈)

1₈

(0·5)

La Motte
(8)   La Trouce   (8)

0₉
Pignonet

6₇

5₈   2₇

Nipple Rk
(9₇)

2₇

4₉
•(1) •(2)

3₃
YB

9₅

8₈

Fl.G.3s
Bell
(1₂) Ruaudière Rk
G

10

7₃

(3)

(4)

0₉

Noirs Hommes
(0₆)
(0₆)

Grunes St Michel 0₃
(1₅)

(3)✳   0₆
R   Fl(4)R.15s

4₉

2₇

(3)

(3)

3₄
Red
•(4)

7₈

La Sambue
(8)

0₉
Grunes aux Dardes
✳1₈

1₂
(0₉)

Hinguette

(3)

(4)
Violet ✳ **Bank**

4
2₁

Fairway Rk

2₇

Demie de Pas
Mo(D)WR.12s
11m14/10M
Horn(3)60s

La Frouquie
(2)

(11)

8₈

Les Poches à Suie
0₃

1₂ Danger Rk   4₃   4₃

4₃

Les Têtards   1₈

2₇
✳2₇

(5₈)   (2₁)

(7₃)

12

7₉

White

12

Danger Rock Passage

Red and Green Passage

023

Electric Passage

South Passage

Eastern Passage

Traffic Control Signals

On the port control tower

Oc or Fl.G – Vessels may enter

Oc or Fl.R – Vessels may leave

Oc or Fl.G and R – No vessel may enter or leave harbour

Q.Y – Vessels under power and under 25m may enter or leave, keeping to the starboard side of the pierheads, contrary to the light signal exhibited

St Helier Marina

Green light outside – Clear for entry.

Red light inside – Clear for exit.

Red and green together – No entry or exit, or sill gate closed.

The red light inside and the green light outside will be on at the same time. Responsibility for collision avoidance lies with the individual skipper.

Entrance and berths

There is no need to call on Ch 14 provided the traffic control signals are followed but a listening watch should be kept while in the vicinity of the entrance. Yachts must keep clear of all commercial movements. The Red and Green passage line leads right up to the inner entrances. When the port control tower is abeam to starboard turn hard a starboard into La Collette or St Helier harbour.

La Collette Two red buoys mark the shallow water in the entrance on the E side. Keep well to the W side on entry. Visitors' berths are on the first pontoon inside to port. Dredged to 1·8m in entrance and basin.

St Helier Marina There is a pontoon outside the marina entrance for waiting; otherwise use La Collette. The sill depth is 3·5m above CD. A bottom-hinged gate rises 1·4m above this sill to retain 2·4m inside although this is not uniform and there are shallower patches particularly at the N and W sides. The gate is automatic and entry is possible about 3 hours either side of HW. There is a tide gauge by the entrance which shows depth of water over the sill.

Elizabeth Marina Not for visitors without prior arrangement. It is reached by a buoyed channel running N by W from a red buoy to the N of Small Road port-hand buoy. Access is approximately 3 hours either side of HW. There are yellow waiting buoys outside and light control of the entrance; basically it is Green – Go, Red – Stop.

Moorings and anchoring

There are no moorings in St Helier nor is anchoring allowed or advisable in the harbours.

Facilities

Water and electricity On the pontoons at St Helier and La Collette.

Fuel Diesel and petrol from the fuel berth in St Helier on south pier opposite the entrance.

Showers and heads At both St Helier and La Collette.

Yacht club St Helier Yacht Club is on South Pier and welcomes visitors.

Chandlers and engineers Both nearby.

Shops and laundry Near St Helier marina and open long hours; this is the nearest one to La Collette.

Travel There are daily passenger/RoRo ferries to Portsmouth and fast ferries to Poole and Weymouth, although the latter are more weather dependent. There are fast ferries to Granville, St-Malo and Guernsey. There are daily or more frequent flights to Gatwick, Stansted, Manchester, Exeter, Southampton, Guernsey and Dinard.

Departures

To the NW The stream turns to the N on the W side of the island 2 hours before HW but only turns fair on the S side at HW. The later the departure in this bracket, the greater likelihood of overfalls in the vicinity of La Corbière. If passing Guernsey to the W, a departure 2 hours before HW would be favourable to carry the W-going stream along the S side of that island. A later departure at HW if going to St Peter Port should carry the last of the N-going stream up the Little Russel.

To the N Departure 3 hours before HW and proceeding eastabout through the Violet Channel will give nearly 7 hours fair stream along the S coast and then northerly to reach Alderney or clear the race before it turns foul.

To the W or SW Departure 1 hour after HW will give the most favourable tidal conditions for 6 hours.

To the S or SE Departure time will depend on whether the Minquiers are to be passed to the W or E. If passing to the W, departure at 1 before LW will give 2 hours of W-going stream to clear the Minquiers followed by five hours generally favourable to reach St-Malo or Granville around HW. The streams do not serve so well going to the east of the Minquiers but a departure at 1 hour after LW will carry 3 hours of generally favourable stream.

JERSEY EAST COAST

N

Depths in Metres

La Coupe

Verclut Pt House

11₇

0₉ Pillon Rock

1₈

1₉

St Catherine Fl.1·5s18m13M

Kempt Martello Tr (13)

St Catherine Bay

1₆   3₃

5₃

15

Le Fara
BYB (2₆)

St Catherine Bank

Archirondel Tr (16)

La Crête Pt

2₃   7₉

8₅

Anne Port

1₂

Bramble Cottage

0₁

8₅   Les Arch Bn   North Ridge

250°

12

250°   Oc·G   230°

GOREY   Mont Orgueil
Spire (65)   Cas (67)

G   Très Grunes   0₉

3₆   Banc du Château

Oc.R.5s24m8M

Equerrière Rk

Oc.RG.5s8m 12M

0₉

Fort William   Azicot Rk   Écureuil Rk

5₉

0₄   Middle Bank

2₄   Q.G   Outer Road

3₈   BW   Les Burons   18

Grouville Bay   1₆   1₇   South Ridge

Grune du Port

4₇   0₈   1₂

49° 11′ N   GROUVILLE   5₃

2₉

Grouville Mill (69)

Horn Rk
(4₇)

2₇   3₈
(2)

6

Oc.R   298°

(0₄)

Le Giffard

4₄

2₁

La Noire
(4₅)

St Clements 10′ Bay   La Rocque Pt
Plat Rocque Pt

(2)

Little Seymour
(2)

0₂

2₄   R
1₃   Le Cochon

9₁

11

7

Seymour Tr (20)

1₅

Icho Tower (14)   2

1₄   Karamé
(1)

8   Brett Bn
(0₉)

0₆

1   8   (0₈)

0₃

L'Echiquelez (2)

2₈   (0₅)   1₈   (1₅)
Seal Rks

West Rk   2₃   0₆   Petite Anquette

La Conchière
(2)   (1₂)

(1₇)   5   1₄   1₂   0₃

La Route en Ville   Violet Channel

5₉   8₆   Violet
LFl.10s
RW

11

9₅

Conger Rk
Q(9)15s
YBY

(1)   La Rousse Platte
5₁   Pierre d'Enfants

(3₃)   (4₆)

02′   **01′**   **2°W**   **59′**   **58′**   **57′**

Gorey

General

A drying harbour on the E coast sheltered from the N and W with a large village dominated by the much photographed Orgueil Castle. With St Catherine Bay just to the N, it provides shelter in strong westerlies if further progress westward either to the N or S of the island is not favoured. Customs may be cleared here.

Data

Charts

Admiralty *1138* (ARCS), *2669* (ARCS), *3655* (SC) (ARCS)
Imray *C33A, C33B*

Tidal information

As for St Helier.

Lights

St Catherine breakwater Fl.1.5s18m13M White framework tower.
Gorey Ldg Lts 298° *Front* Oc.RG.5s8m12M 304°-R-353°-G-304° White tower on breakwater head *Rear* 490m from front Oc.R.5s24m8M White square, orange sides on stone wall
Inner Road buoy starboard Q.G

Search and rescue

As for St Helier. An inshore lifeboat is stationed at St Catherine.

Communications

The piermaster monitors Ch 74 around HW during daylight hours April to October.
Pier office ☎ 01534 853616.

Customs

May be cleared here.

Approaches

From the N and E Provided Banc du Château has sufficient water over it (least depth 0·4m) navigate to the vicinity of the Inner Road buoy and pick up the leading line 298° by day or night. Coming from the N by day and with insufficient water over the Banc du Château consult chart *1138* which shows two transits to lead into the Outer Road and thence to the leading line. By night or coming from the E, navigate to pick up the leading line outside the 15m line and follow it closely to leave the Inner Road buoy and Ecueriel beacon (G, triangle topmark) close to starboard. After passing the Ecueriel beacon borrow a little to starboard to avoid the drying 2·7m patch close to port of the line.

From the S Identify the offshore distant mark Violet buoy (RW ball topmark, Fl.10s) to navigate thence N through the Violet channel. From here either pick up the transit shown on chart *1138* to lead up the Outer Road, or stay outside the 10m line leaving the unlit Le Cochon buoy (port), La Noire Beacon (E cardinal), Le Giffard buoy (port) and Horn Rock beacon (red, can topmark) all to port to

Pierhead

Jersey. Gorey looking NW at LW

pick up the Gorey leading line in the vicinity of the Inner Road buoy.

Entrance and berths

The outer part of the pier is used by ferries from Port Bail and Carteret as the tide serves. Alongside berths are not usually available.

Mooring and anchoring

Some moorings are maintained for visitors to the S of the harbour entrance. Anchor clear of these and of the approach to the outer end of the pier.

Facilities

Water Tap on the pier.
Fuel Garage nearby.
Showers and *heads* On the pier.
Crane On the pier.
Shops, restaurants, banks and post office All in the town.

Other anchorages

There are a number of partially sheltered anchorages around the coast which can be found in *The Channel Islands* by the Royal Cruising Club Pilotage Foundation or from study of charts *1136*, *1137* and *1138*. Two that may be useful as alternatives are:

St Catherine Bay Lies 1½ miles to the N of Gorey. Sheltered from the N and W by a long breakwater. The approaches from the N and E are clear of immediate off-lying dangers. Anchor as far in as depth and moorings allow to the S of the breakwater. There are underwater rocks along the length of the breakwater. There is a landing slip, a sailing club and café but otherwise no facilities.

St Aubin Bay A wide bay close to the W of St Helier which provides shelter from the SW through N to E. Turn off the Western Passage in the vicinity of Ruardière buoy towards Diamond Rock buoy, thence select an anchorage in this large bay where tide and wind direction dictate. There are landings at St Aubin harbour on the W side, or through La Vrachère boat passage to the N of Elizabeth Castle.

3. St-Malo to Lézardrieux and Pontrieux

Introduction

This part of the coast, embracing the wide and sandy bay of St-Brieuc with its scattered rocks lying well offshore, has major ports at the E and W ends and several attractive anchorages and minor harbours in between. Because it is off the direct track between St-Malo or Jersey and Lézardrieux, it is less frequented by yachtsmen although an excellent area for exploration by bilge-keelers or shallow draught yachts. The deeper keeled are well catered for from Dahouet to the westward although with the exception of St-Quay-Portrieux all harbours are tidal limited until Lézardrieux is reached. The tidal streams slacken off appreciably in this large, wide bay.

St-Malo, Dinard and La Rance

General

St-Malo is the most important port on the north coast of Brittany with a steady flow of commercial traffic, many ferry movements, a busy fishing fleet and major yachting facilities. It can be entered at all states of the tide by day or night in any weather although entry into the basin is limited to approximately 2½ hours either side of HW, entry to the marina at Port de Bas Sablons to approximately 5 hours either side of HW and entry through the barrage for approximately 4 hours either side of HW in daylight hours.

Dinard on the W side of the estuary is a large

Planning guide
Cherbourg – Channel Islands – Tréguier

	Cherbourg	A de St-Martin	Goury	Alderney	Diélette	Guernsey	Carteret	Port Bail	Jersey (St H)	Granville	Is Chausey	Cancale	St-Malo	St-Briac	St-Jacut	St-Cast	B de Fresnaie	Erquy	Dahouet	St-Brieuc	Binic	St-Q/Portrieux	Paimpol	Ile Bréhat	Lézardrieux	Pontrieux	Tréguier
Cherbourg		12	16	24	26	42	37	41	57	69	69	86	89	89	89	89	90	92	97	103	105	104	87	82	87	93	93
A de St-Martin	12		4	12	14	30	25	29	45	73	73	74	77	77	77	77	78	80	85	91	93	92	75	70	75	81	81
Goury	16	4		10	10	27	22	26	42	70	70	71	74	74	74	74	75	77	82	88	90	89	72	67	72	78	78
Alderney	24	12	10		17	22	28	32	40	62	62	71	72	72	73	73	73	76	80	85	81	79	67	64	69	75	75
Diélette	26	14	10	17		28	13	17	33	48	48	61	64	67	69	72	74	68	73	80	83	85	68	63	68	74	74
Guernsey	42	30	27	22	28		30	32	28	54	47	58	54	52	52	52	51	50	54	57	54	51	44	43	48	54	50
Carteret	37	25	22	28	13	30		4	22	35	35	43	44	46	48	51	53	63	68	73	73	72	63	62	67	73	73
Port Bail	41	29	26	32	17	32	4		21	31	31	39	42	44	46	49	51	61	66	73	73	73	62	60	65	71	71
Jersey (St H)	57	45	42	40	33	28	22	21		30	25	34	35	35	35	35	35	37	43	48	48	45	44	42	47	53	60
Granville	69	73	70	62	48	54	35	31	30		10	13	22	26	28	31	33	43	48	55	65	65	74	77	82	88	91
Is Chausey	69	73	70	62	48	47	35	31	25	10		13	14	18	20	23	25	35	40	47	57	58	67	70	75	81	84
Cancale	86	74	71	71	61	58	43	39	34	13	13		17	21	23	26	28	38	43	50	60	61	70	70	75	81	84
St-Malo	89	77	74	72	64	54	44	42	35	22	14	17		7	9	12	14	24	29	36	36	37	46	46	51	57	60
St-Briac	89	77	74	72	67	52	46	44	35	26	18	21	7		2	5	7	17	22	29	29	30	39	39	44	50	53
St-Jacut	89	77	74	73	69	52	48	46	35	28	20	23	9	2		3	5	15	20	27	27	27	28	37	42	48	51
St-Cast	89	77	74	73	72	52	51	49	35	31	23	26	12	5	3		2	12	17	24	24	25	34	34	39	45	48
B de Fresnaie	90	78	75	73	74	51	53	51	35	33	25	28	14	7	5	2		10	15	22	22	23	32	32	37	43	46
Erquy	92	80	77	76	68	50	63	61	37	43	35	38	24	17	15	12	10		5	12	14	14	25	25	30	36	40
Dahouet	97	85	82	80	73	54	68	66	43	48	40	43	29	22	20	17	15	5		7	10	11	25	23	28	34	39
St-Brieuc	103	91	88	85	80	57	73	73	48	55	47	50	36	29	27	24	22	12	7		6	9	24	24	29	35	42
Binic	105	93	90	81	83	54	73	73	48	65	57	60	36	29	27	24	22	14	10	6		3	18	17	22	28	31
St-Q/Portrieux	104	92	89	79	85	51	72	73	45	65	58	61	37	30	28	25	23	14	11	9	3		15	14	19	25	28
Paimpol	87	75	72	67	68	44	63	62	44	74	67	70	46	39	37	34	32	25	25	24	18	15		8	13	19	22
Ile Bréhat	82	70	67	64	63	43	62	60	42	77	70	70	46	39	37	34	32	25	23	24	17	14	8		5	11	18
Lézardrieux	87	75	72	69	68	48	67	65	47	82	75	75	51	44	42	39	37	30	28	29	22	19	13	5		6	18
Pontrieux	93	81	78	75	74	54	73	71	53	88	81	81	57	50	48	45	43	36	34	35	28	25	19	11	6		24
Tréguier	93	81	78	75	74	50	73	71	60	91	84	84	60	53	51	48	46	40	39	42	31	28	22	18	18	24	

Distances are given over the shortest navigable route and are measured to and from inner harbour or anchorage

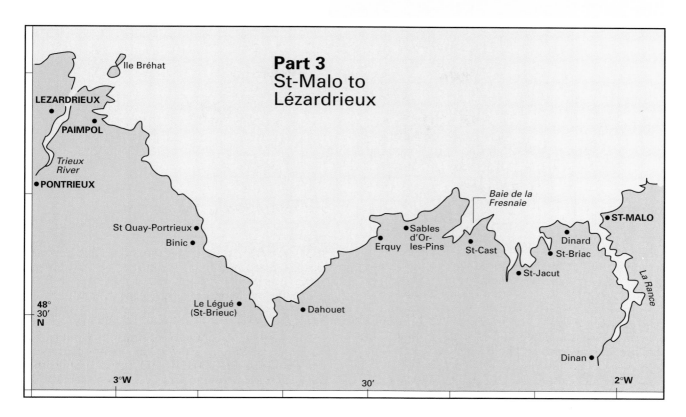

**Part 3
St-Malo to
Lézardrieux**

holiday resort off which an anchorage may be found at neaps.

La Rance, a pleasant river in mainly rural surroundings, is entered through the barrage and is navigable for 4 miles by deep draught yachts to St-Suliac. A further 5 miles to Châtelier can be taken when there is sufficient water, the height of which is regulated by the barrage (see page 61 for details). There is a lock at Châtelier where the Canal de l'Ile et Rance starts and vessels drawing 1·5m or less and 15m or less air clearance can proceed a further 2 miles to Dinan. Above this masts have to be lowered and a draught of 1·3m or less needed to reach Rennes, Nantes or Redon.

There are excellent facilities at both St-Malo and the marina at Port des Bas Sablons for yachts and their crews; either are good places to change crews or to leave the boat with good links by rail, road, sea and air with the UK, Channel Islands and the rest of France.

Data

Charts

Admiralty *3659* (SC) (ARCS), *2700* (plan) (ARCS)
Imray *C33B* (plan)
SHOM's *7130* and *4233* also cover La Rance to
   Châtelier
If intending to use any other than the main approach channels from the NW charts *2700* or SHOM *7130* would be essential. SHOM *4233* is essential if going above the barrage.

Tides

St-Malo is a Standard Port

MHWS	MHWN	MLWN	MLWS
12·2m	9·3m	4·2m	1·5m

Spring range 10·7m, neap range 5·1m, MTL 6·8m.
St-Malo times of HW and LW are 45 minutes after St Helier taking into account any time differences between France and the Channel Islands during DST.

Tidal streams

1M to the NW of Le Grand Jardin in the approaches streams start as follows:

−0430 St Helier (−0515 St-Malo)	E
−0040 St Helier (+0005 St-Malo)	W

The maximum rate in either direction is 2½ knots.

Between Le Grand Jardin and Le Buron in the main approach channel the streams set across the channel but align with the channel to the SE of Le Buron. Off Dinard the stream start as follows:

−0530 St Helier (−0445 St-Malo)	SSE
HW St Helier (−0045 St-Malo)	NNW

The maximum rate in either direction is 2½ knots but the timing and the rate are greatly influenced by the operation of the sluice gates in the barrage.

Lights

Les Courtis close SW of the outer approach to the
   Chenal de la Petite Porte. Fl(3)G.12s14m7M Green
   tower
La Platte to N of the town and NW of the E approach
   channels Fl.WRG.4s11m10·7M Green tower. 140°-
   W -203°-R-210°-W-225°-G-140°
Le Grand Jardin Ldg Line 089°
   Front Fl(2)R.10s24m15M Grey tower, red top
   Rochebonne *Rear* DirF.R.40m24M Grey square
   tower, W face white, red top 088°-intens-090° Leads
   through Chenal de la Grande Porte from the W

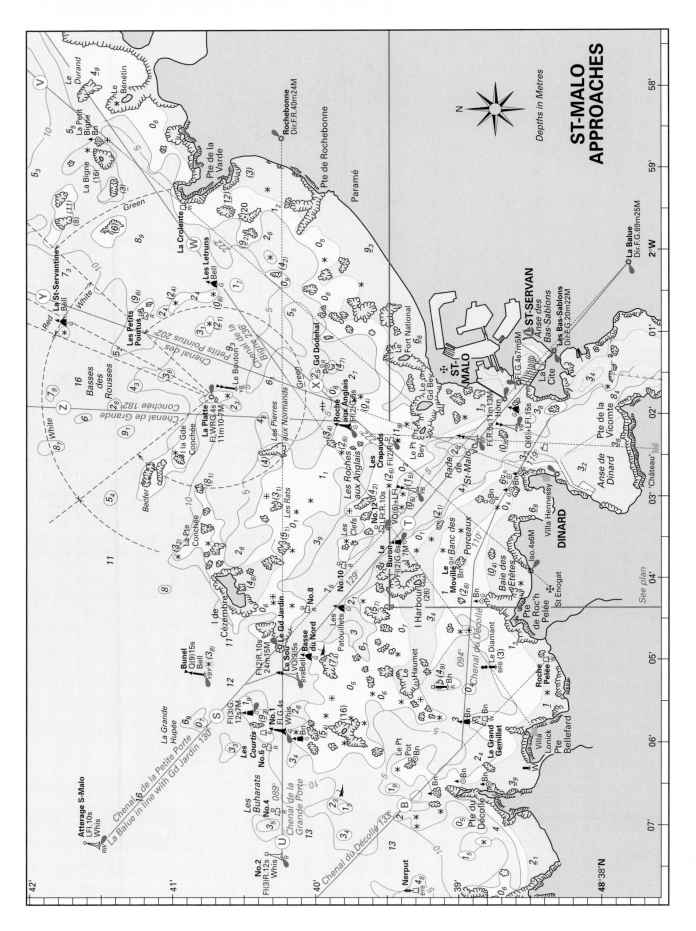

ST-MALO
APPROACHES

Depths in Metres

Le Buron Fl(2)G.6s15m7M Green tower
Mole des Noires head Fl.R.5s11m13M White tower, red top
Les Bas Sablons Ldg Lts 129° *Front* DirF.G.20m22M White square tower, black top
La Balue *Rear* DirF.G.69m25M Grey square tower 128°-intens-130°
This line leads up the channel from Le Grand Jardin inwards
Ecluse du Naye Lock Ldg Lts 070° *Front* F.R.7m3M white circle, purple border
Rear F.R.23m7M, white circle, red border on white column.
Les Bas Sablons Marina head Fl.G.4s7m5M Grey mast
La Rance
La Jument Fl(5)G.20s6m3M Green tower
Barrage entrance NW corner Fl.G.4s6m5M Green pylon on dolphin
NE corner Fl(2)R.6s6m5M, red pylon on dolphin.
SW corner Iso.G.4s
SE corner Oc(2)R.6s

Buoys
There are many lit and unlit buoys in the approaches and harbours which are shown on chart *2700*. The following assist in the outer approaches to Chenal de la Petite Porte if the leading line cannot be distinguished at a distance:
Basse NE du Vieux Banc N cardinal Q Bell
Landfall red and white, ball top Fl.10s Whis

Search and rescue
St-Malo is at the E end of the CROSS Corsen region and the nearest substation is at Cap Fréhel which will respond to calls on Ch 16 or activation of GMDSS on Ch 70, as will Jersey Radio.
There are all-weather and inshore lifeboats at St-Malo. There is a hospital in the town.

Weather forecasts
The area is Manche Ouest.
Cap Fréhel on Ch 79 in French and English at 0545, 0803, 1203, 1633, 2003 LT.
Météo France ☎08 36 68 08 35.
Two weather maps per day at the *Bureaux du Port* in the marina and Bassin Vauban.
Navtex Corsen (A), Niton (S) or (K).

Communications
Bureau du port Ch 9 ☎ 02 99 81 71 34.
Ecluse du Naye Ch 12, 2½hours either side of HW.

Customs
Office near the lock.

Consul
There is a British Consul at Dinard – La Hulotte, 8 Boulevard des Marechaux, 35800 Dinard ☎ 99 46 26 64.

Approaches
Apart from the extensive Minquiers to the N there are few off-lying dangers to bother a yacht in the approaches. Le Vieux Banc with a drying 1·8m rock on it just SW of the Chenal de la Petite Porte and 3M from the entrance is somewhere to avoid in heavy weather and strong tides even with water to clear it. The extensive shallows and rocks to the N and NE of the entrance are all clearly shown on chart *2700* and this would not be an area to navigate in poor visibility.
There are six entrances that can be used, three by day and night and three by day only. They are:

From the W – Chenal de la Grande Porte The deepest but not the main channel. The best to use if visibility precludes seeing the leading marks, as buoys and beacons are close together.

From the NW – Chenal de la Petite Porte The main channel and the most used but subject to strong cross streams. A possibility if the leading marks cannot be seen but a minimum of 1M needed for safety, or a radar.
The least depth in both these channels is 5·8m.

From the N – Chenal de la Grande Conchée The channel used by the fast ferries from the Channel Islands. A radar or a minimum of 1M visibility needed for safety.

From the E or NE by day only – Chenal des Petits Pointus and Chenal de la Bigne Both need 1M+ visibility for safety.

St-Malo. Le Grand Jardin lighthouse with St-Malo spire right centre bearing 118°

Chenals Grande Conchée, Petits Pointus and la Bigne all have a least depth of 0·5m in the final stages – nearly 5m at MLWN – but have shallower dangers close to the lines.

From the W – Chenal de Décollé An interesting navigation exercise otherwise of no advantage over Chenal de la Grande Porte.

Chenal de la Petite Porte – by day (Lines S and T) Navigate to a position close to the NE of the landfall buoy 2M to the NW of Le Grand Jardin lighthouse. From here the leading line of Le Grand Jardin and La Balue lighthouse (grey square tower on the skyline behind the town) 130° (Line S) should be visible. Follow this line to leave:

> **Grand Houpée** rock 0·7m 200m to port
> **Bunel** W cardinal bell buoy 600m to port
> **Le Courtis** lighthouse (green) 300m to starboard.

When Le Courtis bears 280° leave this line and steer 160° for 400m and pick up Line T which is Les Bas Sablons lighthouse (white square tower with black top 20m high) in line with La Balue lighthouse on the skyline bearing 129°. This leaves:

> ***Le Grand Jardin** lighthouse 180m to port. A port beacon stands 100m SW of the lighthouse and must also be left to port
> **Le Sou** E cardinal spar buoy 300m to starboard
> **Basse du Nord** starboard buoy 250m to starboard
> **No.8** port buoy 250m to port
> **Les Patouillets** starboard buoy 190m to starboard
> **No.10** port buoy 300m to port
> **Le Buron** starboard light tower 120m to starboard
> **No.12** port buoy 100m to port
> **Les Grelots** S cardinal buoy 300m to port.

The channel now approaches Plateau de la Rance, a shoal containing drying rocks, which may be left on either hand. (See plan on page 58.)

For St-Malo or Sablons Marina continue on Line T to leave the shoal to starboard and the end of Môle des Noires 100m to port. Steer then for the lock gates on 070° or for the Marina entrance behind the ferry terminal berthing jetty extension.

For Dinard or La Rance leave Line T when 400m past the last S cardinal buoy and steer 170° to leave both buoys marking the Plateau de la Rance 300m to port, and so in to Rade de Dinard.

Chenal de la Petite Porte – by night In good visibility Line S, Le Grand Jardin Fl(2)R.10s and La Balue (the upper of the two fixed green lights) 130° can be picked up a long way to seaward. This line leaves Le Vieux Banc N cardinal lit bell buoy 150m to starboard and the landfall light and whistle buoy about 180m to starboard. At some stage a yacht will lose La Balue behind Le Jardin lighthouse and when this occurs borrow to starboard to keep La Balue green on the edge of the tower.

When Les Courtis (Fl(3)G.12s bears 280° with Le Jardin then some ¼M ahead, alter to 170° for 300m to align the two fixed green lights of La Balue and Le Bas Sablons on 129°; La Balue is intensified 1° either side of 129°. This line leaves the following:

> ***Le Grand Jardin** 150m to port (also the unlit port beacon to the SW)
> **Le Sou** VQ(3)5s to starboard
> **Le Buron** tower Fl(2)G.6s to starboard
> **No.12** buoy LFl.R.10s to port
> **Les Grelots** S cardinal buoy (VQ(6)+Fl.10s).

If going to the locks or the marina leave:

> VQ N cardinal on Plateau de la Rance to starboard
> **Head of Môle des Noires** Fl.R.5s to port
> **Le Crapaud** starboard buoy Fl(4)G.15s to starboard.

The three fixed red lights lead on 070° into the locks. See below under Entrance for the lock signals.

The W end of the marina entrance is marked by a Fl.G.4s and the depth gauge is lit.

If going to Dinard or up La Rance, alter to 170° after passing Les Grelots S cardinal VQ(6)+Fl.10s and leave the two buoys on Plateau de la Rance (N cardinal VQ, S cardinal VQ(6)+Fl.10s) well to port to enter Rade de Dinard. See under Lights above for guidance to the barrage.

St-Malo. Leading marks for Chenal de La Bigne, 222°. La Crolante white beacon tower on the NW edge of Le Grand Bey island. Le Petit Bey fort to the right

St-Malo. Second transit for Chenal de la Bigne, line W, 236°. Le Buron green tower in line with Lonick Villa. The white stripe is midway between Le Buron and Ile Harbour fort

Chenal de la Grande Porte – by day or night (Line U)

This channel cuts a small corner if coming from Cap Fréhel or Banchenou buoy, passing inside Le Courtis. It is also a safer channel in poor visibility than any of the others.

Navigate to a position ¼M to the W of No.2 light (port Fl(3)R.12s) and whistle buoy. From here Le Grand Jardin lighthouse (Fl(2)R.10s) will be in line with Rochebonne lighthouse (white faced, square tower elevation 40m DirF.R bearing 089°). Le Grand Jardin will shortly obscure the latter so borrow a little to the S to just open it clear. Leave the following marks:

No.2 port pillar buoy Fl(3)R.12s 50m to port
No.4 Les Buharets port bell buoy 50m to port
No.6 Pierres des Portes port can buoy to port
Le Boujaron starboard beacon tower 300m to starboard
No.1 starboard whistle pillar buoy Fl.G.4s close to starboard
Pierres des Portes port beacon tower 200m to port
Les Courtis green lighthouse Fl(3)G.12s 300m to port
Le Sou E cardinal VQ(3)5s 100m to starboard.

When Le Sou is abeam start to turn on to Line T – Les Bas Sablons lighthouse, front (white square tower with black top F.G) and rear, La Balue lighthouse (square tower on skyline F.G intensified on 129°) on 129°. Proceed then as from * in the sections above *Chenal de la Petite Porte by day, or night* (page 54).

Chenal de la Grande Conchée – by day (Lines Z and X)

Navigate to a position 1M N of La Platte lighthouse (green tower) and identify Ile Cézembre and La Grande Conchée which has a small fort on it. The line is 182° on Le Petit Bey which has a more conspicuous fort on it. When on the line a new château-like building with a tower at each end will be just to the right of Le Petit Bey and a group of four electricity pylons to the left.

Proceed down this line leaving:

La Grande Conchée (4m high) 400m to starboard
La Platte green beacon tower 400m to port

Le Bouton S cardinal buoy 450m to port
Les Pierres aux Normands starboard beacon 350m to starboard
Les Roches aux Anglais starboard beacon 300m to starboard
Les Roches aux Anglais starboard buoy close to starboard.

200m past Les Roches aux Anglais buoy turn to make good 222° to leave Les Crapauds port buoy to port. When Le Petit Bey is abaft the beam, course may be altered to head between the Plateau de la Rance and the head of Môle des Noires and so to the locks or marina.

Chenal de la Grande Conchée – by night

There are no leading lights for this channel but it is wide and lends itself to the use of parallel index on radar.

Navigate to a position 1M N of La Platte light (Fl.WRG.4s) in the white sector and set up a parallel index of 350m from La Platte on this track. If no radar, make good 182° passing through the white sector of La Platte into the green. Les Roches aux Anglais buoy (Q.G.6s) should then be visible ahead at 1M. Continue on this track to leave it close to starboard. When 300m past it turn to 222° to leave Les Crapauds port buoy (Fl.R.6s) close to port or use a parallel index of 450m on Le Petit Bey on this track. Shortly after Les Grelots S cardinal buoy (VQ(6)+Fl.10s) is abeam, turn to port to align the two fixed green lights on the Bas Sablons/La Balue leading line on 129°.

Then proceed as from # in *Chenal de la Petite Porte – by night* (page 54).

Chenal des Petits Pointus – by day only (Line Y)

A wide and easy channel with only one danger (Les Petits Pointus) close to the line. Like La Grande Conchée it lends itself to the use of parallel index if a radar is carried.

Make a position ¼M E of La Servantine starboard bell buoy. The line then is 202° on Le Petit Bey with its conspicuous fort and Villa Hennessy, a prominent villa in the NE part of Dinard. Make good this track to leave Le Petit Pointus port beacon 150m to port or set up a parallel index on La Platte of 650m on a track of 202°. Once Le Petit Pointus is passed leave:

La **Platte** green lighthouse 650m to starboard
Le **Bouton** S cardinal buoy 400m to starboard
Grand Dodehal port beacon 400m to port.

Shortly after passing the latter alter to 222° to leave Les Roches aux Anglais starboard buoy 200m to starboard and Les Crapauds port buoy close to port with a parallel index of 450m on Le Petit Bey on this track. Course may be altered to port when clear of Le Crapaud to pass between Plateau de la Rance and the head of Môle des Noires, and so into the locks or marina.

Chenal de la Bigne – by day only (Lines V,W and Y) This is the most direct channel from the E. There is a narrow part at the E end but once past this there are no particular dangers or difficulties.

Navigate to a position where Rochefort W cardinal beacon tower bears 260° 0·7M. This is on the first leading line of Le Crolante white beacon tower in transit with the NW edge of Le Grand Bey bearing 222°. The latter is the larger of the two islets with forts on them just to the NW of St-Malo town. Keep close to this line to leave:

Basse aux Chiens E cardinal buoy 100m to starboard
Basse du Durand shoal with a least depth of 0·7m 200m to port
La Petite Bigne starboard beacon 80m to starboard.

200m beyond La Petite Bigne alter to 236° on to Line W to leave:

Le Crolante beacon tower 300m to port
Les Létruns starboard buoy close to starboard.

The marks on this line are difficult to distinguish. The easiest is to keep Le Buron green beacon tower open to the left of Ile Harbour's ruined fort by the width of the fort.

½M past Le Létruns buoy alter back to 222° and follow Line X as for Chenal La Conchée and Petits Pointus.

Chenal de Décollé – by day only (Line B) This is an interesting exercise in navigation but saves no time or distance if coming from the W to St-Malo, over using Chenal de la Grande Porte.

Chart *2700* shows the lines and tracks to be followed. There are no difficulties initially provided the first leading line of Le Grand Gemillet white beacon tower, front and Roche Pelée white beacon, rear on 133° can be positively identified before commitment. The difficulties occur at the E end to the N of Pointe de Dinard where the channel is narrow, there is no established leading line and the sands and channel constantly change.

It would be prudent to reckon on a least depth of drying 1m and to make the passage on a rising tide with the aid of chart *2700* or SHOM *7130*.

St-Malo

Anchorage

Anchoring is prohibited anywhere in the main channels from Le Grand Jardin and La Grande Conchée inwards up to Baie du Solidor. The only exception is a narrow strip outside the moorings in Rade de Dinard where the streams run strongly and the bank from drying into deep water is steep. There are waiting buoys to the W of the lock, outside the marina and to the N of the lock to the barrage. The best plan is to time arrival between 2 hours either side of HW.

Docks

There are four interconnected basins with a common access through Ecluse du Naye. They are maintained to a depth of about 5·4m and shown on the plan on page 58. Yachts use Bassin Vauban with an overflow into Bassin Duguay-Trouin if needed.

Entry procedure

The locks are worked 2½ hours either side of HW. The gates are often left open from 1½ hours before to HW and this is the best time to pass through. Take note of the traffic signals and beware of a strong N set outside the gates before and just past HW, and if the barrage is discharging seawards. Unless the lock is very crowded, a yacht should secure on the side on which an attendant is standing. There are ladders in the sides; the attendants will sometimes pass down a line to take up warps.

Entry signals
Normal lock working

G		
W		Vessels may not enter until authorised
G		
G		
G		Vessels may enter
G		
R		
R		Vessels may not enter. Keep 200m clear of
R		the gates

Both gates open

G	Y	Vessels may not pass until authorised.
W		Beware of the current
G		
G	Y	Vessels may pass through.
G		Beware of the current
G		
R	Y	Vessels may not pass through.
R		Keep more than 200m from the lock
R		

Navigation control signal

Y	G	Vessels may not move in the Avant Port until
	W	authorised.
	G	This also applies to Port de Bas Sablons

Other communications

Capitainerie and Ecluse du Naye Ch 12. This should be watched when underway anywhere in the port.
Bureau du port Vauban Ch 9.

Waiting buoys for marina | Yacht berths in Bassin Vauban | Marina entrance | Ferry berth | Cruise liner in Ecluse du Naye lock | Marina. Port de Bas Sablons

St-Malo looking N

Berthing

Speed limit in the basins is 3 knots. Yachts berth alongside the pontoons at the N end of the Bassin Vauban, smaller yachts to the W, larger yachts to the E. Yachts double or treble up provided a passage is left between the pontoons.

For yachts longer than 12m or if the pontoons are full, the W wall under the city walls is available and usually attracts no charge.

During a special event the pontoons and the quay may fill when a berth may be found in Bassin Duguay-Trouin. The lifting bridge over the busy main road should respond to a long blast during lock opening times. Duguay-Trouin is also a bit quieter and nearer to the casino.

Facilities

Water and electricity On the pontoons. Occasional points and taps on the quay.
Fuel From fuelling berth in Port des Bas Sablons. Credit card with chip needed.
Showers and heads Next to the *bureau du port* at the N end. Pass needed to access.

Yacht club Societé de la Baie de St-Malo (SNBSM) is situated by the pontoons and is known world wide. They welcome visitors and host a number of races from the UK and elsewhere.
Chart agent Librairie Maritime, 5 rue Broussais; also another in Port de Bas Sablons.
Slips, cranes, engineers, electricians and *repairs* All such facilities available in Port de Bas Sablons.
Bureau du port and tourist office These are close together at the N end of Bassin Vauban and are mines of information. The former on port information and particularly the details of intended water levels above the barrage, and times of sluice openings; the latter on the myriad of leisure activities available in the area.
Shops Many of all qualities and varieties, mostly in the old town (intra muros).
Restaurants, bars and hotels An infinite variety from the Duchesse Anne just inside Porte St-Vincent, to those to satisfy very much more modest tastes and pockets. They are mostly intra muros and although a large number are situated near Porte St-Vincent a further exploration is worthwhile.

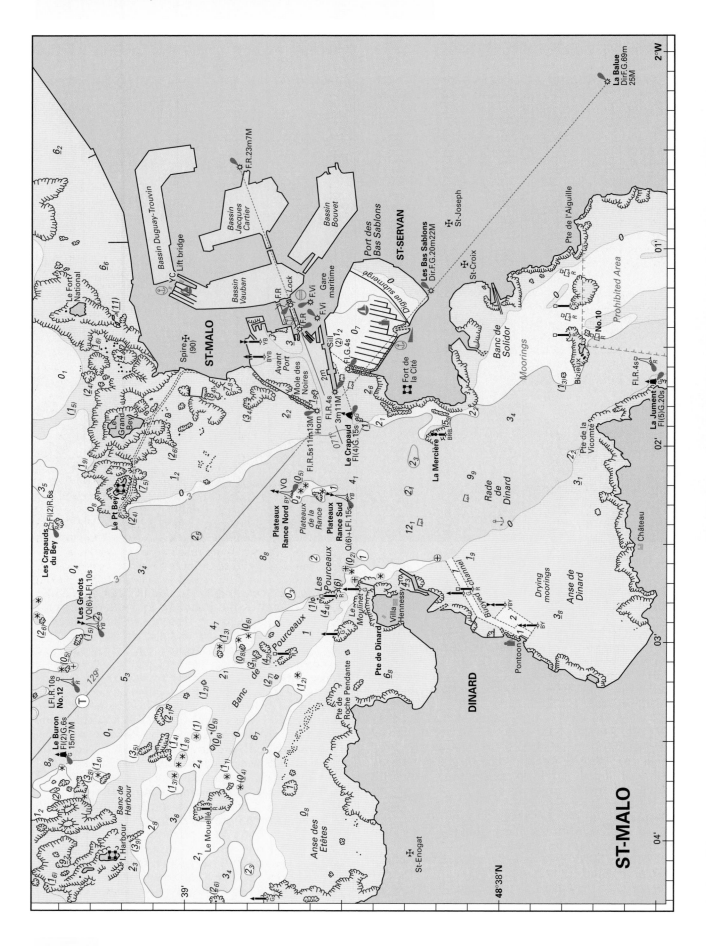

ST-MALO

Hotel de l'Univers in Place Châteaubriand is a traditional yachtsman's watering hole.

Travel Train to Rennes whence there is a high speed link to Paris; the station is ½M E along the road across the lifting bridge. Bus timetables and details from the tourist office; the bus station is just beside it. Airport at Dinard-Pleurtuit has flights to Channel Isles and Exeter and connections to Paris. Rennes airport also connects to Paris. Ferries daily to Jersey, Poole, Portsmouth and less frequently to Plymouth and Rosslare; the ferry terminal is to the SW of the lock. *Vedettes* to Dinard and elsewhere run from the quays to the N of the lock.

Leisure A visit to the tourist information office to find the wide variety of entertainments on offer is worthwhile and should satisfy the most fractious family or crew. If only here for a day, the least that should be tried is a walk round the walls (¾ hour easy stroll) from which a lot can be gleaned of the town's history, together with a visit to the museum in the Hotel de Ville in the E corner of Intramuros near which there is a small aquarium.

A longer stay should include the magnificent new Grand Aquarium (on the outskirts, bus or taxi) which is in a world class and a visit to Châteaubriand's tomb on Le Grand Bey but don't get caught there by the tide – you stay there. There are splendid beaches on the W and N sides of the town.

Historical

The town itself started when it was an isolated rock with a monastery founded in the 6th century by a monk named Aaron. He was succeeded by a Celt of Welsh origin St-Maclou (or St-Malo) who was Bishop of what is now St-Servan. The latter declined as a powerful walled town grew on the isolated rock and the inhabitants, known as Malouins became famous seamen, *corsairs* and explorers. In the 16th century and later they forced all shipping coming up the channel to pay tribute and also brought wealth from further afield. Jacques Cartier who started the colonisation of Canada lived in and sailed from here. They were the first colonists of the Falklands – hence the Argentine name of Las Malvinas. They declared St-Malo as an independent republic in 1590 – *Ni français, ni Breton, Malouins suis.*

As the centuries passed the walled town took its present form with massive fortifications and fine granite mansions for the wealthy merchants and sea captains, and the causeway Le Sillon was built to join it to Paramé.

The town resisted four attempts by the English to take it, one in 1758 when the Duke of Marlborough landed with 15,000 men near Cancale. In the 19th century the docks were developed to the SW of Le Sillon and the Malouins developed more peaceful pursuits such as fishing where they were one of the leaders in the cod fishery off Newfoundland.

In 1944 80% of the old town was destroyed by General Patten and the USAAF before the Germans surrendered. The subsequent restoration has been remarkable in the detail of its faithfulness to the original state.

Port des Bas Sablons (St-Servan Marina)

Anchorages and moorings

Anchorage is prohibited in the channels and Avant Port from Le Grand Jardin inwards with the exception of narrow strip to the NE of the moorings in Rade de Dinard. The streams run strongly here and the bank is steep. There are two waiting buoys off the marina entrance and also waiting buoys in the Avant Port for the lock. The happiest arrangement is to time arrival for when there is enough water over the sill which dries 2m which, with a 2m draught should allow entry from about 1¼ hours after LW to 4½ hours after HW.

Entrance

The entrance to the marina is to the S of the ferry terminal berthing jetty extension. Leave Le Crapaud starboard buoy (Fl(4)G.15s) and the end of the mole (Fl.G.4s) to starboard. Large illuminated screens show the depth over the sill. The waiting buoys between Le Crapaud and the entrance have 2m under them but it dries 2m just to the W of them.

Three red lights displayed on a mast by the sill prohibit movement in and out of the marina while a ferry is (un)berthing at the adjacent ramp.

There are 1216 places in the marina, maximum length 12m. There are 86 visitors' berths on pontoons A and B, the first inside the entrance. The marina is dredged to 2·5m but less at the inner end. The visitors' berth numbers on pontoon A are from 36–66 and 43–75, and from 92–102 and 91–101 on pontoon B. At busy periods marina staff may visit yachts waiting outside to allocate berths other than at these pontoons.

The marina is sheltered in all weathers although some movement may be felt around HW in strong northwesterlies.

Communications

GWG vertical lights with a yellow to the left of the top G shown by Ecluse du Naye prohibits movement in the Avant Port and applies to entry and departure from the marina.

Capitainerie and locks Ch 12 which should be watched when underway in the harbour.

Bureau du Port des Sablons is on Ch 9 although there is no need to call them before going to a berth.

Facilities

The marina is fully equipped to meet almost any demand.

Fuel Diesel and petrol at the root of pontoon K. A credit card with a chip is needed to work the pumps. Ask at the *bureau du port* if one is not held, and pay cash.

Water and electricity On the pontoons. French 2-pin plug needed, available from chandlers.

Shower and heads By the roots of pontoons E and F.

Travel-lift 30-tons plus crane to cope with masts or engines. The slip it uses can be used for launching trailed craft and also to dry out against on a hard bottom.

Engineers, electricians, shipwrights, chandlers and chart agent All available on site.

Launderette In rue des Bas Sablons outside the marina.

Shops Within short walking distance. Market on Tuesday and Friday mornings.

Restaurants, cafés and bars A number of all qualities and prices in Bas Sablons and St-Servan.

Travel See under St-Malo for details. Only the ferry terminal is within walking distance, unless fit and energetic.

Leisure See under St-Malo. A visit to tourist information office at St-Malo would be worthwhile if staying for a few days. There is an Olympic swimming pool open all the year round nearby and the Tour Solidor, a short walk to the S, has a museum of Cape Horners; it is open in French working hours except on Monday. Nearby in the old Fort d'Aleth is a Second World War Museum. The striking Grand Aquarium is on the hill above St-Servan and well worth a taxi ride.

History

St-Servan is more ancient than St-Malo and is near the site of the Gallo Roman town of Aleth. The quarter immediately to the S of the marina still bears this name. Aleth remained the bishopric and the dominant of the two towns until the 12th century when it declined in relation to St-Malo with its powerful defences and ambitious inhabitants.

The Tour Solidor, of three towers arranged in plan like an ace of clubs, was built in 1392 to guard La Rance.

Dinard

Approaches

See under St-Malo, Chenal de la Petite Porte.

Anchorage

At neaps it is possible to work well in to the Anse de Dinard with enough water to stay afloat, out of the stream and clear of the moorings. At springs the bank drops steeply from drying down to 7m and although the holding is good it will not be possible to get out of the stream which can be strong when the barrage sluices are open; also subject to swell with onshore winds.

Bilge keelers or those able to take the ground can select a berth anywhere in the middle of the bay on sand and mud and clear of the many moorings.

A marked channel, dredged to 1m runs in to the yacht club almost parallel to the shore on the N side of the bay. This culminates in a pool or wet basin with between 1m and 2m. The channel is used by the *vedettes* and the area is covered with moorings. Visitors are not catered for unless by previous arrangement. There are plans to build a marina here (2000).

Facilities

Fuel There is a fuel berth in the wet basin.

Water From the yacht club or slips, in cans.

Landing slips At the yacht club or *vedette* slips. The slip on the E side never dries.

Yacht club The large Yacht Club de Dinard is well known for its hospitality to British yachts and can provide showers. It is rather more formal than many French yacht clubs.

Shops, cafés, restaurants and hotels Many of all qualities, sizes and prices in the town.

Travel See under St-Malo. There is no bus to the airport from Dinard and a taxi must be taken.

History

Dinard became a holiday resort much patronised by the English and Americans in the Victorian age and the architecture and ambience in the town still reflect these prosperous times. Picasso painted here

St-Malo. Drying moorings at Dinard which is out of picture to the right. On the skyline, water tower conspic from seaward and to the left château-like building with twin towers which is a leading mark for Chenal de la Grande Conchée

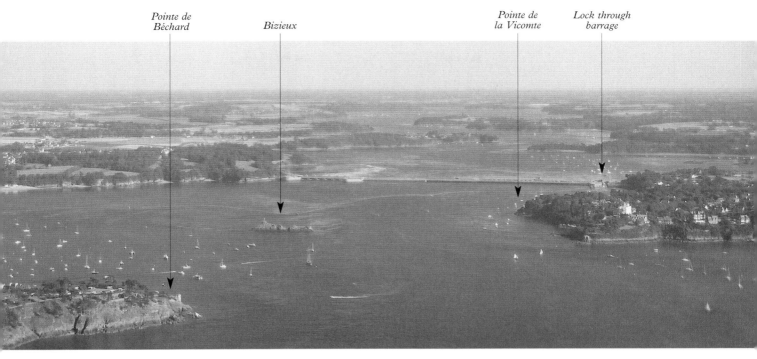

Pointe de Béchard *Bizieux* *Pointe de la Vicomte* *Lock through barrage*

St-Malo looking S to barrage and La Rance

in the 1920s and a strange statue of Alfred Hitchcock commemorates the town's annual festival of English language films.

There are a number of British graves in the cemetery near the top of the town, many from the loss of HM Ships *Charybdis* and *Limbourne* in 1943.

La Rance to Dinan

General
The barrage was built in 1966 to harness the power of the high tides and continues to supply electricity to the national grid. As a further benefit a large area of navigable water was created and the navigation to Dinan improved.

Before entering this part of La Rance, the annual pamphlet showing the regulations and the times and heights of HW between June and September should be obtained either from the *bureaux des ports* at Vauban, Bas Sablons or at the lock to the barrage. This shows the times when the water level will be 4m or 8·5m above CD in the river. The rate of rise and fall is variable but the normal does not exceed 4m per hour. This can be exceeded in exceptional circumstances when fierce currents can be generated both above and below the barrage. It is therefore difficult to calculate the depth needed when anchoring and a good margin for safety should be added.

Warning
The prohibited areas above and below the barrage marked by buoys joined in some places by ropes, must not be entered due to the currents from the sluices.

Charts
SHOM *4233*

Approach
From Rade de Dinard pass between Pointe de la Vicomte and the islet of Bizeux; leave La Jument starboard beacon tower 50m to starboard and continue up the narrowing channel between the prohibited area and the shore. If early for the lock, an anchorage may be found out of the stream just S of La Jument but the waiting buoys outside the lock where there is 1·5m, may be more convenient.

From seaward, yachts should try to arrive off the lock 20 minutes before the exact hour.

Lock working
The locks work when the height of the water outside exceeds 4m and from 0430 to 2030. A telephone call to 02 99 16 37 37 and two hours' notice may get them to open outside these times. The gates will open for incomers on the hour and for outgoers at the half hour. Be prepared to pass your draught and mast height to the lock keeper on demand.

Signals at the lock

3 greens	Vessels may pass
3 reds	No entrance
2 greens and a white	No movement until instructed

Signals on the barrage (on masts at centre and E end)

2 cones point up, white above black	Sluices open to flow inwards
2 cones point down, black above white	Sluices open to flow seawards

Signals to indicate exceptional flow

At Chatelier lock	2 red lights
At Mordreuc slip	5 red lights arranged as in St-Andrew's cross

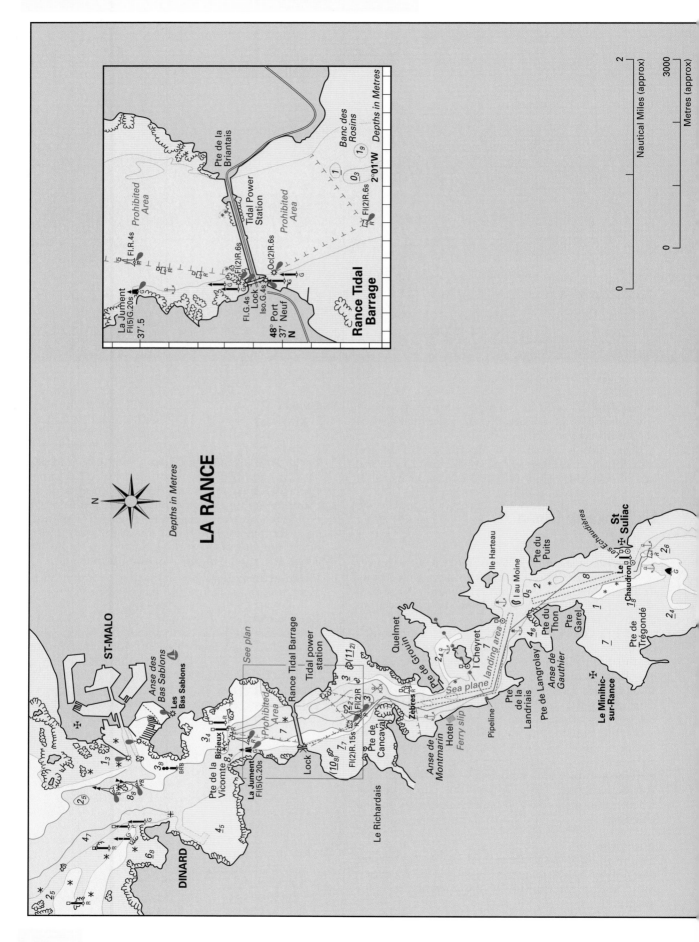

LA RANCE

Depths in Metres

N

ST-MALO

Anse des Bas Sablons

⚓ **Les Bas Sablons**

DINARD

See plan

Pte de la Vicomte

Bizieux

La Jument Fl(5)G.20s

Lock

Rance Tidal Barrage

Tidal power station

Pte de Cancaval

Le Richardais

Fl(2)R.15s

Fl(2)R

Zebres

Quelmet

Pte de Grouin

Anse de Montmarin

Hotel

Ferry slip

Sea plane

Pipeline

landing area

Ile Harteau

l'au Moine

Pte du Puits

I Cheyret

Pte de la Landriais

Pte de Langrolay

Anse de Gauthier

Pte du Thon

Pte Garel

Le Minihic-sur-Rance

Pte de Trégondé

Le Chaudron

St Suliac

Les Echaudieres

Rance Tidal Barrage

Fl.R.4s

Prohibited Area

Pte de la Briantais

Tidal Power Station

La Jument Fl(5)G.20s

37'.5

Fl.G.4s

Lock

Iso.G.4s

48° Port
37' Neuf
N

Oc(2)R.6s

Fl(2)R.6s

Prohibited Area

Banc des Rosins

2°01'W

Fl(2)R.6s

Depths in Metres

Nautical Miles (approx)

Metres (approx)

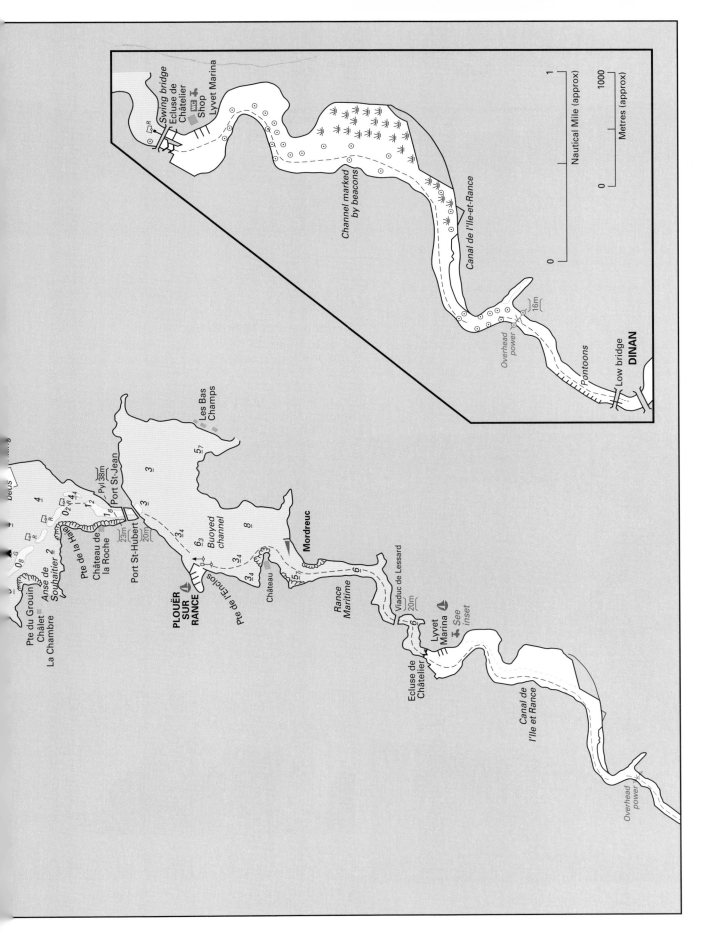

St-Malo. La Rance. Looking up-river to the two road bridges across Port St Hubert narrows

Fishing boats and *vedettes* take precedence at the locks over yachts.

Yachts with masts coming from seaward should precede those without; those with masts going seaward should let those without enter first. This is because the lifting bridge at the N end of the lock clears mastless boats and can then be lowered sooner.

Ropes hang down from the sides of the lock and it is not necessary to make fast securely as there is little turbulence.

From barrage to St-Suliac

A yacht taking the first lock from seaward between 2 and 1½ hours before HW should have plenty of time to reach the lock at Chatelier before the level starts to fall.

On leaving the barrage lock, leave three port buoys and the prohibited area close to port. The last port buoy (Fl(2)R.6s) is the only navigational light above the barrage. The channel to St-Suliac carries a least depth of 2m above CD. There is a certain amount of *vedette* traffic in the river.

SHOM *4233* is now essential for further navigation although there is plenty of water in the channel as far as St-Suliac. Note that anchorage is prohibited N of Les Zebres port beacon tower except for a small area on Bancs des Rozins, that there is a prohibited anchorage area on either side of a pipeline which crosses to the SE of Ile Cheyret and which is marked by beacons, and that there are three seaplane landing areas. Anchoring in the latter is prohibited.

Anchorages

With the prohibitions above in mind, it is possible to anchor almost anywhere out of the channel where

The two bridges   *Plouër marina*

St-Malo. La Rance looking NE over Plouër

St-Malo. La Rance. Château opposite Mordreuc looking downstream to the two bridges

St-Malo. La Rance. Plouër marina entrance bearing 284°

depth allows. However it is advisable to get as close to the shore as possible and to avoid the headlands where the current runs strongly. The bays are often filled with local boats at moorings but there are sometimes white mooring buoys with no name or number on them available for visitors.

1. Anse de St-Martin at the S end of the bay in 4m or closer. Good landing slip near the hotel conspicuous.
2. In the pool N of Ile Cheyret in 2m+.
3. In the bay to the N of Ile au Moine and Ile Notre Dame.
4. In the bay opposite between Pointe de Longrogley and Pointe du Ton. There are many moorings here and it is difficult to get far enough in out of the strong current. Slip and yacht yard, and a restaurant at Le Minihic ½M up the hill.
5. S of Les Echaudieres off St-Suliac in 1m+. There are 3 visitors' moorings in 2m off the slip at St-Suliac.

St-Suliac is a small, sleepy country town with a post office and a shop or two; also a restaurant and a *crêperie*. There is a good dinghy landing at the slip but it dries to wet mud at LW. There is a water tap here.

On Saturday in mid-August the Pardon of St-Suliac takes place with a candle-lit procession up to the pagoda-shrine of Our Lady of La Rance on the point N of the village.

St-Suliac to L'Ecluse du Châtelier

The charts show the run of the deeper water of the steadily decreasing channel. The buoys however show the direct route in shallower water, least depth drying 0·8m which should present no problems with 4m+ rise. This leads to the power line and the two bridges crossing the narrowest part of the river

La Rance looking WSW up final reach to Dinan

Lyvet Marina

La Rance. Châtelier looking ESE. The swing bridge is opening
to let the yacht in the lock through

La Rance. Early morning at Dinan

between Port St-Hubert and Port St-Jean. The lowest clearance is 20m below the S bridge. The pool below the bridges is the last one possible to anchor in and stay afloat but the current runs fiercely through it and an anchorage as close to the side as possible should be sought. There are landing slips on either side.

Above here a least depth in the channel of drying 6m should be assumed. The channel is narrow and winding and close attention should be paid to the buoys and beacons marking it.

Port de Plouër-sur-Rance

This yacht harbour in the old mill pool is 1M above the bridges and maintains 2m inside a sill. The gate opens when there is 8·2m depth, with 1·5m over the sill. The entrance is between Nos50 and 52 port buoys on a line of Plouër church bearing 284° between the entrance beacons. Red and green lights indicate when the gate is open. There are waiting buoys outside the entrance. *Bureau du port* watches Ch 9 during working hours. There are 10 places for visitors on pontoon B which is the first inside the gate.

There is water and electricity on the pontoons, showers and heads, a bar/restaurant nearby and another in the village where there are shops, banks and a post office.

Mordreuc

A small village on the E bank above Plouër with a landing slip and a small bar/restaurant. Warning lights are shown here if exceptional currents are to be expected.

Le Châtelier

The Lessard Viaduct with a clearance of 20m crosses the river ¼M below the lock and bridge at Le Châtelier. The channel is marked by port and starboard poles between the viaduct and the lock. The sill is 6·43m above datum but there has been some silting and the lock and bridge are usually operated when the level reaches 10m at St-Suliac. Mooring lines are provided which should be kept taut until the turbulence, which can be considerable has subsided. The lock is 39m long and 7·9m wide. Ch 14 is watched when the lock is working. ☎ 96 39 55 66 for lock opening times or further details.

Le Châtelier to Dinan – Canal de l'Ile et Rance

It is as well to check on the depth of water above the lock before proceeding. In early 2000 there were a few 1·5m patches between it and Dinan and some sign of dredging over winter. Dry spells will lower the water level appreciably.

Above the lock on the E bank is a small marina at Lyvet where there is a water tap and a small food store. There are pontoons here with 2m under them and 10 places for visitors on pontoon B.

When leaving the lock, turn slowly to port to pass between the pair of red and black posts on the first bend, thence between the red posts and the towpath. See plan on page 63 showing the general run of the canal to Dinan. The clearance under the power line just below Dinan is 16m.

At Dinan there are quays and a pontoon with short (6m) fingers on the W bank. All are crowded in the summer and there is a steady stream of *vedettes* when the lock is open.

Facilities at Dinan

Dinan has a far longer and important history than its almost-namesake Dinard. The centre of the town has many ancient houses and the ramparts date back to the 13th century. The church of St-Sauveur is well worth a visit for its Gothic extravagance and there are many other mediaeval gems to be seen. The ubiquitous Duchesse Anne, twice Queen of France to different kings, had connections with the town.

Water and electricity On the pontoons; occasional tap on the quays.

Showers, heads and launderette At the *bureau du port*.

Restaurant and shops Some on the quay otherwise it is a steep climb up the hill through cobbled streets and mediaeval houses to the main town where there is an abundance.

Crane For masts up to 400kg.

Travel Buses and railway to Rennes. Nearest airports Rennes and Dinard.

Further travel by canal

Masted navigation ceases at Dinan. The depth in the canal to Rennes is stated as 1·3m but may well be less after a scarcity of rain. There is little point in continuing to Nantes as the Vilaine River can be navigated from there to Redon and so to the sea.

No inland waterway documentation is required to reach Dinan but will be if proceeding further and rules and regulations for French inland waterways will apply. The minimum requirement for any vessel of less than 15m is that the helmsman must possess a RYA Helmsman's Overseas Certificate of Competence and that a current tax disc (*vignette*) is held. Details of the latter may be obtained from Voies Navigable de France, rue Ludovic Boutleux, 62400 Béthune, France. The French Government Tourist Office, 178 Picadilly, London W1V 0AL ☎ 0906 824 4123 can help further and can supply any details of closures (*chômages*). The following references may be of further help:

Cruising Association's *Introduction to the French Inland Waterways*.

Cartes-Guides Navicartes No.12 Canaux Bretons by Grafocarte which has strip maps of the canals and is available from Imray, Laurie, Norie and Wilson.

RYA *Book of Euroregs for Inland Waterways* Marian Martin. Adlard Coles Nautical.

Inland Waterways of France David Edwards-May Imray, Laurie, Norie and Wilson.

St-Briac

General

This small, drying bay should not be confused with St-Brieuc with its associated port Le Légué 25 miles to the W. The harbour, as such, is formed by the mouth of the Rivière de Frémur nearly all of which dries but it does have a sectored light to lead in at night. There is an anchorage off it in easterly or settled weather and some rather spread out facilities ashore in a pleasant and unspoilt resort.

The harbour is within an area where a risk is still thought to exist from the Second World War mines when anchoring, fishing or taking the ground. Such a risk, particularly in well frequented areas must now be very small.

Data

Charts

Admiralty 3659 (SC), 2669 (ARCS)
Imray C33B
SHOM 7129 and 7133 are on a larger scale.

St-Briac looking W through entrance at LW

Tides

Within 5 minutes and 0·2m of those at St-Malo.

Lights

Embouchure du Frémur DirIso.WRG.4s13-11M
White mast on hut 122°-G-125°-W-126°-R-130°

Approaches

By day Coming from the N in the vicinity of the starboard Banchenou pillar buoy, identify Ile Agot to the E, Portes des Hébihens group of rocks of which the most northern is 9m high and behind them, the tower on Ile des Hébihens. From a position 0·3M N of Portes des Hébihens turn on to 125° to pass between Les Herplux port beacon and La Moulière N cardinal beacon. From here the line of port and starboard beacons leading in to the harbour can be seen and it should be possible to identify the white sectored light pillar. This is at the end of a wall which leads round to the bridge. The latter does not become visible until into the harbour. Keep the light pillar bearing 125° and pass the port and starboard beacons on the appropriate side until a suitable depth to anchor or dry out is found.

By night Make good a southerly track from the Banchenou starboard buoy (Fl(5)G.20s) to pick up Le Briac sectored light (Iso.WRG.4s). The red sector is to the N and 4° wide followed by the even narrower white sector of 1° and the green sector to the S. Follow the white sector exactly on 125° but the visibility must be such to see and identify the beacons which are very close to this line.

Anchorage

Deep draught yachts may find an anchorage in fine weather in 1m or more S of Ile du Perron. Bilge keelers or shallow draughts can continue in to good shelter and dry on sand and mud although the best places have been taken by moorings. Rocks run out from the wall along the E side of the harbour.

Entrance

St-Briac looking S up Rivière du Frémur

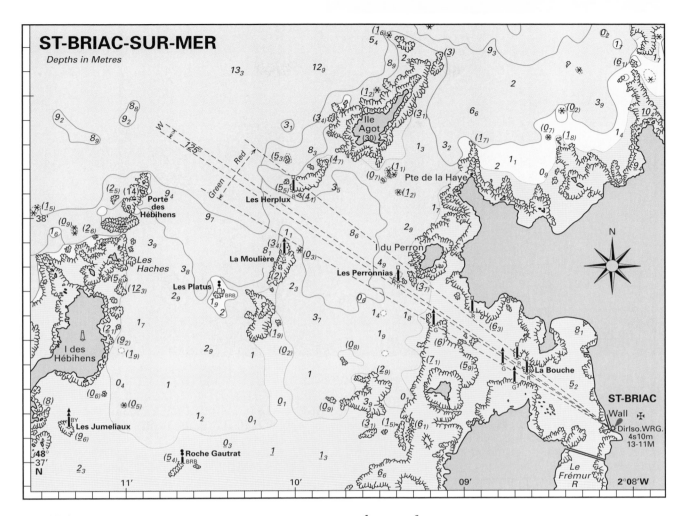

ST-BRIAC-SUR-MER
Depths in Metres

Ile Agot (30)

Pte de la Haye

Porte des Hébihens

Les Herplux

Les Haches

La Moulière

I du Perron

Les Platus

Les Perronnias

I des Hébihens

La Bouche

ST-BRIAC

Wall
Dirlso.WRG.
4s10m
13-11M

Les Jumeliaux

Roche Gautrat

Le Frémur R

48° 37' N

11'   10'   09'   2°08'W

Facilities

An unspoilt holiday resort with some small hotels, a restaurant and modest shops all rather scattered through the village.

St-Jacut – Baie de Lancieux

General

A large drying bay with an open anchorage to the E of Ile des Hébihens. Even for those able to take the ground, a place near the shore will be hard to find close to the E of St-Jacut village because of moorings. Minimal facilities but fun for children.

The whole Baie de Lancieux is in an area in which a risk still exists if anchoring, fishing or taking the ground due to remains of Second World War mines. Such a risk must now be very small particularly in well used and frequented areas.

Data

Charts

Admiralty *3659, 2669* (ARCS)
Imray *C33B*
SHOM *7129* There are no plans.

Tides

Within 5 minutes and 0·2m of St-Malo.

Approaches

By day only Identify Porte des Hébihens rock (see under St-Briac above) and from a position 100m E of it make good a track of 164° leaving Platus isolated danger beacon 200m to port. From here an anchorage in 1m–2m can be found as close to the E

St-Jacut looking NE. The tiny harbour has partly filled with sand over the winter gales. Moorings and anchorage to the right

St-Jacut anchorage looking SW. The small harbour and slip are right centre

of Ile des Hébihens as depth and moorings allow. If continuing to St-Jacut drying anchorage, leave another isolated danger beacon to starboard and bring up outside the moorings on the NE side of the Baie de Lancieux. There is a tiny harbour here which dries 8m (see photograph). The bay is all hard sand with the occasional rock patch and from the S end of Ile des Hébihens dries from 2m to 7m.

Facilities
Ile des Hébihens is private but landing is permitted. Just above the small harbour at St-Jacut is a white wooden shack housing the yacht club. From here it is a mile up the hill to the scattered village which has a few cafés and shops.

St-Cast – Baie de L'Arguenon – Port Le Guildo
See plan page 72

General
St-Cast lies 3M SE of Cap Fréhel on the E side of Pointe de St-Cast. The port is a mile from the town but with enough facilities to satisfy most needs. The harbour area is occupied by fore and aft moorings but there is room to anchor although not well protected from the E and S.

The Baie de L'Arguenon lies in an area where there is still thought to be a risk from the remains of Second World War mines when anchoring, fishing or taking the ground. This risk must now be very small, and non-existent in the vicinity of St-Cast harbour.

Baie de L'Arguenon dries from 2M to the SE of St-Cast and leads via the channel of the river L'Arguenon in the sands to the port of Le Guildo where there is a quay drying 7·6m used by coasters drawing up to 4·5m. There is no reason why yachts which can take the ground should not find their way up there but the quay is grubbily commercial and right on the main road.

St-Cast
Data
Charts
Admiralty *3659* (SC), *2669* (ARCS)
Imray *C33B*
SHOM *7129* (No plan)

Tides
Within 5 minutes and 0·2m of St-Malo.

Lights
Breakwater head Iso.WG.4s11m11/8M Green and white structure 204°-W-217°-G-233°-W-245°-G-204°

Buoys
Les Bourdinots Unlit E cardinal 1M to the NE in the green sector of the light

Search and rescue
An inshore lifeboat is maintained here. The semaphore station on the point above is manned.

Communications
Bureau du port Ch 9 during working hours. ☎ 02 96 41 88 34.

Approaches
By day Coming from the Banchenou buoy to the NE, avoid the Bourdinots rock drying 2m and

Bec Rond

St-Cast looking WNW

marked by an E cardinal spar buoy. Enter the harbour between the pierhead and Le Bec Rond port beacon.

By night Identify the light on the end of the breakwater Iso.WG.4s and approach in one of the white sectors, between 204° and 217° or 233° and 245°. The green sector between covers the

Bourdinots rocks and the buoy there is unlit. Le Bec Rond beacon at the harbour entrance is also unlit.

Anchorages
1. To the SE of Bec Rond in 2m clear of moorings.
2. 1M to the S, to the SSE of Pointe de la Garde is a good anchorage sheltered from the S through W to NW. There is a slip and yacht club nearby.

Bec Rond

St-Cast looking E at LW

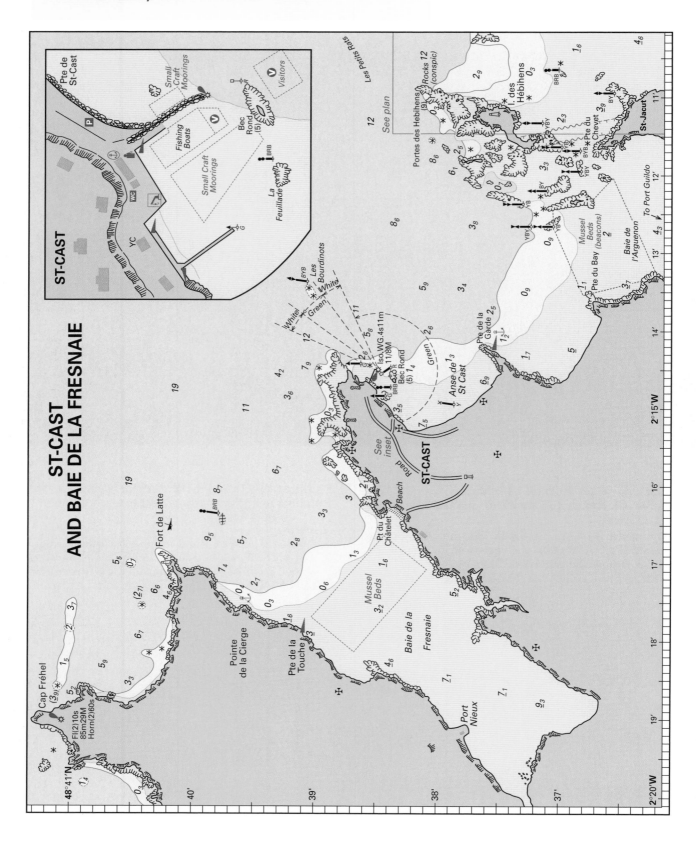

ST-CAST
AND BAIE DE LA FRESNAIE

Moorings

There are 10 moorings for visitors, maximum 13m. Yachts should pick up a buoy or anchor to seaward of the fishing boat moorings or off Bec Rond, and come in by dinghy to arrange a mooring at the *bureau du port* at the root of the slip in the NE corner of the harbour. The harbourmaster is keen to oblige. Alternatively call on Ch 9 if your French is good enough, French working hours only.

The first two rows of yellow mooring buoys parallel to the breakwater are for fishing boats. This and the yacht section immediately to the SW are dredged to at least 1·6m so there is access at all stages of the tide.

Facilities

Water and fuel At the root of the breakwater.
Showers and heads At the SW end of the block of shops/flats by the harbour.
Slip Up to 10 tons.
Cranes Up to 12 tons.
Launderette In the town about 1M away.
Chandler By the harbour.
Cafés, bar and crêperie By the harbour.
Shops Basic provision shops and others by the harbour. Supermarket in the town.
Travel Nearest station is at Lamballe with bus connections. Nearest airport at Dinard. Taxi ☎ 02 96 41 86 16.

Baie de la Fresnaie

General

A wide and deep bay, most of which dries, lying some 2M E of Cap Fréhel. It offers an anchorage sheltered from the W under Pointe de la Latte surmounted by an impressive castle.

The whole of the bay lies in an area in which there is still thought to be some risk from the remains of Second World War mines when anchoring, fishing or taking the ground. The risk must now be very small particularly in areas such as the anchorages shown below which are well frequented.

Baie de la Fresnaie. Anchorage 1M S of Fort de la Latte. Note shellfish farm grids on drying sand

Data

Charts

Admiralty *3659* (SC), *2669* (ARCS)
Imray *C33B*
SHOM *7129* (there is no plan)

Tides

Within 10 minutes and 0·5m of St-Malo.

Baie de la Fresnaie. Fort de la Latte from NW

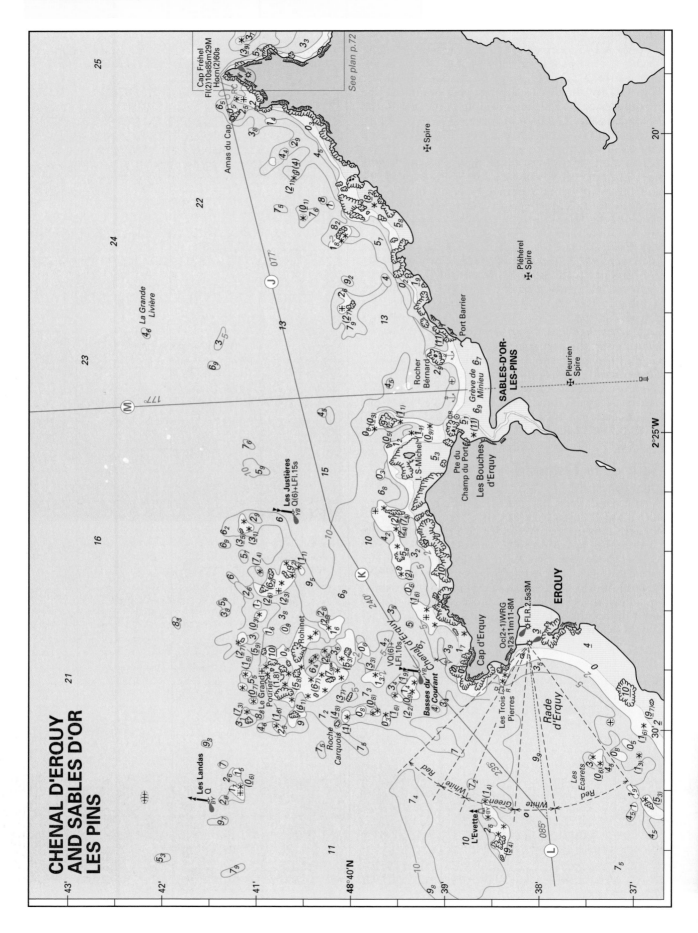

CHENAL D'ERQUY AND SABLES D'OR LES PINS

Cap Fréhel
Fl(2)10s85m29M
Horn(2)60s

See plan p.72

Amas du Cap

077°

J

La Grande
Livière

Les Justières
VB Ql(6)+LFl.15s

M 177°

K 240°

Rohinet

Le Grand
Pourier

Roche
Carquois

Les Landas
Q

L'Evette

Chenal d'Erquy VB
VQ(6)+
LFl.10s

Basses du
Courant

Les Trois
Pierres R

Rade
d'Erquy

Les
Ecarets

Red
White
White
Green

White
Green
085°

ERQUY

Oc(2+1)WRG
12s11m11-8M
Fl.R.2.5s3M

Cap d'Erquy

Port Barrier

SABLES-D'OR-
LES-PINS

Grève de
Minieu

Rocher
Bérnard

Pte du
Champ du Port
Les Bouches
d'Erquy

S-Michel

Plèhèrel
Spire

Pleurien
Spire

Spire

L

48°40'N

43'
42'
41'
30'
38'
37'

25
24
23
22
21
16
15
13
11
10

2°25'W
20'

Buoys

An isolated danger buoy marks a dangerous wreck ¾M SE of Pointe de la Latte.

Approaches

Straightforward once Fort de la Latte has been identified and the dangerous wreck avoided.

Anchorages

There is an anchorage in 3m sand and mud, and very good holding with Fort de la Latte bearing 010°, 0·6M just off Pointe de la Cierge.

1M to the SW is a small landing slip with some moorings off it where it dries 3·5m (see photograph).

A further 1½M up the bay is Port Nieux which has a quay and small jetty where alongside berths dry 7·8m.

On the SE side of the bay, an anchorage can be found in 2m to the NW of Pointe du Châtelet. To the S of the point is a beach, some moorings off it, a caravan site and a road up to St-Cast from where it would be possible to obtain supplies if desperate.

Facilities

None except for the above and Fort de la Latte which is worth a climb up from the sea. The tower which contains a cannon-ball factory, can only be reached over two drawbridges and is a favourite with film makers. Guided tours only.

Sables d'Or-les-Pins – Grève de Minieu

General

A wide, sandy bay open to the N affording some shelter from the W but less from the E. It has two very small quays and a lively resort at the back of the beach. A lot of *les pins* suffered in the great winter gale of 1999.

Data

Charts

Admiralty *3674* (SC), *2669* (ARCS)
Imray *C33B* No plan.

Tides

Within 10 minutes and 0·5m of St-Malo.

Approaches

Identify Ile St-Michel with a diminutive chapel on the summit. There is an unmarked rock drying 9·7m shaped like an inverted saucer ½M NE of Ile St-Michel. Identify Pleurien belfry and the conspicuous water tower behind and bring them into transit 177° (Line M); this is well open of the large hotel on the *plage* (see photograph). Follow this line in to a suitable depth of water to anchor. Do not stray to the E of this line to avoid a dangerous rock near the middle of the beach 600m SW of Rocher Bénard (7m).

Anchorages

Anywhere in the bay in a suitable depth clear of the dangerous rock, mostly sand but some rock patches.

There is an anchorage to the SE of Rocher Bénard in 2m–4m, sand but beware of Rocher Fournel drying 11m further to the SE at the end of a spit from the shore.

Berths

There are two small harbours in the bay not really suitable for yachts:

Port Barrier at the E end is a substantial jetty built for loading stone from the nearby quarries. Although it has silted it is still used occasionally for aggregates. It would be possible to dry against but a recce first would be advisable as the bottom alongside has become uneven and permission should be asked at the *capitainerie*. It is a good walk to the village.

A small river flows into the bay at its W end and there is a small jetty at Pointe du Champ du Port which dries 5m with a number of moorings off it.

Facilities

There is no slip except at Pointe du Champ du Port which is cut off from the village by the river and estuary; land anywhere on the sands in the bay.

The village sprawls along the beach and up the road inland. The *capitainerie* is in the sailing school at the W end where there is a water tap. Two garages, a chandler and a supermarket lie up the road. There is a casino and several cafés/restaurants near the beach, and a large hotel.

Sables d'Or-les-Pins. Leading marks centre, just out of line

Hotel (conspic)

Sables d'Or-les-Pins. Pointe du Champ du Port from NW at LW. The small breakwater, slip and moorings at W end of the bay

Sables d'Or-les-Pins. Port Barrier from the N at LW. The drying jetty is just visible behind the breakwater

Chenal d'Erquy

General

This channel lies between Cap d'Erquy and the large group of rocks to the N. It is ¼M wide at its narrowest and carries a least depth of 3·5m. The two cardinal buoys near each end are lit so it is possible to transit at night. The tidal streams set true through it.

Data

Charts

Admiralty 2669 (ARCS) 3674 (SC), 3672 (Erquy approaches)
Imray C33B

Tides

Subtract 10 minutes from the times of HW St-Malo and 20 minutes from the times of LW St-Malo for the times at Erquy; subtract 0·8m from the heights of HW and 0·2m from the heights of LW St-Malo for those at Erquy.

Tidal streams

Streams in the channel start at:

–0540 HW St Helier (–0625 HW St-Malo) ENE
HW St Helier (–0045 HW St-Malo) WSW

Maximum rates are 2¾ knots in either direction.

Lights

Cap Fréhel Fl(2)10s85m29M Horn(2)60s Brown square tower, green lantern
Erquy breakwater end Oc(2+1)WRG.12s11m11-8M 055°-R-081°-W-094°-G-111°-W-120°-R-134°

Buoys

There are two cardinal buoys marking the N side of the channel:

Basses du Courant S cardinal VQ(6)+LFl.10s at the SW end of the channel
Les Justières S cardinal Q(6)+LFl.15s at the NE end of the channel.

Approaches and passage

By day Approaching from the E, having passed N of Cap Fréhel and of Amas du Cap, a large rock which lies to the W of the cape, close the shore until the S edge of Amas du Cap is touching the end of Cap Fréhel bearing 077° (Line J, see photograph). Steer 257° to hold this stern transit and leave Les Justières S cardinal spar buoy 800m to starboard.

When this buoy is abaft the beam and Cap d'Erquy bears 230°, alter course to make good 240° (Line K) leaving the Basses du Courant S cardinal spar buoy 100m to starboard.

If continuing W, when the Basses du Courant is abeam alter to 235° to leave L'Evette N cardinal beacon tower 0·4M to starboard. When Erquy lighthouse (red and white circular tower 10m high on end of the breakwater) bears 085°, alter course to make good 265° so as to keep that bearing astern (Line L). This line passes well N of Plateau de Jaunes, a group of rocks lying WSW of Erquy just off the W edge of plan page 74.

By night Navigate to a position 3M W of Cap Fréhel light and identify Les Justières light buoy (Q(6)+LFl.15s). Close it on a westerly course and identify Basses du Courant buoy bearing SW (VQ(6)+LFl.10s). Should the latter not be sighted at this stage when in the vicinity of Les Justières buoy, it would be wise to abandon the passage and return seaward to the NE. If radar is available a parallel index of 650m from Cap d'Erquy/Les Chatelets on a track of 240° will take one through.

From the vicinity of Les Justières make good 240° with Basses du Courant buoy on the starboard bow and in the green sector of Rohein light (VQ(9)WRG.10s). Alter to 235° when Basses du Courant is abeam. The red sector of the Erquy breakwater light will then be entered followed by a white sector, a green sector and then another white. When the light bears 085° in this sector alter to 265° and keep it bearing 085° in the white sector. This course will lead clear of Plateau des Jaunes to the S and Rohein group of rocks to the N.

If bound for Erquy, approach the light in the first white sector between 111° and 120°.

Chenal d'Erquy leading line. Cap Fréhel in transit with right-hand edge of Amas du Cap 077°

Erquy
See plan page 74

General

An active, drying fishing port protected by two short breakwaters from a 12-mile fetch to the W. Provided strong westerlies are not foreseen there is a good, flat drying area for bilgekeelers but any sea from the W will make grounding and floating unpleasant and possibly dangerous. The drying quays are occupied by fishing boats and *vedettes* in the season and yachts are not catered for alongside. The shops are some way from the port but there are some cafés and restaurants by the harbour which may be worth a long dinghy ride from the deep water anchorage.

Data

Charts

Admiralty *2669* (ARCS), *3674* (SC), *3672* (plan)
Imray *C33B*
SHOM *7310* (plan)

Tides

Subtract 10 minutes from the times of HW St-Malo and 20 minutes from the times of LW for the times at Erquy; subtract 0·8m from the heights of HW St-Malo and 0·2m from the heights of LW for the heights at Erquy.

Tidal streams

See under Chenal d'Erquy for the streams outside the harbour. Off the breakwater ends a W-going stream starts at HW -0200, continues to HW and can reach 2 knots.

Outer breakwater   Inner breakwater

Erquy from SSW at half-tide

Erquy looking N. Inner breakwater at LW

Lights and buoys

See under Chenal d'Erquy. In addition to those mentioned, an unlit port buoy marks the W extremity of Les Trois Pierres rocks ½M WNW of the root of the outer breakwater.

Approaches

By day From the E. Sail along Line K until Pointe d'Erquy is abeam 0·3M and follow the coast round at about this distance to leave Les Trois Pierres port can buoy to port. When Erquy lighthouse bears 090°, course may be altered to the anchorage.

From the N Leave Les Landas N cardinal spar buoy to port and L'Evette N cardinal beacon tower at least 400m to starboard.

From the W Pass 1¼M S of Rohein lighthouse (white tower, black top 13m) and make good 085° on Erquy lighthouse. This will leave Plateau des Jaunes ½M to the S and Plateau des Portes d'Erquy on which stands L'Evette N cardinal beacon tower, over ½M to the N.

By night The best approach is from the W. The southerly white sector of Le Grand Lejon (Fl(5)WR.20s) leads between the Roches de St-Quay and Rohein, after which course should be altered to 085° to stay in the middle of the S white sector of Erquy light.

Anchorages

Yachts must not anchor in the white sectors of Erquy light by day or night. At night an anchor light must be shown.

The recommended anchorage is with the breakwater lighthouse bearing less than 080° and Cap d'Erquy bearing 350°. The bottom is gently shelving and flat so that one can get further inshore with safety at neaps. The part of the harbour inside the inner breakwater is covered with mooring chains; this dries 3m for the most part.

It would be possible to anchor off the end of the inner breakwater on a rising tide (but buoy the anchor) and to go ashore to shops or for a meal over HW.

Facilities

Landing slip At the sailing club by the root of the inner breakwater.
Water Tap at the *bureau du port* near the sailing club.
Shops ½M away in the town.
Fuel At garage ½M away in the town.
Restaurants and cafés Some along the harbour.
Transport A bus service from the town; nearest railway station at Lamballe. Taxi ☎ 02 96 72 13 70.

History

Erquy was the scene of a smart little action by Sir Sydney Smith in 1796 in the frigate *Diamond* with a brig and lugger in support. A French convoy of a corvette, four brigs, two sloops and three luggers were seen in Erquy under the protection of the shore batteries. A landing party of seamen from *Diamond* stormed the batteries and the whole convoy was burnt with the exception of one lugger which was sunk defending her charges to the last. The British lost 3 killed and 5 wounded.

Dahouet

See plans on pages 80 and 81

General

An unusual drying harbour with a marina inside lying in a gap in the cliffs 1M S of Pointe de Pléneuf. The entrance dries up to 4·5m and the sill of the marina dries 5·5m to maintain 2·5m inside. A few fishing boats still use the outer harbour. Open to the W and NW, it will be dangerous to enter or leave in any weather from these directions. Some facilities ashore but a long way to the shops.

Data

Charts

Admiralty *3674* (SC), *2669* (ARCS)
Imray *C34*
SHOM *7310* (plan)

Tides

Subtract 10 minutes from the times of HW St-Malo and 25 minutes from the times of LW for the times at Dahouet; subtract 0·8m from the heights of HW St-Malo and 0·2m from the heights of LW for the heights at Dahouet.

Tidal streams

The streams start at the following times off the Plateau des Jaunes:

    −0430 HW St Helier (−0515 HW St-Malo) ESE
    +0010 HW St Helier (+0055 HW St-Malo) W

Lights

Dahouet Fl.WRG.4s10m9-6M Triangle on green and white tower 055°-G-114°-W-146°-R-196°
Entrance Fl(2)G.6s5m1M, green metal pylon. 156°-vis-286°

Buoys

Le Dahouet N cardinal unlit spar buoy 1M to WNW marking a rock drying 0·3m.

Approaches

By day Approach from the N or W and identify Verdelet, a conical island 42m high to the NNW of Pointe de Pléneuf. Leave Plateau des Jaunes whose W side is marked by a W cardinal unlit beacon, well to the E and Le Dahouet N cardinal spar buoy 200m to the S. Approach La Petite Mouette white and green lighthouse on a course of 120° to leave it close to starboard and a red perch to port. Then steer 148° on a port beacon to leave two white posts below a pagoda shrine to port. These posts mark the outer edge of a slip (see photograph). There is a tide gauge showing the depth over the sill to starboard. Keep over to the N side until the marina entrance becomes visible to starboard.

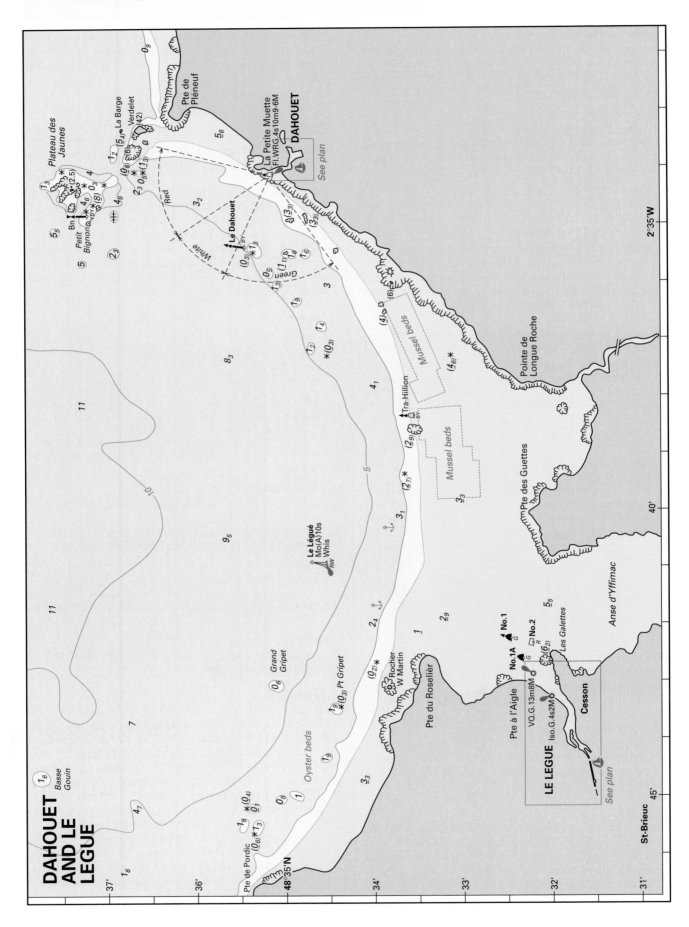

DAHOUET AND LE LEGUE

DAHOUET

Basse Gouin 1_6

4_7

Pte de Pordic

1_8 $*(0_4)$
$(0_6)*(1_3)$ 0_1

0_3

1

Oyster beds

1_9

1_9 (0_3)
$*$

0_6 Grand Gripet

(0_2) Pt Gripet

Rocher W Martin

Pte du Roselier

3_3

11

$16'$

11

7

9_5

8_3

10

Le Légué
Mo(A)10s Whis
RW

Le Dahouet BY

Plateau des Jaunes

1_3 $*$ $*$ 4
$2(2.5)$ 0_3
4_6 (8)
BY

5_5

Petit Bignon 5

2_3

1_2 (5_4) La Barge
$(5(6)$ Verdelet
(0_6) $*(1_3)$ (42)
2_3 0_5 $*$

Pte de Pléneuf

0_9

5_6

La Petite Muette
Fl.WRG.4s10m9-6M

DAHOUET

See plan

White

Red

3_2

Green

(0_3)
1_3 0_5
$*1_3$
$(1)_1$ 1_6
1_8
1_6

1_9

1_4

1_2 (0_3)
$*$

3

3_3

(3_3)

4_1

5

3_1

2_4

1

2_9

(4)

(6)

Mussel beds

Tra-Hillion BY
(2_9)

3_3

(2_7) $*$

Mussel beds

(4_6) $*$

Pointe de Longue Roche

Pte des Guettes

5_5

Les Galettes

Anse d'Yffiniac

No.1 G
No.2 R
No.1A G
(6_2)
Pte à l'Aigle VQ.G.13m8M
Cesson
LE LEGUE Iso.G.4s2M

See plan

St-Brieuc

$2°35'W$

$40'$

$45'$

$37'$

$36'$

$48°35'N$

$34'$

$33'$

$32'$

$31'$

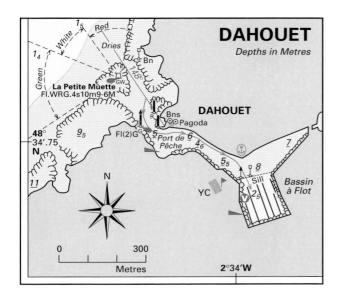

DAHOUET
Depths in Metres

La Petite Mouette
Fl.WRG.4s10m9-6M

DAHOUET

Pagoda

Fl(2)G

Port de Pêche

Bassin à Flot

Sill

YC

0 — 300
Metres

2°34'W

are 20 visitors' berths (max 12/13m) alongside the E side of the pontoon to starboard inside the entrance and it is usual to double up. Do not attempt to go on the other side between pontoon and slipway.

In the outer harbour, fishing boats berth two or three abreast on the quay but it may be possible to find a drying alongside berth here or on the wall in the inner harbour. The latter is packed with drying moorings. Ask at the *capitainerie* which is on the knuckle on the N wall opposite the marina entrance.

Facilities

Water and electricity On the pontoons.

Showers and heads Access card needed from marina office at end of slip.

Cranes One 15 ton and one 8 ton.

Fuel Diesel by a long hose from garage at head of inner drying harbour; petrol by can.

Shops A baker, chandler and fish from the cold store near the marina otherwise it is 1km to Val André to the NE but a pleasant walk along the cliffs.

Cafés/bars A couple by the harbour.

Travel The nearest railway station is at Lamballe (13km) and the nearest airport at St-Brieuc (35km). Taxi ☎ 02 96 72 25 04.

Leisure Not much, but the local tourist office by the harbour may be able to help. There are *vedette* trips every four or five days when the tides serve to Ile de Bréhat.

By night This is not recommended unless an entrance has been previously made by day. Navigate in to the white sector of La Petite Mouette light with it bearing between 114° and 146° and approach to leave it to starboard with the Fl(2)G.6s light inside ahead on 158°. The visibility must then be good enough to see the unlit marks as above for daytime.

Entrance and berths

The entrance to the marina is marked by red and green posts each side of the sill drying 5·5m. There

Dahouet light   Pagoda shrine

Dahouet looking SE at half-tide

Visitors' pontoon   Marina entrance   Bureau du Port

Dahouet looking NW

Dahouet at LW. Entrance channel looking inwards. White tide gauge on right. Marina beyond

History

The port was used by the Vikings over a thousand years ago but all traces of them and subsequent historical events appear to have vanished.

Yacht berths on N side   Lock Boatyard   No.1 Basin

Le Légué looking ENE

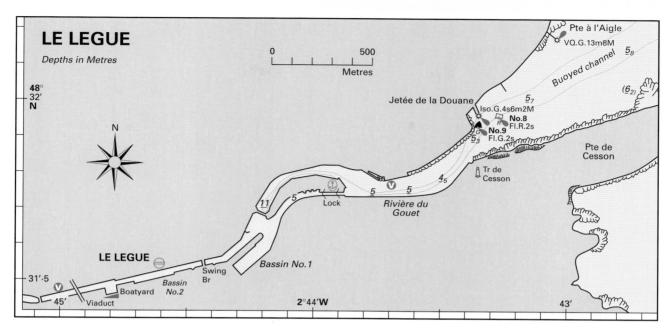

St-Brieuc
Port Le Légué

General

Le Légué is the port of St-Brieuc and lies about 1M up from the mouth of Le Gouet river at the head of the Anse d'Yffiniac. During strong northerlies the sea breaks right across the head of the bay and no attempt should be made to enter, but the approach is sheltered during the prevailing west and southwesterlies and, with sufficient rise of tide, is easy.

The port is entered through a lock with a sill that dries 5·1m. The entrance channel dries about 5m. The port is a commercial one with some facilities for yachts in the inner (No.2) basin. There are some shops, bars and cafés beside this basin but the surroundings are not attractive and it is a long walk up (300 feet) to the town which is a good mile away.

St-Brieuc is the major city of the district, industrialised on the outskirts and a focus for rail and road links. It is divided by two deep, wooded valleys which are crossed by several viaducts.

Data

Charts

Admiralty 3674 (SC) (plan), 2669 (ARCS)
Imray C34 (plan)

Tides

Subtract 10 minutes from the times of HW St-Malo and 20 minutes from the times of LW St-Malo for those at Le Légué; subtract 0·8m from the heights of HW St-Malo and 0·2m from the heights of LW St-Malo for those at Le Légué.

The heights of the tide is influenced by the wind and can vary by up to 0·7m.

Tidal streams

At the entrance to Anse d'Yffiniac streams start as follows:

−0430 HW St Helier (−0515 HW St-Malo) S
HW St Helier (−0045 HW St-Malo) N

Lights

Pointe à l'Aigle VQ.G.13m8M White tower, red top
Jetée de la Douane Iso.G.4s6m2M White column, green top

Buoys

Le Légué red and white Mo(A)12s Whis
From **No.1** starboard buoy about ½M ENE from Pointe à l'Aigle inwards there are some 10 lateral buoys, some lit, indicating the channel.

Communications

Bureau du port Ch 12 and 16 up to 2 hours either side of HW ☎02 96 33 35 41.

Customs

There is an office on the N side of the basin.

Approach

By day From the N or W see under Paimpol, Portriex and Binic.

Le Légué looking down-river from lock. Tour de Cresson on skyline

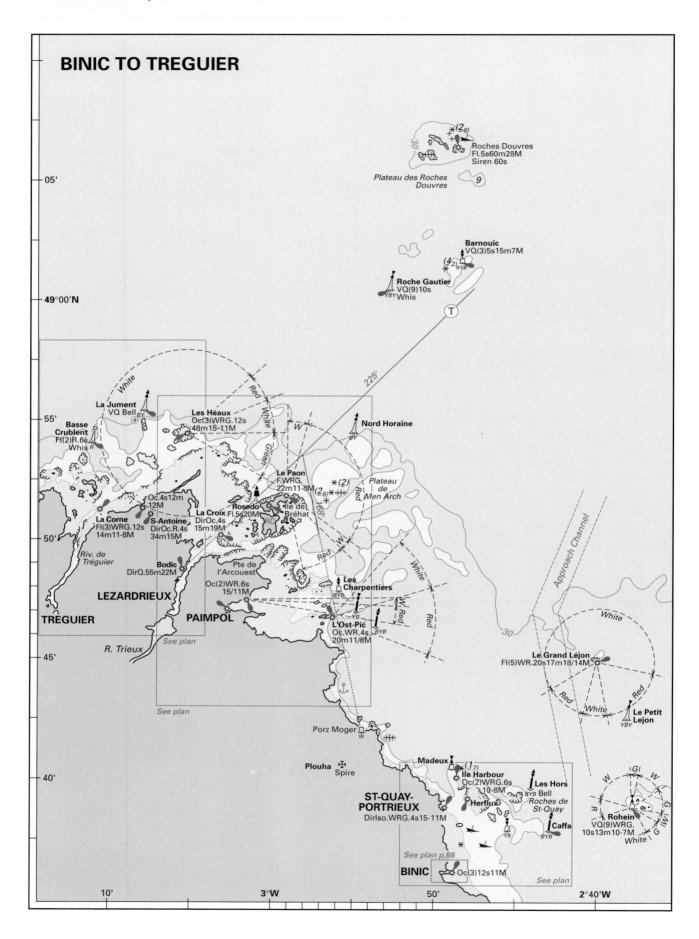

BINIC TO TREGUIER

Roches Douvres
Fl.5s60m28M
Siren 60s

Plateau des Roches Douvres

30

9

(2₆)

05'

49°00'N

Barnouic
VQ(3)5s15m7M

(4₂)
BYB

Roche Gautier
VQ(9)10s
Whis
YBY

T

225°

White

La Jument
VQ Bell
BY

Red White

Green

W

Les Héaux
Oc(3)WRG.12s
48m15-11M

Nord Horaine
BY

Basse
Crublent
Fl(2)R.6s
Whis R

55'

Le Paon
F.WRG.
22m11-8M

Plateau de Men Arch

(2₆)

(2)

198°

Oc.4s12m
12M

La Croix
Fl.5s20M

Rosedo
Île de
Bréhat
RC

La Corne
Fl(3)WRG.12s
14m11-8M

S-Antoine
DirOc.4s
DirOc.R.4s
34m15M

Red

W

50'

Riv. de Tréguier

Bodic
DirQ.55m22M

Pte de l'Arcouest
Oc(2)WR.6s
15/11M

Les
Charpentiers
BYB

W/
Red

White

Red

Approach Channel

30

White

LEZARDRIEUX

TRÉGUIER

PAIMPOL

YB

L'Ost-Pic
Oc.WR.4s
20m11/8M
BYB

45'

R. Trieux

See plan

Le Grand Léjon
Fl(5)WR.20s17m18/14M

Red

White

Le Petit
Lejon
YBY

Red

See plan

Porz Moger
W

Madeux
(1₇)

40'

Plouha
Spire

Île Harbour
Oc(2)WRG.6s
10-8M

Les Hors
BYB Bell

Gl

W   W

R

Herflux

Roches de St-Quay

ST-QUAY-
PORTRIEUX
DirIso.WRG.4s15-11M

YB

Caffa
BYB

Rohein.
VQ(9)WRG.
10s13m10-7M
White

G W

G

See plan p.86

BINIC
Oc(3)12s11M

See plan

10'   3°W   50'   2°40'W

From Le Légué landfall buoy make good 202° with sufficient rise of tide to allow for it drying 5m in the channel, and leave No.1 starboard-hand buoy off Pointe de l'Aigle close to starboard. Then proceed along the buoyed channel to the lock gates. The lock works from 1 to 2 hours either side of HW depending on the height of tide. Vessels may secure to the wall on the S side immediately outside while waiting.

By night From seaward pick up Pointe á l'Aigle jetty light (VQ.G.8M) and bring it on to a bearing of 208° with Rohein W cardinal beacon tower (VQ(9)10s) astern. This leads to Le Légué landfall buoy (Mo(A)12s) whence, with sufficient rise of tide to allow for drying 5m in the channel, and good visibility to pick up unlit No.1 starboard buoy, proceed up the channel. The light on Jetée de la Douane (Iso.G.4s) will assist and a number of the channel buoys are lit.

Entrance

The lock is 85m long and 14m wide and the sill is 5·1m above CD. Bassin No.1 is to port about 600m from the lock and is commercial. Basin No.2 which is formed by the canalised part of Rivière de Gouet is entered through a swing bridge which only opens twice a day. Proceed through it and secure to the N side of the basin.

The tide gauge on the N side of the entrance indicates depth over the sill, the gauge on the S side indicates depth above CD.

The interaction between fresh water from the river and sea water creates some turbulence in the lock, and a delay before entering after the gates open is advisable.

Anchorage

In settled weather and offshore winds, a yacht awaiting the tide can anchor in a suitable depth S of Le Légué landfall buoy.

Facilities

Water Occasional points on the quays; also from the boatyard or bars.
Fuel In cans from a garage on the N side of the basin.
Travel-lift and cranes Travel-lift to 30 tons, cranes to 10 tons.
Repairs and chandlery From the boatyard on the S side of the basin.
Shops A small *supermarché*, baker, chemist and post office on the N side of the basin.
Cafés/bars A few on the N side of the basin, otherwise a long walk up a steep hill to the town for a decent restaurant.
Travel Good rail and road connections with the rest of France. Flights to Paris from the local airport twice a day. Taxi ☎ 02 96 94 70 70.

Historical

The inundation of the Baie de St-Brieuc by the sea has only occurred in the last 2,000 years. In Roman times forests and cultivated land existed where there is now only drying sand. The Tour de Cesson, on the hill above the entrance at its narrowest part, was built originally in 1395 but has been blown up, knocked down and rebuilt over the centuries.

St-Brieuc is an old cathedral town named after the Celtic monk who arrived with his disciples in the 5th century, and converted the district to Christianity. Much of the cathedral is 13th and 14th century.

Le Légué was formerly the base for a fleet of *goëlettes*, the fine two-masted topsail schooners that fished off Greenland and Iceland until the last century.

Binic

See plans on pages 84 and 86

General

An attractive little port with a wet basin in the centre of the town which is a minor and pleasant tourist resort with good beaches in rural surroundings. There are drying moorings in the outer harbour, the sill at the gate to the basin dries 5·5m and opens when the tide rises to 9·5m until HW. It may not operate near neaps. There is some fishing activity mainly confined to the S outer jetty with the basin given over to yachts.

Binic tries hard to please yachtsmen and is a good deal more agreeable from their point of view than Le Légué although rather more tidal limited; St-Quay-Portrieux just to the N is much more expensive but accessible at all stages of the tide.

Data

Charts

Admiralty *3674* (SC), *3674* (ARCS), *2669*
Imray *C34*
SHOM *7128* (plan)

Tides

Subtract 10 minutes from the times of HW St-Malo and 20 minutes from the times of LW to find these times at Binic; subtract 0·8m from the heights of HW at St-Malo and 0·2m from the heights at LW to find the heights at Binic.

Tidal streams

Tidal streams start at the following times off the port:

−0430 HW St Helier (−0515 HW St-Malo)	SSE
HW St Helier (−0045 HW St-Malo)	NNW

Lights

N mole head Oc(3)12s 2m11M White tower, green gallery

Buoys

La Roselière W cardinal VQ(9)10s2M to the NE of Binic
Caffa E cardinal Q(3)10s4M to the ENE of Binic

Communications

Bureau du port Ch 9 (1100-1200, 1500-1600) ☎ 02 96 73 61 86.

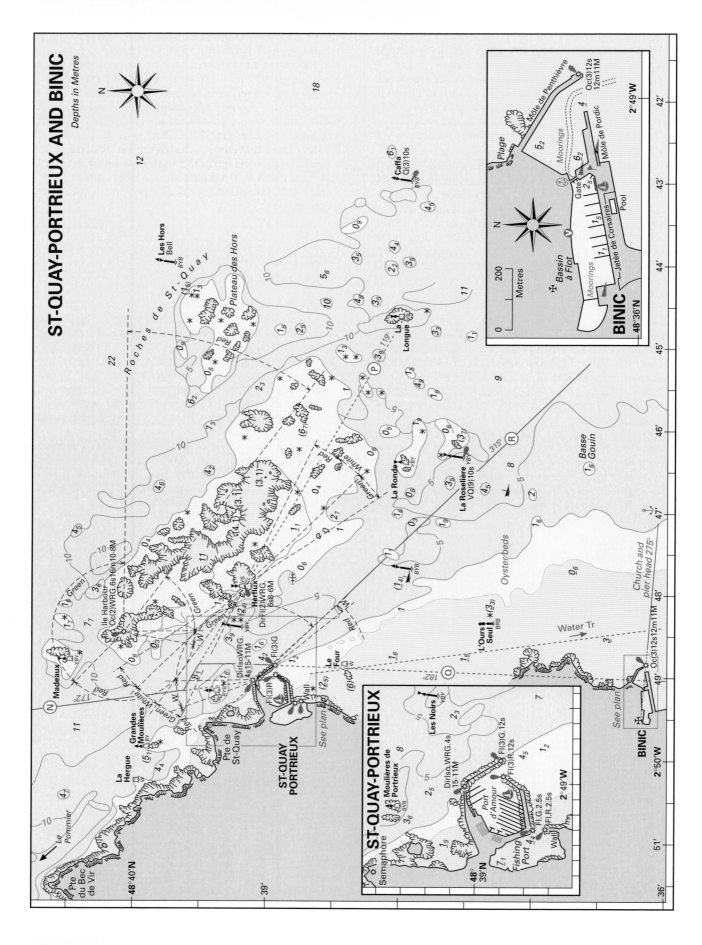

ST-QUAY-PORTRIEUX AND BINIC
Depths in Metres

BINIC
48°36'N
2°49'W

Môle de Penthièvre
Oc(3)12s 12m11M
Plage
Moorings
Môle de Pordic
Gate
Bassin à Flot
Pool
Jetée de Corsaires
Moorings

200
Metres

ST-QUAY-PORTRIEUX
48°39'N
2°49'W

Semaphore
Mouilières de Portrieux
Les Noirs
DirIso.WRG.4s 15-11M
Fl(3)G.12s
Fl(3)R.12s
Port d'Amour
Fl.G.2.5s
Fl.R.2.5s
Wall
Fishing Port

BINIC
2°50'W

Oc(3)12s12m11M
See plan
Church and pier head 275°

Roches de St. Quay

Les Hors
Bell
BYB

Caffa
Q(3)10s
BYB

Plateau des Hors

La Longue

Basse Gouin

La Ronde
La Roselière
VQ(9)10s

L'Ours Seul
BRB

Water Tr

Oysterbeds

Herflux
DirFl(2)WRG. 6s8-6M

Ile Harbour
Oc(2)WRG.6s16m10-8M

Madeaux

Grandes Mouilières

La Hergue

Le Pommier
Pte du Bec de Vir

Pte de St-Quay

DirIsoWRG. 4s15-11M
Fl(3)R
Fl(3)G
Le Four
Wall

See plan

48°40'N
39'
36'

Approaches

By day or night See under Paimpol or Portrieux if coming from the N.

There are no dangers in the immediate vicinity of Binic except Basse Gouin a rock about 1½M ENE of the harbour with a depth of 1·6m over it which should not present a problem unless anchoring in the area.

The least depth on any approach from the E sector is drying 5m with a shallow and steady gradient from the 5m line. The breakwater end and its light Oc(3)12s are readily identifiable.

Anchorage

In westerly or settled weather an anchorage may be selected in a suitable depth of water anywhere off the port except in the vicinity of Basse Grouin.

Entrance

The outer harbour has many moorings in it on the N side but a fairway is kept clear for access to the gate, and to the S pier for fishing boats.

The gate opens when the tide rises to 9·5m and stays open until HW. It will not operate outside these limits so take care not to be caught inside if approaching neaps. Red and green lights control entry and exit. A timetable of opening is displayed outside the *bureau du port*. There is a sliding bridge by the gate which is operated by the harbourmaster.

Berths

There is no provision for visitors on the moorings in the outer harbour but a drying berth may be found alongside the N mole drying 4·5m, sand and mud where it is quieter than in the basin.

There are 60 visitors' berths either on the first pontoon inside the gate (max 10m) or alongside the long pontoon running along the N wall (max 15m). Depths in the basin vary from 2·5m near the gate to 1·5m further in.

Facilities

Water and electricity On the pontoons; water point on the N quay.

Showers and heads 4 of each behind the *bureau du port* which is just N of the gate.

Fuel From garage 300m away in town.

Launderette Near the basin.

Crane 10-ton mobile.

Slip At head of basin.

Chandlery There are two close by.

Mechanics, electricians, sailmaker Ask at the *bureau du port*.

Shops and banks Many close by in the town.

S jetty for fishing boats   Visitors' pontoon on N side   Lock   Bureau du Port

Binic looking W at LW

Binic. The basin from the lock

Hotels and restaurants A good selection of all qualities and prices.

Yacht club There is an active yacht club housed in an unusual building just S of the gate.

Travel There is a bus service to St-Brieuc whence there are frequent departures in all directions by road or rail. The nearby airport has twice daily flights to Paris. Taxi ☎ 02 96 70 59 46.

Leisure The Zoological Gardens of Brittany are 6km W with many wild animals in natural surroundings; open 1000–1900 in the season. Good beaches to the N and S.

Historical

Binic used to be a considerable port and was the first to break the Basque monopoly of the Newfoundland cod fishery. Hundreds of *terre-neuviens* made the round trip of several months each year to the fishery and then to the south of France to sell their catches.

St-Quay-Portrieux
(Port d'Amour)

General

A traditional, drying fishing port that has had a large new marina added (Port d'Amour). The latter is accessible at all stages of the tide and in all weathers with a least depth of 4m in the approaches and 3m inside. The port is approached from the NW or the SE inside the extensive Roches de St-Quay which provide protection to the E. The marina includes a large fishing facility and fishing boat berths along the N side. The investment in this considerable project is reflected in the charges which are at the top end of the European average.

Most facilities required by yachtsmen are in the marina area but the nearby small resort town of Portrieux has more shops and leisure facilities.

Data

Charts
Admiralty *3674* (SC), *3672* (plan), *2669* (ARCS)
Imray *C34*

Tides
Subtract 10 minutes from the times of HW St-Malo and 20 minutes from the times of LW to find the times at St-Quay-Portrieux; subtract 0·8m from the heights of HW at St-Malo and 0·2m from the heights of LW to find the heights at St-Quay-Portrieux.

Tidal streams
The streams start in the channel between the harbours and Roches de St-Quay as follows:
    −0430 HW St Helier (−0515 HW St-Malo) SSE
    +0115 HW St Helier (+0030) HW St-Malo) NNW
The maximum rate is 2 knots.

Lights
Le Grand Lejon 9M NE Fl(5)WR.20s17m18/14M Red tower, white bands 015°-R-058°-W-283°-R-350°-W-015°

Herflux Roches de St-Quay DirFl(2)WRG.6s10m8-6M S cardinal beacon tower 115°-G-125°-W-135°-R-145°

Ile Harbour Roches de St-Quay
  Oc(2)WRG.6s16m10-8M White tower and dwelling, red top 011°-R-133°-G-270°-R-306°-G-358°-W-011°

Marina elbow DirIso.WRG.4s16m15-11M Concrete tower 159°-W-179°-G-316°-W-320°-R-159°

Marina N entrance Fl(3)G.12s10m2M Green tower

Marina S entrance Fl(3)R.12s10m2M Red tower

Old harbour N entrance Fl.G.2·5s11m2M White and green octagonal tower

Old harbour S entrance Fl.R.2·5s8m2M White mast, red top

Buoys
La Roselière W cardinal VQ(9)10s2M SE of port.

Search and rescue
St-Quay is in the CROSS Corsen area which will respond to distress calls on Ch 16 or activation of Ch 70 on GMDSS. The nearest manned substation is at the Sémaphore at Pointe de St-Quay.

An inshore lifeboat is maintained at St-Quay.
The nearest hospital is at St-Brieuc.

Weather forecasts
Bodic (CROSS Corsen) on Ch 79 at 0533, 0745, 1145, 1615, 1945 LT in French and English.
Météo France ☎ 08 36 68 08 14.
Daily weather map at the marina office.
Navtex Corsen (A) or Niton (S) or (K).

Communications
Marina office (C/S *Port d'Amour*) Ch 9 0700–2000.
  ☎ 02 96 70 81 30.

Approaches

From the N by day This entrance has a least depth of 4m provided the recommended tracks are followed but a 1·6m patch is passed close in the later stages.

First identify Madeux W cardinal beacon tower and behind it the Ile Harbour lighthouse, a white tower with a red top on a house. These are on the

Moulières de Portrieux   Marina office   Fish quay   Ile Harbour   Old harbour entrance   Marina entrance

St-Quay-Portrieux looking NE

northernmost rocks of the Roches de St-Quay group. To the W is the conspicuous sémaphore building on Pointe de St-Quay and it should be possible to identify the massive marina breakwater with the Moulières de Portrieux E cardinal beacon tower in front of it. Approach the latter on a track of 172° (Line N) until Herflux S cardinal beacon tower comes into transit with La Longue S cardinal beacon tower (both on the Roches de St-Quay) bearing 119° (Line P). Keep on this transit for about 0·3M until Le Four white beacon tower to the S of the breakwater end bears 182° and is in line with Pordic belfry (Line Q). Follow this until the breakwater end is abeam when course may be altered to enter the marina or the old harbour.

If intending to proceed on S to go to Binic or Le Légué, a course of 135° (Line R) will lead out of the Rade but passes close to a 0·3m patch and over a 1·1m patch. To avoid both, pass close to the E cardinal spindle buoy marking a wreck 1M SE of the breakwater end and keep the latter bearing 325°. The least depth on this track is 1·9m.

By night Approach in the white sector of the

Marina Elbow light (Iso.4s) bearing 170°. Note that in the red sector you will be too far to starboard, not port.

Shortly after Herflux light (Fl(2)WRG.6s) turns from red to white alter to 120° to bring it ahead and continue until the white sector of Ile Harbour light (Oc(2)WRG.6s) on the port quarter is entered, when head for the marina breakwater end (Fl(3)G.12s). Les Noirs E cardinal unlit buoy lies on the E edge of the white sector of Ile Harbour light. The least depth on this approach is 1·6m.

If intending to pass on S to go to Binic or Le Légué, get into the (20°) white sector of the Marina Elbow light and make good 145° until La Roselière buoy (VQ(9)10s) is abeam to port.

From the S by day This passage carries a least depth of 1·1m along Line R but it passes close to a 0·3m patch and it would be prudent for a stranger to regard this as the least depth.

First identify La Ronde W cardinal beacon tower, taking care not to confuse it with La Longue S cardinal beacon tower which lies 1M further E. Navigate to a position where La Ronde bears 035°

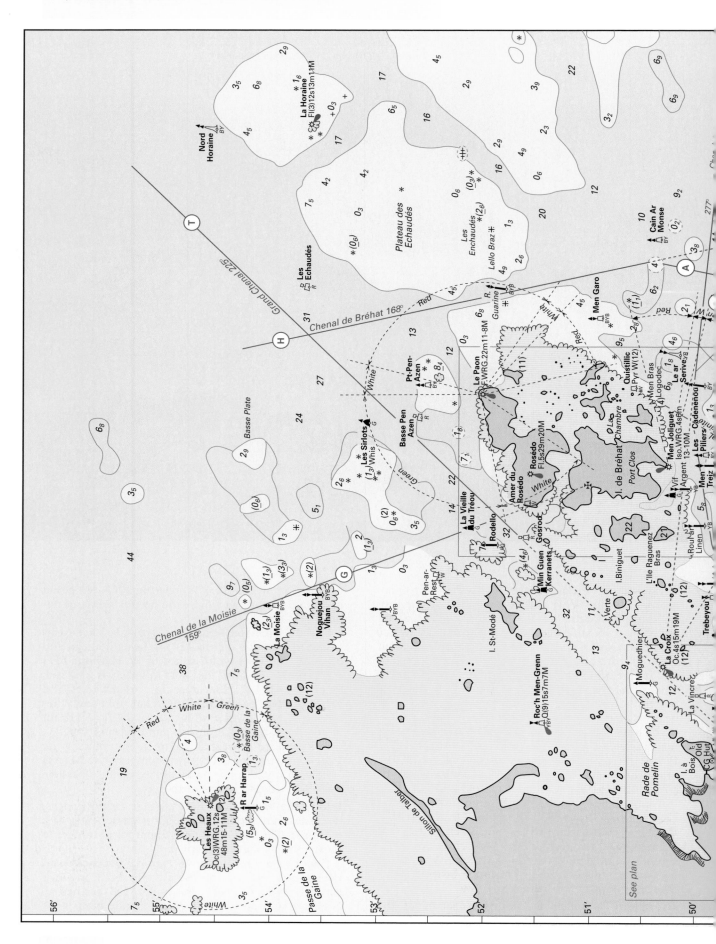

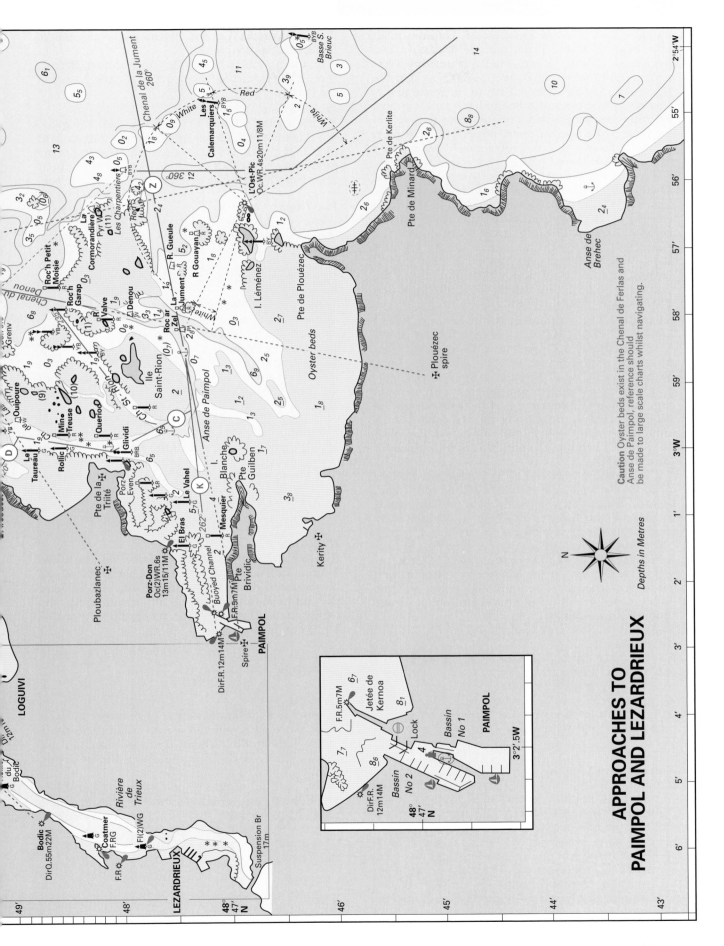

LOGUIVI

Bodic ☼
DirQ.55m22M

Coatmer
F.RG
F.R ☼

Fl(2)WG

Rivière de Trieux

LEZARDRIEUX

48°
47'
N

Suspension Br
17m

Ploubazlanec ☩

Porz-Don
Oc(2)WR.6s
13m15/11M ☼

Buoyed Channel

F.R.5m7M Pte
Brividic

DirF.R.12m14M ☼
Spire ☩

PAIMPOL

Pte de la Triité ☩

Le Taureau

Rollic

Queriou

Glividi

Treuse

Mine

Ouipoure

Grenv

Chenal du Denou

Roc'h Garap

Roc'h Petit Moisie

La Cormandiere

Les Charpentiers

Pyr

Roc ar Zel

La Jument

Denou

Valve

R

Ile Saint-Rion

St-Rion

El Bras

Le Vahel

Mesquier

Porz Even

Pte Blanche

Pte Guilben

Kerity ☩

Anse de Paimpol

R Gouayan

R. Gueule

I. Léménez

Pte de Plouëzec

L'Ost-Pic
Oc.WR.4s20m11/8M

Les Calemarquiers

White

Red

Chenal de la Jument 260°

360°

Z

Basse S. Brieuc

Pte de Kerlite

Pte de Minard

☩ Plouëzec spire

Oyster beds

Anse de Brehec

Caution Oyster beds exist in the Chenal de Ferlas and Anse de Paimpol, reference should be made to large scale charts whilst navigating.

Depths in Metres

N

APPROACHES TO PAIMPOL AND LEZARDRIEUX

F.R.5m7M

Jetée de Kernoa

Lock

Bassin No 1

Bassin No 2

DirF.R. 12m14M ☼

PAIMPOL

48°
47'
N

3°2.5W

49'   48'   48°47'N   46'   45'   44'   43'

2°54'W   55'   56'   57'   58'   59'   3°W   1'   2'   3'   4'   5'   6' distance ½M and La Roselière W cardinal pillar buoy bears E 300m. From here the leading marks for Line R will be in line – the conspicuous white sémaphore building on Pointe de St-Quay and the N breakwater end light structure, a green tower, bearing 315°. Follow this line to leave an E cardinal spar buoy marking a wreck about 400m to port and Le Four white beacon tower about 800m to port. When Le Four is abeam, course may be altered into the marina or the old port.

If intending to proceed N to Paimpol or Bréhat, when Le Four bears 182° and is in line with Pordic spire, alter to the reciprocal 002°. Hold this until Herflux S cardinal beacon tower aligns with La Longue S cardinal beacon tower bearing 119° and steer 299° to keep the two on a stern transit for about 0·3M. When Moulières de Portrieux E cardinal beacon tower bears 172°, make good the reciprocal 352° until Madeux W cardinal beacon tower is clear abaft the beam.

By night The most southerly white sector of Grand Léjon (Fl(5)WR.20s) leads between Roches de St-Quay and Rohein W cardinal beacon light tower. Approach Binic breakwater light (Oc(3)12s) on a westerly course until St-Quay marina elbow light (Iso.WRG.4s) changes from green to white when alter up it on a course of 317°. This leaves La Roselière cardinal light buoy to starboard and an unlit E cardinal buoy to port. On close approach steer for the lights at the entrance to the marina or the old harbour.

If intending to proceed N to Paimpol or Bréhat, when Ile Harbour light (Oc(2)WRG.6s) turns from green to white alter to keep the light on 007° in this sector and clear the unlit Les Noirs E cardinal buoy which is on the E edge of this sector.

On entering the white sector of Herflux beacon tower light (Fl(2)WRG.6s) turn to steer 310° in this sector until in the northerly white sector of marina elbow light when steer out of the Rade in this sector on a course of 350°. The least depth on this track should be regarded as 1·6m.

Anchorage

An anchorage can be found to the E of the southern old harbour breakwater in any desired depth and clear of the entrance, sand and mud, good holding. Avoid the area of the 1·2m sounding S of the marina entrance on the chart and plan, which is rock. The tidal stream falls off appreciably the further W one can go.

Entrance and berths
Marina

Turn to port inside the entrance, leave all the yacht pontoons to port and secure to the arrivals pontoon which is the middle one at the W end. The one to the N of this is used by *vedettes* and the one to the S of it is the fuelling pontoon. Go to the marina office above to be allocated a berth. There are 100 visitors' berths up to 18m and multihulls are catered for. Visitors are usually put on pontoon 7 and most of

the area is dredged to 3m. Berthing is on substantial fingers on the pontoons.

In addition to *vedette* traffic which runs to Bréhat, there is considerable fishing activity in the N side of the harbour.

Old harbour

Yachts are not allowed to berth alongside the quays but those with bilge keels or legs can dry out on hard sand in the harbour, clear of the entrance and many moorings. There is not much room. The harbour dries from 3·5m at the entrance to 7m at the beach.

Facilities

Water and electricity On the pontoons.

Fuel Diesel and petrol from the fuelling berth which requires a credit card with a chip to work the pumps.

Showers and heads 20 of each situated at the W end of the S mole.

Slip In the NW corner.

Ice From the marina office.

Bicycle hire Through the marina office.

Chandler On the marina.

Shops Some on the marina but the nearest *supermarché* is on the front by the old harbour where there also a number of other food shops.

Restaurants, cafés, bars, hotels Some in the marina but otherwise a good selection of all styles and qualities in the town.

Travel A bus runs to St-Brieuc where there are connections to the national road and rail networks in France. Twice daily flights to Paris from St-Brieuc airport.

Leisure The usual divertissements of a bustling holiday resort but little of cultural interest.

Historical

Another Brittany port whose history is steeped in fishing. Like Binic, it was in the forefront of the Newfoundland fishery and there was once a large fleet of *terre-neuviens* many of whom spent the winters hauled well up the beach in the old port.

Paimpol

General

Paimpol is a substantial town surrounding a locked harbour which is still active with fishing and some commercial traffic. There are good facilities for yachts. The least depth in the approaches is drying 4·9m.

The port lies at the W end of an extensive bay which mostly dries and has several winding channels across it. Approaches may be made to the harbour from the E (Chenal de la Jument), NE (Chenals du Dénou and St-Rion) or N (Chenals de la Trinité and Lastel).

Paimpol. Leading line for Chenal du Dénou. Dénou white beacon tower and Plouézec spire in transit bearing 193°

Data

Charts

Admiralty *2668* (SC), *2669*, *3670* (ARCS), *3673* (plan)
Imray *C34* (plan)

Tides

Subtract 10 minutes from the times of HW St-Malo for the times at Paimpol and 35 minutes from the times of LW St-Malo. Subtract 1·6m from the heights of MHWS at St-Malo, 1·1m from the heights of MHWN St-Malo and 0·3m from the heights of LW St-Malo to find the heights at Paimpol.

Tidal streams

1. For tidal streams in the outer approaches see under Ile Bréhat and St-Quay-Portrieux.
2. Tidal streams start at the following times between La Jument and Le Denou beacon towers:

   −0340 HW St Helier (−0425 HW St-Malo) SSE
   +0405 HW St Helier (+0320 HW St-Malo) NNW
   The maximum rate in each direction is 3½ knots.
3. At the N ends of Chenals Trinité, Lastel and Dénou, the S-going streams start about 15 minutes earlier and the N-going 15 minutes later than the times above.
4. At the W end of the bay the streams start at the following times:

   −0515 HW St Helier (−0430 HW St-Malo) W
   +0215 HW St Helier (+0300 HW St-Malo) E
   The maximum rate is 1½ knots.
   There is a S-going eddy across the head of the outer jetty of up to ½ knot during the W-going (flood) stream which ceases when the water level reaches 10m.

Lights

L'Ost-Pic Oc.WR.4s20m11-8M Two white towers, red tops 105°-W-116°-R-221°-W-253°-R-291°-W-329° 4M E of Paimpol

Pointe de Porz Don Oc(2)WR.6s13m15/11M White house 269°-W-272°-R-279° 1M NE of Paimpol

Kernoa Ldg Lts 262° *Front* F.R.5m7M White and red hut

Rear DirF.R.12m14M White pylon, red top 260°-intens-264°

Buoys

There are no lit buoys in the Anse de Paimpol. There is one port-hand buoy approximately ½M E of La Jument beacon tower marking Roche Gueule, and a number of port and starboard buoys marking the channel in the final approach to the port.

Search and rescue

Paimpol is in the CROSS Corsen area and will respond to calls on Ch 16 and to activation of GMDSS on Ch 70. The nearest manned substations are at the sémaphores at Pointe de St-Quay to the S and Ile Bréhat to the N.

The nearest all-weather lifeboats are at Ile de Batz and St-Malo. There is an inshore lifeboat at St-Quay-Portrieux.

There are hospitals at Paimpol and St-Brieuc.

Weather forecasts

Corsen CROSS (Bodic) on Ch 79 at 0535, 0745, 1145, 1615, 1945 LT in French and English.

Météo France ☎ 08 36 68 08 14.

Daily weather map at the bureau du port.

Navtex Corsen (A).

Communications

Maison des Plaisanciers guard Ch 9 2½ hours either side of HW.

Customs

There is an office in Paimpol.

Paimpol. L'Ost-Pic lighthouse bearing 240°

Outer approaches

The outer approaches to the Anse de Paimpol are via:

- **Chenal de Bréhat** from the N
- **Chenal de Ferlas** from the W

The approaches from the E and S past L'Ost-Pic lighthouse are straightforward and run in to Chenal de la Jument.

Chenal de Bréhat by day only (Line H)

Good visibility is needed for navigation of this channel by reference to the leading marks the rear one of which is more than 12M away. The stream runs nearly up to 6 knots in the channel at springs so timing is important. The SSE-going stream starts in the Chenal at about −0145 HW St-Malo/Paimpol which is very convenient to carry a fair stream from the N up to the lock at Paimpol.

Initially pick up the Trieux leading marks which are Bodic light structure and La Croix lighthouse (see photos on page 102) bearing 225° (Line T). Follow this line to leave:

Nord Horaine N cardinal spar buoy 0·8M to port
La Horaine lighthouse 1·4M to port.
Les Echaudés port buoy 0·5M to port.

¼M after the latter is abeam alter course to bring the white daymark at Porz Moguer (distant 12M) in line with the white pyramid on La Cormorandière (distant 5·5M) bearing 168°. This line will be just to the E of L'Ost-Pic lighthouse (Line H). This line leaves:

Roc'h Guarine which dries and is marked by an E cardinal spar buoy (to be left close to starboard)
Lello Bras about ½M to port which also dries and is unmarked.
Men Garo E cardinal beacon tower ½M to starboard.

At this point the leading line for Chenal du Dénou should be identifiable (Line A). If not, a track of 168° must be maintained leaving Cain ar Monse N cardinal beacon to port to pass to the E of La Cormorandière and Les Charpentiers to reach Chenal de la Jument outer leading line (Line Z).

Chenal du Ferlas by day only (Line B)

Proceed up the Grand Chenal de Trieux (page 90-91) until Veille de Loguivi W cardinal beacon is abeam to port and alter on to the first transit for Chenal de Ferlas which is Rompa isolated danger mark beacon in line with Les Piliers N cardinal beacon tower bearing 084°. Proceed until 150m from Rompa when alter course to 095° to leave Rompa at least 100m to port as there is a rock drying 3m 50m to the S of Rompa beacon, and head for Roc'h Rouray (3m high). After 400m alter course to make good 070° on the transit of the S cardinal beacons of Roul-ar-Linen and Vif Argent. This line leaves Trebeyou S cardinal beacon tower 200m to port and Receveur Lihan S cardinal beacon 100m to port.

Shortly after passing Receveur Lihan, Rompa will come into transit with Roc'h Levret astern bearing 259°. Keep these in line steering the reciprocal 079° to leave:

Roul-ar-Linen S cardinal beacon 100m to port
Vif Argent S cardinal beacon 230m to port
Roc'h Ourmelec N cardinal beacon 500m to starboard
Men Joliguet 500m to port
Les Piliers N cardinal beacon tower 300m to starboard.

At this point there is a choice of five inner approaches to the main channel.

Inner approaches

The two main and deepest approach channels are:

Chenal de la Jument from the E Least depth 1·2m in to Mouillage de Paimpol.
Chenal du Dénou from the NE Least depth 0·6m in to Mouillage de Paimpol.

The minor channels are:

Chenal St-Rion from the NE Least depth drying 0·4m in to Mouillage de Paimpol.
Chenal de Lastel from the NNE Least depth 1·2m in to Mouillage de Paimpol.
Chenal de la Trinité from the N Least depth drying 2·2m in to Mouillage de Paimpol.

Chenal de la Trinité by day only (Line D)

This is the most direct route in to Paimpol from the W and Chenal de Ferlas but is the shallowest although this should not present a problem above half tide if drawing 2m.

Navigate to a position where Les Piliers beacon tower bears 270° 400m. From here Quistillic white pyramid (12m) will be open to the right of Men Bras Logodec (a rock which never covers 4m) on a bearing of 032°. Make good the reciprocal 212° keeping Quistillic open to the right to avoid Lel-Ouene rock drying 2·2m if the depth is not sufficient to clear (Lel-Ouene is the least depth in this approach). This leaves:

Men Treiz E cardinal beacon 280m to starboard
Roc Château 240m to port
Roc'h Lème E cardinal beacon 360m to starboard
La Madelaine W cardinal beacon 200m to port.

At this point alter to 120° and keep on this track until Le Taureau starboard beacon bears 215° when course should be altered to about 195° to leave Le Taureau beacon 150m to starboard. Then proceed as for the latter part of Chenal de Lastel, below.

Chenal de Lastel by day only (Lines E and C)

This leads in from the NE, has a least depth of 1·2m and is subject to cross sets.

After passing Les Piliers beacon tower bring La Croix lighthouse astern into line with Ile Raguenez Bras bearing 277° and steer to make good the reciprocal 097°, leaving Cadenenou N cardinal spar buoy 140m to starboard. When Men Gam E

Entrance lock

Anse de Paimpol looking E at LW

cardinal beacon tower is abeam 600m, alter course to make good 136°. This track should align La Cormorandière white pyramid with Les Charpentiers E cardinal beacon tower.

When Ouipoure white beacon tower bears 235°, alter course to keep it on this bearing until Ploubazlanec spire bears 242° and steer towards it to leave Ouipoure white beacon tower 150m to port. From here shape a course towards Le Taureau starboard beacon and, when 250m from it make good 185°. This leaves:

Rollic starboard beacon 100m to starboard
Min Treuse port beacon 60m to port
Roc Queroic port beacon 130m to port.

When Pointe de la Trinité bears 335° alter course to make good the reciprocal 155° when Roc ar Zel port beacon will be ahead on this course. This leaves Glividi isolated danger beacon 200m to starboard and leads in to the main channel.

Chenal St-Rion by day only (Lines A and C)

From Les Piliers beacon tower proceed as for Chenal de Lastel and continue making good 136° until the leading marks for Chenal du Dénou (Plouézec belfry and Dénou white pyramid) come into transit bearing 193° when course should be altered to make this. When La Cormorandière white pyramid comes into line with Roc'h Petite Moisie port beacon, alter course to make good 235°. From now on this channel has no leading marks. Hold this track to leave:

Roc'h Garap (4m) 200m to port
Le Boisseau starboard beacon 150m to starboard
An un-named starboard beacon 50m to starboard
Grand Francais N beacon 100m to port.

Pass between Roc'h Vras group of rocks to the NW and Ile St-Rion and its out-liers to the SE.

Les Fillettes port beacon 50m to port.

Then make good 215° to join the main channel.

Chenal du Dénou by day only (Line A)

Proceed as for Chenal St-Rion continuing down the leading line of Plouézec belfry in line with Dénou white pyramid on 193° and leave Dénou beacon 100m to port. Course may then be altered to 205° to join the main channel.

Chenal de la Jument the main inner approach channel by day or night (Lines Z and K)

All the above channels lead into La Jument which carries a least depth of drying 3m in the very narrow channel. However the slightest deviation will give a least depth of drying 4·9m and it would be prudent to allow for this in the final 2M.

Reference should be made to chart *3670* if approaching from the S or E to avoid, if necessary the off-lying submerged dangers to seaward of L'Ost-Pic lighthouse.

Navigate to a position 030° 1M from L'Ost-Pic lighthouse with Les Charpentiers unlit E cardinal beacon tower 300m to the N. By day identify the

Basin No 1

Arrival and
visitors' pontoon

Paimpol entrance and basins looking SSE

Paimpol lock entrance at half-tide. The public slip is on right

first leading line of Paimpol church spire in transit with Pointe Brividic (a woody hill in front of Paimpol town) bearing 260° and follow this. At night the F.R leading lights are intensified between 261° and 266° and lead right up to the breakwater end. Reference should be made to chart *3673* to see how Pointe de Porz-Don light (Oc.WR.6s) can assist but in general the white sector indicates clearance from La Jument rock until it has been passed, after which its bearing in the red sector will indicate progress along the leading line.

By day or night, these lines will leave:

Les Charpentiers E cardinal unlit beacon
tower 300m to starboard
Roc Gueule port unlit buoy 200m to port
La Jument port unlit beacon tower 150m to port
Roc ar Zel unlit port beacon 300m to port.

By day just before reaching Roc ar Zel beacon identify the inner leading line which is a white hut with a red top on the end of the outer breakwater and a higher white tower with a red top behind it bearing 264° (Line K) and follow this line.

The final 1½M to the entrance will leave:

La Vahel unlit starboard beacon 200m to
starboard
Mesquier unlit port beacon 300m to port
El Bras unlit starboard beacon 150m to port.

Thereafter the channel is marked by unlit port and starboard buoys (with reflective strips) and beacons up to the breakwater end.

Entrance

Turn close round the breakwater end and secure on the W side of the lock if it necessary to wait for it. The lock works for up to 2½ hours either side of HW, is 60m long and 12m wide with a sill depth of drying 3m. At neaps the lock is only opened at HW. With the depth above 8·5m the gates are left open over HW for varying times depending on the height of tide. In this situation before HW there is often a strong in-going current through the gates.

Berths

Basin No.1 is on the E side of the docks and is reached through another lock which is usually left open. It is for fishing and commercial vessels.

Basin No.2 is for yachts and has 20 visitors' berths. The reception pontoon is 'A' and the first one ahead from the lock to the W of the *bureau du port* on the centre quay. Maximum length 20m.

Anchorage in the approaches

Anse de Bréhec is 3M S of L'Ost-Pic with a long sandy beach and sheltered from S through W to NE. It can be approached from Le Taureau beacon tower (isolated danger) 1M to the E.

Anchorages in Anse de Paimpol

It is possible to anchor almost anywhere in Anse de Paimpol clear of the oyster beds although there are few sheltered areas for yachts. The following are possibilities:

Paimpol inner basin No 2 with the schooners *La Belle Poule* and *L'Etoile*

1. Near Line K with La Jument bearing E and Ile St-Rion bearing N in a suitable depth 0–8m. Take care to avoid the 0·7m rock near this position. Little shelter and a long way from anywhere.
2. NNE of Pointe Guilben at the head of the deep channel with restricted swinging room. It is roughly on the following transits:

    La Vierge de Kerroch monument (to the W of Pointe de Porz Don) open to the right of Le Vahel beacon.

    Kerity church and the W side of the hillock on the end of Pointe Guilben.

    An anchor light at night would be a wise precaution as this is on or close to the leading line. There is a dinghy landing on the N side of Pointe Guilben above half tide.
3. Off Porz Even in 2·7m with Glividi beacon bearing 190° 200m to the E of the moorings. This is the most sheltered anchorage from the W. Dinghy landing at Porz Even, a small drying harbour for fishing boats.

Facilities

Water and electricity On the pontoons and quays.
Fuel Available in the marina and garages close by.
Showers and heads By the *bureau du port*.
Slip Public slip into drying harbour at N end of basin.
Cranes Up to 45 tons.

Repairs and chandlery There are several private yacht yards and chandlers around the basin. It would be a good place to lay up at although the security arrangements when ashore may be suspect.
Shops Many around the basin; supermarket at S end of No.2 basin who will deliver.
Restaurants, cafés and hotels Many to suit all pockets.
Leisure A lively town with a tangle of narrow streets lined by grey granite houses. The harbour is still very much the centre of things.
Travel Rail and bus connections to St-Brieuc and westwards. Airport at St-Brieuc whence there are twice daily flights to Paris. Taxi ☎ 02 96 2205 87. Airport ☎ 02 96 94 95 00.

Historical

Paimpol used to be the great base for the Icelandic cod and whaling fleets that left every February for these waters. Their departure was the occasion of a famous pardon. Until September the town would be empty of young men whose return would be greeted by great celebrations. The ships were either *goëlettes* (topsail schooners) or *dundees* (ketches). Hand lines were worked from the ship herself, hove-to in deep water.

The fishery started in 1852 and grew to as many as 50 vessels with 25 men in each. The last of the *goëlettes*, *La Glycine*, made her final voyage to Iceland in 1935.

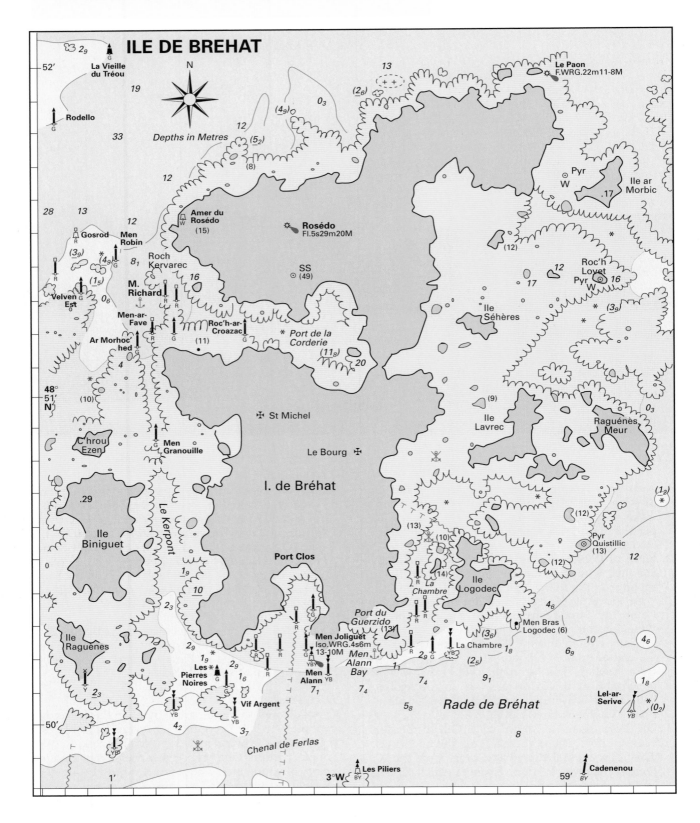

ILE DE BREHAT

La Vieille du Tréou

Le Paon
F.WRG.22m11-8M

Rodello

N

Depths in Metres

Pyr
W

Ile ar Morbic

Gosrod

Men Robin

Amer du Rosédo
(15)

Rosédo
Fl.5s29m20M

Roc'h Loyet
Pyr
W

Velven Est

Roch Kervarec

M. Richard

SS
(49)

(12)

Ile Séhères

Roc'h-ar-Croazac

Men-ar-Fave

Ar Morhoc' hed

Port de la Corderie

48° 51' N

Men Granouille

St Michel

Ile Lavrec

Raguénès Meur

Chrou Ezen

Le Bourg

I. de Bréhat

Ile Biniguet

Le Kerpont

Port Clos

La Chambre

Ile Logodec

Pyr Quistillic
(13)

Ile Raguénès

Les Pierres Noires

Men Joliguet
Iso.WRG.4s6m 13-10M

Port du Guerzido

Men Alann Bay

La Chambre

Men Bras Logodec (6)

Lel-ar-Serive

Vif Argent

Men Alann

Rade de Bréhat

Chenal de Ferlas

Les Piliers
BY

Cadenenou
BY

3°W

59'

Ile de Bréhat

General

An enchanting and still unspoilt little island in spite of the mass of visitors that come from the mainland every summer. Only few stay overnight and peace descends after the last *vedette* leaves in the evening.

There are plenty of sheltered anchorages for bilge keelers or those able to take the ground but for deep keeled craft a visit at neaps only will find some shelter. At springs there is a restricted anchorage at La Corderie at the N end of the Kerpont channel or in the Rade de Bréhat at the S end of the island in strong streams, open to E and W and liable to any swell.

Limited provisions can be obtained at Le Bourg in the centre of the island.

Data

Charts

Admiralty *3670* (ARCS), *2668* (SC), *3673*
Imray *C34* (plan)

Tides

As for Lézardrieux.

Tidal streams

1. Near the Plateau de la Horaine at the NE corner of Bréhat the SE-going flood stream starts at +0524 HW St-Malo and the NW-going ebb starts at −0040 HW St-Malo. The streams are strong in the gap between Barnouic and Bréhat and can reach 3·8 knots at springs. There can be severe overfalls in wind over tide conditions and where there is an uneven bottom.
2. In the Chenal du Ferlas on the S side, the flood runs E from Rivière de Trieux starting at +0524 HW St-Malo and the ebb W starting at −0040 HW St-Malo reaching 3¾ knots at springs.
3. In Le Kerpont Channel on the W side of the island the S-going flood and the N-going ebb start at the same times and achieve the same rates.

Lights

See Lézardrieux for the offshore lights and Paimpol for lights to the S and the Ferlas Channel leading lights.
At N end Le Paon F.WRG.22m11-8M Yellow tower 033°-W-078°-G-181°-W-196°-R-307°-W-316°-R-348°
NW side Rosedo Fl.5s.29m20M White tower, green gallery
S side Men Joliguet Iso.WRG.4s 6m13-10M E cardinal 255°-R-279°-W-283°-G-175°

Buoys

See Lézardrieux for the buoys to the N and W of the island.
To the E of the island
   Chenal de Bréhat E cardinal
To the S and E of the island from E to W
   Lel ar Serive S cardinal
   Cadenénou N cardinal

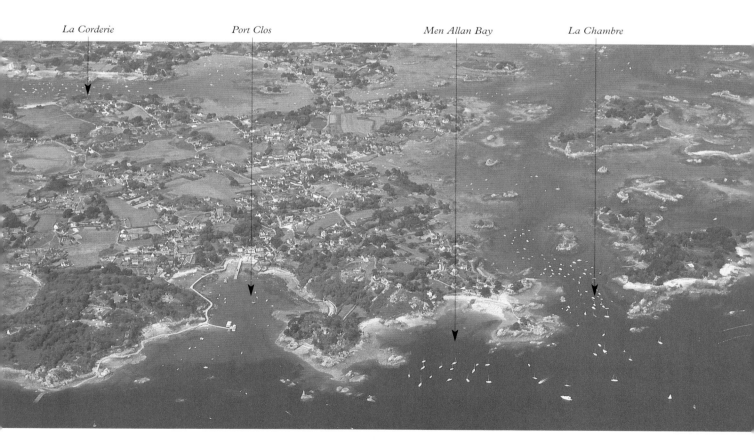

La Corderie   Port Clos   Men Allan Bay   La Chambre

Ile de Bréhat looking N

Ile de Bréhat. La Chambre looking N

Search and rescue, weather forecasts, communications

See Lézardrieux or Paimpol.

Approaches
By day from the N

1. The outer approaches and Grand Chenal are shown on page 106 under Lézardrieux and page 94 under Paimpol.
2. **To enter La Corderie** When La Vielle du Tréou starboard beacon tower bears N, alter course to port to so as to pass midway between Gosrod port beacon tower, leaving it to starboard, and Amer du Rosédo white pyramid (see plan page 98). Then steer to leave Men Robin starboard beacon to starboard, Roc'h Kervarec about 50m to port and Moncello Richard, the first port beacon about 100m to port.

   Alter course then to port into the anchorage, passing between a further pair of port and starboard beacons.
3. **For Port Clos or La Chambre** There are a choice of four passages:
   a. **By Chenal de Bréhat and the Ferlas Channel**
      See pages 94–96 – Paimpol approaches.
   b. **By outer E approach and the Ferlas Channel**
      See pages 94–96 – Paimpol approaches.

   c. **By Grand Chenal and Ferlas Channel from the W**
      See pages 94–96 – Paimpol approaches.
   d. **Le Kerpont Channel** This provides and interesting short cut but only by daylight and near HW. An indication when entering from the S is that the passage is clear for a 1·8m draught when the slip on the SW corner of Bréhat is covered. The stream runs hard through the channel but always true to the fairway. From the N, proceed as for La Corderie but instead of altering to port for the anchorage, steer so as to pass between Men-ar-Fave port beacon and Morhoet starboard beacon and then leave the following marks on the sides indicated:

   Men Granouille starboard beacon about 10m to starboard. This is the narrowest and shallowest part of the channel. When the top of the concrete base of the beacon is awash, there is said to be 0·9m in the channel.

   The isolated rock on the E side of Ile Beniquet 60m to starboard.

   The isolated rock of Ile Beniquet's SE corner 100m to starboard and then follow the deep water round to the N of Les Pierres Noires starboard beacon tower, taking care to avoid

Ile de Bréhat. Port Clos at LWS looking SSW

the end of the slip to the N and the rocks to the SE of the beacon tower. And so into the Rade de Bréhat.

By day from Lézardrieux or Paimpol

See Lézardrieux and Paimpol and Ferlas Channel on pages 94–96.

Moorings

Visitors' moorings are placed in the season just S of La Chambre and E of Men Allan beacon which is just SE of Men Jolinguet beacon. They are subject to swell.

Anchorages

Anchorage is prohibited in:

a. The area in Le Ferlas Channel and at the S end of Le Kerpont shown on chart *3763* and on plan page 98, due to telegraph cables.

b. In La Chambre to the N of the last port-hand beacon. This area is also shown on plan page 98 and chart *3673*.

La Corderie This small drying harbour on the W side of the island offers a restricted anchorage to deep draught yachts at springs but there is considerably more scope at neaps. The inner

Ile de Bréhat. Port de la Corderie looking E at LW

harbour dries about 2·4m which gives about 1·2m at MLWN. Deeper draught yachts can anchor to the SW of Roc'h Kervarec, sounding in as far as possible on the W or E sides of this pool to avoid the streams that rush through this channel. At neaps it may be possible to find enough water to the E of the port and starboard entrance beacons clear of moorings and out of the stream. Bilge keelers or yachts with legs can proceed further E to dry out on the bottom which, except in a few rocky places, is hard sand. A power line is laid across La Corderie shown on plan page 98 and while it is well dug in, it would be advisable to avoid anchoring in its vicinity. The landing slip is on the N side of the harbour but if the beach or rocks on the S side are used it is closer to the shops.

An anchor light is recommended if staying overnight especially in Le Kerpont channel as this is sometimes used by fishing boats.

La Chambre A small drying harbour on the SE corner of the island in some ways preferable to Port Clos. It is now very crowded with moorings and difficult to find an anchorage out of the stream even at neaps; a trip line should be used as there are many new and old chains on the bottom.

An anchorage outside will be subject to strong streams and any swell.

Craft with legs or bilge keelers have more possibilities but should keep clear of the prohibited area at the N end. There is a landing slip on the W side and another at the N end which is nearer to Le Bourg.

Another anchorage nearby at neaps is to the W of the islet on the W side of the entrance to La Chambre and to the E of Port Clos (Men Allan Bay). To avoid the stream and swell, sound in as far as depth allow.

Port Clos Another small drying harbour on the S side of the island which is much used by the vedettes carrying visitors to and fro. Do not obstruct the slips or jetties. At MLWN 2m or more can be found to the NW of Men Jolinguet beacon tower. Craft able to take the ground can use the inner harbour where there is perfect shelter. Note the prohibited anchorage which covers the W side of the outer harbour. The vedette traffic ceases in the evening. Land at any of the slips.

Facilities

The island is worth walking over. There is no traffic apart from the occasional small tractor. There are fine views from St-Michel chapel over the surrounding and varied seascape. Le Bourg in the centre has a post office and a surprising number of shops and *crêperies*. There are restaurants here and at Port Clos where there is also an hotel. There is small but thriving sailing club at La Chambre.

The chaplain of HMS *Charybdis*, sunk in 1943 off Les Sept Iles is buried in the churchyard.

Lézardrieux (Rivière de Trieux)

General

Lézardrieux has been popular with yachtsmen, especially the English since the beginning of the 20th century. The Grand Chenal can be taken at any state of the tide by day or night in any weather except bad visibility; however the approaches can be rough in wind over tide conditions. The two other approaches can only be taken in daylight.

Rivière de Trieux is wooded and attractive. The marina and club at Lézardrieux welcomes visitors and the village can supply most needs. The river continues for another 3 miles to the country town of Pontrieux where there is a wet lock and many alongside berths in peaceful surroundings.

There is much sheltered water to the NW of the entrance, round the Isles Bréhat and in the Anse de Paimpol for a few days family holiday.

Lézardrieux. Leading marks for Chenal de la Moisie just open right. St-Michel chapel and Rosédo white beacon tower. La Vieille du Trou starboard beacon tower on right

Lézardrieux. Leading marks for Grand Chenal. La Croix lighthouse with Bodic on skyline to right

Grande Chaise   Wet basin for locals   Petite Chaise   Visitors' moorings   Visitors' pontoon

Lézardrieux yacht harbours looking WNW

Data

Charts

Admiralty *3670* (ARCS), *2668* (SC), *3673* (plan)
Imray *C34*
SHOM *7127* (plan)

Tides

Subtract 10 minutes from the times of HW St-Malo for the times at Lézardrieux and 45 minutes from the times of LW St-Malo. Subtract 2·0m from the heights of MHWS St-Malo, 1·5m from MHWN, 0·6m from MLWN and 0·2m from MLWS at St-Malo to find the heights at Lézardrieux.

Tidal streams

1. See page 99 for the tidal streams round Ile Bréhat, Le Kerpont and Le Ferlas channels.
2. In the outer approaches to the estuary, outside Pen Azen to the N of Ile Bréhat the SE stream starts at +0524 HW St-Malo and the NW-going stream starts at −0040 HW St-Malo. The spring rate attains 3¾ knots.
3. To the SW of Pen Azen the SE-going stream turns S towards Bréhat and into the Kerpont channel, and the NW stream turns N towards the Plateau des Sirlots.
4. In the Rivière de Trieux the in-going stream starts at the same time as the outer SE-going stream, and the outgoing at the same time as the outer NW-going. The average spring rate is 2½ knots with 3¾ knots under the bridge above Lézardrieux.

Lights

Offshore

Roches Douvres Fl.5s60m28M Siren 60s Pink tower with green roof on dwelling
Barnouic VQ(3)5s15m7M E cardinal on octagonal tower

La Horaine Fl(3)12s13m11M Grey octagonal tower on black hut

In estuary from NE to SW

Rocher Men-Grenn Q(9)15s7m7M W cardinal beacon tower
La Croix *Front* DirOc.4s15m19M Two grey round towers, joined, white on NE side, red tops 215°-intens-235°
  Bodic *Rear* DirQ.55m22M White house with green gable 221°-intens-229°
Coatmer Ldg Lts 219° *Front* F.RG.16m9M White gable 200°-R-250°-G-053°
  Rear F.R.50m White gable. 197°-vis-242°
Perdrix Fl(2)WG.6s6/3M Green tower 165°-G-197°-W-203°-G-040°

Buoys

There are no lit buoys in the approaches or river. There are many unlit beacons and towers and four unlit buoys in the outer reaches on either side of the outer leading line:
Nord Horaine N cardinal spar
Les Echaudés port
Les Sirlots starboard, whis
Basses des Pen Azen port

Search and rescue

The nearest station controlled by CROSS Corsen is at Bodic, close W of the river. It will respond to calls on Ch 16 and to activation of Ch 70 on GMDSS.
The nearest inshore lifeboat is at Loguivi at the river entrance.
There is a small hospital at Lézardrieux and a larger one at Paimpol.

Weather forecasts

Bodic on Ch 79 at 0533, 0745, 1145, 1615, 1945 LT in French.
Météo France ☎ 08 36 68 08 14.
Daily weather map at bureau du port.

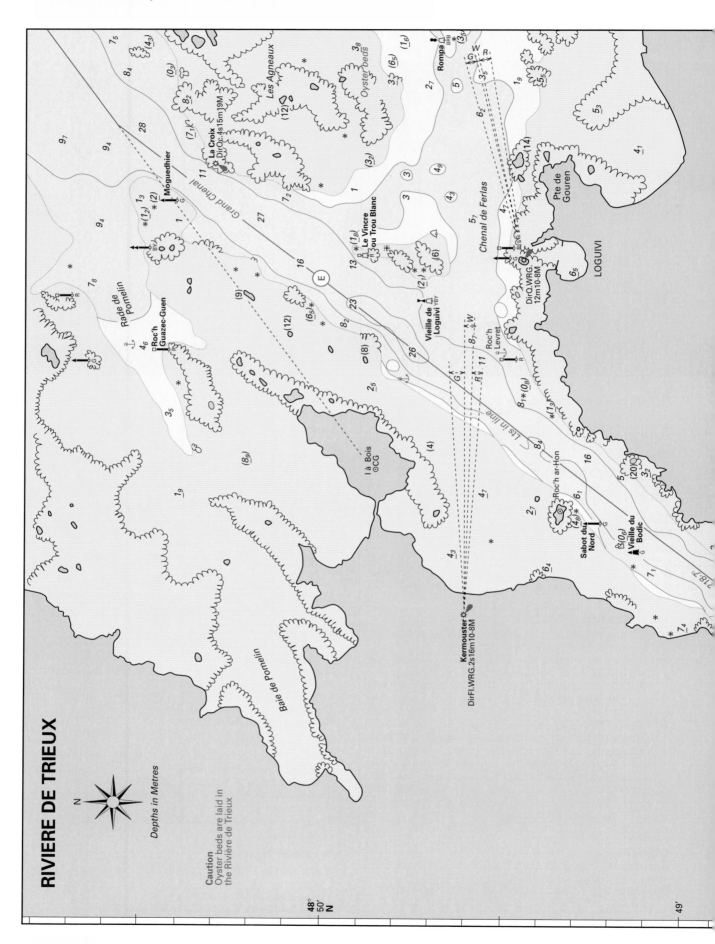

RIVIERE DE TRIEUX

N

Depths in Metres

Caution
Oyster beds are laid in
the Rivière de Trieux

48°
50'
N

49'

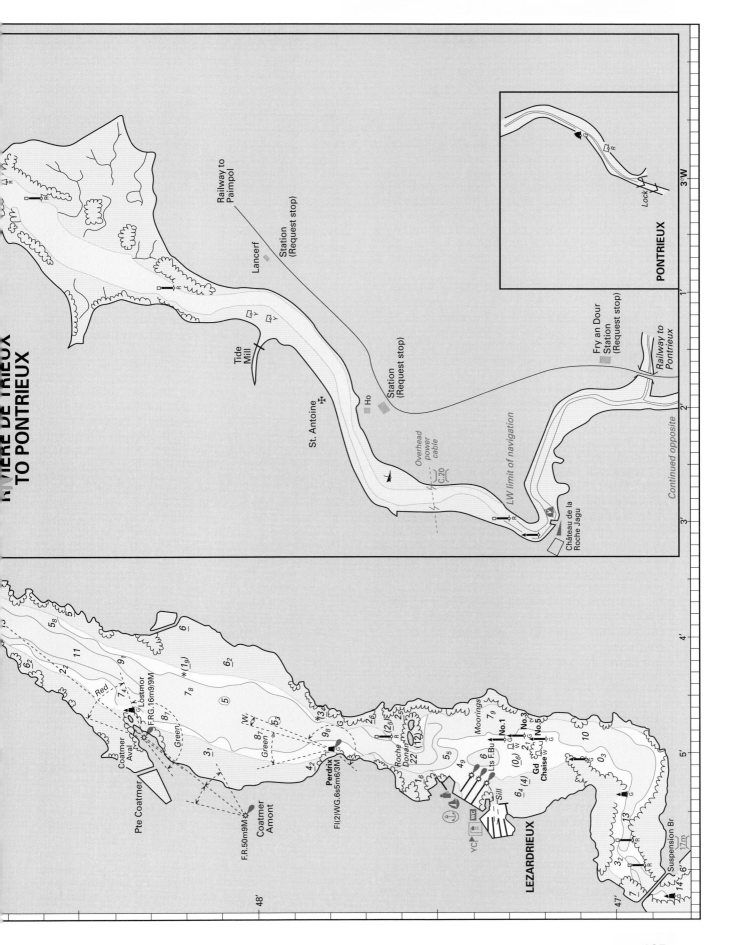

RIVIÈRE DE TRIEUX
TO PONTRIEUX

Railway to Paimpol

Lancerf

Station
(Request stop)

Tide
Mill

St. Antoine

Ho

Station
(Request stop)

Overhead
power
cable

C.20

LW limit of navigation

Fry an Dour
Station
(Request stop)

Railway to
Pontrieux

Château de la
Roche Jagu

Continued opposite

PONTRIEUX

Lock

3°W

Pte Coatmer

Coatmer
Aval

F.R.G.16m9/9M

Lostmor

Red

Green

Green

F.R.50m9M

Coatmer
Amont

Perdrix
Fl(2)WG.6s5m6/3M

Roche
Donan
22

YC

WC

Sill

Gd
Chaise

Lts F.Bu

Moorings

No.1

No.3

No.5

LÉZARDRIEUX

Suspension Br

48'

47'

4'

5'

6'

3°W

105

Navtex Corsen (A) or Niton (S) or (K).

Communications

Bureau du port Ch 9 working hours.

Customs

The nearest office is at Paimpol.

Approaches

By day from the N The Grande Chenal carries a least depth of 3·2m as far as Lézardrieux.

Navigate to a position with La Horaine lighthouse, grey octagonal tower with black bottom bearing 195° 3M from where the first leading marks can be picked up. They are – La Croix double white towers with red tops (front) and Bodic light structure on the skyline (see photos) bearing 225° (Line T on plan page 90–91). Follow this line to leave:

> **Nord Horaine** N cardinal spar buoy 0·8M to port
> **La Horaine** lighthouse 1·4M to port
> **Les Echaudés** port buoy 0·5M to port
> **Les Sirlots** starboard buoy 300m to starboard
> **Petit Pen Azen** N cardinal beacon tower 0·5M to port
> **Basse des Pen Azen** port buoy 0·2M to port
> **Vielle de Tréou** starboard beacon tower 0·25M to starboard
> **Rodello** starboard beacon on base of old tower 0·2M to starboard
> **Rosédo** white pyramid 0·3M to port
> **Gosrod** port beacon tower 200m to port
> **Min Guen Kerranets** starboard beacon tower 300m to starboard.

When about 1M from La Croix, leave Line T steer for the red-roofed old Customs House building (not CG as on chart *3673*) or Moguedhier starboard beacon to pick up the marks for Line E which are – Coatmer Aval light structure (front), a white gable elevation 16m, and Coatmer Amont a similar white gable elevation 50m bearing 219°. This line leaves the following marks on the sides indicated:

> **Moguedhir** starboard beacon 120m to starboard
> **La Croix** lighthouse 180m to port
> **Vincre** port beacon tower 300m to port
> **Vielle de Loguivy** W cardinal beacon tower 150m to port
> **Ile à Bois** (Custom House island) 500m to starboard
> **Olénoyère** port beacon tower 100m to port.

When the latter is abeam, the leading line can be left and a convenient course taken up the channel to leave Lostmor starboard beacon tower and Perdrix starboard beacon tower 100m to starboard before rounding the prominent Roches Donan 30m to port. From here the way is clear to head for the Port de Plaisance. If proceeding further up river, follow the channel to port round the Roches Donan and leave the outlying rocky shoal of La Chaise, marked by Nos 1, 3 and 5 starboard beacons and La Grande and La Petite Chaise white beacon towers, all to starboard. There are many moorings in this area and to the W of La Chaise but generally the channel has been kept clear of them.

300m above La Grande Chaise white beacon tower is a starboard beacon followed by Bec-an-Arvor starboard beacon tower where the channel takes a sharp turn to starboard. Leave Bec-an-Arvor 50m to starboard, the next Min Kéraoul port beacon tower 100m to port and follow the curve of the river round to port leaving two port beacons to port, and line up with the centre of the bridge which has a clearance of 17m. To proceed further, see the section on Pontrieux.

By day from the E For the leading marks for the Ferlas channel to the S of Ile Bréhat see under Paimpol approaches (page 94). When La Veille de Loguivi W cardinal beacon tower has been left to starboard, alter to port on to the Coatmer leading line and proceed as above.

By day from the W via the Moisie channel This approach carries a least depth of 1·3m and is useful as a short cut from Tréguier to Lézardrieux, Paimpol or the S side of Ile Bréhat. Its only limitations are the difficulty in seeing the leading marks in hazy conditions and the prevalence of fishing floats in the area. It would be prudent to allow a least depth of drying 2·3m if there was any doubt about losing sight of the line on an outward passage or if attempting it without initially seeing the leading marks on an inward passage.

Navigate to a position with Les Heaux lighthouse bearing 270° 1·75M whence the leading marks on Ile Bréhat will be in line. They are Rosédo white pyramid in line with St-Michel chapel, a small building with a red roof and a small red spire at its W end (see photo) bearing 159°. (Line G plan page 90–91). Before following this line, check that it passes about 150m E of Roche Moisie E cardinal beacon tower, then follow it closely. It leaves:

> A shoal drying 0·5m very close to the NE
> **La Moisie** beacon tower 150m to starboard
> **Nougejou Bihan** E cardinal beacon 50m to starboard. A shoal drying 2m very close to the NE
> **Pen ar Rest** white beacon tower 0·4M to starboard.

Then steer to leave La Veille du Tréou 100m to starboard and turn to join the La Croix/Bodic transit.

By night from the N If passing to the W of Roches Douvres, keep in the fixed white sector of Le Paon light (F.WRG) bearing between 181° and 196° until the leading lights for the Grand Chenal come into line (Line T). These are La Croix (front) Oc.4s and Bodic (rear) Q bearing 225°. La Croix is intensified 215° to 235° and Bodic from 221° to 229°.

If passing SE of Plateau de Barnouic, keep the white sector of Les Heaux (Oc(3)WRG.12s) bearing between 247° and 270° until the leading lights come into line. Note that Bodic light will dip behind La

Croix towers in the later stages and when this happens, borrow slightly to the W to open it.

When Men Grenn (Q(9)15s) which is WSW of Ile Modé is abeam to starboard, leave the leading line and steer 235° for about 0·25M to bring Coatmer Aval and Amont lights (both F.R in this sector) into line on 219°. Follow this line (Line E) until Olénoyère beacon tower is abeam to port when leave the leading line and steer to leave Perdrix light (Fl(2)WG.6s) about 100m to starboard. Perdrix light now in the G sector in transit with Coatmer Aval also in the G sector astern will now lead in to the marina, but close to Roche Donan; the latter however should be visible against the lights of the marina and village behind it.

The ends of the pontoons at Lézardrieux no longer have individual lights but the pontoon area is well lit and will be visible on a close approach.

Anchorages

1. In the outer reaches, the Rade de Pommelin lying W of Moguedhier starboard beacon offers a temporary anchorage in 3·5m to 4·5m, mud and shells, sheltered from NW through S to E.
2. Off Loguivi in up to 7·5m sand, clear of the moorings and *viviers* but in strong streams and open to the E. Loguivi is a small drying harbour to the SE of Vieille de Loguivi beacon tower and is actively used by fishermen and maintains an inshore lifeboat. Little concession is made for yachts and there are few facilities ashore.
3. At the side of the main channel between Bodic and Roche Donan, clear of the oyster beds and any moorings, mostly mud and sand.
4. To the E of the pontoons and moorings above Roche Donan.

Moorings

1. There are some visitors' moorings between Perdrix and Roche Donan but check with the *bureau du port* after picking one up.
2. The main visitors' moorings for those not using the marina pontoons are between the marinas and La Chaise. Some have pontoons on them to berth on and some are of the dumbbell type. They attract a charge. Most of this area carries at least 3m and the stream runs strongly through it.

Berths

The wet basin to the SW of the three main pontoons has no accommodation for visitors. Access is controlled by a gate.

The three main pontoons have 70 spaces for visitors, maximum length 15m. There appears to be at least 2·5m at these pontoons except at the fuel berth which is at the inner end of the most northerly arm. Visitors' reception is at the end of the first (N) pontoon with the *bureau du port* at the inner end. There are fingers on the pontoons and slack water is recommended for berthing although the stream running through them is not as strong as at Tréguier.

Facilities

Water and electricity On the pontoons.

Fuel Diesel and petrol at the root of the N pontoon.

Dinghy landing On the pontoons and at the slip to the N of them.

Slip and crane To the N of the pontoons; max 50T.

Yacht club By the pontoons, is welcoming and has a bar but no catering; there are showers and heads.

Launderette Machine at the yacht club.

Shops All in the small country town ½M up the hill, also a garage. There is a *supermarché* on the far side of the square.

Restaurants and cafés A café near the harbour but there is a selection of restaurants and *crêperies* in the town with one well known restaurant just over the bridge. There is a new town hall which can be hired for larger functions.

Travel The town is on the main E/W coast road between St-Brieuc and Morlaix. The nearest railways stations are at Paimpol and Pontrieux.

Pontrieux
(Upper reaches of Rivière de Trieux)

General

The lock at Pontrieux is 3M above the bridge at Lézardrieux. HW Pontrieux is the same time as HW St-Malo and the lock opens 2¼ hours before to 1¾ hours after HW. It is an attractive trip with few difficulties if taken on the flood.

The basin at Pontrieux is 1M long with plenty of berths alongside and also on moorings. There are all the facilities of a small country town and it would be a suitable and safe place to leave the boat or to change crews.

Data

Charts

There are no official charts above the bridge but the plan on page 104–105 indicates the run of the channel.

Tides

See Lézardrieux. HW Pontrieux is 10 minutes later and the same time as HW St-Malo.

Lights

There are no navigational lights above the bridge.

Communications

Bureau du port, Pontrieux Ch 12, working hours. Call sign *Port de Pontrieux* ☎ 02 96 95 34 87.

Lock keeper Ch 12 or 16 during lock opening times. Call sign *Ecluse de Pontrieux* ☎ 02 96 95 60 70.

Approaches and entrance

The bridge at Lézardrieux has a clearance of 17m and above this are two beacon towers marking the side of the channel before the valley opens out. Provided this section is taken during the first half of the flood the channel will be visible for the first mile after which the banks close in and the channel follows the outside of the bends. A high tension

Slip crane   Bureau du port   Boatyard   Lock (behind trees)   Aggregate works

Pontrieux basin looking NNW

cable crosses the river just above a wreck on the E bank whose clearance is believed to be 20m+. 1½M above the bridge, the river takes a sharp turn to port under Château Roche Jagu where there is sometimes a mooring and is a convenient anchorage to await the lock opening. Beware if staying over a tide as the banks are steep and it is possible to swing on to a drying bank as the tide falls, even at the mooring. See 'Facilities' below for more details of the château.

An anchor light should be exhibited if staying in the river overnight as there is occasional coaster, dredger and *vedette* traffic.

Above the château, take the right fork for the lock (the other arm is spanned by the railway). There are port and starboard buoys 200m below the lock which should be left 5m on the appropriate sides.

Pontrieux. Château Roche Jagu showing moorings and slip

Lézardrieux. The bridge above the town (17m clearance)

Bridge above Lézardrieux

Château Roche Jagu

Pontrieux looking NE

Just outside the lock the river takes a sharp turn to port round a port beacon. There is a waiting buoy here. The bed of the river is rocky and uneven and if it is necessary to dry out the best place is alongside the wall by the entrance to the gates. The sill dries 3·5m. The lock is 65m long and 11m wide and the gates will stay open if the tide level exceeds 10m. The high tension cable over the lock has a clearance of 25m. The basin has between 2m and 4m in it throughout the length.

It is usual to leave Pontrieux at HW but the lock keeper will advise.

The port is used by the occasional coaster serving the aggregate works situated above the weir 200m up the basin on the W bank.

Pontrieux. The lock into Pontrieux basin looking WNW. The river dries at LW from the spillway downwards

Pontrieux. The locks from downstream. The yachts are waiting to enter

Berths

There are 160 berths with 40 reserved for visitors, maximum length 25m round the first bend after the aggregate works. There are also moorings in the middle of the basin. It is customary to double up at most berths and moorings.

Tell the harbourmaster if there are children or elderly on board and he will try to put you alongside.

Facilities

Water and electricity Available at points on the jetty.

Showers and heads 3 of each near the harbour office.

Slips and crane A slip above the harbour office and a fixed 5-ton crane. A 20-ton travel-lift is available.

Fuel From garage in town but delivery is possible; ask at the *bureau du port*.

Shops None near the quay but plenty in the town. Turn right over bridge at end of basin and then left ½M up the hill to the town. Market day is Monday.

Restaurants There are two in the vicinity of the quay and a selection in town.

Laying up Either ashore or afloat; security is said to be adequate and *gardiennage* can be arranged. Masts can be removed.

Travel The town is on the railway (5 trains/day) which connects via St-Brieuc with the main network, and to Morlaix and Brest to the W. (4 hours to Paris). The station to use is 'Pontrieux Gare' not 'Pontrieux Halte'. Buses to St-Brieuc and Morlaix, and beyond. Nearest airport at St-Brieuc.

Visits and leisure There are excursions to Château Roche Jagu which has a programme of theatrical and musical events between 1 June and 31 August. It is worth a visit to see the house and gardens even if not associated with an event. The restaurant stays open till 1900 and the one on the road outside the gates to the usual hours.

Fêtes There is a torch lit procession and funfairs in the town on the third Sunday in July.

4. Tréguier to Ile d'Ouessant

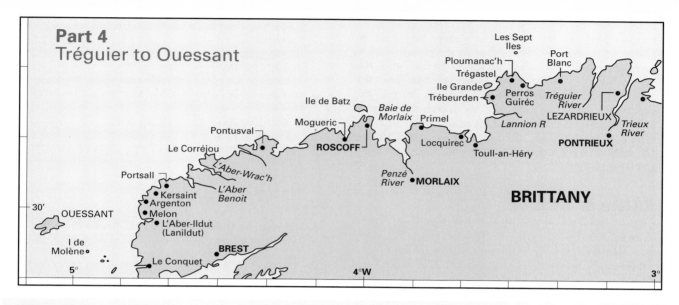

Part 4
Tréguier to Ouessant

Les Sept Iles • Ploumanac'h • Trégastel • Port Blanc • Ile Grande • Trébeurden • Perros Guirec • Tréguier River • LEZARDRIEUX • Trieux River • Ile de Batz • Baie de Morlaix • Primel • Lannion R • PONTRIEUX • Mogueric • ROSCOFF • Locquirec • Toull-an-Héry • Pontusval • Penzé River • MORLAIX • BRITTANY • Le Corréjou • L'Aber-Wrac'h • Portsall • L'Aber Benoît • Kersaint • Argenton • Melon • L'Aber-Ildut (Lanildut) • OUESSANT • I de Molène • BREST • Le Conquet • 30' • 5° • 4°W • 3°

Planning guide
Guernsey – Tréguier – Ile d'Ouessant

	Guernsey	Tréguier	Port Blanc	Perros Guirec	Ploumanac'h	Les Sept Isles	Trégastel St-A	Trébeurden	Lannion	Primel	Morlaix	Penzé River	Roscoff	Ile de Batz	Moguéric	Puntusval	Le Corréjou	L'Aber Wrac'h	L'Aber Benôit	Portsall	Argenton	L'Aber-Ildut	Le Conquet	Ile de Molène	I d'Ouessant
Guernsey		51	49	53	54	53	58	62	66	71	82	78	75	77	81	90	100	105	108	109	113	116	124	124	129
Tréguier	51		15	19	21	21	24	28	32	37	48	44	41	44	49	61	72	79	80	81	85	88	96	96	101
Port Blanc	49	15		7	8	8	11	15	19	24	35	31	28	31	36	48	59	64	67	68	72	75	83	83	88
Perros Guirec	53	19	7		6	6	9	13	17	22	33	29	26	29	34	46	57	62	65	66	70	73	81	81	86
Ploumanac'h	54	21	8	6		3	4	8	12	17	28	24	21	24	29	41	52	57	60	61	65	68	76	76	81
Les Sept Isles	53	21	8	6	3		5	9	13	18	29	25	22	25	30	42	53	58	61	62	66	69	77	77	81
Trégastel St-A	58	24	11	9	4	5		4	12	19	24	21	18	20	25	37	48	53	56	57	61	64	72	72	77
Trébeurden	62	28	15	13	8	9	4		4	14	23	20	17	19	24	36	47	52	55	56	60	63	71	71	76
Lannion	66	32	19	17	12	13	12	4		12	23	20	17	19	24	36	47	52	55	56	60	63	71	71	76
Primel	71	37	24	22	17	18	19	14	12		11	8	6	8	13	25	36	41	44	45	49	52	60	60	65
Morlaix	82	48	35	33	28	29	24	23	23	11		11	11	13	18	30	41	46	49	50	54	57	65	65	70
Penzé River	78	44	31	29	24	25	21	20	20	8	11		6	8	13	25	36	41	44	45	49	52	60	60	65
Roscoff	75	41	28	26	21	22	18	17	17	6	11	6		2	7	19	30	35	38	39	43	46	54	54	59
Ile de Batz	77	44	31	29	24	25	20	19	19	8	13	8	2		5	17	28	33	36	37	41	44	52	52	57
Moguéric	81	49	36	34	29	30	25	24	24	13	18	13	7	5		12	23	28	31	32	36	39	47	47	52
Puntusval	90	61	48	46	41	42	37	36	36	25	30	25	19	17	12		11	16	19	20	24	27	35	35	40
Le Correjou	100	72	59	57	52	53	48	47	47	36	41	37	30	28	23	11		5	8	9	13	16	24	24	29
L'Aber Wrac'h	105	77	64	62	57	58	53	52	52	41	46	42	35	32	28	16	5		3	4	8	11	19	19	24
L'Aber Benôit	108	80	67	65	60	61	56	55	55	44	49	45	38	35	31	19	8	3		1	5	8	16	16	21
Portsall	109	81	68	66	61	62	57	56	56	45	50	46	39	36	32	20	9	4	1		4	7	15	15	20
Argenton	113	85	72	70	65	66	61	60	60	49	54	50	43	40	36	24	13	8	5	4		3	11	11	16
L'Aber-Ildut	116	88	75	73	68	69	64	63	63	52	57	53	46	43	39	27	16	11	8	7	3		8	8	13
Le Conquet	124	96	83	81	76	77	72	71	71	60	65	61	54	51	47	35	24	19	16	15	11	8		7	17
Ile de Molène	124	96	83	81	76	77	72	71	71	60	65	61	54	51	47	35	24	19	16	15	11	8	7		10
I d'Ouessant	129	101	88	86	81	82	77	76	76	65	70	66	59	56	52	40	29	24	21	20	16	13	17	10	

Distances are given over the shortest navigable route and are measured to and from inner harbour or anchorage

Introduction

La Côte de Granit Rose from Port Blanc to Trébeurden deserves its name not only for the colour of its rocks but the strange shapes that wind and weather have fashioned them into. From Lannion onwards the more sombre grey granite is evident and the coast becomes rockier and more rugged until the most western outlier of France is reached at Ile d'Ouessant. In between there is no major port apart from the ferry terminal at Bloscon/Roscoff but a number of deep harbours in river estuaries such as Morlaix, Penzé and the Abers. The tidal streams ease off but are still significant especially round Ouessant where the Atlantic swell can combine to create unpleasant seas. Industry has not made its mark on this part of Brittany; agriculture, fishing and accommodating the holiday trade are the chief pursuits in an unspoilt rural region.

Rivière de Tréguier

General

An attractive estuary with an entrance which can be taken in all weathers by day and night. 6 miles up a pretty and wooded river lies the old cathedral town of Tréguier. There is a small marina which can be reached at all states of the tide with a least depth in the river of 2m. There are no leading lights once in the river but the upper 4 miles are well lit by buoys and a night passage up to the town should be possible.

Data

Charts

Admiralty *3670* (ARCS), *2668* (SC), *3673* (plan)
Imray *C34*

Tides

Subtract 10 minutes from the times of HW St-Malo for the times of HW Tréguier and subtract 45 minutes from the times of LW St-Malo for those at Tréguier. Subtract 2m from the heights of MHWS St-Malo, 1·5m from MHWN, 0·6 from MLWN and 0·2m from MLWS to find these heights at Tréguier.

Tidal streams

1. Outside the estuary to the N of Basse Crublent and La Jument des Heaux buoys the streams turn as follows:

−0350 HW Brest	To the E
+0200 HW Brest	To the W

   Maximum spring rate in each direction is 3¾ knots

2. In Passe de la Gaine S of Les Heaux light the streams turn as follows:

−0450 HW Brest	To the ENE
−0025 HW Brest	To the WSW

3. In the river above Les Trois Pierres the streams start as follows:

−0425 HW Brest	In-going
+0130 HW Brest	Out-going

Lights

Les Heaux de Bréhat Oc(3)WRG.12s48m15-11M Grey round tower 227°-R-247°-W-270°-G-302°-W-227°

La Corne Fl(3)WRG.12s14m11-8M White tower, red base 052°-W-059°-R-173°-G-213°-W-220°-R-052°

Grande Passe Ldg Lts 137°
   Porte de la Chaine *Front* Oc.4s12m11M White house 042°-vis-232°
   San Antoine *Rear* DirOc.R.4s34m15M Red and white house 134°-intens-140°

Buoys

Basse Crublent Fl(2)R.6s port Whis
La Jument des Heaux VQ N cardinal Bell
There are a number of unlit buoys in the approaches which may be seen on charts *3670, 3670* and plan on page 114–15. ¾M above La Corne the lit (Fl) port and starboard buoys are spaced at regular intervals.

Search and rescue

The nearest CROSS Corsen station is at Bodic, some 5M to the E. It will respond to any distress calls on

Tréguier. Outer approach to Grande Passe. From Le Crublent buoy, left foreground keep Pleubian spire (front) in transit with water tower (rear) on 154°

Spire
Water tower

Tréguier. Pointe de la Chaine and St-Antoine leading lights/marks for La Grande Passe (just open left)

Tréguier. La Corne light tower with Skeiviec white beacon open left. Banc de Taureau buoy to left of yacht on far right

Ch 16 or activation of GMDSS on Ch 70. The nearest inshore lifeboat is at Loguivi on Rivière de Trieux.

Weather forecasts
Bodic on Ch 79 at 0533, 0745, 1145, 1615, 1745 LT in French and English.
Météo France ☎ 08 36 68 08 22.
Daily weather map in bureau du port.
Navtex Corsen (A). Niton (S) or (K).

Communications
Capitainerie, Tréguier Ch 9, working hours ☎ 02 96 92 42 37.

Customs
The nearest office is at Paimpol.

Approaches
There are three approaches to the estuary:
Grande Passe in all conditions by day or night in visibility of 2M or more.
Passe de La Gaine which is narrow and dependent on seeing the leading marks at 5M or more. By day only.
Passe du Nord-Est Not so narrow as Passe de La Gaine but 10M visibility needed to see the rear leading marks.

Grande Passe
By day The leading marks for this channel are the light structures of Port de la Chaine (front) and St-Antoine (rear) bearing 137°. Port de la Chaine is a white house with a red lantern near the shore, and St-Antoine is a white house with a small red lantern elevation 34m. Due to other houses and trees these are very difficult to identify and another line may be used in the early stages. This is Pleubian Water Tower (not on chart *3670*) and Pleubian spire in transit 154° which runs through a position close SW of Le Crublent buoy. (See photograph page 112.)

This transit leads between Le Corbeau port buoy and Pierre a l'Anglais starboard red buoy from here the Port de la Chaine and St-Antoine transit 137° should be identifiable. Continue on it and do not get

to the E of the line to keep clear of the Basse du Corbeau shoal. This leaves the Pen-ar-Guézec beacon tower and beacon 400m to starboard. Round Penn-ar-Guézec starboard-hand buoy closely and alter to 215° to keep the E edge of La Corne white lighthouse with red base in line with Skeiviec white beacon tower (see photograph). This leaves the following marks on the sides shown:

Two starboard beacons on the E side of Ile d'Er 600m to starboard.

Men Noblance black and white pyramid, the front mark for Passe de la Gaine ½M to starboard.
Les Trois Pierres N cardinal beacon tower 100m to port. Note that Banc de la Pie has only 1·1m over it close NW of the line just before reaching Les Trois Pierres if entering near LW springs.

When Les Trois Pierres is abeam, alter to leave La Corne lighthouse 200m to port which will leave Le Petit Taureau starboard beacon 200m to starboard. When La Corne is abeam alter to leave Banc de Taureau starboard-hand buoy close to starboard.

Round this buoy and steer 234° keeping Les Trois Pierres beacon tower touching the W side of La Corne as a stern transit. This leaves:
Skeiviec small white beacon tower on a rocky shoal 200m to port
Laouenan beacon 300m to starboard
Guarivinon port light buoy (the first of the lit buoys) to port.

Do not cut close round after this buoy as there is a rock just upstream from it. From here the channel can be seen as one proceeds from the buoys marking it and the beacons marking the occasional rocks outside it. The increasing number of moorings at the sides, especially in the vicinity of the village of La Roche Jaune, and occasional fish farms also give indications of the run of the channel. Keep well to the W bank to round Banc de Ven just below the town. From here the channel is marked by frequent buoys to the pontoons.

Grande Passe (Line A)
By night The 30m line keeps clear of any outlying dangers until the leading lights can be aligned. They are synchronised with front Port de la Chaine Oc.4s12M and rear St-Antoine DirOc.R.4s15M on 137°. The rear light is intensified from 134° to 140° (Line A). For radar equipped vessels Basse Crublent, Pierre à l'Anglais and Pen Guézec buoys all have radar reflectors.

This line will pass through the red, then green sectors of La Corne light (Fl(3)WRG.12s) and enter its white sector bearing 213° close to the unlit Pen Guézec buoy. Alter to starboard round this buoy and stay in the white sector of La Corne between 213° and 220° until Les Trois Pierres beacon tower is abeam to port. Then alter to starboard to pass round W of La Corne light in its red sector leaving it about 100m to port. When the narrow white sector is reached, keep on its S edge steering 234° to avoid the unlit starboard Banc de Taureau buoy which must be left to starboard. From here the S

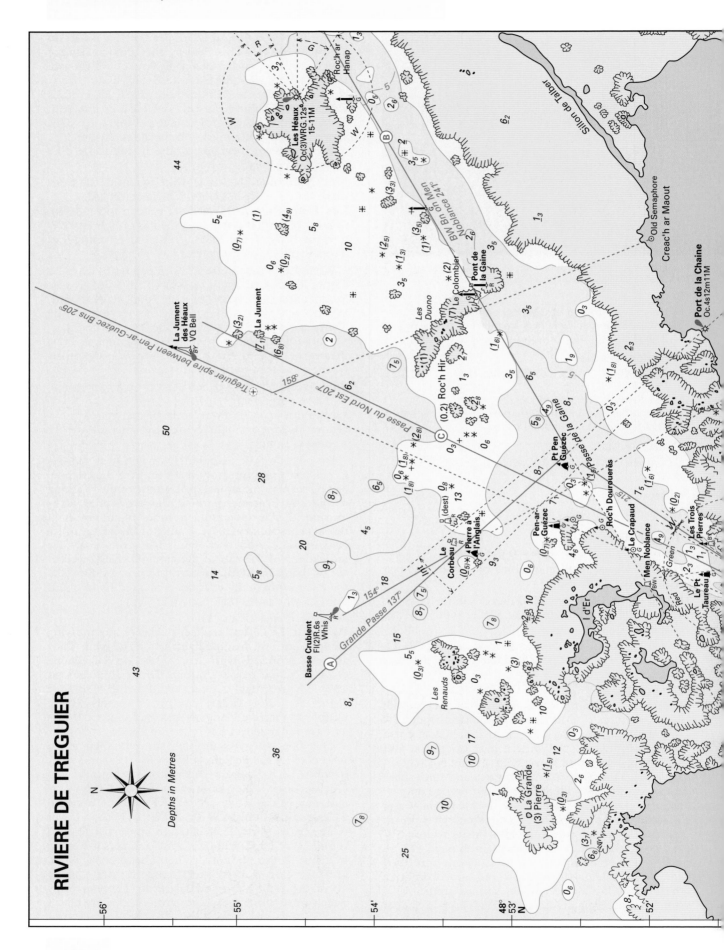

RIVIERE DE TREGUIER

N

Depths in Metres

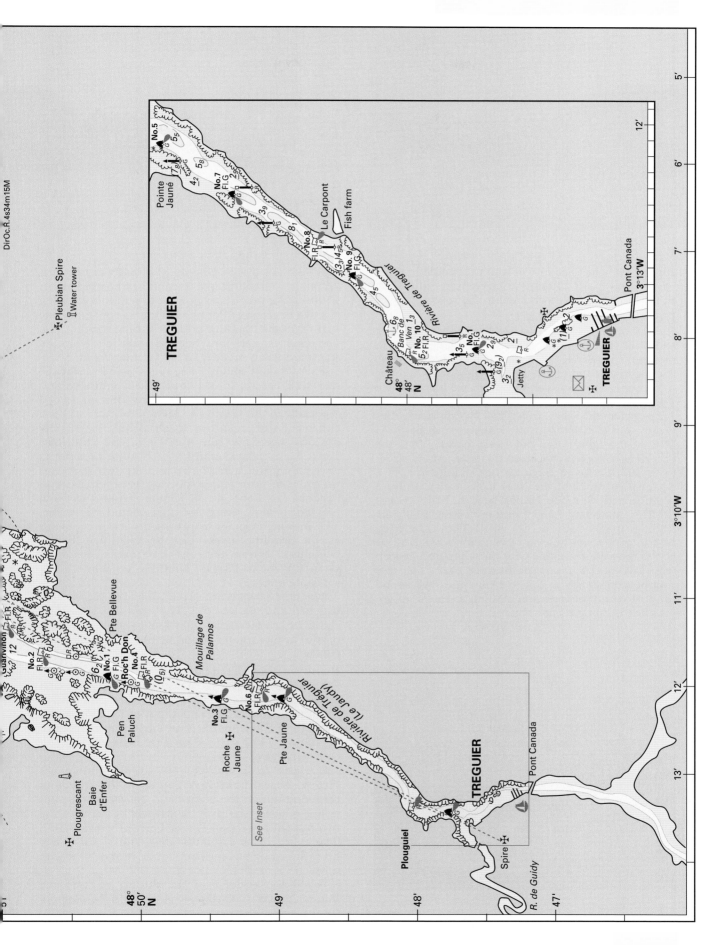

DirOc.R.4s34m15M

⌖ Pleubian Spire
ꝉ Water tower

TREGUIER

No.5
✦ G 5
7 8
G 5 8
4 2
No.7 2 9
Pointe Fl.G
Jaune 3 9
8 1
No.8 3 14 5
Fl.R No.9 5
G 5
Le Carpont 4 5
Fish farm

Château 6 8
Banc de
48° Ven 1 3
48' R **No.10**
N 5 Fl.R
No.1 2 9
G Fl.G 2
1 3 5 2
G 3 2
Jetty G 9 2
* Rivière de Tréguier

✦ * 11 2
* G
R G
⚓ **TREGUIER**
⚓ ⊠ ꝉ
Pont Canada
3°13'W

TREGUIER

Guarynnon
12
No.2 6 2 **No.1**
Fl.R G Fl.G **No.4**
G Roc'h Don
Pte Bellevue

Pen 10 5
Paluch Fl.R
Mouillage de
Palamos
No.3 **No.6**
Fl.G Fl.R
Roche ꝉ G
Jaune
Pte Jaune

See Inset
Rivière de Tréguier
(Le Jaudy)

TREGUIER

Plouguiel
Pont Canada

Spire ꝉ
R. de Guidy

ꝉ Plougrescant
Baie
d'Enfer
Plougrescant

48°
50'
N

49'

48'

47'

Approaching Tréguier

edge of the white sector will lead to the first lit port-hand buoy off Roche Guarivinon and the subsequent lit buoyed channel to the town.

Passe de la Gaine (Line B)

By day only This pass can be taken only in daylight and clear visibility. The leading marks are harder to pick out in the late afternoon if it is sunny. If the leading marks are followed exactly, the least depth is 0·3m but a divergence of 35m from the line will give 2·1m less in two places.

To enter the pass from the E, approach Les Heaux and identify Roc'h ar Hanap which lies ¼M SSE of the lighthouse and never covers. It is the outermost of several rocks on this side, and is steep-to to the SE. Avoid Basse de la Gaine (dries 0·5m and just to the S of the line) if necessary. From a position with Roc'h ar Hanap bearing N 400m and the first starboard-hand beacon bearing 290° the leading marks will be in line. They are Men Noblance a white beacon tower with a black stripe across the middle, in line with the white wall beacon with a vertical black stripe bearing 241°. The rear wall beacon stands in a field below the skyline and the first clump of trees some 500m to the W of the prominent Plougrescant church.

Marina   *Spire*

Tréguier looking S

Follow this line leaving the first starboard beacon 200m to starboard, the second starboard beacon 150m to starboard and pass in the middle between the two beacons at Pont de la Gaine leaving the line slightly to the N at this point to hit the middle. The Pen Guézec starboard buoy is then left 100m to starboard when proceed as for Grande Passe.

The difficulty about Passe de la Gaine is that the rear wall beacon is 6M from the E entrance and Men Noblance 4M and they are difficult to see especially in the afternoon. Men Noblance has been enhanced with reflective material but this is only obvious when the sun is on it in the mornings. However in calm conditions it is quite possible to navigate by Roc'h ar Hanap and the two starboard beacons on entry, then steering between the two beacons at Pont de la Gaine using the Men Noblence mark which by then should be visible. The passage from W to E presents fewer problems as the leading marks can be identified before becoming committed and alternative exits by Grande Passe or Pass du Nord Est are immediately available options.

The tidal streams are strong and cross set must be watched and allowed for. The extensive rocks and shoals of Les Heaux and Les Duono are an effective barrier at most states of the tide to any swell in the passage.

Passe du Nord Est (Line C)

By day only This is an alternative for vessels approaching from the Channel Islands especially if late afternoon sun prevents the identification of the Passe de la Gaine marks. Visibility however needs to be about 10 miles to see the rear mark of Tréguier cathedral spire.

Navigate to pass 100m NW of La Jument des Heaux N cardinal buoy whence the Tréguier cathedral spire (the right-hand of the two spires visible between the river banks) will be between the two beacon towers on Pen ar Guézec bearing 205°. The S beacon is a spindly affair and if not visible keep the cathedral spire just open of the N beacon tower. Follow this line for about 0·75M.

When the summit of the middle rock in the Duono group is in line with the old Sémaphore

Tréguier. Leading marks for Passe de la Gaine (just open left) on a clear day. Plougrescant spire far left

building on the Creac'h ar Maout bearing 158°, steer to follow this line for about 0·3M until Skeiviec white beacon comes into line with the cathedral spire bearing 207° (Line C). This line can then be followed until La Corne is reached but it passes very close to a drying 1·5m rock. If necessary to be sure to avoid this, turn to port on to the Grande Passe leading line before reaching the rock, turn to starboard round Pen ar Guézec starboard buoy and continue as for Grande Passe.

Anchorages
It is possible to anchor in good holding almost anywhere in the channel but room must be left for the occasional coaster, fishing boats and fish farm boats. A riding light is advisable. The following positions are recommended:

1. Near the Guarivinon buoy in 5m and sandy mud. Avoid the rock to the S of the buoy.
2. Towards the W of the channel between Pen Paluch and Roc'h Don beacon in 5m, mud.
3. Clear of the moorings and fish farms in the vicinity of La Roche Jaune village (see Facilities below).
4. Under the château opposite Banc de Ven in 5m, mud but the banks are steep-to and the channel narrow.

Anchorage is prohibited between the château and the bridge above the pontoons.

Moorings
There are no visitors' moorings nor are there any in the upper reaches. A private mooring of the many in the vicinity of La Roche Jaune may be available for a short stay.

Berths
There are 5 pontoons with 330 berths, 130 for visitors. Maximum length 12 m and the outer berths are dredged to 2m but this shallows towards the wall. The fingers are only 7m long. There is one berth only for a longer boat at the end of the first pontoon and doubling up is not encouraged especially at springs. The stream runs strongly through the pontoons. It is advisable to arrive or

leave near slack water and the inner berths should not be attempted except at these times. If an arrival coincides outside slack water times, always berth head to the stream, adjusting the berth as necessary before departure.

With permission from the *capitainerie*, it might be possible to take the ground alongside the commercial quay downstream of the pontoons.

Dinghy landing
The only practical dinghy landing at all stages of the tide for those coming upriver by dinghy to the town is at the root of the pontoons.

Facilities
Water On the pontoons.
Fuel Diesel only from the fuelling pontoon, petrol from garage opposite.

Only berth suitable for 10m plus

Tréguier yacht berths

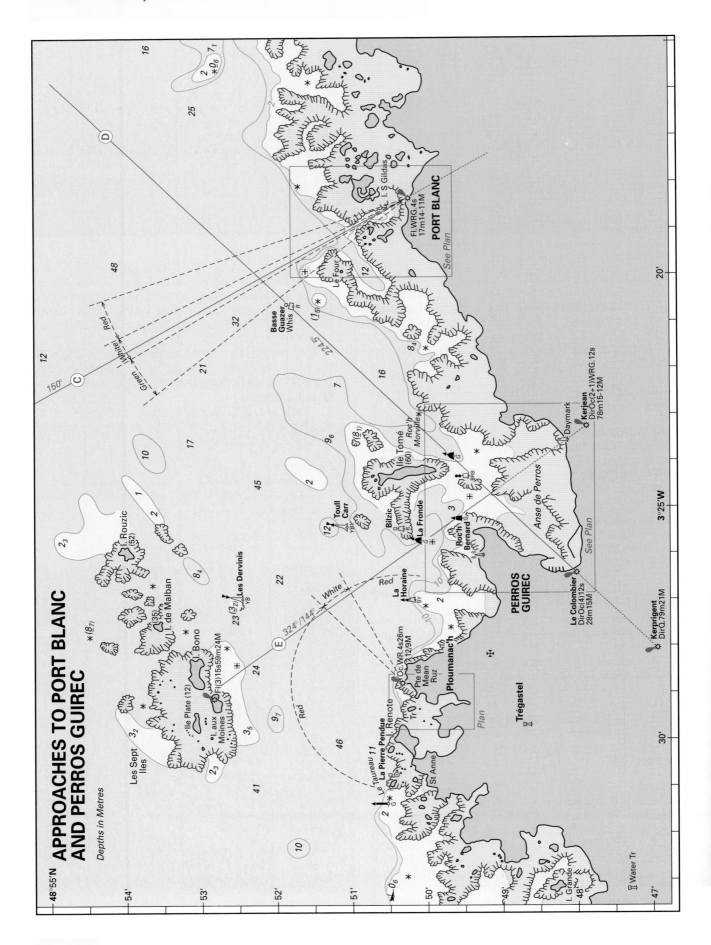

APPROACHES TO PORT BLANC AND PERROS GUIREC

Depths in Metres

48°55'N

Showers and heads In the yacht club.

Launderette In rue St-André.

Chandlers One at each end of the quay.

Electricity At some points on the pontoons.

Post office Up the road to the town.

Shops and banks There is a wide variety of shops and banks towards and in the centre of the town which is a 15-minute walk from the pontoons.

Hotels and restaurants A few near the quay and more up in the town.

Yacht club At the base of the pontoon and welcoming to visitors.

Travel Buses to Paimpol via Lézardrieux and to Lannion railway station. Small airfield at Lannion.

Historical and leisure

This pleasant, quiet old town traces its history back to the monastery of Trécon, founded by St-Tugdal in the 6th century. There are many 17th-century buildings in the town. The fine church, formerly a cathedral, was founded in the 9th century but mostly rebuilt in the 14th; there is an 11th-century tower on its northern side. The strange granite spire, a sort of honeycomb of irregular openings, was finished in 1787. St-Yves, the friend of the poor, lived in Tréguier in the 13th century. A procession from Tréguier church to his birthplace in the nearby village of Minihy takes place each year on 19 May and is known as 'The pardon of the poor'. Tréguier is the birthplace of Renan to whom there is a memorial near the quay.

Port Blanc

General

A small natural harbour halfway between Rivière de Tréguier and Perros Guirec. It is well sheltered except from the N sector. The approach could be dangerous and the anchorage untenable in strong winds from this direction. The entrance is straightforward if a little difficult to identify by day but it can be taken at any state of the tide by day or night. An attractive and unspoilt holiday and minor fishing village with few facilities apart from local provision shops.

Data

Charts

Admiralty *3670* (ARCS), *2668* (SC), *3672* (plan)
Imray *C34* (plan)

Tides

Subtract 30 minutes from the times of HW St-Malo for the times of HW at Port Blanc, and subtract 1 hour 5 minutes from the times of LW St-Malo. Subtract 2·4m from the heights of HW St-Malo and 0·5m from the heights of LW to get the heights at Port Blanc. For more accurate predictions, see Perros Guirec (page 121).

Tidal streams

The tidal stream turns to the E at −0450 HW Brest and to the W at +0120 HW Brest off the entrance and the maximum spring rate is 2½ knots.

Lights

Le Voleur Fl.WRG.4s17m14-11M White tower 140°-G-148°-W-152°-R-160°

Ile St-Gildas white pyramid — White house — Le Voleur — Sailing school — Ile du Château Neuf white pyramid — Yacht on approach course

Port Blanc looking SSW

Port Blanc. Conspicuous house and Le Voleur light structure

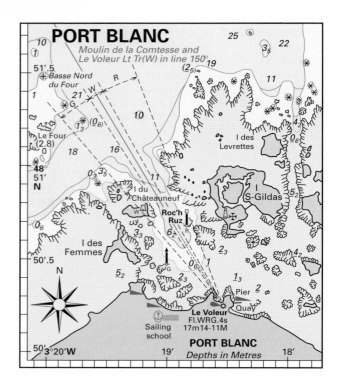

Search and rescue and weather forecasts
See Tréguier (page 112) or Perros Guiréc (page 121).

Communications
Capitainerie Ch 9 (working hours) ☎ 02 96 92 64 96.

Approaches
By day The leading line is not easy to pick out by day and identification of Le Voleur lighthouse will depend on how recently it has been painted and the trees cut back round it. The rear mark of a disused windmill on the line of 150° is now hidden. Le Voleur is a white tower with a square window at half height. However the following features are all more conspicuous and will help to establish Le Voleur's postion:

Ile du Château Neuf with a conspicuous white pyramid to the W of the line.

A white house with a grey slate roof near the shore line just to the E of Le Voleur; the W end is white and particularly visible in the afternoon sun.

A white pyramid on the W side of Ile St-Gildas.

The 30m line clears all dangers outside comfortably until Line C 150° can be identified and followed.

By night The E approach leading lights to Perros Guiréc can be used to approach the Port Blanc entrance from either direction (Line D on plan page 118) until the white sector of Le Voleur (Fl.WRG.4s) on 150° is opened up (Line C).

Entrance
Le Voleur lighthouse or its white sector on 150° will lead right into the anchorage passing the following on the sides indicated:

> **Basse Gauzier** port whistle buoy 0·7M to starboard
> **Le Four** white painted rock 0·5M to starboard
> **Ile du Château Neuf** and white pyramid 300m to starboard
> **Ile St-Gildas** and its white beacon 300m to port
> **Roc'h Ruz** port beacon 100m to port.

Anchorage
The W part of the inner anchorage is occupied by a number of white mooring buoys to the W of Run Glas starboard beacon, one of which may be vacant. If not, there is room to anchor clear of them in depths of 1 to 3m, sand.

Facilities
There is a slip and a small jetty drying 1·3m alongside, just round the corner to the E of Le Voleur. This could be used to dry out against after a recce. This slip can be used to land or the beach anywhere between Le Voleur and the sailing school. There is another slip well to the W of the sailing school which is a long building 300m W of Le Voleur. The *capitainerie* is in this building.

Water From a tap at the E slip or from the sailing school.

Fuel From a garage at Penvenan ½M inland by taxi from the café.

Heads There are two public WCs, and showers at the sailing school.

Shops A butcher and baker to the S of the E slip.

Hotel Grand Hotel has a restaurant, and the post box is in its side wall.

Historical
The 16th-century chapel of Notre Dame de Port Blanc stands above the village, and is the scene of a pardon held on 8 September and attended mainly by fishermen and seafarers.

Anatole le Braz, the author of several classics of Breton traditions and legends, lived here.

One of the local legends tells of a long procession of drowned seamen, led by a woman, which can sometimes be seen landing on the beach of Ile St-Gildas in search of fresh water, while the shape of their vessel is dimly seen in the offing.

Perros Guirec

General

The Anse de Perros is a large shallow bay much of which dries above CD. There is a substantial marina in the SW corner with a sill drying 2·5m. The entrance to the marina is 6m wide which would prevent entry to some multihulls. The gate may not open around neap tides. Both the E and N approaches are well lit by leading or sectored lights. There are anchorage or moorings sheltered from the W under Ile Tomé or Pointe du Château in the approaches. A lee could be found under Ile Tomé in easterly weather to await the tide for entry to the marina. There are all the facilities expected in a marina and a wide variety of shops in the town up the hill.

Data

Charts

Admiralty *3670* (ARCS), *2668* (SC), *3672* (plan)
SC *2668*
ARCS *3670*
Imray *C34* (plan)
SHOM *7125* (plan)

Tides

	Time differences			Height differences			
	H W	LW		MHWS	MHWN	MLWN	MLWS
St-Malo							
0100	0800	0300	0800				
and	and	and	and	12·2	9·3	4·2	1·5
1300	2000	1500	2000				
Perros							
−0030	−0040	−0115	−0055	−2·9	−1·9	−0·8	−0·2

Tidal streams

In Passe de l'Ouest the streams start as follows in relation to HW Brest:

−0435	SE
+0250	NW

Maximum spring rate 2¾ knots
In Passe de l'Est the streams start as follows in relation to HW Brest:

−0435	ENE
+0250	WSW

Maximum spring rate is also 2¾ knots.

Lights

Kerjean. Passe de l'Ouest 144°
DirOc(2+1)WRG.12s78m 15-12M 133·7°-G-143·2°-W-144·8°-R-154·3° White tower, black top
Passe de l'Est Ldg Lts 224°
Le Colombier *Front* DirOc(4)12s28m15M White

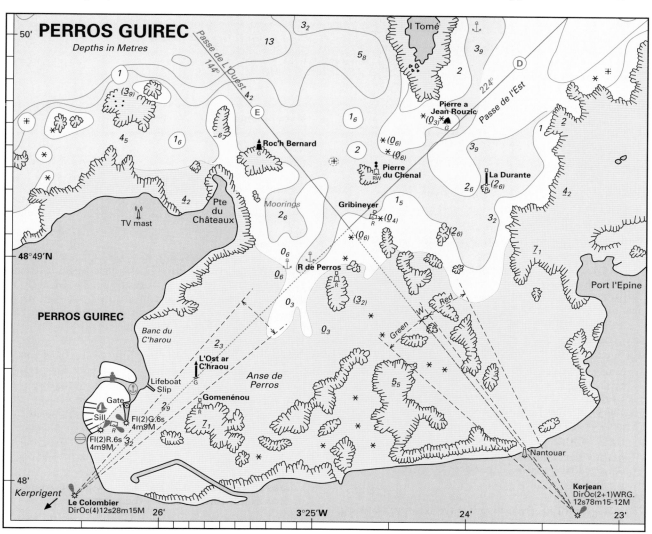

Gate to marina

Perros Guirec looking W at LW

house 214·5°-intens-234·5°

Kerprigent *Rear* Dir Q.79m21M 221°-intens-228°
Jeteé Est (Linkin) head Fl(2)G.6s4m9M White pile, green top
Môle Ouest head Fl(2)R.6s4m9M White pile, red top

Buoys

In Passe de l'Est from the E:
Basse Guazer port Whis
Pierre à Jean Rouzics S of Ile Tomé starboard
Gribineyer S of Pierre du Chenal Bn port
In Passe de l'Ouest from the N:
Toull Carr WNW of N end of Ile Tomé W cardinal
La Fronde starboard
Gribineyer port
Just to the W of Linkin Head is a Fl.R.5s buoy which should be left to port on entry.

Search and rescue

Sémaphore Ploumanac'h near to Méan Ruz lighthouse monitors Chs 16 and 11 for 24 hrs and is controlled by CROSS Corsen. The nearest GMDSS stations to respond to calls on Ch 70 are at Bodic 15M to the E and Ile de Batz 25M to the W. There is an inshore lifeboat maintained just to the E of Ploumanac'h sémaphore.

Weather forecasts

Ile de Batz on Ch 79 at 0515, 0733, 1133, 1603, 1933 LT in French and English.
Bodic on Ch 79 at 0533, 0745, 1145, 1615, 1945 LT in French and English.

Météo France ☎ 08 36 68 08 22.
Daily weather map at capitainerie.
Navtex Corsen (A).

Communications

Capitainerie Ch 16 and 09 ☎ 02 96 49 80 50.

Customs

The nearest office is at Paimpol.

Approaches
Passe de l'Est (Line D)

By day The leading line (D on plans pages 118 and 121) carries a least depth until the final ½M of 0·4m if it is followed exactly but a small diversion, as below, will increase this least depth to 2·1m. The final ½M dries to a least depth of 2·9m.

The leading line is formed by Le Colombier, a white house light structure on which the name appears 5m high, elevation 28m, and Kerprigent lighthouse, a white tower 14m high among the trees on the skyline bearing 224°. These marks are difficult to pick out especially in the afternoon but there is enough latitude in the early stages to navigate by the buoys and beacons.

The leading line leaves the following on the sides shown:

Basse Guazer port whistle buoy 200m to port
Roc'h Morville (dries 1·5m) the seaward end of a dangerous unmarked shoal, 300m to port

Pierre à Jean Rouzic starboard buoy 50m to starboard
La Durante port beacon 400m to port
Pierre du Chenal isolated danger beacon tower 150m to starboard
Gribineyer port buoy 100m to port.

The line passes over a 0·4m patch shortly after this. To avoid it alter to 270° just before reaching this buoy and continue until Roc'h de Perros beacon tower bears 180° when the line may be regained.

Continuing along it if the tide serves leave:

Roch de Perros port beacon tower 250m to port
Lost ar C'hraou starboard beacon 50m to starboard.

The depths now shallow to drying 2·9m and after leaving Gomenénou port beacon tower 200m to port slightly greater depths can be found to the NW of the line. Once round the head of Jetée du Linkin, the deeper water is close to the jetty.

By night Navigate to reach the leading line to the E of Ile Tomé which is formed by Le Colombier (front) DirOc(4)12s (220°-intens-230°) and Kerprigent (rear) DirQ (221°-intens-228°) (Line D), bearing 224·5° and follow it as by day. If the Gribineyer buoy cannot be seen and the 0·4m patch is to be avoided, alter sharply to starboard as soon as the Kerjean light (DirOc(2+1)WRG) to port starts to change from red to white and keep in the white sector for 150m before turning back to a converging course of 215° to rejoin the leading line. Then proceed as by day.

Passe de l'Ouest (Line E)

By day Navigate to a position about ½M SW of Toull Carr W cardinal buoy and identify leading line (E on plan page 121) which consists of a white house with a former light tower on its roof near the foreshore in line with Kerjean, a white light tower elevation 78m with a grey roof amongst the trees on the skyline, bearing 144°. This line carries a least depth of 1m. Follow the line leaving the following on the side indicated:

Bilzic port beacon tower 200m to port
La Fronde starboard buoy 250m to starboard
Roc'h Bernard starboard beacon tower 250m to starboard

Perros Guirec. Yacht leaving the narrow gate. Note that wall to left of gate is well covered

Pierre du Chenal isolated danger beacon tower 400m to port.

As soon as Pierre du Chenal is abeam alter to 190° to pick up the Passe de l'Est leading line and follow it in to the entrance.

By night Note that the white sector of Méan Ruz light Oc.WR.4s near Ploumanac'h clears all dangers between Les Sept Iles and the mainland. Navigate to pick up the narrow white sector of Kerjean light (DirOc(2+1)WRG.12s) on 144° which is flanked by a green sector to the W and red to the E. Follow this line as for by day and alter course to starboard to 190° as the Kerprigent DirQ light becomes intense until this aligns with Le Colombier light DirOc(4)12s on 224° following this to the entrance.

Anchorages
There is generally good holding throughout the Anse de Perros and shelter from the SE through S to NW.
a. With Roc'h de Perros tower bearing 130° 250m. Least depth 2·4m, sand.
b. With Roc'h de Perros tower bearing 120°, and with Bilzic port beacon tower just open W of Roc'h Bernard tower in a least depth of 0·6m.
c. At neaps anywhere to the SW of these anchorages as depths allow.
d. In westerly weather on the SE side of Ile Tomé about 200m offshore in 3·5m, sand and shells. The island is precipitous and uninhabited.

Moorings
There are 5 white visitors' buoys in a minimum of 3m just to the E of Pointe du Château but they can be uncomfortable around HW. There are three waiting buoys outside the harbour entrance, drying about 3m.

Entrance and berths
The marina is enclosed by a wall that dries 7m and is marked by a few red and white poles. The narrow (6m) entrance is at the NE end of the wall and dries 2·5m. The gate is opened between 1½ hours before to 1½ hours after HW at springs but this time reduces towards neaps to only 30 minutes before HW. At slack neaps it will not open and may be closed for up to 2 to 3 days; beware of being caught inside. 2·5m is maintained throughout most of the basin.

There are 70 berths reserved for visitors and unless directed otherwise these are on the most northern pontoon. There are also some moorings in the basin.

The W side of Jetée de Linkin outside the gate dries and is used by fishing boats and the occasional commercial craft.

Facilities
Water and electricity On the pontoons.
Fuel Diesel and petrol from the fuel berth in the NE corner.

Showers and heads Included in berthing price but access card needed from the *capitainerie*.

Launderette Within 50m of the *capitainerie*.

Mobile crane (40-ton), slip and chandlers.

Shops, restaurants, cafés and banks Basic requirements around the marina. Nearest *supermarché* is up the hill towards the church and there is a wide variety of shops in the town.

Leisure There is an interesting 12th-century church and some nice coastal and cliff walks. In a park, close uphill from the town centre, is a small memorial to 500 lost in the sinking of HM Ships *Charybdis* and *Limbourne* to the N of Les Sept Iles in 1943. Many of the bodies were buried where they came ashore between here and the Channel Islands.

Ploumanac'h

General

The entrance to Ploumanac'h lies between dramatic pink sandstone rocks about ¼M west of Mean Ruz lighthouse and leads to a beautiful, shallow and almost landlocked bay. Its beauty, however has made it very popular and led to restrictions such as prohibited anchorage between the inner harbour and the outer entrance. The sill of the inner harbour dries 2·55m and retains a depth of 1·5m to 2m inside. There are dumbbell moorings inside but almost always occupied. Yachts drawing 2m or more may not find a berth but it is a well worthwhile port of call for shallow draught craft or bilge keelers.

Data

Charts

Admiralty *3670* (ARCS), *2668* (SC)
Imray *C34*
SHOM *7125* (plan)

Tides

Subtract 30 minutes from the times of HW St-Malo and subtract 1 hour 5 minutes from the times of LW. Subtract 2·4m from the heights of HW St-Malo and 0·5m from the heights of LW. See Perros Guirec page 121 for more exact predictions.

No.2 port beacon   No.1 starboard beacon   Sill at entrance   Château Costaérès

Approach line 215°

Ploumanac'h looking S

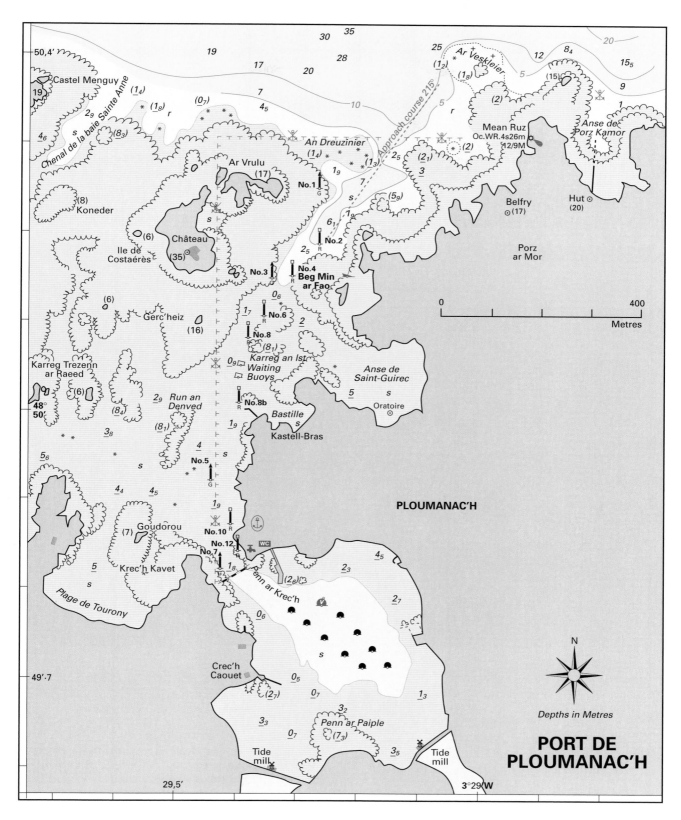

PORT DE PLOUMANAC'H

Depths in Metres

Tidal streams

Off Mean Ruz the E-going stream starts at about −0435 HW Brest and the W-going at +0130 HW Brest. The maximum spring rate is 2½ knots but will be much stronger out in the Chenal towards Les Sept Iles.

Lights

Ploumanac'h Méan Ruz Oc.WR.4s26m12/9M Pink square tower 226°-W-242°-R-226°

Search and rescue

The Sémaphore at Méan Ruz (Ploumanac'h) operates

Ploumanac'h entrance bearing 215° with boat ahead in channel.
Château Costaérès far right

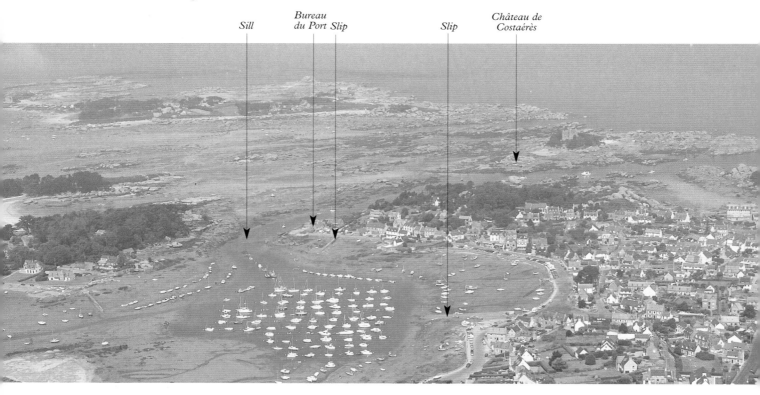

Sill   Bureau du Port   Slip   Slip   Château de Costaérès

Ploumanac'h looking WNW

under CROSS Corsen control on Ch 16 and 11 ☎ 02 96 91 46 51.

An inshore lifeboat is maintained on a slip just to the E of the Sémaphore.

Communications

Harbour office ☎ 02 96 91 44 51 also Ch 16 and 09.

Approaches

From a position 0·3M W of Méan Ruz lighthouse approach the lighthouse on a track of 110° until the first port beacon bears 215° when turn onto this bearing and follow it until the first starboard beacon is abeam. The conspicuous Château Costaéres will be seen on the starboard bow. Because there is no leading line a least depth of drying 2·1m should be assumed for safety.

A night approach except after one in daytime and with some moon, is not recommended.

Entrance

Chart *3670* at that scale does not show the true position at the entrance for which the plan on SHOM *7125* or the plan above should be consulted. Deviation out of the approach channel carrying 2·5m before the first starboard beacon is reached will find rocks drying 1·3m to starboard, and drying up to 2·1m to port. The channel shallows after the second port and starboard beacons to drying 0·6m and progressively shallows to drying 1·9m outside the sill.

There are 11 numbered beacons marking the channel, numbers 8 and 12 having tide gauges

Ploumanac'h. Château Costaérès from inner entrance looking NW. The black-hulled boat is at the waiting buoys

showing depths over the sill. The gauge on No.12 covers near HW (there is no No.11) when there will be at least 2m over the sill. There are two white waiting buoys between Nos 8 and 8b beacons but it is unlikely to find them free. The sill, drying 2·55m is between Nos 7 and 12 beacons.

Anchorage and fishing is prohibited S of a line running W from Mean Ruz lighthouse and E of a line running S from the château on Ile Costaéres.

If intending to enter the basin, an entry to the harbour should be timed with enough water to pass straight over the sill. Waiting anchorages outside may be found at Trégastel St-Anne (page 128) to the W, Les Sept Iles (page 127) to the north or off Perros Guirec (page 121) to the E.

Berths

Inside the sill will be found several rows of dumbbell moorings. There is up to 2m on the outer middle ones but fishing boats tend to occupy them. The water shallows progressively towards the SE corner. There are ostensibly 20 places for visitors, maximum length 12m.

For those able to dry, an anchorage on a generally flat, sandy bottom inside the basin and clear of the moorings will be possible, or to the W of the approach channel and clear of the prohibited area above, on sand.

Facilities

Water From a tap by the harbour office at the N end of the sill and convenient to the slip.

Fuel A garage a good kilometre to the SW.

Hotels, cafés and bars A few around the harbour.

Shops A few scattered about the village.

Slips The main slip by the harbour office has been extended almost to LW and there are two other slips around the harbour.

Travel Buses to Perros Guirec and to Lannion railway station. There is a small airport at Lannion.

Les Sept Iles

General

The group consists of four principal islands which are uninhabited except for the lighthouse keepers on Ile-aux-Moines, and many islets. There are a number of isolated rocks and the tidal streams run strongly through the group but there is no difficulty in entering the anchorage between Ile-aux-Moines and Ile Bono in suitable conditions.

The islands are a bird sanctuary. No navigation is permitted amongst them (see chart 3670 for the prohibited area) nor is landing allowed anywhere except at the pier on the E side of Ile-aux Moines. This pier is in frequent use by *vedettes* in the season.

Data

Charts

Admiralty *3669* (ARCS), *3670* (ARCS), *2668* (SC)
Imray *C34*
SHOM *7125* (plan)

Tides

Subtract 30 minutes from the times of HW St-Malo for the times of HW at Les Sept-Iles, and subtract 1 hour 5 minutes for the times of LW. Subtract 2·4m from St-Malo HW, and 0·5m from heights of LW. See Perros Guirec for more precise predictions.

Tidal streams

In the middle of the Chenal des Sept-Iles the ENE-going stream starts at −0320 HW Brest and the WSW-going stream starts at +0250 HW Brest. The maximum spring rates are 4¾ knots in each direction to the SW of Ile-aux-Moines but this reduces to 2¾ knots at the E end of the Chenal.

The seas are high and steep in the Chenal des Sept-Iles in wind over tide conditions especially at springs. The shallower areas such as Basse Meur 1M S of Ile-aux-Moines should be avoided in these conditions.

Lights

Les Sept-Iles Fl(3)15s59m24M Grey tower and dwelling. Obscured by Ile Ruzic and E end of Ile Bono between 237° and 241°

Ploumanac'h Mean Ruz Oc.WR.4s26m12/9M Pink square tower 226°-W-242°-R-226° Obscd by Pointe de Trégastel, and partially obscd by Les Sept-Iles and Ile Tomé

Kerjean DirOc(2+1)WRG.12s78m15-12M 133·7°-G-143·2°-W-144·8°-R-154·3°

Buoys

Les Dervinis S cardinal

Search and rescue

See Ploumanac'h.

Approaches

By day From the east navigate to a position close S of Les Dervinis S cardinal buoy to avoid this shoal and those of Les Noires de Rouzic which run to the NE from there. From Les Dervinis make 285° on Ile-aux-Moines lighthouse and hold this bearing with accuracy as it passes between a rock with 0m CD to the SW and one drying 1·3m to the NE of

Lighthouse on Ile-aux-Moines   Jetty   Ile Bono anchorage

Les Sept Iles looking N

this track. When the W end of Ile Bono bears 345° alter on to it in to the anchorage. This final leg passes between a shallow with 0·3m over it and another with 0·8m over it which can be disregarded for practical purposes unless it is near LW springs.

From the west pass ½M S of Le Cerf and Ile-aux-Moines keeping outside the 30m line until an approach to the anchorage on 345° can be made as above.

By night The white sector of Pointe de Mean Ruz (Oc.WR.4s) bearing SW leads clear into the Chenal until the sectored light at Kerjean (DirOc(2+1)WRG.12s) is picked up. This has a narrow white sector of between 143·2° and 144·8° flanked by a red sector to the E and a green sector to the W. Keep in the white sector on a track of 324° noting that while it will keep clear of the dangers to the E, passes very close to the rock with 0m CD and over the one with 0·8m over it.

Anchorages

The main anchorage lies SE of the gap between Ile-aux-Moines and Ile Bono with the lighthouse bearing about 270° and the W end of Ile Bono about 000°. There is a mooring buoy in the anchorage which is used by the *vedettes*.

Anchor between the buoy and the pier which has a beacon on the end of it. Do not proceed far N of the buoy towards the strand between the islands as there are two rocks which cover towards HW. The anchorage is protected from the NNE and NE by Ile Bono and from the W by Ile-aux Moines. The strand of sand, stones and rocks which dries out between the islands, breaks the seas from that direction but otherwise it is quite open to southerly winds and should only be used in settled weather. The anchorage is often crowded in the daytime especially at week-ends.

Land at the pier/slip whence a track leads up to the lighthouse and fort.

Another less frequented anchorage lies to the S of the centre of Ile Bono which is less sheltered from the W. Chart SHOM *7125* is needed to avoid the drying rocks (drying 0·7m and 0·1m) to the S and a rocky area drying 2·2m off the centre of the beach; landing is not allowed on Ile Bono.

Amenities

The only inhabitants are the lighthouse keepers on Ile-aux-Moines although at one time the islands were the resort of *corsairs*. The old fort at the W end was occupied until 1875 and is worth a visit if for nothing else than the striking views over the archipelago.

In the season a *buvette* is opened on the terrace overlooking the anchorage.

Les Sept Iles looking NNE

Trégastel St-Anne

General

This Trégastel should not be confused with the Trégastel near Primel 13M to the SW.

An open anchorage in a bay with a small and well frequented seaside resort which has more shelter than could be surmised from the chart. There are some visitors' moorings and it would be a pleasant overnight stop or for an interlude on the sandy beaches amongst the strange and attractive rocks, provided there was no N in the wind or appreciable swell.

Data

Charts

Amiralty *3669* (ARCS), *3670* (ARCS), *2668* (SC)
Imray *C34*

Tides

As for Trébeurden or Ploumanac'h.

Tidal streams

In the offing and S of Les Sept Isles the SE-going stream begins at −0435 HW Brest and the NW-going at +0130 Brest with the maximum spring rate of 4¼ knots.

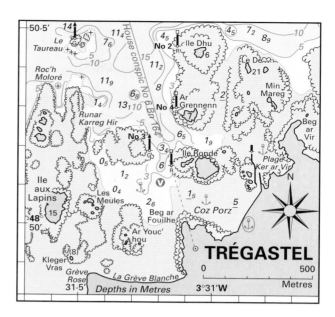

Approach

By day only Navigate to a position 1½M W of Méan Ruz lighthouse and identify the prominent overhanging rock La Pierre Pendue (see photograph). About ¼M W of the rock lies the low

E bay and slip   Ile Ronde   West bay anchorage and moorings

Trégastel St-Anne looking WSW

rocky Ile Dhu and to the W of that Le Taureau beacon. This is on a dangerous rock which dries 4·6m. The beacon marking it is sometimes removed by the winter gales but the base remains in situ. This must be identified before attempting to enter.

Proceed to a position halfway between the red beacon to the W of Ile Dhu and Le Taureau and make 164° on a prominent house in transit with No.6 port beacon (the third port beacon in), allowing for any cross stream. Leave:

Le Taureau N cardinal beacon 300m to starboard
Ile Dhu port beacon (No.2) 100m to port
No.4 port beacon 100m to port
No.3 starboard beacon 50m to starboard
No.6 port beacon to the W of Ile Ronde 50m to port.

Anchorage
The western bay is full of white moorings for locals but outside these is a row of red mooring buoys for visitors. To the S of the last two beacons depths shallow from 6m between them to 1·2m further S. This area is sheltered from the E through S to SW. There are no lights to facilitate a night departure if the wind comes away from the N and the anchorage would be dangerous in these conditions or with any swell from that direction.

The bay to the E of Ile Ronde dries 1·1m and also has many small boat moorings in it.

Facilities
Water By can from the café.
Fuel The nearest garage is at St-Anne ½M inland.

Trégastel St-Anne. La Pierre Pendue from the slip in E bay

Landing There is a slip on the sands.
Restaurants and hotels On the front.
Shops Several including supermarkets at St-Anne.
Leisure The bay is almost completely landlocked at LW and a good place for children where all the more strangely shaped stones have names. There is an interesting little aquarium in caves under a pile of rocks aptly called The Turtles which is topped by a saintly figure in white.

Ile Grande

General
Ile Grande lies 1½M N of Trébeurden and has an anchorage at neap tides for deep draught boats reasonably sheltered all round and particularly from

Ile Grande. Looking S over Ile Grande slipway towards Trébeurden

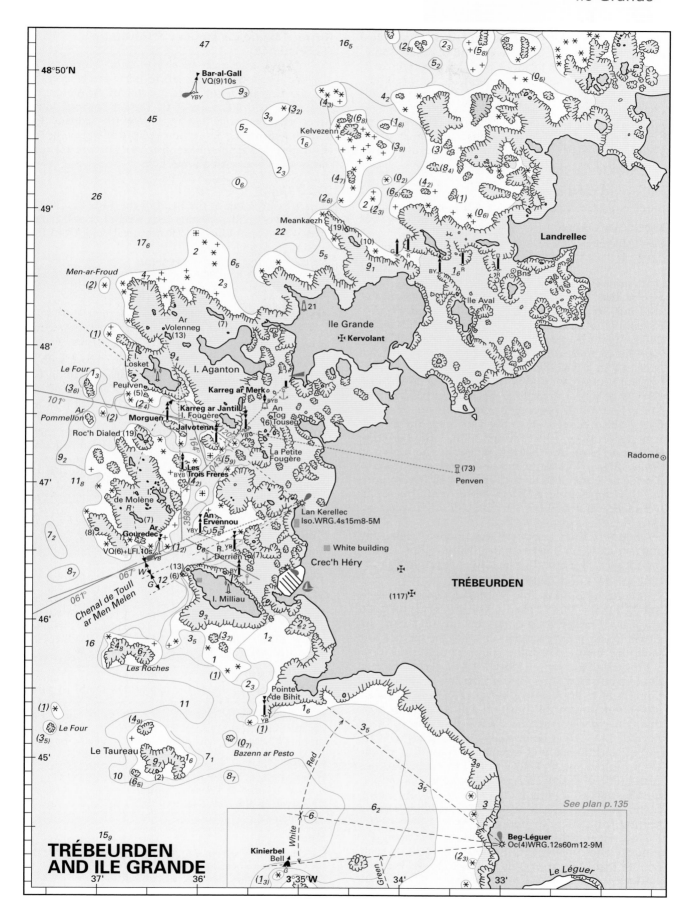

48°50'N

47   16₅   (2₉)   (2₃)   +(5₈)
                                5₂   +
Bar-al-Gall
VQ(9)10s
YBY   9₃   4₃   4₂
45   3₉ (3₂)   (0₅)
       5₂   (6₈)   (1₆)
               Kelvezenn   (3₉)
                1₆   (3)   (8₄)
       26   (4₇)   (0₂)   (4₂)   (1)
49'   22   (2₆) (6₅)   (0₆)
17₆   Meankaezh (19)   Landrellec
        2 +   (10)   G R
Men-ar-Froud 6₅   5₅   9₁   BY   1₆ R
(2)   4₇   2₃   R
       2₃   21   Bns   Ile Aval
    Ar
48'   Volenneg (7)   Ile Grande
       (13)   ⊕ Kervolant
    I.   9₄
Le Four Losket   I. Aganton
1₃
(3₆)   Peulven   Karreg ar Merk
(5)   BYB   An
Ar   (2₄)   Karreg ar Jantill YB   Tog
Pommellon (2) Morguen I. Fougère   (6) Touseg
    Roc'h Dialed (19) Jalvotenn   La Petite   (73)
9₂   (5₉)   Fougère   Penven
11₈   BYB Les   (4₂)
       Trois Frères
    I.   Lan Kerellec
    de Molène R   An   Iso.WRG.4s15m8-5M
7₂   (8) (7) YBY Ervennou 5₃
    Ar   White building
    Gouredec (1₂) 6₈ R YB
VQ(6)+LFl.10s YB Derrien (7) Crec'h Héry   TRÉBEURDEN
8₇   (13)   (117)
       (6)
    Chenal de Toull   I. Milliau
    ar Men Melen 067° W 9₃
061°   G 12   2₂
16   3₅ (3₂) 1₂
    Les Roches 1
       (1)   2₃   Pointe
       de Bihit   1₆
11   YB 3₅
(1)   (1)
Le Four (4₉)   Red   3₉
(3₅)   (0₇)   3₅
    Le Taureau 1₆ 7₁ Bazenn ar Pesto   3
       9₇   3   See plan p.135
10 (6₅) (2)   8₇   6₂
15₉   Beg-Léguer
                     Oc(4)WRG.12s60m12-9M
TRÉBEURDEN   Kinierbel   (2₃)
AND ILE GRANDE Bell   G (0₁)
       (1₃)   3°35'W 34'   33'   Le Léguer
37'   36'

any swell. It is a delightful and still unspoilt area for a family holiday in a bilge keeler and there are some shops, a garage and facilities on the island which is joined by a causeway to the mainland.

Data

Charts

Admiralty *3669* (ARCS), *2668* (SC)
Imray *C34*
SHOM *7124* and *7125* cover the area on a large scale.

Tides and tidal streams

See Trébeurden, Trégastel St-Anne or Ploumanac'h.

Lights and buoys

See Trébeurden. There is a lit approach to Trébeurden but no lights further north.

Approaches

From the S by day Follow the directions for entering Trébeurden by day until the vicinity of An Ervennou W cardinal beacon is reached, leaving it 200m to starboard heading N. This should bring Les Trois Frères E cardinal beacon (NE of Ile Molène) in transit with the E edge of Ile Losket bearing 358°. Follow this line for about ¼M until Karreg ar Jantil S cardinal beacon and Karreg ar Merk E cardinal beacon tower are in line bearing 043°. This line leads in to the anchorage but passes very close to a rock drying 2·2m, and between Karreg ar Jentil and Karreg ar Merk, another rock drying 2·4m. The latter may be avoided by leaving Karreg ar Jentil close to port, then borrowing to port and leaving Karreg ar Merk close to starboard. It would be safer however, to have enough water to clear these two drying rocks.

Once N of Karreg ar Merk beacon tower, select an anchorage in an appropriate depth clear of the moorings to the S of the slip and jetty on the island.

Chenal de Toull ar Peulven

From the N by day It is recommended that either SHOM chart *7124* is used for this passage, or that one leaves rather than enters on the first visit. In either event it is essential that all the marks are identified before becoming committed.

Proceed to a position 1M W of Ile Losket which is flat, steep-sided and has a low building and a number of radio masts on it. Identify Penven water tower which from this position will appear just S of the conspicuous radome. With the water tower bearing 101° it will be in transit with the right-hand end of Ile Fougère and over the grey roof of a long white building with two rows of windows behind the island. Proceed down this transit with any allowance for a set across, leaving Le Four rocks (drying 3·6m) 100m to port and Morguen N cardinal beacon (drying 3·4m) 50m to starboard.

Now steer 120° to pass midway between Ile Fougère and Ar Jalvotenn E cardinal beacon to pick up the transit bearing 043° of Karreg ar Jantil S cardinal beacon and Karreg ar Merk E cardinal beacon tower as above into the anchorage off Ile Grande.

From Chenal de Toull ar Peulven to Trébeurden

Follow the entrance as above until Morguen N cardinal beacon has been left to starboard when pick up the transit on the port quarter of Ar Volenneg just clear of the E edge of Ile Losket bearing 344°; steer 164° on this line to follow the transits for entrance from the S on their reciprocals, leaving An Evennou W cardinal beacon to port before turning on to the Trébeurden approach.

Facilities

Water From a tap at the head of the slip.
Shops Two small supermarkets, a butcher and baker at Kervolant which is 15 minutes' walk from the slip.
Restaurant and café At Kervolant.

Trébeurden

General

Trébeurden is an upmarket seaside resort with a large marina which usually has ample berthing for visitors. The sill at the entrance dries at 2·1m above CD with the least depth in the close approaches drying 1·1m. A yacht drawing 2m will therefore be able to proceed straight in to the marina once there is sufficient water over the sill. The harbour is lit and a night entrance is possible. There is an annual race here from the River Yealm and a close association between the two yacht clubs.

Data

Charts

Admiralty *3669* (ARCS), *2668* (SC)
Imray *C34*
SHOM *7124* (plan)

Tidal

Add 1 hour 5 minutes to the times of HW Brest for the times at Trébeurden and 1 hour 10 minutes to the times of LW Brest. Add 2·0m to the heights of HW Brest for those at Trébeurden and 0·5m to heights of LW.

Tidal streams

Off Le Crapaud buoy in the approaches the SE/E-going stream begins at −0405 HW Brest and the SW/W-going at +0220 Brest both reaching 2 knots at springs. The streams turn some 15 minutes earlier in the channel running N from the NW corner of Ile Milliau.

Lights

Pointe de Lan Kerellec Iso.WRG.4s8-5M 058°-G-064°-W-069°-R-130° Grey tower
Breakwater N head Fl.G.2·5s6m1M White column green top

Buoys

Le Crapaud W cardinal Q(9)15s
Ar Gouredec S cardinal VQ(6)+Fl.10s
S of Ar Evennou beacon port Fl(2)R.6s
N of Ile Milliau starboard Fl(3)G.10s
Roche Derrien port Fl(3)R.10s

Trébeurden. Approaching from SW. Ile Milliau bearing ENE

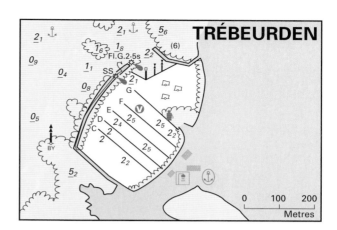

Search and rescue

Trébeurden is in the CROSS Corsen region and the nearest station on the network is Ile de Batz which will respond to calls on Ch 16 or activation of GMDSS on Ch 70. The Sémaphore at Ploumanac'h also keeps watch on Ch 16.

There is an inshore lifeboat kept at Trébeurden.

Weather forecasts

Ile de Batz on Ch 79 at 0515, 0733, 1133, 1603, 1933 LT in French and English.

Daily weather map at the *capitainerie*.

Navtex Corsen (A).

Communications

Bureau du port Ch 9 0600–2400.
Bureau du port ☎ 02 96 23 64 00.

Customs

The nearest office is at Lannion.

Entrance   Waiting buoys and anchorage   Ile Milliau

Trébeurden looking S at LW

Trébeurden marina from NE. Ile Milliau on right

Approaches

By day from the W Navigate to a position 1½M SE of Le Crapaud buoy and keep outside the 20m line at this stage to avoid the outliers of Le Crapaud bank. Make good a track of 065° to leave the distinctive Ile Milliau to starboard. This line leads on Lan Kerellec lighthouse which is a grey tower in the trees and not very conspicuous. When between the NW end of Ile Milliau and Ar Gouredec S cardinal buoy alter to about 080° to leave the red buoy S of An Evennou W cardinal beacon to port. Alter then to about 100° to leave:

> **Men Radenec** S cardinal beacon 100m to port
> A starboard-hand buoy to starboard
> **Roch Derrien** port buoy to port
> **Roch Du-Hont** S cardinal beacon 200m to port.

Steer then for the end of the marina breakwater. Note that there is 1·6m drying and rocky patch 100m WNW of the breakwater end but there will be water to carry over it if the sill can be crossed.

By night from the W Navigate to the SE of Le Crapaud buoy (Q(9)15s) as for by day and make good 065° up the white sector of Pointe Lan Kerellec sectored light (Iso.4s). When Ar Gouredec buoy VQ(6)+Fl.10s is abeam, alter to about 080° to leave the first Fl(2)R.6s buoy to port and enter the green sector of Lan Kerellec light. Steer then about 100° to pass between the Fl(3)G.10s buoy and the Fl(3)R.10s Roc'h Derrien buoy. On passing the latter head for the marina breakwater end Fl.G.2·5s noting the caution above about the rocky patch off it.

By day from the N See the directions for Chenal du Toull ar Peulven under Ile Grande on page 130. The use of this rock strewn and winding route if coming from the N will barely save one mile in distance rather than using the main channel.

Entrance

Call the *bureau du port* on Ch 9 on the approach.

The end of the breakwater is marked by three spindly starboard beacons and there is a 90° turn round them to line up with the gate. This should be taken slowly in case of boats, which may not have masts, leaving. The control lights 100m along the breakwater from the outer end are:

3 reds vertical	Entry and departure prohibited
2 green, 1 white vertical	Entry and departure allowed (1·5m+ over the sill in the gate)

The maintained depths in the marina are from 2·4m near the entrance to 2m towards the S end. The water is retained by a wall which dries 3·8m and the height of the sill in the entrance dries 2·1m above CD. The wall on either sides of the entrance is marked by posts. The entrance is marked by port and starboard beacons and there is a lit depth gauge showing depth over the sill on both sides. The pontoon for visitors is the second one (F) and there appears to be 2·5m along its length.

There is considerable turbulence near the outer ends of the first and second pontoons for up to 10 minutes after the gate is opened. Yachts here should be well secured and movements through the gate should not be attempted during this time.

Moorings

There are a number of moorings to the N of Ile Milliau 10 of which are for visitors. The yellow ones marked 1 to 10 are specifically for those waiting to go into the marina.

Anchorage

Anchor on sand where there is water to the N of Ile Milliau between the moorings and the approach channel. At springs this will be in a position exposed to the W and the whole area is open to any NW swell particularly near HW. There is a slip to land at on Ile Milliau on the N side but beware the rock drying 4·2m just to the N of it marked by a N cardinal beacon.

Facilities

Water and electricity On the pontoons.
Fuel At the fuel berth in the E corner of the marina.
Showers and heads By the marina office.
Launderette Nearby in rue de Trozoul.
Slip and crane Up to 20 tons.
Shops Mostly up the hill in the town; the large supermarket is some distance.
Restaurants and crêperies Some by the marina but more up the hill.

Leisure This is a good place for a family in a bilge keeler. SHOM chart *7124* would allow full use to be made of the area. 3 miles away is the conspicuous radome of the Satellite Telecom Centre where there are guided tours (in French); there is also a modern planetarium on this site with exciting effects and hourly shows ☎ 02 96 91 83 78.

Travel Nearest railway station is at Lannion which connects with the national network. There is a small airfield near Lannion and bus services to there and the rest of France.

Lannion

General

Lannion town lies 4 miles up the narrow and winding Rivière Léguer which dries 5m at the town but carries 0m at CD in the outer entrance channel. There are a number of deeper holes in the river due to dredging so a vessel drawing 2m can enter at LW neaps and find somewhere to lie afloat in the river although Lannion town where it dries 5·5m can only be reached towards HW springs.

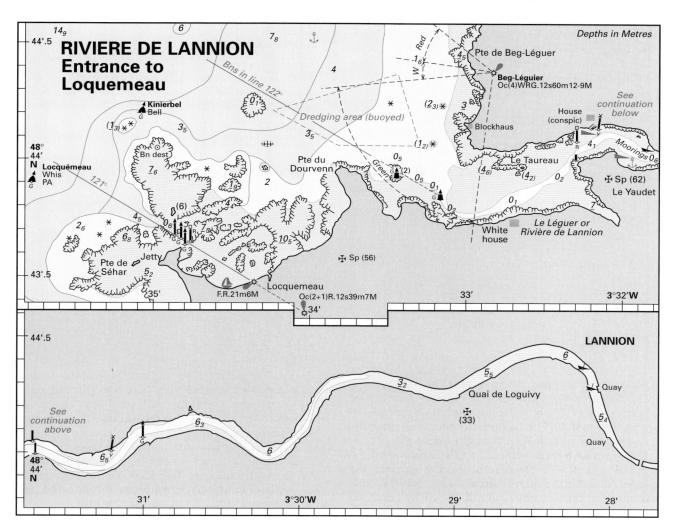

Lannion. The last reach below bridge. Looking downstream from quay on S side

It has an attractive and unspoilt estuary and the river winds through wooded countryside. Lannion is a pleasant country town but few berthing facilities for yachts. There is a quay to berth alongside over HW springs but not to dry out on without a prior recce. The deeper parts of the river have unfortunately been occupied now with moorings but there are still places with enough water to tide over inside the bar.

Warning
Strong westerlies, especially with any N in them will cause the sea to break right across the entrance and entry should not be attempted in these conditions. There is no leading line and the entrance channel shifts in position and width from year to year. That shown on the plan is the result of a run of soundings

in autumn 1999 and was confirmed by SHOM data in 2000.

Data

Charts
Admiralty *3669* (ARCS), *2668* (SC)
Imray *C34*
SHOM *7124* (river plan)

Tides
Add 1 hour 5 minutes to the times of HW Brest for the times of HW at the river entrance; add 1 hour 10 minutes to the times of LW Brest. Add 1·8m to the heights of HW Brest for those at the river entrance and 0·5m to the heights of LW. The flood at Lannion town is not felt until at least 1 hour after it commences at the entrance and the rise is less.

Tidal streams
At Le Crapaud light buoy the SE/E-going stream begins at −0405 HW Brest and the SW/W-going at +0220 Brest. At the river entrance the in-going stream begins at −0600 HW Brest and the out-going at −0045 Brest. The ebb in the river runs for about 7 hours and attains 2½ knots at springs off Le Yaudet; the flood rate does not exceed 2 knots.

Lights
The river is not lit but there is a sectored light just to the N of the entrance which would allow a safe approach to the bay in the dark.
Beg-Léguer Oc(4)WRG.12s60m12-9M 007°-G-084°-W-098°-R-129° West face of white house, red lantern

Search and rescue, weather forecasts, communications
See Trébeurden.

Customs
There is an office in the town.

Approaches and entrance
By day Navigate to a position 2M S of Le Crapaud

Lannion. Lannion river entrance looking E

Lannion entrance looking W. Le Yaudet village and slip left centre

W cardinal buoy (Q(9)15s) and make good 095° on Ben-Léguer light structure which is a white house amongst the trees on the ridge N of the river entrance. This will leave Kinierbel green buoy 400m to starboard. To avoid a drying 0·1m rock patch, continue until the two green beacon towers are open or the W one bears 150° or more and turn towards the W one to leave it 100m to starboard then altering to leave the second one 50m to starboard. Keep about 100m off the S bank until the white house amongst the trees is abaft the beam and slowly turn to head for the slipway and house on the N bank, leaving Le Petit Taureau islet 200m to port and the beacon on the W point close to starboard. The moorings will then show where the channel lies.

By night Navigate to the same position 2M S of Le Crapaud W cardinal buoy (Q(9)15s) when the white sector of Ben-Léguer light should be visible. Stay in this sector steering about 095° and the Locquémeau leading lights (F.R and Oc(2+1)R.12s) will be crossed. Continue, to leave the Kinierbel unlit starboard buoy well to starboard and sound in to a suitable depth to anchor on mostly sand and sheltered from N through E to S.

Anchorage, moorings and berths
1. Between Le Taureau and the W point and SW of the slip before the moorings start.
2. Above the slip, where there is an active sailing school, outside the moorings. Care will have to be taken at the turn of the tide not to foul boats at nearby moorings.
3. In the pool E of Le Yaudet slip in 1·2m+ but

again care will be needed at the turn of the tide.
4. Sound until a pool is found or ask the dredger skipper who will know where they are. It does not appear that any exist above about ½M above Le Yaudet. In some parts the bed of the river is rocky.

Berths
There are three quays projecting from the rough, sloping stone walls that line both sides of the last mile of river. Only one is of any practical use with safety.
1. The old sand dredger jetty at Loguivy on the S bank but not to dry out on as the bottom is very uneven; it is two miles from anywhere.
2. The small jetty on the N bank just before the town. There is the remains of a wreck alongside it which is submerged above half tide and the quay should not be used.
3. A longer jetty above this on the S side and 200m below the first bridge has a reasonable surface, a ladder and a couple of bollards. It might be possible to dry alongside on steep, soft mud but a recce first would be advisable whatever the keel configuration.

Facilities
At Lannion
Water A hydrant on the quay.
Fuel From a garage nearby in the town.
Shops, banks and restaurants There are a number nearby in this large town and a daily outdoor market.

Leisure A yacht drawing 2m should have enough water for a 3 hour run ashore before returning down river. The Place de Centre is flanked by 15th- and 16th-century houses and the 12th-century church at Brévélenez with its granite spire is worth the climb up to it.

At Le Yaudet

Shop There is sometimes a mobile shop in the mornings up the hill from the slip.

Restaurant and crêperie One of each up the hill; the restaurant is in the hotel which is a Logis de France.

Leisure There is a picturesque little church near the hotel with a curious statue of the Virgin Mary in bed with the infant Jesus.

Travel Lannion is on a branch line; buses connect to St-Brieuc, Morlaix and beyond. There is a small airfield nearby.

Locquémeau

General

A small haven which dries entirely but has some alongside drying berths in relative shelter. The few, small fishing boats kept there hardly seem to justify the leading lights and marks which lead in through the very narrow entrance. No facilities apart from a restaurant.

Warning

Not to be contemplated in strong N/NW winds or significant swell.

Data

Charts

Admiralty *3669* (ARCS), *2668* (SC)
Imray *C34*
SHOM *7124* (largest scale)

Lights

Ldg Lts 122° *Front* F.R.21m6M White lattice pylon, red top 068°-vis-228°
Rear Oc(2+1)R.12s39m7M White gabled house, red gallery 016°-vis-232°

Approach and entrance

Locate the starboard-hand unlit Locqémeau buoy

Locquémeau looking NE towards Lannion entrance. N drying side of jetty on left

Leading light structure

Slip, entrance and jetty

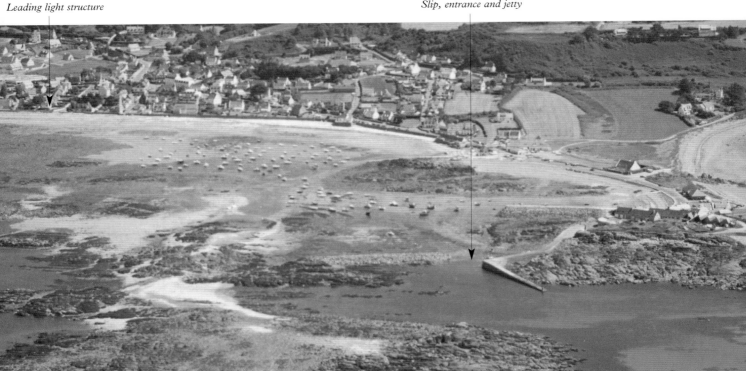

Locquémeau at LW

which has a powerful whistle. From a position just to the N of it identify the leading line 121° and proceed down it. There is 0m CD at the outer starboard beacon and it shallows gradually from there in. The first starboard beacon marks the outer end of the slip/breakwater and the second its elbow and the leading line must be borrowed on to port to leave these two to starboard. As soon as the second is abeam take a jink to starboard to regain the line and pass between the next port and starboard beacons. Continue then until the line of the inner jetty opens up and go alongside on the S side. It has a smooth surface, there are bollards and it dries about 5·5m. The bottom is hard, smooth sand and shingle.

Facilities
Restaurant By the jetty.
Sub post office In the net store.

Locquirec – Toull an Héry

General
An open bay with two small drying harbours, Toull an Héry being about 1M up the Rivière Douron which is crossed by a low bridge above the village. There is a deep water anchorage sheltered from the W to the SE of Pointe de Locquirec.

Data
As for Primel or Lannion. There are no lights. SHOM chart *7124* is the largest scale available.

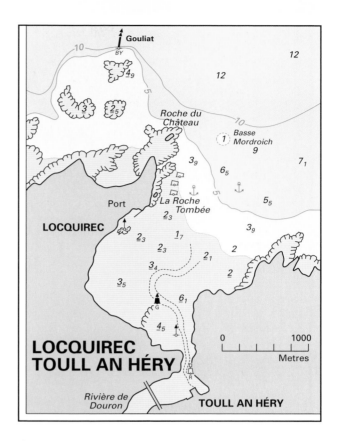

Approaches
Chart *3669* shows the dangers in the offing – Plateaux des Triagoz, Plateau de la Méloine and Le Crapaud to the E off Trébeurden. Closer in Roc'h Gouliat to the N of Pointe de Locquirec (Pointe du

Locquirec. The bay at LW showing run of channel to Toull an Héry

The harbour at Locquirec near LW looking SW

Toull an Héry. The jetty looking N to final beacon on approach

Château) is marked by a N cardinal unlit buoy. The Roche du Château is conspicuous. Steer to leave it 200m to the W to avoid Basse Mordroick with 1m 400m to the E.

Anchorage and mooring

There are 30 moorings to the E of Pointe du Château, 8 for visitors and some in deep water. Either pick one up or anchor to the E clear of them.

If proceeding further in to the bay or to the small port approach on a course of not less than 230° from outside the moorings to avoid rocks drying 3m on the approaches and leave La Roche Tombée (8m) 30m to starboard. The harbour has a short jetty bordered by rocks on the SE side and dries 5m. If there is no swell, it is safe to berth on the inner side of the outer wall or against a wall opposite, which is smooth and has ladders.

Toull an Héry

A very small harbour on the E bank of the river Douron. The channel leading to it is encumbered with sandbanks but is marked by two conspicuous beacon towers and a beacon shown on chart *3669*, plan page 139 and SHOM *7124*. The harbour consists of a jetty with berths on its E side drying 5m. There is only 10m between this jetty and the mud which borders it. The substantial jetty is smooth faced but the bottom is not and a recce before drying out is advisable It would be unwise to enter here without one and on a rising tide (see photograph).

The sand between the jetty and the bridge above it is flat and firm outside the channel.

Facilities
Locquirec
Water Tap on the jetty.
Fuel Garage in the village.
Shops A baker and chemist but light on provision shops.
Tourist office By the harbour.
Toull an Héry
Restaurant and crêperie near the quay. No shops.

Primel

General
A natural harbour open to the N but protected to some extent by a breakwater. It is a busy fishing port with few facilities for yachts but some shops and hotels. There are dangers in the approaches but the entrance is deep and it has a good lit leading line.

Warning
In strong northerlies the sea breaks right across the entrance and entry should not be attempted. A yacht should leave if these are forecast or becoming apparent as there is little shelter inside except possibly behind the breakwater where space will be at a premium.

Data
Charts
Admiralty *2745*, *3669* (ARCS), *2668* (SC)
Imray *C34* (plan)
SHOM *7905* has the same scale and coverage as *2745*.

Tides
Add 1 hour 5 minutes to the times of HW Brest for the times at Primel and 1 hour 10 minutes to the times of LW. Add 1·9m to the heights of HW Brest and 0·5m to the heights of LW Brest for the Primel equivalents.

Tidal streams
About 6M N of Primel the E-going stream begins at −0300 HW Brest and the W-going at +0315 HW Brest. The greatest rate of the E-going is attained at about HW Brest and the W-going at LW Brest spring rates are up to 2½ knots, neap rates up to 1 knot.

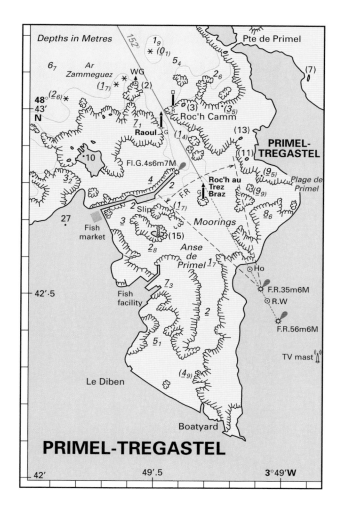

Depths in Metres

48° 43' N

42'·5

42'   49'·5   3°49'W

Ar Zammeguez

WG

Roc'h Camm

Raoul

Fl.G.4s6m7M

PRIMEL-TREGASTEL

Pte de Primel

F.R

Roc'h au Trez Braz

Plage de Primel

Moorings

Anse de Primel

Fish market

Fish facility

Slip

27

Ho

F.R.35m6M

R.W

F.R.56m6M

TV mast

Le Diben

Boatyard

PRIMEL-TREGASTEL

There is a local eddy setting NE during much of the W-going stream outside the entrance between Pointe de Primel and the Roches Jaunes to the W.

Lights

Ldg Lts 152° *Front* F.R.35m6M White pylon with red stripe 134°-vis-168°
   Rear F.R.56m6M White patch on wall, red stripe
Breakwater head Fl.G.4s6m7M White column, green top, on hut

Search and rescue

See Roscoff.

Weather forecasts

See Roscoff.
An inshore lifeboat is maintained at Primel.

Communications

Port radio Ch 9 during working hours.

Approaches

There are three dangers in the outer approaches :

Les Tres Pieds An area of rocks 3 miles to the N which is the western-most extension of the Plateau de la Méloine and marked at the W end by a W cardinal buoy.

Basse Brien A 5·4m patch two miles N of the entrance which should be avoided in a swell.

Le Rater A 4·5m patch 2¼M to the NW with the same restriction in a swell.

By day Pointe de Primel on the NE side of the entrance is prominent. Navigate to a position ½M to the NW of it and align the leading marks on 152° which are:

Pointe de Primel   Roc'h *Fishing boat on*   *Boatyard and*
                  Cramm *leading line*   *chandlers*

Ar Zammeguez (white and green patch)

Primel looking SSE

Ar Zammeguez

Roc'h au Tres Bras   *Pointe de Primel*

Primel looking NNE

Primel. Leading line 152°, just off to the right

1. The white chimney of Réprédou farm.
2. A white pylon with a vertical red stripe which is the front leading light.
3. A large white board with a vertical red stripe.
4. A smaller white pylon with a vertical red stripe which is the rear leading light.

Follow this line closely noting that the submerged dangers lie to port. Leave:

Ar Zammeguez a prominent rock with a green and white patch and a starboard beacon 30m to starboard

Roc'h Camm a port beacon 30m to port
Raoul starboard beacon 20m to starboard
The breakwater end 50m to starboard watching for any vessels leaving at speed.

By night The Chenal de Tréguier leading line (see Morlaix) leads clear of the W end of Les Trepieds and from this alignment the Primel leading line (2F.R) may be picked up. It is visible from 134° to 168°. Follow it closely especially in the later stages and leave the marks above as for daytime. The breakwater end light is Fl.G.4s and note that Roc'h au Trez Braz beacon inside is not lit but may be picked out against the shore lights.

Anchorages

1. Near the leading line outside the breakwater in 9m. Anchor light essential as there can be much fishing boat traffic.
2. To the SE of the outer breakwater as far from it as depths and moorings allow. 2 anchors probably needed to restrict swing.
3. In the vicinity of Roc'h au Trez Braz where depth and moorings allow.
4. If drying out further up the harbour the line Roc'h au Trez Braz beacon and left-hand edge of Pointe de Primel astern leads up.

Moorings

There are 10 visitors' moorings E of Roc'h au Trez Braz in depths that do not dry and these should be used in preference to anchoring.

Berths

The outer stretch of the breakwater as far as the slip is used by fishing boats but a berth may be found here. Ask at the *capitainerie* at the base of the breakwater. This quay is high and a ladder will be needed unless a berth by one of the ladders is available.

Facilities

Water Tap by the freezer building at the root of the breakwater.

Fuel Nearest garage is over 1M away.

Shops A good walk away in Trégastel.

Dinghy landings At the slip on the breakwater, at the small slip on Plage de Primel and at a slip at Le Diben on the W side.

Fish and shellfish Can often be bought from the freezer building.

Boatyard and chandler At the S end of the harbour.

Morlaix

General

Morlaix is one of the largest towns in Brittany and has many historical connections with England. It lies 8 miles up a tidal river the upper reaches of which dry 2·7m and lead to a lock and basin where all the facilities needed by yachts may be found. There are some anchorages in the outer estuary but none particularly snug or close to civilisation although one sheltered from the W is only a mile from the town of Carantec. The last three miles of the river have no navigational lights.

Data

Charts

Admiralty *2745* (plan), *3669* (ARCS), *2668* (SC)
Imray *C35*
SHOM *7905* is on the same scale and coverage as *2745*.

Tides

Add 1 hour to the times of HW Brest for the times at Château de Taureau and 1 hour 5 minutes to the times of LW. Add 1·8m to the heights of HW Brest and 0·6m to the heights of LW. Times at the lock are about 20 minutes later and 0·2m lower.

Tidal streams

North of the Roches Duon the E-going flood begins at −0505 HW Brest gradually changing clockwise to end +0050 Brest. The SSW-going stream begins at +0140 Brest, changing clockwise through W and ending NNW at −0535 Brest. The SE and NW-going streams can attain 2¾ knots at springs.

In the Grand Chenal and the Chenal de Tréguier the in-going stream begins about −0450 Brest and the out-going about +0105 Brest. The spring rates in the Grand Chenal are up to 2½ knots and up to 2 knots in Chenal de Tréguier.

In the Rade de Morlaix the streams are weak and seldom exceed 1 knot. The in-going stream begins at about −0430 HW Brest and the out-going at about +0200 Brest.

In the upper canalised part the stream nearly always runs N.

Lights

Ldg Lts Chenal de Tréguier 190°
Ile Noire *Front* Oc(2)WRG.6s15m11-8M 051°-G-135°-R-211°-G-051° White square tower, red top
    La Lande *Rear* and rear for Chenal de Tréguier. Fl.5s85m23M Obscd by land when bearing more than 204° White square tower, black top
Ldg Lt Canal de Tréguier 176°
Ile Louet *Front* Oc(3)WG.12s17m15/10M 305°-W-244°-G-305° 139°-vis-223° from offshore except where obscured by islands

Buoys

The first buoy S of Château de Taureau is the unlit starboard La Barre de Flot which marks a 0·3m rock. Thereafter:

No.2 port Fl.R.2s
No.3 starboard Fl.G.2s
No.4 port Fl.R.2s
No.5 starboard Fl.G.2s

From the corner at Dourduff inwards the buoys and beacons are all unlit.

Search and rescue

See Roscoff on page 162.

Weather forecasts

See Roscoff. Daily weather map at *capitainerie*.

Communications

Capitainerie de Port de Plaisance on Ch 09, 16 during lock opening hours ☎ 02 98 62 13 14.

Customs

There is a customs officer at Morlaix ☎ 02 98 88 06 31.

Approaches

The principal entrance to Morlaix is the Grand Chenal due N of Penn ar Lann. Chenal Ouest de Ricard branches from it, its transits are not so clear but it is wider and gives more room if beating in, by day only.

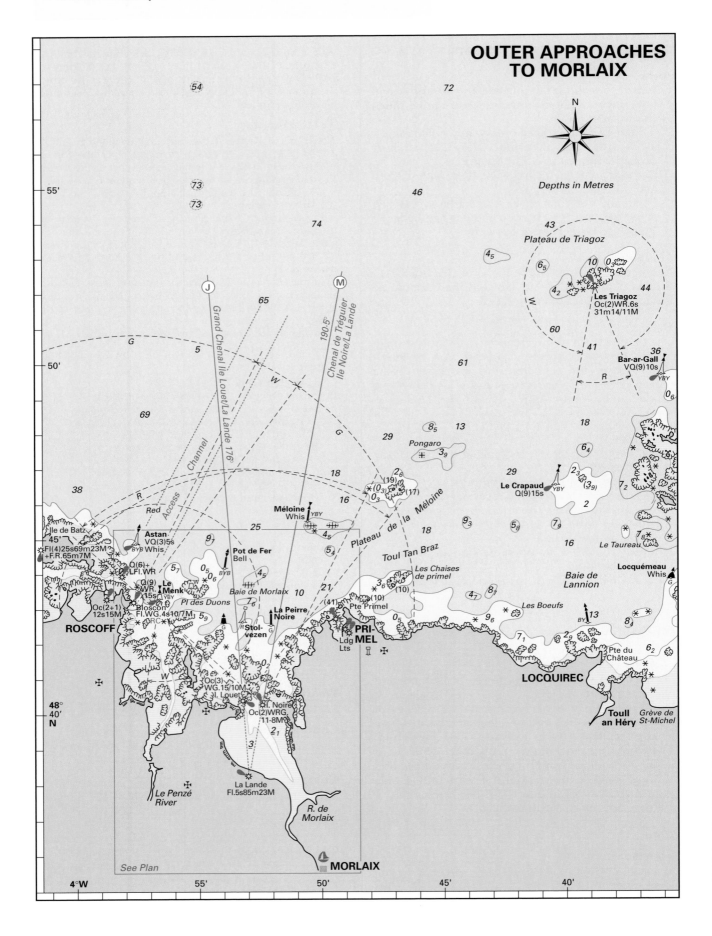

OUTER APPROACHES
TO MORLAIX

N

Depths in Metres

54   72

73   46

73

74   43
                                         Plateau de Triagoz

55'   4₅   6₅   10   0₃
                                                                            44
J   65   M   4₂   Les Triagoz
                                                                Oc(2)WR.6s
                                                                31m14/11M

190.5°   60   41   36
                                                    Bar-ar-Gall
G   VQ(9)10s
50'   YBY
                                                                       0₆
69   61   18

38   29   8₅   13   6₄
                                   Pongaro
                                   3₉   29   2₃   7₂
                               18   Le Crapaud (3₉)
                               16   2₆   Q(9)15s YBY   2
                               (19)   9₃   5₈   7₉   16
Méloine   (0₃) (17)   Plateau de la Méloine   7₅
Whis   YBY   0₃   Le Taureau
Astan   4₅   18
VQ(3)5s   BYB Whis   5₄   Toul Tan Braz   Baie de
25   9₇   Pot de Fer   Les Chaises   Lannion
              Bell   5₇   4₅   de primel   8₇   Locquémeau
Ile de Batz   0₅ 0₆ BYB   3₆   4₇   Whis
Fl(4)25s69m23M   Q(6)+   Baie de Morlaix 10 21 (10) 8₇   Les Boeufs
+F.R.65m7M   LFl.WR   Le   7₆   (41) Pte Primel   9₆ BY 13
         Q(9)   Menk Pl des Duons La Peirre   0₅   8₄
Oc(2+1) WR.   YBY   Noire PRI-   7₁   2₉
12s15M   15s Bloscon   Stol-   MEL   Pte du
         Fl.WG.4s10/7M 5₉ vezen G Ldg   6₂ Château
ROSCOFF   Lts   LOCQUIREC
                          0₂
48°   Oc(3)   Toull   Grève de
40'   WG.15/10M   an Héry St-Michel
N   l. Louet l. Noire
                          Oc(2)WRG
                          11-8M   2₁
                          3
                Le Penzé   La Lande
                River   Fl.5s85m23M
                                   R. de
                                   Morlaix

See Plan   MORLAIX

4°W   55'   50'   45'   40'

Grand Chenal to Rivière de Morlaix (Line J)

By day Navigate to a position 400m E of the Pot de Fer E cardinal buoy which lies about 1M NE of the Roches Duon white beacon tower. From here follow the leading line 176° Ile Louet lighthouse in line with Tour de la Lande, Line J. La Lande is white and just on the skyline at this distance. This leaves the following marks:

Fish farm (not always on station) ½ mile to starboard

Stolvezen port can buoy 200m to port

La Veille starboard beacon tower 800m to starboard

La Fourche starboard beacon 600m to starboard

Le Gouesles a rock painted red and white 200m to port

Le Ricard starboard beacon tower 55m to starboard

La Morlouine starboard beacon tower 50m to starboard

Les Cahers a rock painted red and white 200m to port

Calhic starboard beacon 300m to starboard.

When Calhic bears about 290° leave the leading line and leave:

Le Corbeau starboard beacon tower 100m to starboard

Le Taureau port beacon tower 100m to port.

Then pass midway between Ile Louet and the conspicuous Château de Taureau and steer to pass Barre de Flot starboard buoy to starboard and proceed up the river. If bound for the Penn Lann anchorage leave Barre de Flot buoy well to port.

By night Navigate to keep well clear of the Roches Duon and Plateau de la Méloine to the N which are both unlit, to pick up the leading lights bearing 176° Ile Louet Oc(3)WG.12s17m15/10M in the white sector, and La Lande Fl.5s85m23M. This line is much more visible by night than by day. Follow this line closely as above until just past Calhic beacon tower when the Ile Noire light will change from red to green. Then alter to make good 160° and proceed as for the daylight entry staying in Ile Noire green sector if going to Penn Lann anchorage.

Chenal Ouest de Ricard to Rivière Morlaix (Line K) (See plan page 146)

By day only Proceed as for the Grand Chenal until the fish farm is abaft the beam to starboard. Identify in the bay to the W of Penn ar Lann two small white-painted rocks of the Pierre Carantec in transit with a white wall mark on the shore behind bearing 188° (Line K) and turn down it. Follow this line and leave the following marks:

Stolvezen port buoy 400m to port

La Veille starboard beacon tower 400m to starboard

La Fourche starboard beacon tower 140m to starboard

La Noire starboard beacon 140m to starboard

Ile Noir Château du Taureau Ile Corbeau Louet Penn ar Lann

Morlaix outer estuary looking S

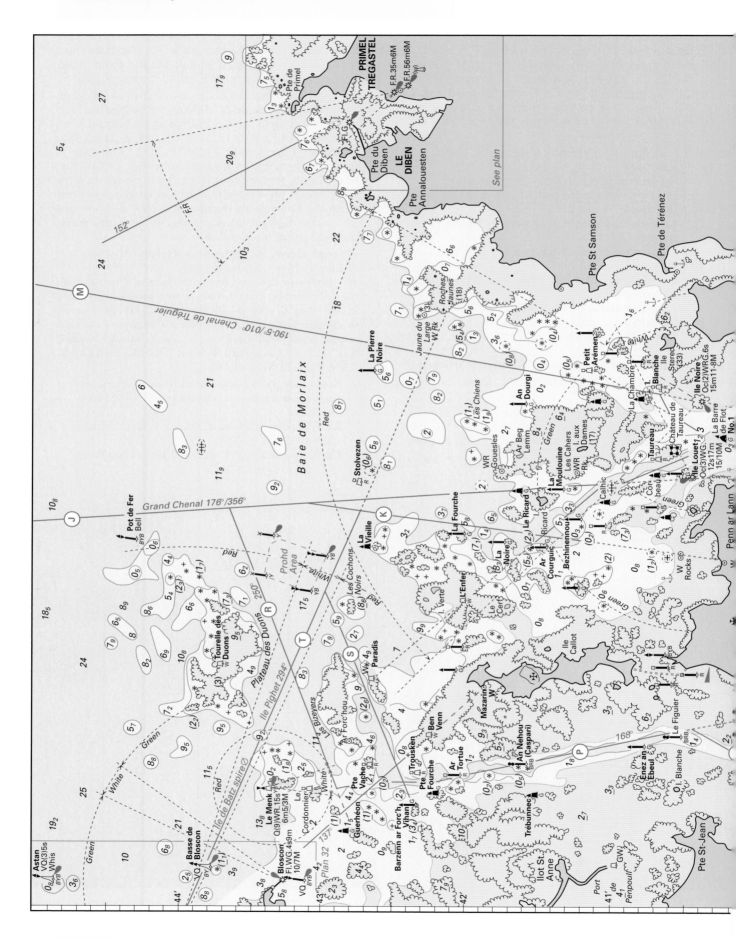

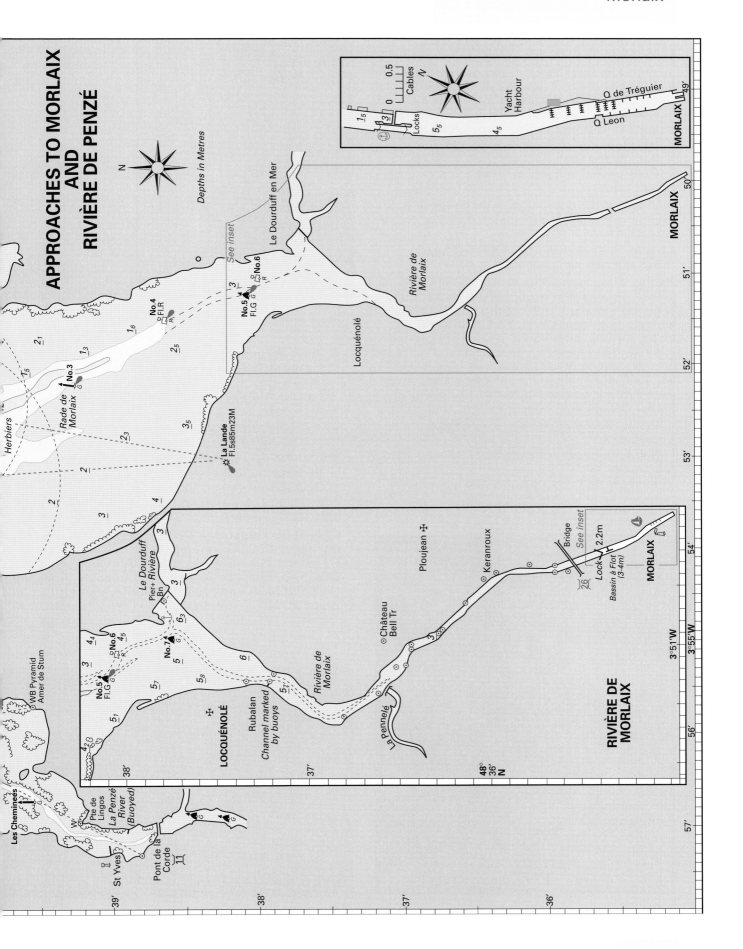

APPROACHES TO MORLAIX AND RIVIÈRE DE PENZÉ

Depths in Metres

N

Inset (Morlaix)

Cables
0   0.5
N
Yacht Harbour
Q de Tréguier
Locks
Q Leon
MORLAIX
49'

Le Dourduff en Mer
See inset
No.4 Fl.R
No.3
Rade de Morlaix
No.5 Fl.G
No.6 R
La Lande Fl.5s85m23M
Rivière de Morlaix
Locquénolé
MORLAIX
50'
51'
52'
53'

Herbiers

RIVIÈRE DE MORLAIX

WB Pyramid
Amer de Stum
No.5 Fl.G
No.6
No.7
Le Dourduff
Pier+ Rivière
Bn
LOCQUÉNOLÉ
Rubalan
Channel marked by buoys
Rivière de Morlaix
La Pennelé
Château Bell Tr
Ploujean
Keranroux
Bridge
See inset
Lock 2.2m
Bassin à Flot (3-4m)
MORLAIX

Les Cheminées
Pte de Lingos
La Penzé River (Buoyed)
St Yves
Pont de la Corde

3°55'W
3°51'W
54'
56'
57'
38'
37'
36'
48° 36' N
39'
38'
37'

147

La Courguic starboard beacon 140m to starboard.

Just before reaching La Courguic alter course to make good 139° to follow the stern transit L'Enfer white beacon tower in line with Le Paradis white beacon tower bearing 319°. At LW Le Paradis is almost hidden by rocks. This line leaves:

Bezhinennou starboard beacon 135m to starboard

Calhic starboard beacon tower 250m to starboard.

As soon as Ile Louet aligns with La Lande again, alter to make good 160° and proceed as for the Grand Chenal.

Chenal de Tréguier to Rivière de Morlaix (Line M) (See plan page 146)

By day This channel should only be used when the tide serves as it contains isolated rocks drying 1m (awash at MLWS). If approaching from the N navigate so as to pass ¼M W of Méloine W cardinal whistle buoy on the W edge of Plateau de la Méloine and identify the leading line of Ile Noire lighthouse, front, white square tower 13m high, and La Lande lighthouse rear, white square tower with black top near the skyline on 190°(Line M). Follow this transit to leave:

Pierre Noire starboard beacon 400m to starboard

Jaune du Large red and white mark on rock 400m to port

Tourghi starboard beacon 400m to starboard

Morlaix. Château du Toureau and Ile Louet looking E

Petit Arémen port beacon 200m to port
Grand Arémen starboard beacon tower 200m to starboard
La Chambre starboard beacon tower 50m to starboard.

Skirt La Chambre at this distance to align it and Petit Arémen beacon astern on 031° and make good the reciprocal 211° to leave:

Ile Blanche port beacon tower 200m to port
Ile Noire lighthouse 300m to port.

This line leads close to La Barre de Flot the first buoy leading upriver.

Chenal de Tréguier to Rivière de Morlaix

By night Navigate to keep well clear of Roches Duon and Plateau de la Méloine which are both unlit to pick up the leading lights front Ile Noire Oc(2)WRG.6s11-8M in the red sector, and rear La Lande Fl.5s23M and align them on 190° (Line M).

Morlaix basin looking NW

Mobile walkway   Bureau du port   Lock

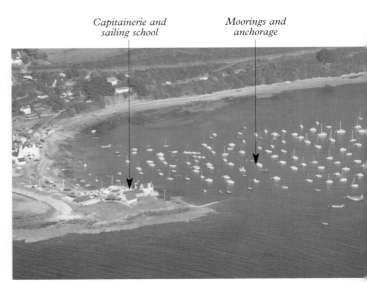

Capitainerie and sailing school   Moorings and anchorage

Morlaix. Térénez looking SE

When between La Chambre starboard beacon tower and Ile Blanche, Ile Louet Oc(3)WG.12s on the starboard bow will turn from white to green. At this point alter to make good 215° for La Barre de Flot buoy which is unlit leaving Ile Noire light 300m to port.

Anchorages

1. The popular spot for yachts is between La Barre de Flot buoy and Penn ar Lann in a depth of choice of 9m or less. This is well sheltered from the W but not from other quarters especially at high water. It is difficult to creep in far enough to get out of the stream. There are sometimes mooring buoys laid here which are ostensibly for visitors. There is a dinghy landing at all states of the tide at the NE corner of Penn ar Lann. From here a footpath climbs the hill and it is then a mile further to the town of Carantec which has shops and facilities.

2. In settled weather and neap tides an anchorage may be found near Pierre de Carantec.

3. In easterly weather and neaps there is an anchorage close S or SW of Pointe de Térénez one mile to the E of Ile Noire where there is about 2·1m at neaps. There is a busy sailing school and a port office at Térénez with some drying moorings for visitors. An anchorage between here and Pointe St-Samson is another alternative. There are two cafés and a restaurant ashore, a water tap but no shops.

4. In the Rade de Morlaix between La Barre de Flot and Dourduff it is possible to anchor in good holding on either side of the fairway but there is no reasonable landing for dinghies near LW. An anchor light should be exhibited at night. Alternatively leave the main channel to the W of No.2 buoy and anchor in the Mouillage des Herbiers (see chart 2745). Anchoring is prohibited in the channel above Dourduff.

Waiting berth   *Waiting berth*

Morlaix. The lock (on the right) from downstream

Rade de Morlaix and the upper river

From Penn ar Lann and La Barre de Flot No.1 starboard buoy the channel in the Rade de Morlaix is wide and deep shallowing from 24m to 2m by No.4 buoy. Inward from here it shallows quickly to drying at CD by No.5 buoy. The alignment of the E side of Château de Taureau and the W side of Ile Ricard on 336°/156° leads down the centre of Rade de Morlaix. From No.5 buoy it shallows progressively to drying 2m by Locquénolé and in general this depth is held to the lock although shallower patches drying 3·6m may be encountered.

The course up the Rade de Morlaix of 156° should be continued from No.5 buoy until the next buoyed channel of 220° is opened up leading towards Loquénolé. From here it is well marked by buoys and beacons until the final stretches when conspicuous transit posts indicate the channel and should be closely kept to. The buoys are all on the edge of the deep channel but some of the beacons are set back from it.

Morlaix looking upstream from the bend above Locquénolé

Morlaix. Alternative waiting berth below lock on W bank, looking downstream. Bridge clearance 26m

Navigation at night above Dourduff is not allowed unless fitted with a searchlight with an effective beam of at least 200m.

Entrance

The lock is 63m long, 16m wide, the lower sill dries 2·2m and the upper sill 3·1m above CD. Vessels of draughts up to 3m at neaps and 4m at springs can be accepted. The gate opens three times each HW – 1½ hours before, at HW and 1 hour after. The tide gauge outside shows the depth over the lower sill. The bridge below the lock has a clearance of 26m at MHWS and not as on chart *2745*; the power line shown on this chart has been removed. Whilst waiting for the gates to open, go alongside the quay on the W side, about 150m from the lower gate. Yachts may safely dry out in this position, but not nearer to the lock where there are rocks which dry. The aggregate jetty below this quay is a better place to go alongside provided it is not occupied by coasters. The best place to dry out is below the weir alongside the east side of the old entrance which is smooth, has two ladders and a soft mud bottom.

When locking through do not be in a hurry to let warps go and proceed. There will be interaction between fresh water from inside and salt water from outside which can cause considerable turbulence which takes a minute or two to subside.

Berths

Depths in the basin which is over ½ mile long vary from 2·4m to 5·4m alongside the quays. At the southern end are the pontoons of the marina. The basin narrows appreciably towards the southern end and large yachts may find some difficulty in turning round if they progress too far in. There is a mobile walkway across the basin halfway down it. There are some 180 pontoon berths and 40 at the quays; maximum length on the pontoons 12m; 30 berths

for visitors. The arrival berth where one should first go to unless directed otherwise, is alongside the W bank before the *bureau du port*.

Facilities

Water From the base of the pontoons (use own hose).

Fuel Pumps on the quay opposite the *bureau du port*.

Showers and heads By the *bureau du port*.

Ice From the *bureau du port*.

Launderette Close by; ask at the *bureau du port*.

Provisions The main shopping centre is beyond the end of the basin under the viaduct. Morlaix is a large town able to provide every possible service.

Hotel and restaurants Many in the town.

Boatyard, chandlers and repairs All is possible. Ask initially at the YC or *bureau du port*. A good place to lay up ashore or afloat. The water in the basin appears to be largely fresh.

Yacht club On the E side of basin; welcomes visitors.

Travel There is a good train service to Roscoff, Brest and Paris with connections to St-Malo and Dinard. Similar bus services. The nearest airport is at Ploujean just outside Morlaix, also at Brest and Dinard. See Roscoff for details of ferries from there.

Historical

In Roman times there was a fortress and the town was called Mons Relaxus and in the Middle Ages it was an important port and shipbuilding town. There were many warlike exchanges with the English. The Fontaine des Anglais on the east bank of the river marks the place where in 1522, 600 English who had disembarked to attack the town were surprised while asleep and killed. They had arrived to find all the inhabitants away at a fair and had helped themselves to all they wanted, especially wine. This is commemorated in the Morlaix coat of arms by the lion facing the English leopard above the legend *S'ils te mordent, mords-les* – If they bite you, bite them.

Ten years later the town was actually captured and for some time occupied by the English but in 1542 the merchants of the town built the Château de Taureau to discourage any further raids.

Rivière de Penzé
Penzé, Carantec and Pen Poul

General

A narrow river, 8 miles from the outer approaches to the town of Penzé which can only be reached after passing a bridge with 11m air clearance; the channel above this bridge dries but is navigable on the tide to Penzé town. Carantec is an attractive town below the bridge and half way up the estuary which is given over to the cultivation of oysters and shellfish. Above Carantec there are now a number of moorings but room can be found to anchor.

Data

Charts

Admiralty *2745, 3669* (ARCS), *2668* (SC)
Imray *C35*
SHOM *7095* is to the same scale and coverage as *2745*

Tides

Add 1 hour to the times of HW Brest for those off Carantec and 1 hour 5 minutes to the times of LW. Add 1·9m to the heights of HW Brest and 0·6m to the heights of LW for those off Carantec.

Tidal stream

The in-going flood begins at about −0450 HW Brest and the out-going ebb at +0105 Brest; the spring rate does not exceed 2½ knots.

Lights

See Roscoff and Morlaix for lights in the approaches otherwise there are no lights or lit buoys in the estuary.

Approaches
From the N to Le Figuer (off Carantec)
(Line P) (See plan page 146)

Leave Basse de Bloscon N cardinal buoy close to the W and proceed S until Bloscon pierhead is 100m to starboard. From here the leading marks Ben Venn, a white pyramid, and Mazarin a white beacon tower on the N end of Ile Callot will be in transit 137°. Follow this leaving:

Guerhéon starboard beacon tower 250m to starboard
Le Cordonnier, a rocky patch drying 1m 100m to port with port beacon tower beyond. This line passes within 150m of two rocks drying 1m and close to one rock drying 0·6m.

After passing Guerhéon beacon look for the river leading line. This is Roc'h Pighet bottle-shaped white pyramid in line with Amer de Stum black and white day mark bearing 168° (Line P on plan page 146–7). These lines may be difficult to see at this distance and if not identified align Ar Tortu port beacon with Caspari BRB beacon on 170°

The following marks should then be left as shown:

La Petite Vache red beacon tower 400m to port
Barzen green beacon tower 250m to starboard
Trousken red beacon tower 200m to port
La Petite Fourche green beacon tower 150m to starboard
La Tortue red beacon tower 20m to port (But note that if beating in there is an alternative course leaving the beacon well to starboard avoiding, if necessary the small rock 180m to the NE with 0·8m)
Caspari isolated danger beacon close either side but alter in time to avoid the rock 0·5m close N of the beacon and the two drying 0·3m close SW of it
Enèz Ebel green beacon (ENE of Pointe St-Jean) 150m to starboard
Le Figuer isolated danger beacon 50m either side.

The channel is also indicated by withies marking the oyster beds. Most of these cover at half tide but are not robust enough to cause damage if hit.

See below if proceeding beyond Le Figuer.

de la Corde *Pointe de Lingos,*
und bend *Port* *leading line just*
ehind trees *buoy* *open right*

Starboard beacon

Rivière de Penzé looking SSW towards St-Yves

From the E, or Morlaix to Le Figuer

By day only Navigate to a position just to the N of La Vieille starboard beacon tower at the N end of Grand Chenal and Chenal Ouest de Ricard. From here there are three routes to follow, none of which is difficult but the first and shortest carries the greatest risk.

1. *S of Les Grandes Fourches*

   From La Vieille make good 245° on Ben Venn white beacon tower until La Verte (12m) islet bears 105° when put it astern on a course of 285°. Leave Les Grandes Fourches group of rocks (7m) 150m to starboard and when Trousken port beacon tower bears 230° alter to 210° to leave La Tortue red beacon close to port. This passes close to a 0·8m patch and a drying 1·1m rock. Then proceed as above up the river.

2. *Between Les Grandes Fourches and Les Bizeyers (Line S)*

   From 400m N of La Vieille proceed along the transit Notre Dame de Bon Secours spire on Ile Batz and the white pyramid on Ile Pighet 294° (Line T) until Barzen starboard beacon bears 248° and turn down this track making adjustment for any cross set to hold the track. This will leave:

   Les Cochons Noirs group of rocks drying 8·6m to port

Les Bizeyers group of rocks (3·1m) to starboard
Paradis white beacon tower to port
Les Grandes Fourches group of rocks (7m) to port
Petite Vache port beacon tower to starboard
Trousken red beacon tower to port.

   After passing Trousken and before reaching Barzen beacon identify the river leading line 168° (Line P) and turn down it. This track passes over a drying 0·3m rock S of Les Bizeyers.

3. *N of Les Bizeyers (Line R)*

   From N of La Veille proceed along the transit Notre Dame de Bon Secours spire on Ile de Batz and the white pyramid on Ile Pighet 294° (Line T) until Guerhéon starboard beacon tower bears 250° and turn towards it to make good this track. Shortly after passing Le Cordonnier port beacon tower to starboard identify the river leading line 168° and turn down it. If this line cannot be identified align La Tortue red beacon and Caspari BRB beacon on 170° and proceed.

Inwards from Le Figuer to Pont de la Corde (Line Q) (See plans pages 146 and 147)

When Le Figuer is abeam alter course to about 200° for 600m, then to 210° to follow the leading line Q (plan 146–147) of a small bottle-shaped white pyramid on Pointe de Lingos and a white rectangular mark on a wall at St-Yves. This line,

Ile Callot   Château du Taureau

Slip and jetty below Carantec town

Entrance to Morlaix

Rivière de Penzé. Carantec looking ESE

Jetty and sailing school on Ilot St-Anne

Causeway to Pen Poul and St-Pol de Leon

Rivière de Penzé. Pen Poul looking SSW

leading on the SE side of the channel, should leave Les Cheminées green beacon 100m to starboard.

On passing Les Cheminées leave the leading line and steer between the first of the buoys. Thereafter the channel is marked by small port and starboard plastic buoys many of whose can and conical topmarks have been knocked off by the oyster boats. There is a least depth of about 0·9m (2·1m at MLWS) from Pointe de Lingos as far as the old ferry slips.

There are numerous moorings between Les Cheminées and Lingos but room to anchor clear of them. There is better shelter further up to the SW of

Lingos pyramid in 2m or just S of the old ferry in about 1m, mud. There are landing hards at each side of the river on the ferry slips at all states of the tide. The noise of the traffic passing over the bridge may be obtrusive if close to.

Pont de la Corde to Penzé Town

The clearance below this bridge is 11m (not 15m as shown on chart *2745*). The river winds through attractive rural surroundings for 5 miles to the town of Penzé. There are occasional buoys and beacons to assist. The railway bridge 2 miles above Pont de la Corde appears to have at least 30m under it and

Rivière de Penzé. The slip at Carantec

Rivière de Penzé. The jetty on W side at Penzé town looking downstream from town bridge

Rivière de Penzé. The railway bridge between Penzé town and Pont de la Corde looking downstream. The channel passes through the right-hand arch

the main channel runs close E of the central pier; port and starboard marks are painted on the piers. 1M above this bridge, the main channel is the E branch which leads to Penzé.

There are some drying moorings just below the town bridge. Do not dry out at the quay on the E side which has a rough and uneven bottom. The quay on the W side has a flat and unobstructed bottom, a smooth surface and two ladders and dries 5m. There is a slip here accessed through the car park (see photograph).

Carantec

Access to Carantec is via a stone jetty and slip below the town and by two yacht yards. The slip dries about 4·6m and bilge keelers can dry alongside (see photograph).

Pen Poul

Pen Poul is a drying bay below St-Pol de Leon with a slip and a hard. The approach is from Caspari beacon on a transit of a green and white beacon at the end of Ilot St-Anne slip, another green beacon and a gatehouse on the shore bearing 230°. There is

Rivière de Penzé. Looking W from Carantec anchorage. Sunset over Kreisker, and Pol de Leon twin spires

a busy sailing school on Ilot St-Anne. It is possible to dry out alongside the outer end of the slip/jetty on the Ilot on its W side where it dries about 4m. The approach dries 3·5m and the rest of the bay which is all flat sand up to 5·5m.

Facilities
Penzé
Shops and restaurants Usual selection of a large village. At St-Yves there is a restaurant on the main road above Pont de la Corde but no shops.
Carantec
Shops and restaurants A good selection up in the town.
Leisure Ile Callot is accessible below half tide from Carantec by the Passe des Moutons (see below).
Pen Poul
The village, which is a good walk from Ilot St-Anne has few facilities and it is a further walk up the hill to the town of St-Pol de Léon.

Historical
On the Ile de Callot stands the pilgrimage chapel of Notre Dame des Victoires, founded in the 6th century to commemorate a victory over Norse pirates. On 15 August each year seamen from the surrounding districts come to pay their devotions.

St-Pol de Léon is an ancient cathedral town which lies about one mile E of the landing at Pen Poul. It has played a leading part in the history of Brittany. Its name is a corruption of St-Paul Aurelian, the first missionary who came from Wales in AD 530. The cathedral is entirely medieval and its twin spires are one of the most distinctive landmarks of the district. Close to the S of the cathedral is the thin spire of Kreisker, 79m high which was built to be the tallest in France, but was subsequently out-built by others.

Ile de Batz
Chenal de l'Ile de Batz

General
As with Ile de Bréhat, the island is very pleasant in the early morning or late evening when the tourists are on the mainland. Most of the island is given over to market gardening and the produce shipped to the mainland. A sheltered harbour for those able to take the ground but only at neaps can deep keeled yachts get far enough out of the channel to avoid most of the stream.

The Chenal Ile de Batz is narrow and unlike the rest of the coast, has few good leading marks and no leading lights. The stream exceeds 3 knots at springs. However there is no great difficulty in transiting provided the visibility is adequate, it is after half tide and there is sufficient water to cover the dangers. It is a useful short cut when going to and from Bloscon and Morlaix.

Data
Charts
Admiralty *2745, 3669* (ARCS), *2668* (SC)
Imray *C35* (plan)
SHOM *7095* is same scale as *2745* but includes a plan of Roscoff harbour and immediate approaches.

Tides
Add 55 minutes to the times of HW Brest and 1 hour to the times of LW to find the equivalent times at Ile de Batz. Add 1·8m to the heights of HW Brest and 0·5m to the heights of LW Brest for the Ile de Batz equivalents.

Tidal streams
In the channel the E-going stream begins at −0435 HW Brest and the W-going begins at +0110 HW Brest. Both streams can reach 3¾ knots in the narrows.

Lights
From W to E (see also under Roscoff)
Ile de Batz Fl(4)25s69m23M F.R.65m7M 024°-vis-059°. Grey tower, black lantern
Ile aux Moutons slip end VQ(6)+LFl.10s S cardinal beacon
Roscoff pier end F.Vi.5m1M White and purple column
Ar-Chaden Q(6)+LFl.WR.15s14m8/6M 262°-R-290°-W-293°-R-326°-W-110°. S conical on masonry tower
Men Guen Bras Q.WRG.14m9-6M 068°-W-073°-R-197°-W-257°-G-068°

Buoys (Off the E approach)
Astan E cardinal VQ(3)5s Whis
Basse de Bloscon N cardinal VQ

Search and rescue
See under Roscoff. An all-weather lifeboat is maintained at Ile de Batz. It is housed at the W end of Kernoch breakwater.

Weather forecasts, communications
See under Roscoff.

CHENAL DE L'ILE DE BATZ

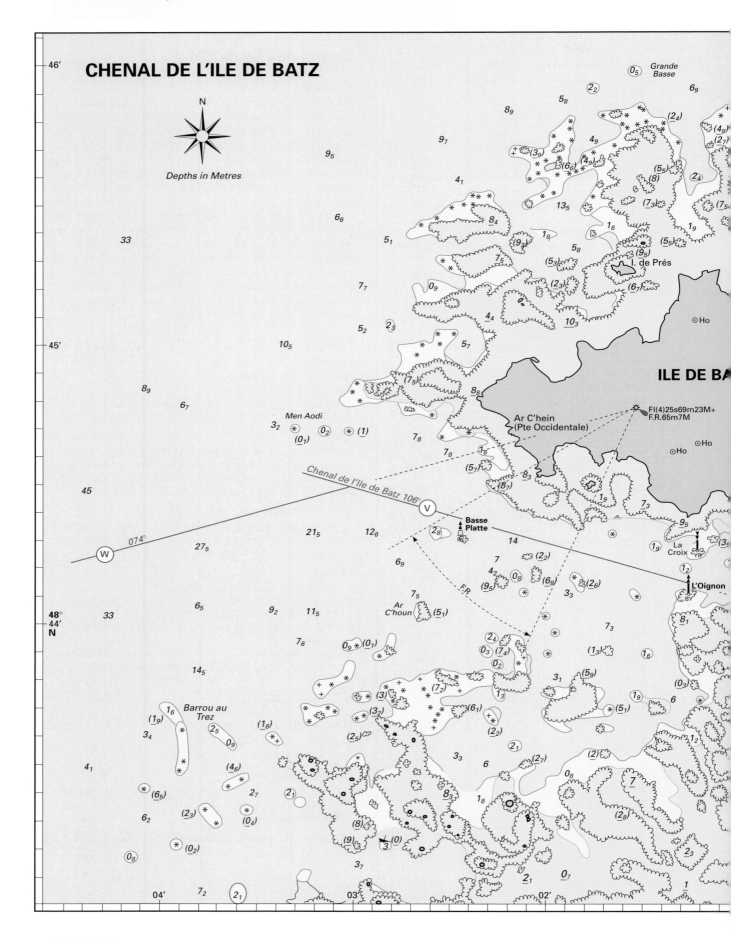

Depths in Metres

Men Aodi

Chenal de l'Ile de Batz 106°

Ar C'hein
(Pte Occidentale)

Fl(4)25s69m23M+
F.R.65m7M

I. de Prés

ILE DE BA

Basse
Platte

La
Croix

L'Oignon

Ar
C'houn

Barrou au
Trez

Grande
Basse

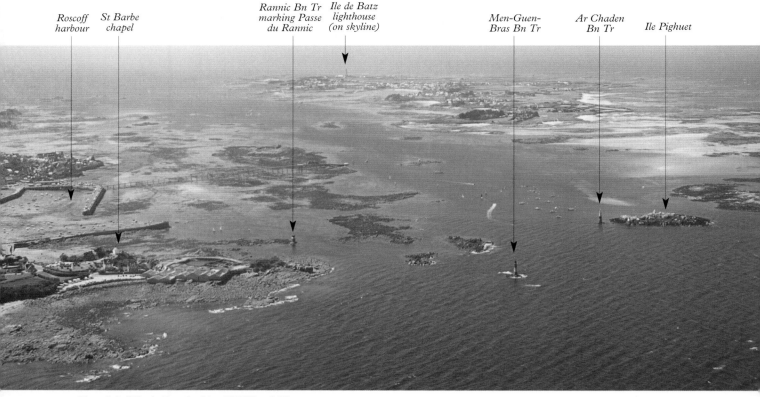

Roscoff harbour   St Barbe chapel   Rannic Bn Tr marking Passe du Rannic   Ile de Batz lighthouse (on skyline)   Men-Guen-Bras Bn Tr   Ar Chaden Bn Tr   Ile Pighuet

Chenal de l'Ile de Batz looking WNW at LW

Men-Guen-Bras   Roscoff church   Ar Chaden   Ile Pighuet

Entering Chenal de l'Ile de Batz from the E

Approaches
Chenal de L'Ile de Batz from the W (Lines V and U)

By day only The visibility limitation for safe transit of this channel is ¾M. In less than this the next mark may not be seen from the previous one.

Approaching from the N, keep over 0·8M from Pointe Occidentale on Ile de Batz and outside the 20m line until Basse Plate N cardinal beacon tower bears 110°, then steer to leave it 100m to starboard. Care should be taken during the E-going flood stream not to be set in to the rocks at the W end of Ile de Batz.

Approaching from the W, keep Ile de Batz lighthouse bearing about 075° until Basse Plate N cardinal beacon tower bears 110° and it can be left 100m to starboard.

From here make good 106° along Line V which is formed by Le Loup, a small steep rock with a white patch on its N end in transit with St-Barbe, a white pyramid just to the S of the conspicuous St-Barbe chapel. If the line cannot be identified steer to pass between La Croix S cardinal beacon and L'Oignon N cardinal beacon leaving a group of rocks the highest of which dries 9·5m and the nearest of which dries 2·2m, 150m to starboard. When between L'Oignon and La Croix beacons, alter to port to

Inner harbour *Roscoff harbour* *End of ferry pier* *Chapel of St Barbe* *Rannic Bn Tr* *Ar Chaden Bn Tr*

Chenal de l'Ile de Batz looking NW at LW

Porz Kernock jetty *Ile aux Moutons jetty*

Ile de Batz harbour looking N at LW

St Barbe chapel   *Leading marks in line 106°. Rear – white pyramid. Front – Le Loup rock*

Entering Chenal de l'Ile de Batz from the W

090° on Per Roch cardinal beacon tower leaving:

Tec'hit Bihan N cardinal beacon 200m to starboard

Malvoch S cardinal beacon tower and Ile aux Moutons S cardinal beacon about 300m to port.

When the latter bears 000°, alter to port to 080° on Pen ar Cleguer the southernmost tip of Ile de Batz. This will pass between two rocks one drying 0·8m which should not present a hazard above half tide.

When An Oan S cardinal beacon comes into line with Ile Pighet white pyramid on 100° alter to follow this line (Line U) leaving Per Roch N cardinal beacon tower 100m to starboard.

When about equidistant from Per Roch and An Oan, alter to leave An Oan 80m to port. Then head for the purple beacon on the end of the long and spindly Roscoff/Batz ferry pier, leaving it 50m to starboard.

Next steer to leave Duslen (An Dreuz Lenn) S cardinal beacon about 50m and Duslen white tower 110m to port. When Duslen is abeam, steer towards Ar Chaden S cardinal lighthouse, leaving Roc'h Zu N cardinal beacon 100m to starboard and finally Ar Chaden lighthouse 30m to port.

Steer hence to leave Basse de Bloscon N cardinal buoy 150m to starboard then, if bound E or for Morlaix bring the white beacon tower on Ile Pighet in transit astern with Notre Dame de Bon Secours bearing 294° (if visible over the trees) (Line T). Make good 113° to follow this line which leads S of the fish farm prohibited area. Then pick up the leading lines for the Chenal Ouest de Ricard or the Grand Chenal for Morlaix (Lines J or K).

If bound for Rivière de Penzé or Carantec, steer to make good 165° with Guerhéon starboard beacon tower fine on the starboard bow until the two beacon towers Ben Venn and Mazarin on Ile de Callot come into line bearing 136° and follow it until Petite Vache port beacon tower bears 045°. This avoids a rock drying 0·2m to starboard. Then turn to starboard and steer 235° to reach the leading line for the Penzé river – Roc'h Pighet and Amer de Stum black and white day mark on 168° (Line P). This track passes close to rocks awash or drying 1m ie covered 0·2m MLWS, 2·4m MLWN.

Chenal de L'Ile de Batz from the E

By day only The minimum visibility for a safe transit is ¾M as the next marks may not been seen from the previous in less.

The approach from the E may be:

a. **From the NE** between Roches Duon and Astan (see plan page 156–157)

b. **From the ESE and the Grand Chenal to Morlaix**, between Roches Duon and the dangers to the S of them by following the line: Ile Pighet white pyramid in line with Notre Dame de Bon Secours spire (if visible over the trees) bearing 294° Line T on plan page 156–157). This line passes S of the fish farm prohibited area.

c. **From the SSE and the Rivière de Penzé**, from a position in which Trousken port beacon tower bears about S ½M make good 317° to carefully follow the stern transit of the white beacon towers Ben Venn and Mazarin on the Ile de Callot (leaving rocks drying up to 1m 100m on either side) until Guerhéon beacon tower bears 180°, then steer to leave Basse de Bloscon N cardinal pillar buoy 150m to port to proceed along Line T as above.

In all the above cases, having reached a position about 150m E of Basse de Bloscon buoy, identify Ar Chaden lighthouse (S cardinal) and approach it on a bearing of about 295° (see plan page 156–157). This line leaves Men-Guen Braz lighthouse (N cardinal) 250m to port.

Steer to pass 50m S of Duslen (An Dreuz Lenn) S cardinal beacon and 120m S of the white beacon tower of the same name, leaving:

Ar Chaden lighthouse about 50m to starboard
Roc'h Zu N cardinal beacon 100m to port.

When Duslen S cardinal beacon is abeam alter course for the trumpet-shaped purple and white beacon at the end of the long, spindly ferry pier. Pass close to this beacon and alter course again to leave An Oan S cardinal beacon 80m to starboard.

When An Oan is on the starboard quarter align it astern with the white Ile Pighet beacon bearing 100° and steer 280°. Do not overshoot this transit, and leave Per Roch N cardinal beacon tower 100m or less to port.

To avoid the rock drying 0·8m which may be a danger at half tide or below, when Ar Porlos Treaz N cardinal beacon bears 160° steer 262° for L'Oignon N cardinal beacon with due allowance for tidal stream. This will leave:

Ile aux Moutons ferry slipway S cardinal beacon and **Malvoch** S cardinal beacon tower 300m to starboard
Tec'hit Bihan N cardinal beacon 300m to port
La Croix S cardinal beacon 200m to starboard.

Just before reaching L'Oignon which is left to port, pick up the stern transit of Le Loup a small steep rock with a white patch painted on its N end and St-Barbe white pyramid just S of the conspicuous chapel of the same name bearing 106° (Line V). Follow this transit out on 287° to leave the Basse Plate N cardinal beacon tower and the rocks before it to the S of the track all to port.

If bound N, follow this line for a further mile to clear the dangers on the W side of Ile de Batz, particularly if the stream is setting E on to them.

If bound W, put Ile de Batz lighthouse on a bearing of 074° and make good 254° which track clears all dangers for the next 10M.

Anchorages

Anchorage is prohibited because of cables in an area between Clocher de Roscoff, Roscoff ferry pier and Pen ar Cleguer the SE point of Ile de Batz. This is shown on chart 2745 and plan page 156–157. Apart from this restriction one can anchor anywhere where there is water in the Chenal but the tidal streams are strong and it will be uncomfortable in a weather-going stream. There are two possible areas to anchor in deep water and a good drying area in Porz Kernock:

1. Between Ar Chaden lighthouse and Duslen beacons as far N as depth will allow. At springs it may be necessary to stay in deep water and strong streams but at neaps it is possible to find a more sheltered position northward clear of the rocks shown on chart 2745. This is uncomfortable in northerly weather near HW. There are some mooring buoys in this area.

2. SW of Malvoch beacon tower (avoiding the 0·1m rock shown on chart 2745) or S of Ile aux Moutons and E of the causeway at neaps. These can be uncomfortable in fresh westerlies and there are a number of moorings in the area much used by fishermen.

3. In Porz Kernock if able to take the ground. A large area of the harbour has been cleared of rocks to make an excellent and fully protected anchorage for those that can dry out. With sufficient water, leave the Ile aux Moutons S cardinal beacon marking the end of the causeway 15m to starboard and steer NNW to leave the white pyramid on Ile Kernock 50m to port, taking care to avoid a number of small moorings and floating fish boxes. Select an anchorage clear of obstructions and anchor bow and stern. There are some residual rocks close to the pier and slip in the NW corner.

Facilities

The pier and slip in the NW corner are used by the flat-bottomed ferry to embark the island produce to take to Roscoff. Can be used as a dinghy landing.
Water and *telephone* Together on the front near the quay.
Showers In the hotel.
Bars and restaurants A few on the front.
Shops Two supermarkets and a baker.

Historical

St-Pol, who arrived on the island from Wales in the 6th century, founded a monastery on the island. In Breton legend, he disposed of a dragon by tying his stole round its neck, leading it to the shore and throwing into the ocean. A fragment of material dating from the 8th century that is kept in the 18th-century church is believed to be part of that stole. The Monster's Hole on the NW shore beyond the lighthouse marks where the dragon was given his comeuppance.

Roscoff and Bloscon

General

Roscoff has many historical connections with the UK and particularly with Scotland. It is an attractive town and well worth visiting but offers little to the yachtsman unless he has a boat that can take the ground. Roscoff harbour dries out and while Bloscon has deep water, it has few facilities and concessions to yachts, and is a long way from the town. In both places there has been talk of creation of marinas but local opposition in this historic town has inhibited any action so far. The terminal at Bloscon for the regular and frequent ferry from Plymouth, however and its position halfway along the N coast makes it a very convenient place to change crews.

Data

Charts

Admiralty *2745, 3669* (ARCS), *2668* (SC)
Imray *C35*
SHOM *7095* is the same scale and coverage as *2745* but has a plan of Roscoff harbour on it.

Tides

Add 55 minutes to the times of HW Brest, and 1 hour to the times of LW Brest to find the equivalents at Roscoff. Add 1·8m to the heights of HW and 0·5m to the heights of LW Brest for the heights at Roscoff.

Tidal streams

Outside Roscoff in the Chenal the E-going stream begins at −0435 HW Brest and the W-going begins at +0110 Brest. Both streams can reach 3¾ knots at springs.

Lights

Bloscon Jetty head Fl.WG.4s9m10/7M 200°-W-210°-G-200° White round tower, green top

Ar Chaden Q(6)+LFl.WR.15s14m8-6M 262°-R-289·5°-W-293°-R-326°-W-110° S cardinal beacon tower

Men-Guen-Bras Q.WRG.14m9-6M 068°-W-073°-R-197°-W-257°-G-068° N cardinal beacon tower

Ldg Lts 209° *Front* Oc(2+1)G.12s7m7M 078°-vis-318° White column, green top
Rear Oc(2+1)12s24m15M 062°-vis-242° Grey square tower, white on NE side

Roscoff Jetty head F.Vi.5m1M White and purple column

Le Menk Q(9)WR.15s6m5-3M 160°-W-188°-R-160° W cardinal beacon tower

Buoys (off E entrance to Chenal)

Astan VQ(3)5s9m6M Whis Ra Refl E cardinal
Basse de Bloscon VQ N cardinal

Search and rescue

Roscoff is in the CROSS Corsen region with the nearest radio station on the Ile de Batz. It will respond to emergency calls on Ch 16 or activation of GMDSS on Ch 70. It also keeps watch on Ch 79.
There is an all-weather lifeboat on Ile de Batz.

Weather forecasts

Ile de Batz on Ch 79 for coastal waters in French and English at 0515, 0733, 1133, 1603, 1933 LT.

Daily weather map at the *capitainerie*.
Navtex Corsen (A).

Communications

Port Radio Bloscon Ch 12 0830–1200, 1330–1800 LT.
Roscoff Ch 09 0800–1200, 1300–1730 LT.
Harbour office, Roscoff ☎ 02 98 69 76 37.

Customs

At Bloscon ferry terminal.

Approaches

From a distance use the directions for Chenal de L'Ile de Batz on pages 156–157. There are two alternative approaches for entry into Roscoff harbour depending of the height of tide.

Passe à l'Est de Benven (Line Y) (See plan page 163)
By day or night Navigate to a position 150m SE of Ar Chaden. Note the rock drying 1m 200m S of Ar Chaden. From here align the leading line/lights on 209°. The front is a white column 7m high on the end of the New Mole Oc(2+1)G.12s and the rear is synchronised with it Oc(2+1)12s on a square tower painted white 24m. Keep close to this line until the end of the E mole is abeam when steer to enter the port.

Passe du Rannic (Line X) (See plan page 163)
By day only From a position 100m N of Basse de Bloscon buoy, follow the transit Rannic N cardinal beacon tower and Roscoff belfry 261°. (Line X on plan page 156–157). This leaves Men-Guen-Bras lighthouse (N cardinal) 100m to starboard after which alter to starboard to skirt round Rannic tower leaving it 30m to port to avoid the rocks which dry some 6m to the N. Bring Rannic tower into transit with Men-Guen-Bras lighthouse astern and keep on this until the end of the eastern jetty is abeam, when course may be altered to enter the port.

Black and white vert.
Lighthouse *stripes on breakwater*

Roscoff entrance from N. Leading line open left

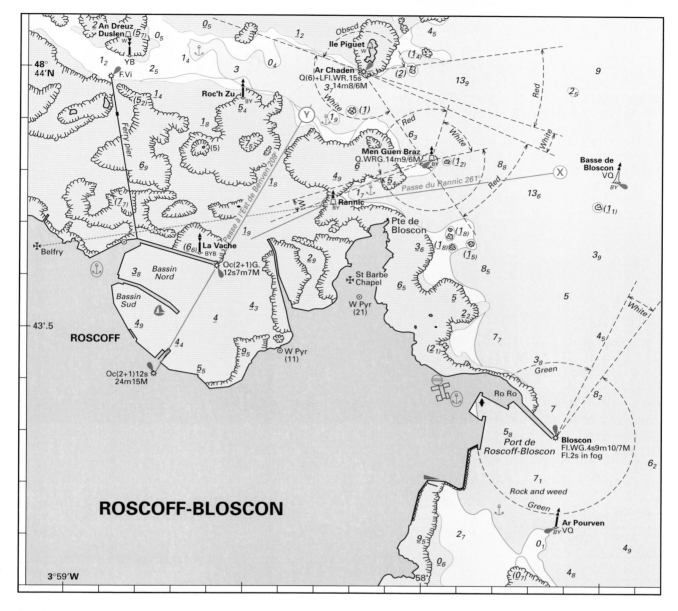

ROSCOFF-BLOSCON

Anchorages outside

No anchorage outside the port is clear of tidal streams except at Bloscon. Selection of a place to await the tide to enter will depend on the wind direction and whether on springs or neaps.

a. Between Ar Chaden and Duslen beacons as described on page 161. Open to the N and only possible to get out of the stream at neaps. There are some mooring buoys in this area.

b. In about 1m just E of the Roscoff leading line with Roc'h Zu N cardinal beacon bearing 285° but note the rock drying 1m close E of this position. Open to the E.

c. East of Rannic beacon tower, using the approach directions above. Fairly sheltered but open to the E.

d. The anchorage at Bloscon is only 1½M away and out of the stream, sheltered except from the E. There may be a mooring free here.

Berths

The outer harbour, Bassin Nord, has good drying berths along its N and W sides drying from 2·4 to 3m on a hard bottom. It is however reserved primarily for fishing boats and the steps are in constant use by *vedettes*. With the harbourmaster's agreement it is possible to lie alongside the second or third ladder where a yacht with 1·8m draught takes the ground just after half tide. If the ladders are occupied one may have to berth alongside the quay elsewhere which, if one does not carry a ladder will need some agility to get ashore when dried out. These are good berths to shop from but for a long stay visitors are expected to use the inner harbour.

The inner harbour dries from 3·6m to 5·1m. The old jetty is rather rough but there are good berths alongside it with 6 ladders and two steps which may be unoccupied even if the outer harbour is full. The wall is high and the use of warps to hold the boat leaning against the wall is preferable to masthead

Ar Chaden Bn Tr   Bloscon   Rannic passage   Roscoff entrance   Ferry pier

Roscoff and E end of Chenal de l'Ile de Batz looking S at LW

Roscoff inner harbour looking W. Visitors lie alongside inner breakwater in centre of picture

lines. Again a ladder is an asset if the built-in ladders are occupied.

The eastern part of the harbour cannot be used for berthing as it is subject to surge if there is any swell.

Facilities

Water From hydrants on the quay. Ask at *bureau du port* to get supply. Otherwise a tap in the showers.

Fuel Duty-free diesel only from pumps on outer end of outer breakwater. Otherwise from garage in town.

Showers and heads Tickets for the municipal facilities can be obtained from the tourist office by the roundabout.

Shops Turn right at the root of the quay for the main street.

Restaurants and hotels A large selection at all prices and styles.

End of Roscoff/Ile de Batz ferry pier   An Dreuz Duslen   Rear leading mark and light   Rannic Bn Tr

Roscoff looking N at LW

Chandlers Near the lighthouse on the S side of the harbour.

Launderette Up the road from the roundabout at the E end of the front.

Engineers and sailmaker Ask at the *bureau du port* for whereabouts.

Leisure The aquarium has many forms of local sea life. It is on the N front and worth a visit as are the church and the Chapel of St-Barbe.

Travel Rail and bus connections with Morlaix and the rest of France. Nearest airfields are at Morlaix (Ploujean), Brest and Dinard. Ferries to Plymouth from Bloscon up to three times daily in the summer but not every day; crossing time 6 hours. There is also a weekly service to Cork.

Historical

Mary Queen of Scots landed at Roscoff in 1548, when she was five years old, to be married to the Dauphin in Paris. Here also came Prince Charles Edward Stuart in a French privateer following the battle of Culloden, and after a number of escapes including from English ships in the channel.

The church has a remarkable Renaissance tower and spire (1550) decorated with carvings of ships and pieces of ordnance.

The pardon of St-Barbe takes place on the third Monday in July and the whole town is *en fête*.

The efficiency of the Brittany ferries in opening up the English markets to the Breton farmer has, alas led to the disappearance of the beret-hatted 'onion men' on their bicycles selling their strings of onions to the English housewife in the summer and autumn.

Port de Bloscon

General

An unattractive artificial harbour a half mile S of the Basse de Bloscon buoy and a one mile walk to Roscoff town. It is completely open to the E but sheltered from N through W to S and out of the stream. It is a commercial port for the ferries, occasional RoRo shipping and some development for fishing boats was started in 1999. Provision of facilities for yachts has been sporadic over the years and in 2000 there were 5 moorings for visitors and some room to anchor. A useful place only to change crews or to wait out a tide.

Data

Charts and tides

See Roscoff.

Tidal streams

These are weak outside the E end of the jetty reaching 1 knot at springs, the S-going beginning at -0300 HW Brest and the N-going at +0300 Brest.

Lights, buoys, search and rescue, weather forecasts, communications, customs

See Roscoff.

Bloscon looking NE showing anchorage and moorings. Slip and ferry terminal buildings off left

Approaches

By day or night Navigate to a position 200m to the E of Basse be Bloscon N cardinal (VQ) buoy noting that this marks a rock drying 0·4m close to the SW. From here steer 180° to give the end of the ferry pier (Fl.WG.4s) a good berth for ferries entering or leaving. Note that the white sector of this light is from 200°-210° and this can be used for the approach.

Anchorage and mooring

Pick up a vacant mooring buoy or anchor clear of them and S of the prohibited area shown on chart 2745. Ar Pourven N cardinal (VQ) buoy marks the SE corner of this area and also a shoal to the S of it.

Facilities

Water A tap by the ferry terminal.
Slipway Available at most states of the tide.
Shops Nothing worthwhile in the terminal. Do not be fooled by the sign '*Supermarché* 500m'; it is a good 2km.

Moguéric and Ile de Sieck

General

Moguéric is a small, drying fishing port in a wide bay into which two small rivers flow. There are leading lights and a fleet of small fishing boats is supported. Ile de Sieck on the N side of the bay has a smaller drying harbour and is connected to the mainland by a sandspit which covers. The only deep water anchorages are open to the W and the only shelter from this quarter in the whole bay is off Moguéric harbour which dries some 5m. There are few facilities but it is a useful anchorage in easterly weather, or for a bilge keeler.

Data

Charts

Admiralty *2745, 3669* (ARCS), *2669* (SC), (*2745* is the largest scale of the bay)
Imray *C35*

Tides

Add 55 minutes to the times of HW Brest and 1 hour to the times of LW Brest to find the equivalent at Moguéric; 1·8m should be added to heights of HW and 0·5m to the heights of LW at Brest for the Moguéric heights.

Tidal streams

To the W of Ile de Sieck the ESE-going stream begins at −0435 HW Brest and the WSW-going ebb at +0125 HW Brest, maximum spring rates 2 and 1 knots respectively.

Lights

Ile de Batz Fl(4)25s69m23M F.R.5m7M 024°-vis-059° Grey tower, black lantern
Moguéric Ldg Lts 162° *Front* Iso.WG.4s9m11/6M 158°-W-166°-G-158° White tower, green top
Rear F.G.22m7M 142°-vis-182° White column, green top

Approaches

By day Navigate to a position 3M W of the Chenal de Batz to pick up the Moguéric leading line bearing 162°. The front mark is a white tower with green top on the jetty and the rear, on the land behind another white beacon with green top (see photograph). In addition Sibiril church spire on the skyline is on the line. It is in wooded country and is the first spire to the left of conspicuous water tower S of Moguéric.

Follow this line to leave Golhédec (just W of and at LW joined to Ile de Sieck) 400m to port, and various dangerous drying rocks 600m to starboard. If proceeding to the Sieck anchorage bear E after passing Golhédec and align the conspicuous ruin on the island with the end of the harbour jetty bearing 053°. S of the jetty is a pile of rocks, Kerrec Levran, which is some 300m long E/W. If proceeding to Moguéric, keep on the transit until about ½M short of the entrance and Ar Skeul W cardinal beacon bears 080° when turn to 160°. When the breakwater end bears 180° alter between the red and green beacons off the entrance. It dries some 5m off the entrance.

By night Pick up the leading lights front Iso.WG.4s with the white sector of 4° either side of the centreline 162° and rear F.G which has a range of

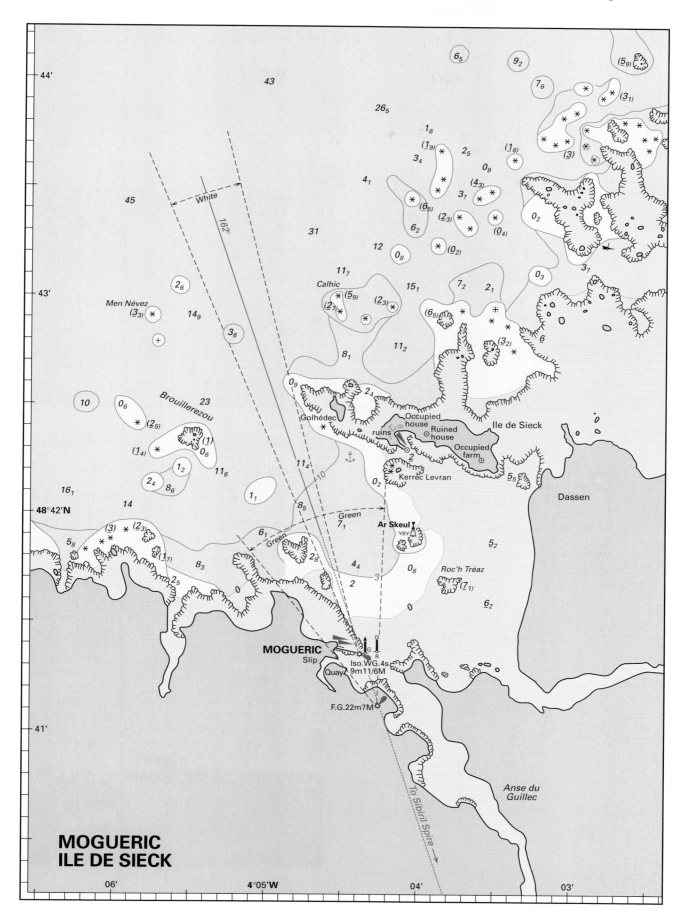

MOGUERIC
ILE DE SIECK

North Brittany & the Channel Islands

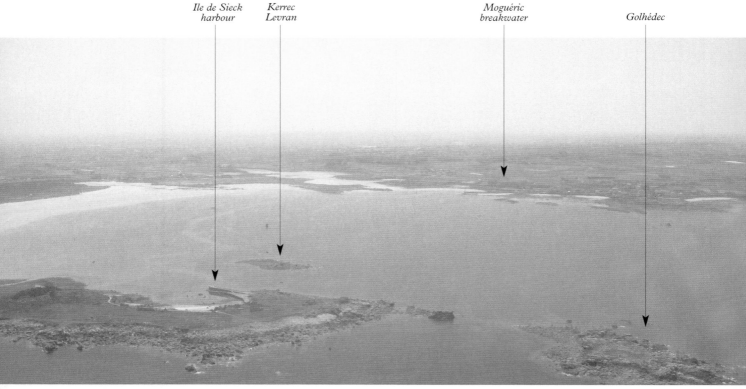

| Ile de Sieck harbour | Kerrec Levran | | Mogueric breakwater | Golhédec |

Mogueric and Ile de Sieck looking S

7M. Follow the line but the moment to leave the line to the E will be difficult to determine unless radar is fitted or the visibility is sufficient to identify Ar Skeul W cardinal beacon bearing 080°; then proceed as for by day. It would be easier leaving by night when, having cleared the red and green beacons off the entrance, a northerly course can be steered and until the white sector is reached it is safe to turn W.

Anchorage
The anchorage off the Ile de Sieck is to the SW of the W end of the island and to the W of Kerrec Levran. The latter's rocks extend some way out from the above-water part and severely restrict the anchorable space and swinging room between it and the island where the bottom dries 2m. Sound in from the W, or between Kerrec Levran and Ar Skeul beacon until a suitable depth has been found on sand. The water is clear and the rock patches visible.

Berths
Ile de Sieck The small harbour is protected by a low breakwater inside of which is a rough jetty. The outer part of this is a slipway running down to the end of the jetty but it is possible for yachts of medium draught to berth alongside it at the inner end at near HW. Look out for loose floating lines on entering. The bottom inside consists of loose boulders and is not a place to dry out in a keeled boat.

Moguéric The harbour lies on the W side of the mouth of the river Guillec. At low water the outflow turns W into the harbour and out along the wall. This often creates (but not every year) a mound of soft sand to the S of the breakwater end on which visitors' moorings are placed and provides a comfortable drying out area. There is a good length of quays to dry out on if they are not occupied with fishing boats.

Facilities
Moguéric
Water tap, heads and telephone All at the head of the jetty.

Moguéric. The harbour at LW looking ENE. The yacht behind the second lamppost from right is dried on the bank to the S of the breakwater end

Rear leading light structure

Breakwater head
Front leading light/mark Bearing SSW

Moguéric looking S

Ile de Sieck harbour near HW. The yacht alongside is berthed above the slip

Hotel/bar and restaurant By the quay.
Shop Sometimes open on the camping site at the W end of the village.
Leisure Many good and unfrequented beaches.

Ile de Sieck

No resources but the sand spit joins it to the mainland (dries about 5·5m) and tide permitting the village of Dossen can be reached. Here there are:
Café/restaurants Two.
Telephone One.
Shops None.

Historical

In 1944, two British airmen parachuted into the sea nearby and, as a reprisal for the help given to them by the inhabitants, all the buildings on the island were blown up by the occupying forces. Another version of the reason for the ruins on the island is that arms and explosives were being landed for the Resistance and cached on the island, causing a predictable reaction on discovery. 17 of the inhabitants, 5 from one family were killed by the Germans and are commemorated on a memorial by the slip at Dossen.

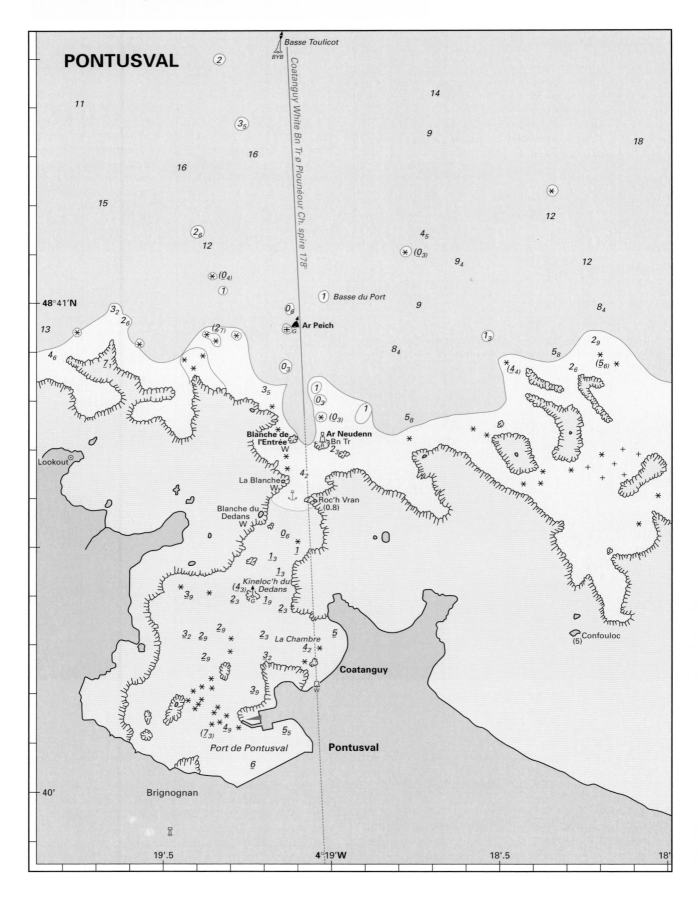

PONTUSVAL

Basse Toulicot
BYB

2

11

3₅

14

16

9

16

18

15

12

2₆

*
12

* (0₄)

4₅

* (0₃)

*
12

1

48°41′N

1 Basse du Port

9₄

9

12

13

3₂

2₆

0₆

*

* (2₇) *

Ar Peich
G

8₄

1₃

2₉

*

4₆

7₁

0₃

5₈

(4₄)

2₆

(5₆) *

3₅

1

0₃

1

**Blanche de
l'Entrée**
W

* (0₃)

5₈

Ar Neudenn
Bn Tr
2₃

Lookout

4₂

La Blanche
W

Roc'h Vran
(0.8)

**Blanche du
Dedans**
W

0₆

1₃

1

1₃

Kineloc'h du
Dedans
(4₃)
G 1₉

3₉ *

2₃

2₃

Confouloc
(5)

3₂ 2₉ 2₉

2₃ La Chambre

5

4₂ *

2₉

3₂

Coatanguy

3₉

W

(7₃) 4₉ *

5₅

Port de Pontusval

Pontusval

6

40′

Brignognan

19′.5

4°19′W

18′.5

18′

Pontusval/Brignogan

General

An anchorage in pretty surroundings in an almost landlocked bay. However most of it dries out to hard sand and occasional rocks and for deep draught yachts it will be a long dinghy trip ashore even at neaps. Not to be contemplated with any north in the wind but sheltered from all other quarters.

Data

Charts

Admiralty *3668* (ARCS), *2668* (SC)
Imray *C35* (plan)

Tides

Add 40 minutes to the times of HW and LW Brest to find the equivalents at Pontusval; add 1·1m to the heights of HW Brest and 0·3m to the heights of LW for the equivalents at Pontusval.

Tidal streams

Off Basse Toulicot the E-going flood stream begins at −0405 HW Brest and the W-going ebb at +0215 HW Brest. Both streams can reach 3 knots at springs but the E/W component becomes weak once to the S of Ar Neudenn beacon tower.

Light

Pointe de Beg Pol (1M to the W)
Oc(3)WR.12s16m10/7M Shore-W-056°-R-096°-W-shore White tower, black top, white dwelling
There are no shore lights at Pontusval.

Approaches

By day only Navigate to Basse Toulicot E cardinal buoy 1M N of the port. It is close to the leading line which is Coatanguy white beacon tower (front) in transit with Plounéour-Trez church spire (rear) 178°. The latter is the E-most of two churches with its spire on the W end of a long straight roof. Follow this line closely to leave Ar Peich starboard buoy close to starboard and An Neudenn port beacon tower close to port. To starboard are three rocks shown on the plan which are painted white from time to time. S of La Blanche, the second one, the channel shoals quickly and a deep draught yacht can only proceed further with sufficient rise of tide.

Anchorages

The deep water anchorage to the SSW of Ar Neudenn is defined by Ar Neudenn, La Blanche, Blanche de Dedans and Roc'h Vran (see plan and photograph) and is rather restricted with rocks on each side drying 0·3m and 6 visitors' moorings. An anchor light would be advisable if staying over either at anchor or on a mooring.

At neaps an anchorage further in can be found by sounding SE of Blanche du Dedans.

For those that can dry the rest of the bay is hard sand with rock patches. An isolated drying rock Kineloc'h du Dedans (dries 4·3m) is marked by a starboard beacon. Most of the bay dries about 3m and La Chambre on the E side where there are

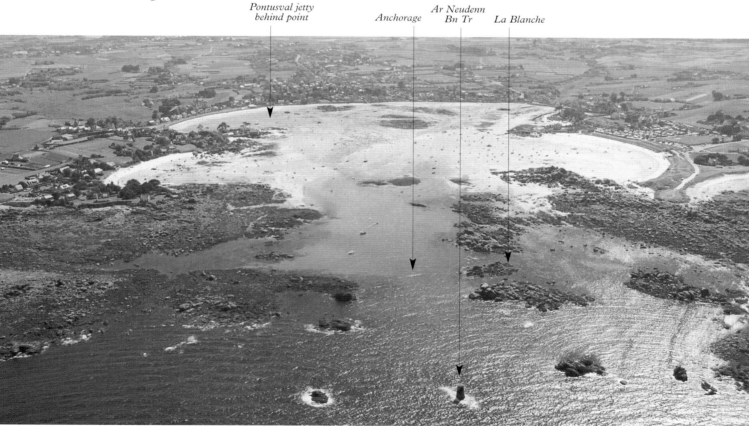

Pontusval jetty behind point   Anchorage   Ar Neudenn Bn Tr   La Blanche

Pontusval looking SSW at LW

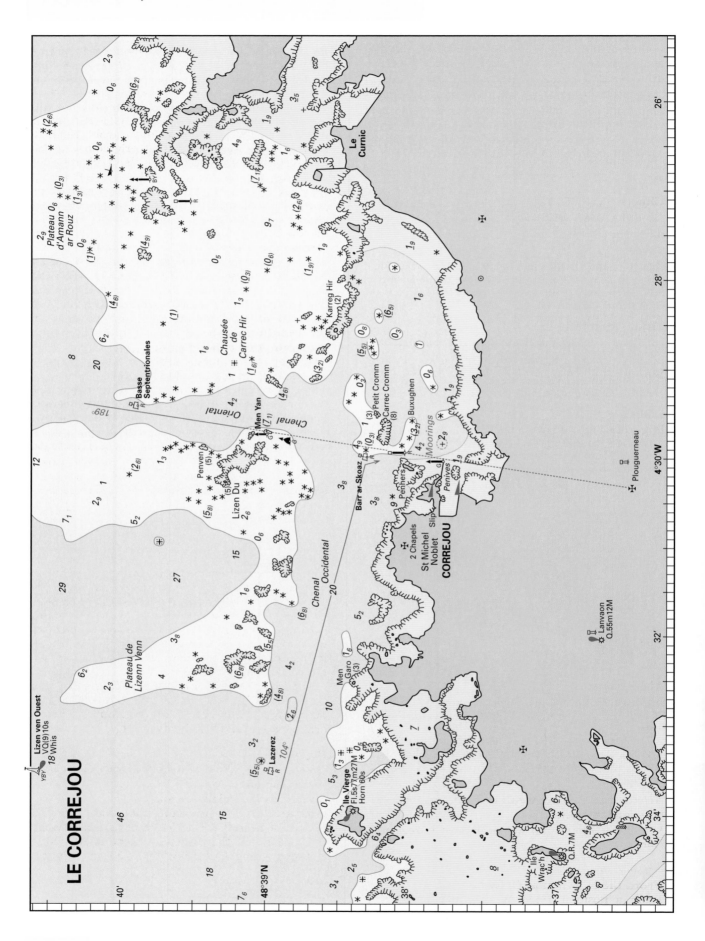

LE CORREJOU

Lizen ven Ouest
VQ(9)10s
18 Whis

Plateau de
Lizenn Venn

Chenal Occidental
20

104°

Lazerez
R

Men Garo (3)

Ile Vierge
Fl.5s77m27M
Horn 60s

Penven Du (5)

Lizen Du

Chausée
de
Carrec Hir

Basse
Septentrionales

Chenal Oriental
189°

Men Yan

Karreg Hir (2)

Barr ar-Skoaz

Penhers

Penives

Petit Cromm
Carrec Cromm (8)
Buxughen

Moorings

CORREJOU
Noblet
St Michel
2 Chapels
Slip

Le Curnic

Plateau
d'Amann
ar Rouz

Lanvaon
Q.55m12M

Plouguerneau

Q.R.7M
Ile Wrac'h

48°39'N

4°30'W

many small boat moorings, dries 4·2m. At Port de Pontusval in the SE corner there is a quay and a slip with rocks on the N side and sand on the S where it dries 5m.

Facilities
Landing slip At Pontusval, or land anywhere over the beaches.
Shops, hotels and post office At the head of the bay at Brignogan.
Leisure There is a pleasant walk over the dunes to Pointe de Pontusval past some standing stones. A good place for a beach holiday with children, but not on a rainy day.

Le Correjou

General
This open bay provides shelter from the S and W to deep keeled yachts and better shelter for those able to dry out. It has a small fishing facility and a local kelp-gathering industry; the latter is loaded from boats into lorries on the slip, or at the jetty at HW. Worth a short stay, but not in easterlies and enter only by day and in good visibility.

Warning
It is still in a danger area for the Second World War mines although the risk from such remains must now be minimal. However, vessels should not anchor between the longitudes of 4°32'W and 4°23·5'W in the area except just to the E of Penhers island and the jetty, where any explosive detritus can be assumed to have disappeared.

Data
Charts
Admiralty *1432, 3668* (ARCS), *2668* (SC)
Imray *C35*

Tides
Add 40 minutes to the times of HW and LW Brest for the same times at Le Correjou; add 1·1m to the heights of HW Brest and 0·3m to the heights of LW Brest for those at Le Correjou.

Tidal streams
In Chenal Occidental the E-going flood stream begins at −0515 HW Brest and the W-going ebb at +0110 HW Brest.

In Chenal Oriental the NE-going flood begins at −0445 HW Brest and the SW-going ebb at +0125 HW Brest.

The maximum spring rates are 2 knots in each direction.

Search and rescue, weather forecasts and communications
See L'Aber Wrac'h. An inshore lifeboat is kept at Le Correjou.

Approaches
From the N – Chenal Oriental
From a position 1·3M W of Aman ar Ross W cardinal pillar buoy, identify Plouguerneau belfry which is just to the W of a prominent water tower. With this bearing 189° identify Men Yann, a small rock drying 7·1m with a green beacon and align this with the belfry on the bearing. Leave Basses Septentrionales port buoy to port and Penven rock 400m to starboard. Then deviate to port from the transit and leave Men Yann beacon 100m to starboard. Continue on a southerly course of less than 190° until 400m S of Men Yann, identify Barr ar Skoaz port can buoy and alter to starboard to leave it close to port. Then turn to port to leave the port beacon 250m E of the N end of Penhers island close to port on a track of 170°. The channel is narrow between Penhers and this port beacon but carries a least depth of 3·9m. This is the entrance used most frequently by the fishing boats and it would be prudent to wait if one is leaving rather than meeting it in the narrows by the beacon.

There is a channel used by fishing boats near HW to the W of Penhers island but it is unmarked and the depths unknown.

From the W – Chenal Occidental
This channel is wider than Chenal Oriental and may be preferred. Navigate to a position ½M N of Ile Vierge lighthouse when the Lazerez port buoy will be close to the E. Leaving this to the N steer about 104° and identify the two pinnacles of Karreg Cromm and Petit Cromm ahead. This course leaves Men Garo (2m) a conspicuous cottage-loaf-shaped rock ¼M to starboard. Chapelle St-Michelle, shown on chart *1432* is hard to pick out in the trees but by then Barr ar Skoaz can be identified and steered for. Leave it close to port and proceed as for Chenal Oriental above.

Anchorage
SE of Penhers island in from 0·6m to 4m sand.

An anchorage between this and the slip/jetty can be found provided the rocks shown on chart *1432* are avoided. The positions of these differ between charts *1432, 3668* and SHOM *7094* but a fisherman will often come and tell you if you have anchored too close to any of them even if they cannot be seen in the clear water. There are many small boat moorings S and E of the slip.

The jetty to the W of the slip has fishery buildings on it and a sailing school. It would be possible to dry out on the end or the E side of it but ask first as fishing vessels and kelp boats use it.

Facilities
Dinghy landing At the slip at all stages of the tide.
Water Tap on the quay.
Showers At the sailing school.
Cafés and bars Nearby on the main road.
Shops The nearest are at Plougerneau, a large village 1½M S but the distance can be shortened by taking a dinghy near HW to the S end of the bay.

The Cromms. Behind them two fishing boats, not beacon towers

Slip

Quay

Penhers

Entrance

Le Correjou looking SW

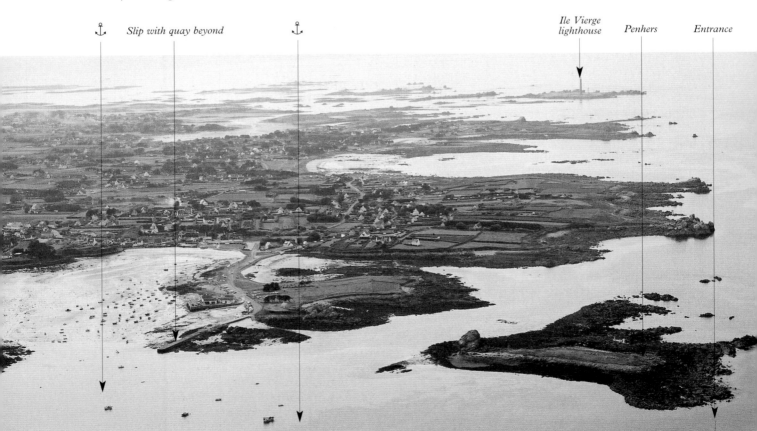

Slip with quay beyond

Ile Vierge lighthouse

Penhers

Entrance

Le Correjou looking W at LW

Le Correjou. Quay at LW looking W

L'Aber Wrac'h

General

This is probably the best harbour between Tréguier and Brest. It is much used by yachts going to and from the Chenal du Four and as a landfall for those crossing from the West Country.

The river can be entered by day or night at any state of the tide but calls for reasonable visibility in order to pick up the leading lines to keep clear of the many off-lying dangers. Approach may be easier by night, but not in bad visibility, as it is necessary to pick up Lanvaon light (55m, 12M) at a range of at least 5M and Ile Wrac'h red light (19m7M) at a range of at least 3M. By day it is possible to enter in less visibility provided the yacht's position can be accurately plotted whilst looking for the outer marks. In bad visibility this entrance lends itself to the use of parallel index on radar.

There are pontoons and moorings for visitors, room to anchor and most facilities at La Palue/Port d'Aber Wrac'h. The pontoons are sometimes removed in the winter months. The river above to Paluden has become increasingly restricted in places by moorings and oyster beds but room can still be found to anchor in peace and quiet.

A good port to change crews and where the boat may be safely left if Brest itself is not used.

Data

Charts

Admiralty *1432* (plan), *3668* (ARCS), *2668* (SC)
Imray *C35* (plan)
SHOM *7094* (same coverage and scale as *1432*).

Tides

Add 30 minutes to the times of HW and LW Brest for the same times at L'Aber Wrac'h. Add 0·8m to the heights of HW Brest for the heights at L'Aber Wrac'h and 0·2m to the heights of LW.

Tidal streams

Off Libenter buoy outside the entrance the ESE-going stream (ebb) begins at −0500 HW Brest and the WNW-going (flood) at +0110 and attains 3 knots at springs. This stream sets across the Grand Chenal approach line until Le Petit Pot de Beurre is passed after which it aligns with the channel and can attain 1½ knots at springs. In the Malouine and La Pendante channels it sets across until the vicinity of Le Petit Pot de Buerre when it aligns with the channel.

Lights

Ile Vierge Fl.5s77m27M 337°-vis-325° Horn 60s Grey tower
Grand Chenal Ldg Lts 100°
Front **Ile Wrac'h** Q.R.20m7M White square tower, orange top, dwelling
Rear **Lanvaon** DirQ.55m12M 090°-intens-110° White square tower, orange triangle on top
La Palue/L'Aber Wrac'h Ldg Lt 128°
DirOc(2)WRG.6s5m13-11M 126°-G-127°-W-129°-R-130° White structure, red top; rear the same
Breac'h Ver Fl.G.2·5s6m3M Triangle on green tower

Buoys

Libenter (outer approach) Q(9)15s8m6M Whis W cardinal Radar reflector
Basse de la Croix Fl(3)G.12s starboard
Enez Terc'h Fl(2)R.6s port

Search and rescue

CROSS Corsen (3M N of Le Conquet) will respond to emergency calls on Ch 16 and to activation of Ch 70 on GMDSS.
There is an all-weather lifeboat and an inshore lifeboat maintained at L'Aber Wrac'h.
There are hospitals in Brest (25 km).

Weather forecasts

Le Stiff on Ch 79 for local areas at 0503, 0715, 1115, 1545, 1915 LT in French and English.
Navtex Corsen (A).
Daily weather map at the *capitainerie*.

Communications

Port Office Ch 16, 09 working hours ☎ 02 98 04 91 62.

Approaches
Grand Chenal (Line D)

By day Navigate to a position ½M W of the Libenter buoy (W cardinal) when La Petite Fourche buoy (W cardinal) will be slightly further away to the SE. Libenter has a powerful whistle which may be heard up to a mile away in any sea or swell. From here identify the leading line front Ile Wrac'h (square white tower with red top on white house) and rear Lanvaon (white square tower with orange triangle on top) 100° (Line D) Plougernau belfry is also on this line and there is a rectangular tower just to the N of it. When Libenter buoy is abeam look for Le Trépied buoy which is ½M away and marks the minimum limit of visibility to proceed further in safety.

Proceeding down the line, leave Le Trépied port buoy to port, Grand Pot de Beurre red beacon, La Petit Pot de Beurre red beacon tower and Plate Aber Wrac'h port buoy all to port. Just before the last is reached the next leading line on 128° up the channel (Line E) should become visible. This consists of two white towers with red tops by the lifeboat house and

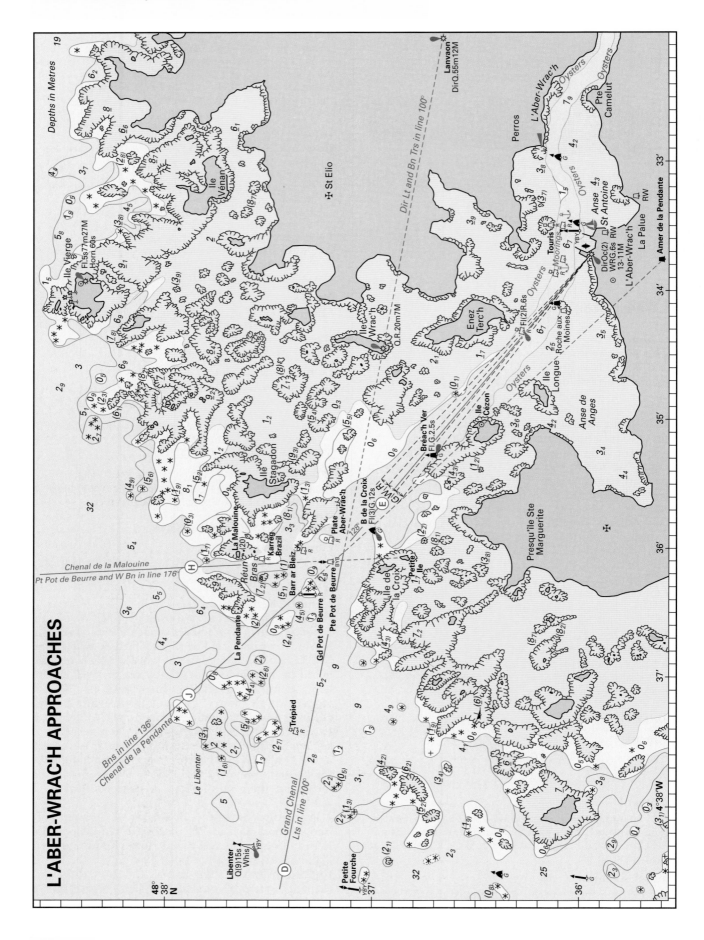

L'ABER-WRAC'H APPROACHES

North Brittany & the Channel Islands

48° 38' N

Depths in Metres

19

Ile Vierge Fl5s77m27M Horn 60s

Lanvaon DirQ.55m12M

Perros

L'Aber-Wrac'h

Oysters

Pte Camelut

Oysters

St Elio

Dir Lt and Bn Trs in line 100°

Ile Wrac'h Q.R.20m7M

Anse St Antoine RW

La Palue RW

Touris Moorings

DirOc(2) WRG.6s 13-11M L'Aber-Wrac'h

Amer la Pendante

Fl(2)R.6s

Enez Terc'h

Roche aux Moines

Ile Vénan

Ile Stagadon

Bréac'h Ver Fl G.2.5s

Ile Cézon

Ile Longue

Anse de Anges

Presqu'île Ste Marguerite

Chenal de la Malouine
Pt Pot de Beurre and W Bn in line 176°

H

La Malouine

Karreg Brazil

Réun Bras

Barr ar Bleiz

Plate Aber-Wrac'h

B de la Croix Fl(3)G.12s

Ile de la Croix

Petite Ile

Pte Pot de Beurre

Gd Pot de Beurre

Bns in line 136°
Chenal de la Pendante

La Pendante

J

Le Libenter

Trépied

Grand Chenal
Lts in line 100°

Libenter Ql(9)15s Whis

Petite Fourche

D

176

Touris beacon tower   *Yacht moorings*   *Yacht pontoon*   *Lifeboat slip and house*   *Roche aux Moines*

L'Aber Wrac'h looking SE

to the right of the yacht moorings but if the visibility is not that far, Basse de la Croix starboard buoy will give an indication. In the next 1½M up the channel, the following will be passed to starboard – Bréac'h Ver green beacon tower, Ile Cézon with a black and white disc on the NW side of the fort, and Roche aux Moines green beacon tower. Before the latter is reached Enez Terc'h port buoy will be passed to port. From here the way is open to the yacht moorings/pontoons or up the river.

Grand Chenal (Line D)

By night Navigate to put Libenter buoy (Q(9)15s radar reflector and whis) ½M bearing E and identify the leading lights front Ile Wrac'h Q.R.7M and rear Lanvaon DirQ.12M 090°-intens-110° and bring them into line on 100°. It would be unwise to proceed if Ile Wrac'h cannot be seen from Libenter buoy.

Follow this line until the green sector of L'Aber Wrac'h directional light Oc(2)WRG.6s appears and alter down the white sector on 128°. An anchorage in the Anse des Anges clear of the oyster beds is an option if finding a berth or mooring in the dark is not attractive.

Chenal de la Malouine (Line H)

By day only This channel is narrow and the stream sets hard across in the outer approaches. However the leading marks are fairly close to the channel and 1½M visibility is enough to identify them before being committed to the passage.

From a position on Line H 1½M W of Ile Vierge lighthouse identify the large rock La Malouine, and a lower rock La Pendante to the W of it. In the gap between these two align Le Petit Pot de Buerre an E cardinal squat beacon tower and the white pyramid on Petite Ile de La Croix on 176°. The red beacon tower Karreg Bazil will be to the left of the line. Follow this line making allowance for any cross set. This channel carries a least depth of 3m but passes very close to an isolated rock drying 1·7m to the NW of La Malouine and to the NE end of La Pendante which has a least depth of 0·7m over it and over which the sea usually breaks at most states of the tide. In heavy weather this broken water is said to extend right across the channel and in this event the Grand Chenal should be used.

The line leaves the following marks on the sides shown:

> **La Malouine** rock 100m to port
> **Karreg Bazilport** beacon tower 100m to port
> **Réan Bras** Rock (dries 6·4m) 90m to starboard
> **Bar-ar-Bleiz** port buoy 100m to port.

When the latter is abeam leave the line and steer between Le Petit Pot de Buerre E cardinal beacon tower and Plate Aber Wrac'h port buoy. From the latter the next leading line up the river can be picked up and proceed as for the Grand Chenal.

Chenal de La Pendante (Line J)

By day only Departure in good conditions is preferable to entry for the first time with this

Lifeboat house *Yacht pontoon*

L'Aber Wrac'h looking NE

channel. The marks are further away than for La Malouine and more difficult to identify. Dangers lie close on each side and the line must be held precisely. The set across the line can be considerable until S of Le Petit Pot de Buerre.

From a position 2½M W of Ile Vierge lighthouse identify Ile Cézon, a small stone fort on an island with a black and white circular mark painted on the wall of the fort, and Amer de La Pendante black tower, with a white stripe and an orange conical top among trees on the skyline. The latter is roughly midway between the conspicuous white fishery school building and a water tower on the skyline. These marks in line 136° mark Chenal de La Pendante (Line J). This channel carries a least depth of 3·6m but passes very close to drying rocks on the NE side of Le Libenter and the SW side of Plateau de La Pendante. It leaves La Pendante an anvil-shaped above-water rock painted white 200m to port. Shortly after this, when Le Grand Pot de Buerre bears 175° leave the line and steer for Bar-ar-Bleiz port buoy. Shortly after Le Petit Pot de Buerre E cardinal beacon tower will come into transit with Ile de La Croix white pyramid (Line H) when alter course to pass between Le Petit Pot de Beurre and Plate Aber Wrac'h port buoy. Thence follow Line E up the river (see Grand Chenal above).

Berths
Maximum length on the pontoons is 12m but is not rigidly enforced. The only restriction is depth of water towards the root of the pontoons. Current practice is to find a berth and then report to the *capitainerie*. Private berths when vacated for a short time may have a line across to prevent access. A brightly illuminated square sign at the end of the access pontoon (hammerhead) is clearly visible at night from the river to locate the pontoons.

There is a patch drying 0·5m between the W cardinal pole beacon and the green buoy just to the NE of the pontoon on which many yachts have grounded.

This pontoon is very exposed to W winds with any N in them, as are most of the moorings; the latter, while safe for a single vessel will be uncomfortable if not dangerous if doubled-up. In these weather conditions, the only safe place is up river.

Moorings
Moorings now extend from off the pontoons almost up to the first starboard-hand buoy opposite Perros. Report to the *capitainerie* if picking up a vacant one. The charges are the same for a mooring as for a berth but the launch service (summoned on Ch 9) comes free. It is common practice for several boats

Beg-an-Toull beacon tower • Paluden quay • Rowing club and slip • Restaurant • Paluden bridge

L'Aber Wrac'h. Paluden looking N

to raft up on each buoy which are well spaced out and substantial.

Anchorages

The anchorage for large vessels between Roche aux Moines and the lifeboat slip in up to 18m is somewhat exposed to the W and N.

An anchorage may be found to the N of and clear of the moorings between Touris beacon and Perros but above Pointe Cameleut as far as Beg-an-Toul there is perfect shelter in depths of 4 to 6m, mud and few obstructions. There is a landing at Pointe Cameleut, mud at LW, whence a road runs to L'Aber Wrac'h. There are a few dumbbell moorings below Beg-an-Toul and more above it to Paluden, but a space may be found in between 4 and 5m, mud. There is often space on the dumbbells in the same depths.

Upriver

There is a quay at Paluden with 0·5m alongside it and a slip beside it. It is possible to dry out on the outer face of the quay where the bottom is flat, but it only has one ladder and two bollards, and there are several large tractor tyres hanging by chains which are mostly submerged at HW. This quay is occasionally used by coasters. There are some visitors' moorings off the quay. There is a slip on the other side of the river. Harbour dues are collected at Paluden. Masted navigation ceases at the bridge above Paluden village.

Facilities
At La Palue

Water and electricity On the pontoon (included in the charges).

Fuel On the quay.

Showers and heads At the yacht club.

Chandler and chart agent Near the pontoon.

Repairs, engineer and electrician Available, ask at bureau du port.

L'Aber Wrac'h. Approaching Perros upstream from L'Aber Wrac'h

L'Aber Wrac'h. Paluden
Paluden quay, slip and dumbbell mooring

Shops The lack of provision shops nearby is the one disadvantage of L'Aber Wrac'h. The nearest is 2km away up the hill. Only oysters and other crustaceans available by the quay, and milk and bread from a souvenir shop to the E of the quay.

Hotels, restaurants and crêperies Several by the quay and along the road to Baie des Anges.

At Paluden

Water and heads On the quay.

Shops A twenty-minute walk up the hill to Lanillis which has a good selection for day-to-day needs.

Showers May be solicited from the rowing club on the quay opposite.

Restaurants Two round the bay towards the bridge on the main road.

Travel Bus or taxi to Brest (25km) whence there are air, rail and bus connections with the rest of France and particularly good services to Paris. L'Aber Wrac'h is a possibility for changing crews or for leaving the boat for a short time if the marina at Brest is not used.

L'Aber Benoît
Stellac'h

General

Lying only 2M SW of L'Aber Wrac'h this little river offers an excellent sheltered anchorage in beautiful surroundings with some lovely beaches. It is known locally as La Rivière de Saint-Pabu from the nearby parish of that name and carries a least depth of 3m as far as Stellac'h. There are few facilities but is a good place to visit for healthy, open air exercise. It can be entered at any state of the tide but in daylight only and in reasonable visibility. The northerly entrance is said to be dangerous in strong winds in the N sector.

Data

Charts

Admiralty *1432, 3668* (ARCS)
SHOM *7094* (same coverage as *1432*)
Imray *C35* (plan)

Tides

Add 30 minutes to the times of HW and LW Brest for the times at L'Aber Benoît; add 0·8m to the heights of HW Brest and 0·2m to the heights of LW Brest for those at L'Aber Benoît.

Tidal streams

Off La Petite Fourche buoy the ENE-going flood begins at −0515 HW Brest and the W-going ebb at +0100 HW Brest; both streams can reach 3 knots at springs.

In the river the stream turns at high and low water and can reach 3 knots.

Lights and buoys

There are no lights or lit buoys in the approaches.

Approaches and entrance

Northern approach (See plan page 182)

Make for La Petite Fourche W cardinal spar buoy and from a position 50m W of it make good 168° (Line C) to leave Rusven Est starboard conical buoy 50m to starboard. Continue on this course until Basse du Chenal port beacon bears about 125° and the highest point of Ile Guénioc is abeam to port. Then steer 134° to leave Basse du Chenal port beacon 150m to port, Karreg ar Poul Doun port beacon 200m to port and Men Renead starboard buoy 30m to starboard.

With Men Renead buoy abeam, alter to starboard to leave the conspicuous La Jument rock, marked with a patch of red paint and a port beacon 40m to port, whence follow the channel on 142° marked by Ar Gazel and Kervigorn starboard buoys and Le Chien isolated danger beacon tower which should be left to port.

After passing Kervigorn starboard buoy and leaving the small craft moorings in Kervigorn bay to starboard, the channel is indicated by yacht and fishing boat moorings. Depths in the channel and upriver are unpredictable due to dredging and the echo sounder should be watched but 3m or more can be expected at LW as far as Stellac'h.

There are oyster beds as far as Stellac'h on the N bank and on both sides above there. The channel turns S at Stellac'h and a drying bank extends halfway across the river from the E bank S of the quay.

Western approach

This is the best approach in bad weather. See Portsall Inner Passages for the approach from this direction.

From the NW pick up the line of Rouellou water tower just below the wood of that name, just open to the right of the prominent rock (see sketch page 182) of Pen Ven on 143° (Line X) and pass within 50m of Rusven Ouest W cardinal spar buoy as there is a 0·6m patch 400m SSW of it. Here turn on to 103° with Landéda belfry in transit with the left-

Le Chien Bn Tr   Stellac'h   Kerrigorn stbd buoy

L'Aber Benoît looking SE.

hand edge of Roc'h Aval (7m) (Line P). Leave the Rusven Sud starboard buoy to starboard and turn to starboard on to 134° when short of Basse du Chenal port beacon. Then proceed as in northern approach above.

The favoured channel for entry used to be to the S of Poul Orvil rocks but the introduction of new buoys and marks has now made the N one easier to follow.

Anchorage

Anchor anywhere in the river clear of moorings which now extend above Stellac'h, or pick up a mooring. There is a wide fairway between the moorings in the lower reaches. There are also anchorages to the NW of Kervigorn in deep water more suitable in offshore winds. There is a good dinghy landing at all stages of the tide at Stellac'h whence it is a ½M uphill walk to the few shops that there are; otherwise land on the sands on both sides down river.

Berths

There is a substantial jetty at Stellac'h with a smooth outer side and two ladders which dries and is used by the occasional fishing boat; a berth may be found here. ½M above this is a yacht yard and slip.

There is also a new jetty with a depth gauge on it on the N bank just inside the entrance large enough to take a 35-footer alongside, together with a slip close by.

Facilities

Small shops, garage, chemist, cafés and small restaurant To the W and at top of hill.

Restaurant, crêperie In St-Pabu village.

Water tap, heads and telephone On the quay at Stellac'h.

Leisure Good beaches. The island of Guénioc near the entrance to the estuary has prehistoric building remains and a balanced stone that many visitors have tried unsuccessfully to dislodge.

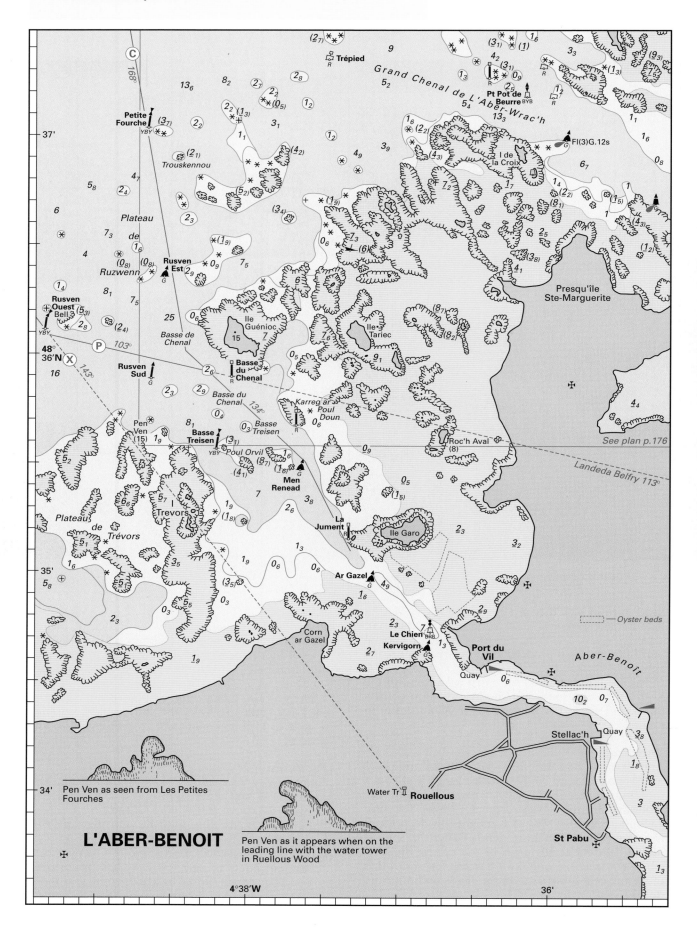

Pen Ven as seen from Les Petites Fourches

L'ABER-BENOIT

Pen Ven as it appears when on the leading line with the water tower in Ruellous Wood

Stellac'h jetty and slip   Outer jetty and slip

L'Aber Benoît looking NW at LW

Portsall inner passage

General

The passages inside the Roches d'Argenton and
Roches de Portsall besides giving access to Portsall
provide an interesting exercise in rock dodging. As a
short cut between Chenal du Four and L'Aber
Wrac'h it only amounts to a saving of less than one
mile in ten on the passage outside. It can only be
used in clear weather and, if sailing, with a fair wind.
The streams are strong especially in the vicinity of
Portsall and a passage at springs is not
recommended for the first time. At low water the
rocks are clear but some of the back leading marks
may be masked for a considerable distance by the
front marks standing high above the water. The
channels carry a least depth of 1·8m but there are
many rocks close to the transits with much less over
them; in places the channel is so narrow between the
rocks that an error would be dangerous and great
care must be taken for the first time which is easiest

from east to west. The optimum time for the
identification of marks is when the tide is 3·6m
above datum.

There are three passages through the islands and
rocks:

1. Chenal du Rélec from the NE (Line A) which
   leads to:
2. The short Chenal du Raous (Line B) which leads
   to:
3. The unnamed and narrow channel between
   Bosven Kreiz and Bosven Aval which leads to:
4. Chenal de Méridional inside Roches d'Argenton
   and Le Four lighthouse (Line C).

The westerly Portsall passage (Line D), Calerec
Passage (Line E) and Chenal du Bosven (Line F) all
lead into Portsall and are described in that section.

PORTSALL INNER PASSAGE

N

Depths in Metres

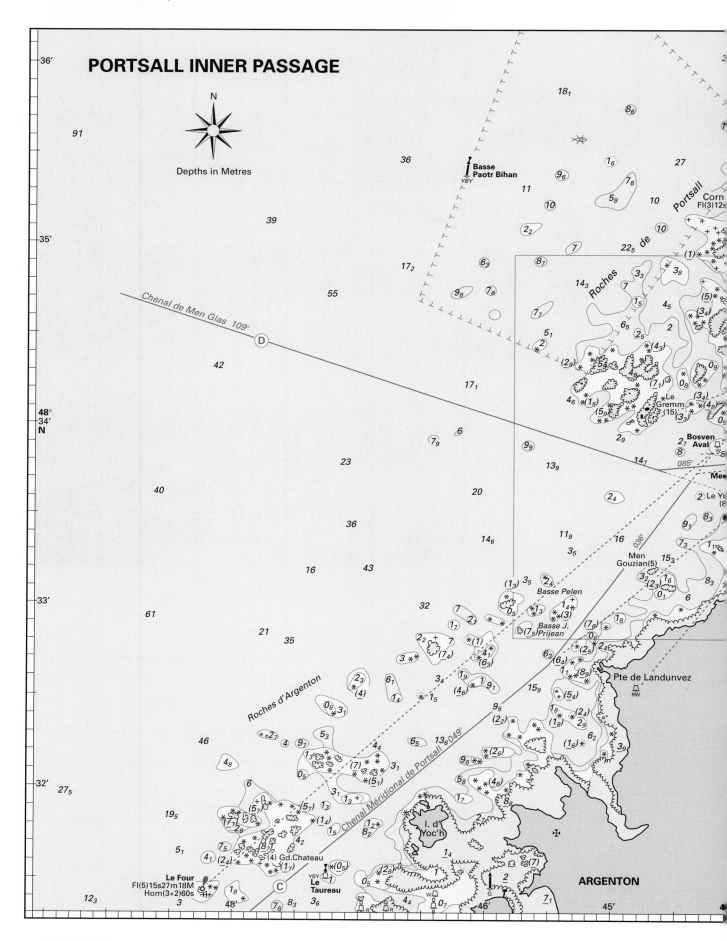

Chenal de Men Glas 109°

Basse
Paotr Bihan
YBY

Portsall
Corn
Fl(3)12s

Roches

de

Roches d'Argenton

Chenal Méridional de Portsall 049°

Le
Gremm
(15)

Bosven
Aval
W

Men

Le Yu
(8

Men
Gouzian(5)

Basse Pelen

Basse J.
Prijean

Pte de Landunvez
RW

I. d'
Yoc'h

Gd.Chateau

Le Four
Fl(5)15s27m18M
Hom(3+2)60s

YBY
Le
Taureau
W

ARGENTON

G

R

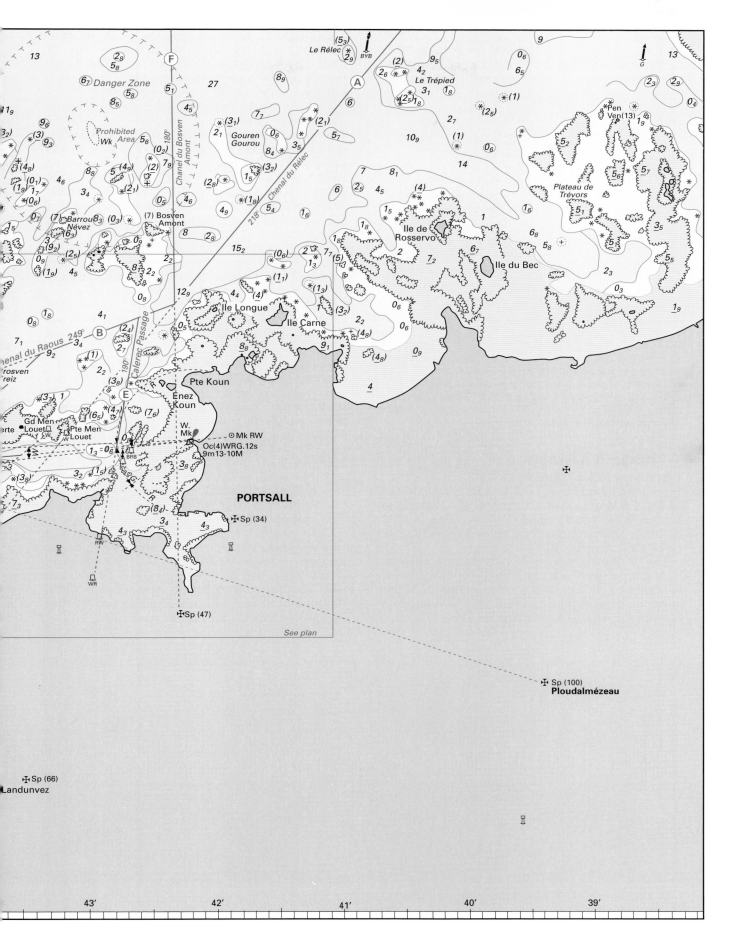

PORTSALL

Ploudalmézeau

Landunvez

Warning

The overfalls in Chenal Méridional and to the W of Ile Verte are severe in wind over tide conditions and are said to compare to those in the Raz de Sein. This is not an area to be in strong westerlies.

Data

Charts

Admiralty *1432, 3668* (ARCS)
SHOM *7094*
Imray *C35*
(*1432* or SHOM *7094* are the only charts of sufficient scale for safe navigation in the channels.)

Tides

Add 20 minutes to the times at Brest for the times at Portsall; add 0·7m to the heights of HW Brest and 0·4m to the heights of LW Brest for the heights at Portsall.

Tidal streams

The rising tide sets to the NE and falling to the SW. The directions and rates are much affected in the channels by the formation of the plateaux and rocks between which they run. They are particularly fast north of Ile Verte and accelerate as LW approaches when the flow is compressed between the island and the drying rocks to the N. They are more moderate in the open parts of the channels.

The NE-going stream begins at HW Brest −0500, the SW at HW Brest +0130. The spring rates in either direction are up to between 3 and 5 knots.

Westbound passage

Chenal du Rélec (Line A)

From Petite Fourche W cardinal spar buoy, situated on the S side of the entrance to Grand Chenal in to L'Aber Wrac'h make good 255° for about 0·75M when the leading marks for Chenal du Rélec should be identified bearing 218°.

The front mark is a tall beacon painted white on its N side on the N side of the steep Petit Men Louet rock or islet. If this cannot be identified from this position the visibility is too poor for a stranger to attempt the passage for the first time.

The beacon stands on the islet E of the Men Louet group of rocks which dry high at low water. It must not be confused with Grand Men Louet beacon on the islet 200m to the W of it which is squat and only painted white on its S side.

The rear mark, distant 5·5M is a white beacon with a red top on Pointe de Landunvez just W of the ruins of a semaphore building, and about 0·2M SE of the headland. The transit is 218° and it should initially be kept with the front Men Louet beacon open to the LEFT of the rear to pass clear of the dangerous Queyn-an-Treis 1·8m shoal which breaks in any swell below half tide. Resume the transit after this is passed to leave Le Rélec buoy and shoal close to starboard and Le Trépied shoal (dries up to 2·5m) close to port. The next danger is the line of scattered rocks Gouren Gourou which lie close to starboard of the transit but there is plenty of water to port at this stage.

The line then leads 0·15M off Ile Longue (3m) which is a rocky area mostly covered at HW. When Ile Longue is abeam alter to 249° on to the transit for Chenal du Raous.

Chenal du Raous (Line B) (See plan page 190)

The line here is Bosven Kreiz (a rock with two apexes and a white beacon) in line with the southernmost high rock (15·8m) of Le Gremm group. At LW the rear rock is hidden behind Bosven Kreiz. When about 0·25M from Bosven Kreiz alter to 228° and keep Le Four lighthouse just open LEFT of Bosven Aval (a rock with one apex and a white beacon). The stream will now be at its strongest, not necessarily in line with the track and the narrowest part of the passage is being entered. The transit should be held precisely.

Only toward LW is the channel clearly defined with the rocks uncovered. The immediate dangers are first to starboard with the Karreg Luth shoal drying 5·2m, the shallows to the W of Ile Verte to port, the extension of Bosven Aval 100m to the E (0·4m) to starboard with Sélédren rock (dries 0·8m) on opposite side of channel. To avoid these:

Portsall inner passage. Le Rélec E cardinal buoy at E entrance.
Le Rélec rock breaking right

Leading marks
Front – white beacon on Petit Men Louet
Rear – white beacon with red top on
Pointe de Landunvez 218°

Grand Men Louet

Le Yurc'h

Portsall inner passage. Chenal du Rélec leading marks
looking SW

1. When Bosven Kreiz is in line with Barrou Nèvez (almost covers at HW) astern bearing 025° alter on to the reciprocal 205° to follow this line until:
2. Men Gouzian rock touches the tip of Pointe de Landunvez bearing 210° when maintain this line until Sèlèdren rock is left safely to port and Bosven Aval 120m to starboard. Navigation then becomes much easier.

Turn to port on to the Portsall leading line 085° if bound there (see Portsall). If continuing W align Bosven Aval and Bosven Kreiz astern on 036° and maintain this line on the reciprocal 216° until W of Pointe du Landunvez. Identify Le Yurc'h rock in passing. This transit should be held exactly in the later stages.

Chenal Méridional de Portsall (Line C)
When the beacon on Grand Men Louet which is painted white on its SW side (Petit Men Louet 200m to its W is grey on this side) is in line with the cleft on the top of Le Yurc'h bearing 049°, alter to make good the reciprocal 229°. The cleft is like a gunsight and except perhaps at HW, the beacon is lost once the yacht deviates to one side or another.

This line leads about 200m N of the prominent Ile d'Yoc'h, about 200m S of Grand Château rock (3m) and leaves Le Taureau W cardinal beacon tower 200m to port. After Le Taureau there is clearer water S of the line. The line then leads into open water about 0·3M S of Le Four lighthouse. Note that there will be extensive overfalls in this area in wind over tide conditions.

Eastbound passage
This passage should not be attempted for the first time with visibility of less than 5M as this will be needed for the last pair of leading marks. However the advantage of an eastbound passage is that it can be taken on a rising tide and usually with a fair wind. Provided the visibility is at least 2M Le Rélec buoy at the N end should be visible ahead to steer for as the stern transit beacons disappear into the haze.

Chenal Méridional de Portsall (Line C)
First identify Le Grand Château rock (3m) lying about 0·4M NE from Le Four lighthouse, and Le Taureau W cardinal beacon tower 0·6M E by N from the lighthouse. The track lies midway between them bearing 049° with Grand Men Louet beacon, painted white on the SW side, in line with the cleft on the top of Le Yurc'h. The cleft is like a gunsight and except perhaps at HW the beacon is lost as soon as the yacht deviates to one side. A help is to keep Men Gouzian (5m) which is easily distinguished just open W of Le Yurc'h.

When Bosven Kreiz and Bosven Aval white beacons come into line bearing 035°, follow this line exactly until Men ar Pic bears 090°, then alter to starboard and, when the E side of Men Gouzain touches the tip of Pointe de Landunvez bearing 210°, steer 030° to maintain this stern transit. Follow this line leaving Sélédran rock (dries 0·8m) close to starboard and Bosven Aval 120m to port. When Bosven Aval is abaft the beam, alter slightly to starboard to avoid Karreg Luth (drying 5·2m) and bring Bosven Kreiz in line with Barrou Névez (almost covers at HWS) bearing 025°. Follow this line until Le Four lighthouse is just open to the left of Bosven Aval astern bearing 228° when alter to hold this stern transit making good 048°. This is the narrowest part of the passage with the strongest streams and care must be taken to hold the transits exactly.

Men Gouzain   *Leading line 049°*   *Le Yurc'h – front*   *Grand Men Louet beacon tower – rear*   *Sabloc*   *Land ez bea*

Portsall inner passage west entrance looking E. Chenal Méridional

Portsall inner passage eastbound, looking N. Bosven Aval (front) and Bosven Kreiz, the second pair of marks

Chenal du Raous (Line B)

When the southernmost rock of Le Gremm is in line with Bosven Kreiz on the port quarter bearing 249°, alter to make good 069° and follow this line until the white beacon with red top on Pointe de Landunvez and the tall beacon painted white on its N side, on the N side of the steep Petit Men Louet rock are in line astern bearing 218°.

Chenal du Rélec (Line A)

Make good 039° to follow this line towards Le Rélec buoy. Initially there is more water to the S of this line but once Gouren Gourou rocks are passed Le Rélec buoy should be left close to port to avoid both Le Rélec rock and Le Trépied close to the S. Once the buoy is passed borrow to port to avoid the dangerous Queyn-an-Treis patch (1·8m) which breaks near LW in any swell. If bound for L'Aber Benoît there is plenty of water between Le Trépied and Queyn-an-Treis to approach the Ruzven Ouest

Portsall Inner Passage. Chenal Méridional. Le Four lighthouse and Le Grand Château rock bearing WNW

cardinal buoy on 085° but pass close to the buoy avoid the 0·6m patch 400m SSW of it.

Portsall and Kersaint

General

A pretty, drying harbour with a drying berth alongside the quay. The deep water anchorage is only sheltered in offshore winds and is a long way from shore. The approaches can be very rough in wind over tide conditions. Some facilities ashore.

Data

Charts

Admiralty *1432, 3668* (ARCS)
Imray *C35*

Tides

Add 20 minutes to the times of HW and LW Brest for those at Portsall; add 0·7m to the heights of HW Brest and 0·4m to the heights of LW Brest for those at Portsall.

Tidal streams

See page 186 for the tidal streams in the Portsall passages.

Between Ile Verte and La Pendante in the outer anchorage the flood begins setting E at HW Brest −0530 and the ebb starts setting W at HW Brest +0100 both reaching 2 knots.

Lights

Le Four Fl(5)28m18M Grey tower.Horn(3+2)60s
Portsall Oc(4)WRG.12s9m13-10M White column, red top 058°-G-084°-W-088°-R-058°

Buoy

Grande Basse de Portsall (3M to the NW) W cardinal VQ(9)10s Whis

Search and rescue

A lifeboat lies at a mooring just to seaward of La Pendante beacon tower when tides are insufficient for it to be housed ashore.

Approaches

Chenal de Men Glas (Line D)

By day From a position 1½M S of Basse Paupiane W cardinal spar buoy (unlit) identify Ploudalmézeau church spire and Le Yurc'h rock; the latter is just S of Men ar Pic starboard beacon tower. Align these on 109° and make good this track down the transit leaving the Portsall Rocks about 0·25M to port. There is deep water to the S on this approach.

When the conspicuous Bosven Aval islet with white beacon on top bears 070° identify the next leading marks bearing 085°. They are two rectangular column beacons on the land; the front is white with silver radar reflector along the top and the rear is white with a red top; they are not easy to distinguish amongst the houses in the vicinity. This transit leaves Men ar Pic beacon tower 150m to

starboard and Ile Verte a similar distance to port. The danger on this approach is Basse Idi to the E of Men ar Pic parts of which dry 2·8m; the leading line leaves these 80m to starboard.

Identify La Pendante N cardinal beacon tower to the right of Besquel isolated danger masonry beacon. When La Pendante is in line with Ségou Braz (9m), which may have a painted white patch, bearing 094° follow this line into the anchorage.

By night Note that the Portsall light (Oc(4)WRG.12s) is obscured on bearings greater than 088° so a more southerly approach will be needed to pick it up. Approach in the 4° white sector as far as the outer anchorage.

Calerec Passage (Line E)

By day only When entering from the NE by Chenal du Relec and Chenal du Raous instead of proceeding to the Bosvens there is a short cut W of Ile Longue which can be used with sufficient rise of tide, over a rock which dries 0·6m and others near which dry 1m.

About 0·25M W of Ile Longue when on the Chenal du Relec or the Bosven Kreiz/Le Gremm transits identify two pyramids (both white with red tops) bearing 190°. Turn down this transit and follow it precisely with La Pendante beacon tower on the port bow. When Besquel isolated danger beacon is abeam and before reaching La Pendante alter in to the anchorage. This channel is very narrow but is considered better locally than the pass from Bosven Kreiz to Bosven Aval which involves a detour and where the seas can be unpleasant. However the latter must be used if there is any doubt in identifying the Calerec leading marks.

Chenal du Bosven Amont (Line F) (See plan page 185)

By day only This approach passes to the E of the sunken remains of the *Amoco Cadiz* which caused such devastating pollution on this coast in 1978.

Portsall looking SE. Old water tower in line with breakwater end 133°

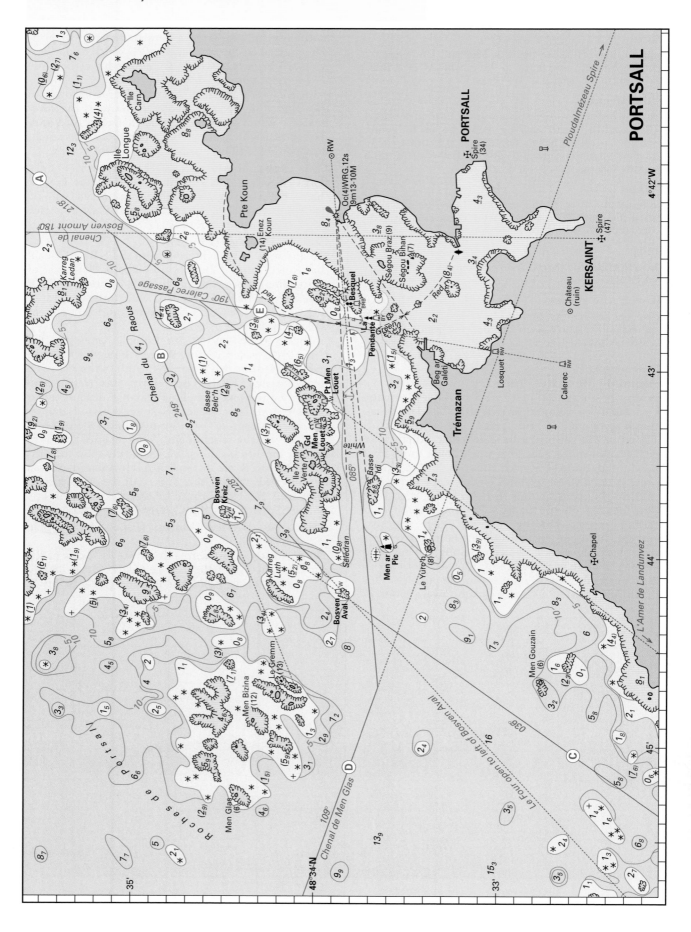

PORTSALL

Lifeboat slip   Yacht club and breakwater   La Pendante Bn Tr

Portsall looking SW at LW

From a position 1M W of Le Rélec E cardinal buoy (unlit) identify the leading line the tower of Kersaint church between Pointe Koun and Enez Koun islet (16m) on a bearing of 180°. This transit leaves Bosven Amont rock (7m) 300m to starboard but with a drying rock halfway between it and the transit.

0·4M past Bosven Amont turn to starboard to join Chenal du Raous with the southernmost of the Roches du Gremm in line with the white pyramid on Bosven Kreiz bearing 249°. The harbour may

then be entered either by Chenal du Raous or the Calerec Passage.

Chenal du Rélec

(Line A)
See page 188 *Portsall inner passage anchorage.*

Anchorage

1. In 2 to 4m sand with La Pendante bearing SSE 100m and Besquel bearing E about 100m clear of the lifeboat mooring. The streams are strong and it is far from the landing slip and harbour.
2. Towards neaps up to 2m can be found to the SE of La Pendante clear of the rocks surrounding the beacon and fishing boat moorings. This is out of the stream and closer to the harbour.

Harbour

Leave La Pendante 50m to starboard and steer 165° until the old water tower standing on four legs is clear of the end of the breakwater. Identify the above-water rock (6m) to the SW of Ile Ségou Bras and leave it 100m to port thence steering to pass close to the end of the mole. Go alongside or anchor. It is all hard sand and grounding and floating off is uncomfortable in any NW sea or swell. In these conditions visit near HW and move out again in plenty of time.

Facilities

Water and heads On the jetty.
Showers In the sailing school.
Fuel Pump on the jetty and requiring a card with chip to operate.

Relic of a past disaster. *Amoco Cadiz's* broken anchor at Portsall

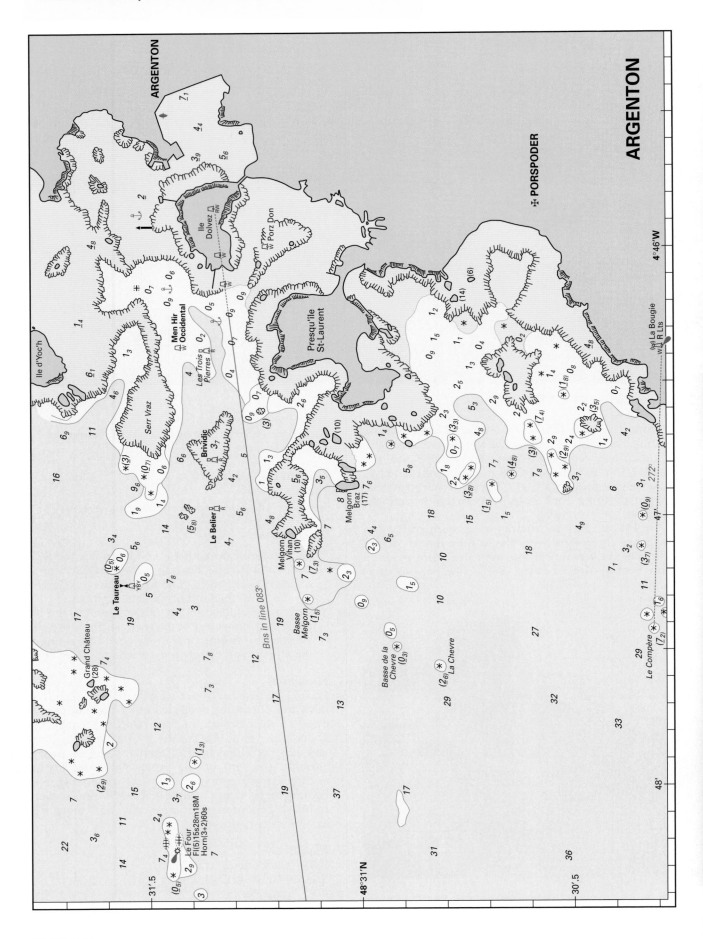

ARGENTON

ARGENTON

PORSPODER

Supermarket and garage At Barr ar Lann between Portsall and Kersaint.

Restaurant and cafés At Portsall and Kersaint.

Sailing school A smart new (1999) sailing school dominates the front at Portsall outside of which is preserved one of the damaged anchors of the Amoco Cadiz which failed to hold her off the rocks outside.

Leisure The 12th-century château outside Kersaint is worth a visit.

Argenton

General

A small village with an open anchorage sheltered from the E through to SSW, and a drying harbour, situated 2 miles E of Le Four lighthouse. An interesting approach in deep water passing close to drying rocks. There is a sheltered landing place behind Ile Dolvez and a few facilities, but more at Porsporder 1 mile to the S.

Warning

A dangerous harbour in strong westerlies; any swell is said to build up to a great height in the approaches. Not a place to be caught in these conditions.

Data

Charts

Admiralty *2694, 3345* (ARCS)
Imray *C35* (plan)

Tides

Add 15 minutes to the time of HW and LW Brest for those at Argenton; LW heights as for Brest, add 0·5m to HW heights at Brest.

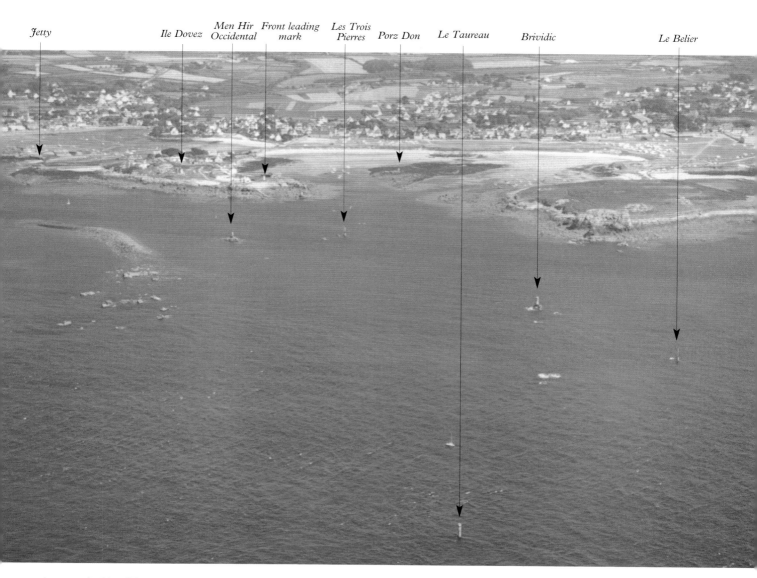

Jetty   Ile Dovez   Men Hir Occidental   Front leading mark   Les Trois Pierres   Porz Don   Le Taureau   Brividic   Le Belier

Argenton looking SE

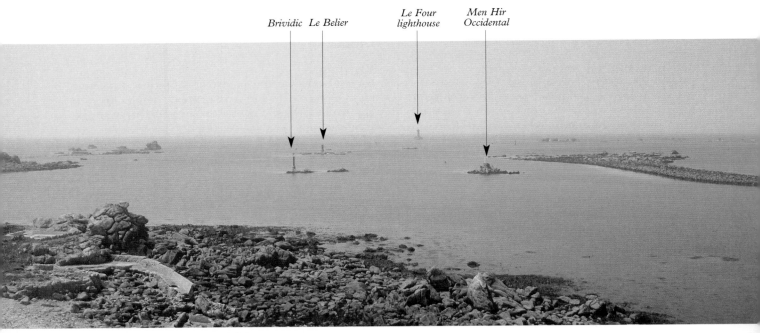

Brividic Le Belier *Le Four lighthouse* *Men Hir Occidental*

Argenton entrance looking W at LW

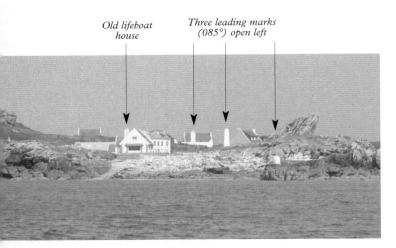

Old lifeboat house *Three leading marks (085°) open left*

Argenton looking E to Ile Dolvez

Light
Le Four Fl(5)15s28m18M Horn(3+2)60s Grey tower

Approaches and entrance
Make a position 0·2M S of Le Four lighthouse and a heading to make good 085°. Identify Le Belier port beacon tower with two further port beacon towers beyond it, and Melgorn Vihan Rock (12m) to starboard. Approach to pass midway between Le Belier and Melgorn Vihan and identify the leading marks on Ile Dolvez. The front mark is a small, white, round beacon tower on the foreshore and the rear is a white pyramid on the island itself; there is a third white mark to the east of this and all line up on 085°. On this line Melgorn Vihan is left 200m to starboard and a strong cross set may be experienced in this area. Keep exactly on the line as there is an isolated rock drying 3m close to starboard and a

shoal round Brividic beacon tower with 0·9m over it to the N. The channel is only some 100m wide to the SE of Brividic beacon and the isolated rock. Once this narrow part has been passed stay on the line leaving Les Trois Pierres beacon tower with Men Hir Occidental beacon beyond it well to port to the anchorage.

If proceeding in to the inner anchorage with sufficient rise of tide, pass midway between Men Hir Occidental and the end of the old lifeboat slip and house on the W end of the island; round Ile Dolvez leaving the starboard beacon and a rock on the N side with a breakwater running to it to starboard. The rocky promontory above the sailing school, slips and jetty is surmounted by a Cross of Lorraine.

Anchorages
Anchor in between 2 and 0·9m anywhere between Les Trois Pierres and Ile Dolvez, mostly sand. The area is more rock free to the N of the leading line than to the S. 0·9m may be found half way between Men Hir Occidental and the starboard-hand beacon to the N of the island. The mooring buoy between Les Trois Pierres and Ile Dolvez is reserved for the lighthouse tender.

For yachts that can dry out the bay to the NE of Ile Dolvez has large areas of weed-covered sand drying 2m which would be covered at LW neaps and is sheltered from all directions except NW.

Harbour
The harbour to the NE of Ile Dolvez consists of two jetties and a slip. The slip to the W is weed covered and now disused. There is a large jetty and slip to the E of this which is used by the sailing school and the occasional excursion boat. It is possible to berth alongside here (dries 4m) and to dry out but ask at

the sailing school. The bay to the SE of this, Porz Don dries 4·4m in its centre.

Facilities
Water From tap on the jetty.
Showers and heads In the sailing school/yacht club.
Shops A baker in Argenton. 1M S in Porspoder there is a Spar supermarket, more shops, a garage (bottled gas), two banks and a post office.
Travel Bus from Porspoder to Brest (15km).

Melon

General
A small drying harbour lying between the island and village of the same name, about a mile N of L'Aber-Ildut. The island is 14m high and bordered by low cliffs. In fine weather there is a deep draught anchorage to the N of Ile de Melon but not in any swell or wind from the N quarter. Shallow draught yachts or those able to take the ground will find more shelter to the E of Ile de Melon or in the small bay to the SE. The only practical approach without local knowledge is from the NW.

Anchorage inside island   *Ile Melon*

Melon looking SSE

Melon. 'La Bougie' tower in transit with Le Compère rock 092°

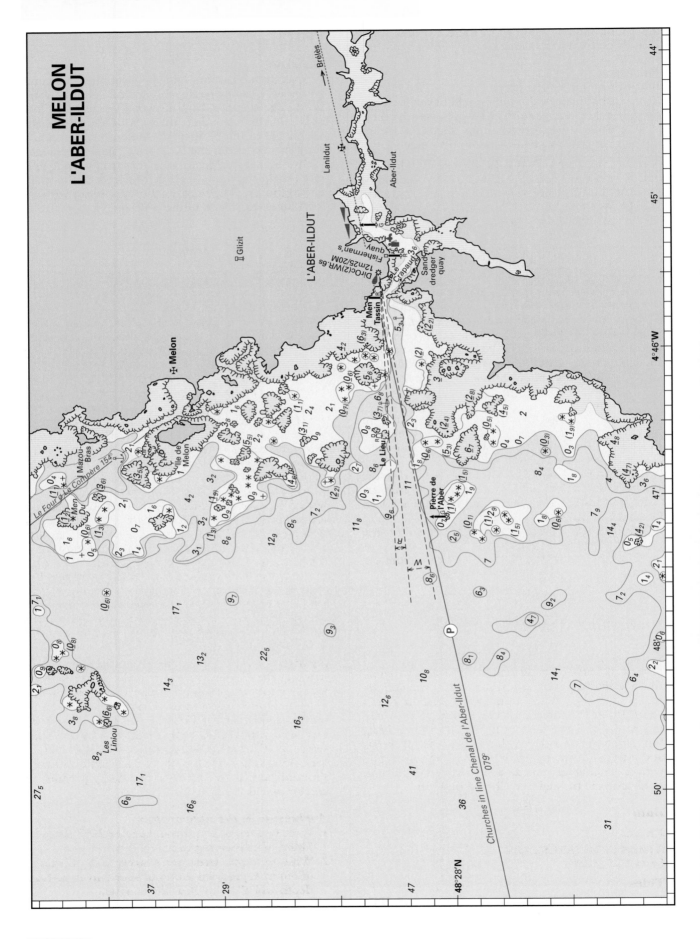

MELON
L'ABER-ILDUT

Data

Charts

Admiralty *3345* (ARCS)
Imray *C35*

Tidal

As for L'Aber-Ildut.

Approaches

The key to the approach is Le Compère rock about 1M N of Ile de Melon. This dries 6·6m and will be covered at HW except towards neaps. The approach should therefore be made at about 2 hours before HW to be sure of locating it.

First identify the tall white radar tower aptly nicknamed La Bougie (the candle) which is shown on chart *3345* in position 0·4M to the SW of Porspoder village. Approach this bearing 092° and when Le Four lighthouse bears 340° Le Compère will be close to the ENE. Pass at least 200m to the SW of it and align it with Le Four lighthouse astern and make good 154° on this transit. There is deep water on this approach line but it passes very close to rocks drying 1·2m and it would be prudent to carry enough water to clear them.

Anchorage

Anchor in a convenient depth on this line in between 8 and 1m to the N of Ile de Melon and with Ile Mazou Braz bearing between 010° and 060° sheltered from the E through to S.

Room may be found in the narrow channel to the E of Ile de Melon but a second anchor may be needed to restrict swinging. A sandy patch needs to be found amongst the weed here.

The harbour contains a number of small fishing boats on drying moorings but has no quays or facilities apart from one restaurant. It dries from 2·5 to 5m.

L'Aber-Ildut (Lanildut)

General

A natural harbour at the confluence of two small rivers that has been deepened and extended by much dredging for sand and aggregates in recent years. It can be entered by day and night provided the marks and the leading light can be identified, but it is crowded inside with dredgers, fishing boats and yachts at many moorings. There is a fine weather anchorage outside and it is a good place to await the tide through the Chenal du Four.

Data

Charts

Admiralty *3345* (ARCS), *2694*
Imray *C35* (plan)

Tides

Times are generally +10 minutes on Brest and HWs +0·4m. LWs the same heights as at Brest.

Tidal streams

The ebb stream from the river can reach 3 knots at springs in the narrows and outside sets to the SW on to the off-lying rocks.

Outside, the rising tide sets N and falling tide S. 2 miles off the entrance the direction changes at about the times of HW and LW at Brest i.e. the stream turns to the southward at HW Brest.

Lights

Le Four Fl(5)15s28m18M Horn(3+2)60s Grey round tower
L'Aber-Ildut DirOc(2)WR.6s12m25-20M 081°-W-085°-R-087°

Search and rescue, weather forecasts

As for Le Conquet.

Communications

Capitainerie ☎ 02 98 04 36 40 (June–September).

Approaches and entrance

By day The traditional approach is to align Bréles church spire with Lanildut church spire bearing 079° Line P but the trees have grown up to make both marks indistinguishable. The three most prominent marks are Glizit Water Tower (62m) to the N which is useful for identifying the position of the entrance, Le Lieu port beacon tower and the square white light structure.

Navigate to get Le Lieu bearing 080° and steer down this bearing leaving Pierre de l'Aber starboard beacon 300m to starboard. Leave Le Lieu beacon tower 100m to port and from here it should be possible to identify Men Tassin port beacon to the left of the light structure. The latter is white with a red section in the left-hand part of it. Keep this bearing 083° with Men Tassin well open to the left until 200m short of Men Tassin when head to leave this no more than 30m to port in the narrowest part of the channel. From here turn to starboard to 117° to leave Le Crapaud rock which juts out from the N bank 15m to port. When the second port beacon is abeam, the river and moorings will open up bearing 020°. The least depth in the entrance channel is 3·6m.

By night Le Four light to the N and the many lights marking the Chenal du Four to the S will help to make a position 2 miles off the port to the W, and to avoid the unlit reefs 1 mile offshore of Le Liniou to the N and Plateau des Foutches to the S. From here pick up the powerful leading light of L'Aber-Ildut, DirOc(2)WR.6s25/20M bearing 083° and stay in the white sector until past Le Lieu unlit beacon. Proceed then as for daytime if visibility permits or anchor outside.

Anchorage in the approaches

1. With Le Lieu beacon tower bearing 275° distance 300m. The least depth here is 7m.
2. With the light structure bearing 075° distance 400m in at least 3m sand but sound in as far S as depth will allow to clear the channel.

Moorings

Further up the harbour are some dumbbell moorings but most are fore and aft. The creek to the S largely dries and is full of smallboat moorings but the outer end has some dumbbell moorings where there may be a vacancy. There is no room to anchor anywhere inside. Least depth in most of the mooring area is 3m.

Berths

It is possible to go alongside the fishing quay on the W side by the fishing boat moorings but it is high and the stream runs fast along it. It would be wise to have someone ashore to take lines if going here for water; there are two ladders in it. There is a short pontoon just above this jetty usually occupied by fishing boats but it is the most convenient place to land someone.

Facilities

Water On the fishing quay.
Fuel Duty-free diesel only on the quay, otherwise a garage in the village.
Showers and heads Three of each.
Shops All the shops are in the village. The best way

Light structure   Le Crapaud rock

L'Aber-Ildut looking NE

Light structure   Le Crapaud rock

L'Aber-Ildut entrance looking E

Light structure   Le Crapaud rock   S jetty

L'Aber-Ildut looking E, the river crowded with moorings above
L'Aber-Ildut jetty

to reach this is to land at the slip below a restaurant 300m upstream from the pontoon which saves a long detour on foot.
Restaurant On the quay.
Engineer, shipwright and repairs Ask at the *bureau du port*.
Crane 10-ton mobile.
Travel Buses to Brest (14km) whence there are rail and air connections with the rest of France. Taxi ☎ 02 98 89 55 50.

Historical
The great disused quarry nearby once supplied stone for the construction of many of the ocean harbours of France and for several works in England, including the Thames Embankment.

L'Aber-Ildut. The jetty and slip looking S at half-tide

Le Conquet

General

Le Conquet is in an attractive position near the S end of the Chenal du Four but although sheltered to some extent by Ile de Beniguet and a breakwater, is open to the W. It is also a busy ferry and fishing port and there are few concessions to visiting yachts. However there is limited space to anchor in the outer harbour and the drying inner harbour is well sheltered for those that can take the ground.

An alternative anchorage to wait the tide or for the fog to clear is in the S part of Anse de Blancs Sablons just over the peninsula to the N of le Conquet. In north or easterly weather the bay of Porz Illien in the NE corner gives shelter (see photograph page 202). Good holding in sand but there are fishing floats in the SW corner of Anse de Blancs Sablons and a swell sometimes finds a way in.

Data

Charts

Admiralty *3345* (ARCS) (plan)
Imray *C36* (plan)

Tides

The times are within 5 minutes of the times at Brest and within 0·1m in height.

Tidal streams

The rising stream is to the N outside the port and the falling to the S. Tidal streams outside the port begin at the following times in relation to HW Brest:
N −0600 The maximum rate in the main channel.
S HW to the W is 5 knots. On the ebb this decreases progressively towards the harbour entrance under the tidal lee of Pointe de Kermorvan.

Lights

La Grande Vinotière LFl.R.10s15m5M Red octagonal tower
Trézien DirOc(2)6s84m20M Grey tower, white on S side 003°-intens-011°
Kermorvan Fl.5s20m22M White square tower
    Front light with Lochrist
    Rear as leading line for Chenal de la Helle
Lochrist DirOc(3)12s49m22M White octagonal tower, red top 135°-intens-140°
St-Mathieu Fl.15s56m29M+DirF White tower, red top 158°-intens-160°
S breakwater end Oc.G.4s5m6M

Buoy

Roche Lochrist Iso.R.4s port with topmark

Search and rescue

Le Conquet is in the CROSS Corsen region with the nearest radio station at Pointe de St-Mathieu which will respond to emergency calls on Ch 16 or activation of GMDSS on Ch 70. CROSS Corsen control is situated 3M N of Le Conquet.
There is an all-weather lifeboat maintained at Le Conquet.
There are hospitals in Brest.

Weather forecasts

On Ch 79 for local areas at the following times: 0503, 0715, 1115, 1545, 1915 LT in French and English.
Fog warnings when required also on Ch 79.
Navtex Corsen (A).

Communications

Bureau du port Ch 08 and 16 0830–1200, 1300–1800 LT
☎ 02 98 89 08 07.

Approaches

See page 204 for the approaches from N and S through the Chenal du Four or by Chenal de la Helle.

By day from the N From the N pass midway between La Grande Vinotière beacon tower (octagonal, red) and L'Ilette leaving Pointe de Kermorvan at least 400m to the E to avoid Petite Vinotière (dries 2·4m) and Pierre Normand (dries 2·2m) just to the NW of Pointe de Kermorvan. The height of the tide on the last of the flood (N-going) may allow one to pass over these dangers to get close inshore to dodge the stream. When La Louve red beacon tower is open of Pointe de Kermorvan and bears 090° or less, alter towards the harbour entrance and make allowance for any cross streams. This should pass well S of an off-lier (dries 2·4m) between Kermorvan and La Louve. The N/S streams will be strong except at slack high and low water but will decrease as the entrance is approached.

By night from the N Approach either down Chenal de La Helle leading line (front Pointe de Kermorvan Fl.5s, rear Lochrist DirOc(3)12s 135°-intens-140°) on 138°, or down Chenal du Four leading line (front Pointe de Kermorvan Fl.5s, rear St-Mathieu Fl.15s+F 158°-intens-160°) on 158° until Grande Vinotière bears 230°. Then alter to the

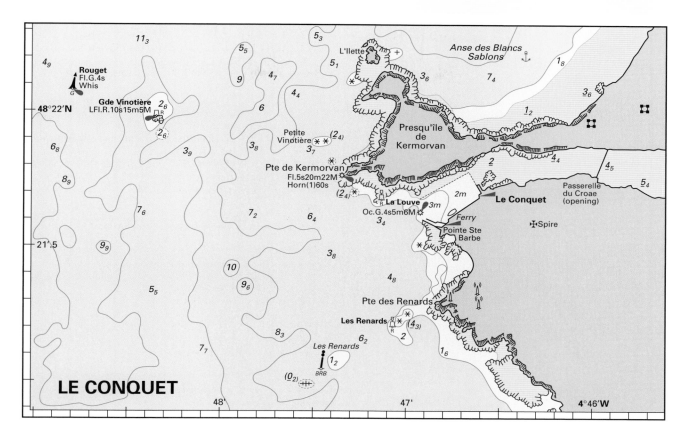

LE CONQUET

S on Roche du Tournant buoy Iso.R.4s to pass midway between Grande Vinotière and Pointe de Kermorvan. When the Oc.G.4s on the S breakwater end bears 080° or more alter course towards it and approach on a steady bearing making any allowance for cross streams.

By day from the S Transits of Pointe de Kermorvan/Pointe de Corsen 358° or Pointe de Kermorvan/Trézien lighthouse 007° will lead up to the entrance. The former is more easily identified by day and leads between Les Renards buoy (BRB 2 spheres) and Les Renards beacon tower (red port topmark). If using the Kermorvan/Trezien line, borrow to starboard before reaching Les Renards buoy to leave it to port. Keep La Louve beacon tower (red, port topmark) ahead until the harbour entrance is opened and turn in.

By night from the S Only the Pointe de Kermorvan (Fl.5s) and Trézien (DirOc(2)6s) leading line on 007° is useable by night. This leads close to Les Renards buoy and a charted *PD* wreck drying 0·2m close to the SW. If there is not enough water to clear this, the line should be kept slightly open to the E to pass safely between Les Renards buoy and beacon, both unlit. When the Oc.G.4s on the breakwater end bears 080° turn towards it.

Entrance

Leave the end of the S breakwater 50m to starboard on entry but watch for any vessels leaving from inside the breakwater. There is 4m on the approach, 3m in the outer harbour and 2 up to the inner jetty beyond the slip.

Berths

The inner side of the breakwater is not suitable for yachts and all of the remaining useable quays are taken by the fishing boats. Fishing boats also occupy the moorings with extensive ground chains in the S and SE part of the harbour. It may be possible to find an alongside berth clear of those used by the ferries but ask at the *capitainerie*.

Anchorage

Either anchor as close in as water permits between La Louve and La Basse du Filet (see plan on chart *3345*) or work in as far as moorings allow in to the N part of the harbour keeping clear of manoeuvring space for the ferries. A trip line is advisable inside the breakwater.

Facilities

Water From a tap in the inner harbour.
Fuel From a garage along the main road.
Shops and restaurants A selection in the town.
Cranes Up to 15 tons.
Slip In the inner harbour.
Chandler At the co-operative.
Travel Bus to Brest (12M) whence there are rail and air connections with the rest of France. Ferries run from Le Conquet to Iles d'Ouessant and Molène. A footbridge crosses the estuary higher up which gives access to the peninsula and Anse de Blancs Sablons.

Anse des Blancs Sablons
Le Conquet on far side *Porz Illien*   *L'Ilette*

Porz Illien and Anse des Blancs Sablons (Le Conquet) looking SW

La Louve   *Outer breakwater end*

Le Conquet entrance looking E

Anse des Blancs Sablons   Pointe de Kermorvan   La Louve Bn Tr   Anse de Bertheaume in Rade de Brest

Le Conquet looking ESE at LW

Historical

Le Conquet has been the scene of many fights with the English who seem to have been generally repulsed. However, in 1558 they sacked the town and burnt all the houses except for eight that belonged to English subjects – they still stand today. The church contains the tomb of Père Michel le Nobletz, the seafaring priest who devoted his life to the conversion of the seafaring inhabitants of Finistère and surrounding islands.

Chenal du Four

General

The Chenal du Four is the normal inshore route for vessels travelling south from the English coast or North Brittany to the Biscay ports, or on the return route. It saves distance and avoids the larger seas and complication of the shipping lanes outside Ouessant. It is wide and well marked but is subject to the Atlantic swell, strong tidal streams, steep seas and the visibility is often poor.

There are two other channels in the area. Chenal de la Helle runs from the NW into the Chenal du Four towards its southern part and merges with it. The directions for it are included here. Passage du Fromveur to the SE of Ouessant is 1½ miles wide at its narrowest, deep and well marked. It has the strongest streams in the area (up to 9 knots at springs) and wind against tide conditions will produce steep seas and violent overfalls. Provided

CHENAL DU FOUR

Depths in Metres

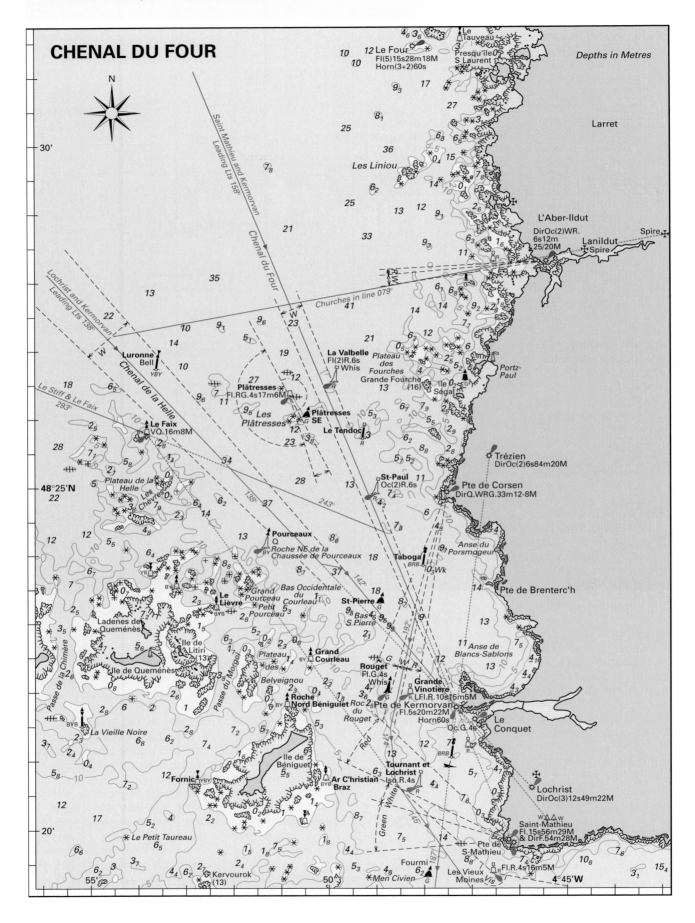

these conditions can be avoided there are no special difficulties in using this passage with chart *2694*. Details of lights and anchorages in the Passage du Fromveur may be found under Ile d'Ouessant.

The worst seas occur not in the Chenal du Four but its northern approaches. Between Ile Vierge and Le Four lighthouse northerly winds often produce a considerable swell which a weather-going stream over an uneven bottom will turn into steep and dangerous seas. The same area is also more effected by any westerly swell from the Atlantic than further south where Ouessant and other islands and rocks provide some lee. The timing of arrival at the exits of the Chenal in strong winds is of some importance to avoid the worst effects of wind over tide as the open sea is regained. These timings are given in the directions below.

Warning

In fog or bad visibility navigation becomes difficult. Once the narrows are reached a yacht with wind and stream astern will be committed. The bottom is too uneven and the rocks too steep-to for the echo sounder to give adequate warning. Speed over the ground is likely to be high, making the buoys themselves a considerable hazard and their lights cannot always be relied on. Radar and DGPS may alleviate the dangers but not remove them.

However if the outer marks have been sighted and the visibility gives no indication of further deterioration, pilotage is possible even if the main leading lines and lights are not visible until closer to them. In very poor visibility it is better to remain in harbour or well out to sea. If caught by a sudden deterioration when in the passage there are two options – feel your way to an anchorage in Anse de Blancs Sablons or call St-Mathieu Signal Station on Ch 16 and ask for radar guidance on Ch 11. The latter is an English speaking service for use in emergency only.

Data

Charts

Admiralty *2694, 3345* (ARCS)
Imray *C36*

Tides

The times of HW and LW are within 5 minutes of those at Brest and the heights within 0·1m.

Tidal streams

The rising stream sets to the N and the falling to the S. The time of flow is much affected by the wind; a S wind will prolong the N-going stream and vice versa. Tidal streams at the following positions begin at the following times in relation to HW Brest (from the N):

1M N of Les Plâtresses
+0600   020°   Maximum spring rates 1 knot
−0100   170°
Basse St-Paul (off Pointe de Corsen)
+0600   340°   Maximum spring rates 2½ knots
HW   170°
Grande Vinotière (off Le Conquet)
−0600   345°   Maximum spring rates 5 knots
HW   185°
Roche de la Fourni (at S entrance)
−0600   000°   Maximum spring rates 3 knots
HW   180°

Depths

The Chenal du Four has a least depth of 5m and Chenal de la Helle 7m on the leading lines.

Lights and buoys (from the N)

Le Four Fl(5)15s28m18M Horn(3+2)60s Grey tower
Chenal du Four Ldg Lts 158·5°
    Front Kermorvan Fl.5s20m20M Horn 60s White square tower
    Rear St-Mathieu Fl.15s56m29M and DirF.54m28M 158°-intens-160° White tower, red top
Les Plâtresses Fl.RG.4s17m6M 343°-R-153°-G-333° White octagonal tower
Valbelle buoy (port) Fl(2)R.6s5M Whis
Basse St-Paul buoy (port) Oc(2)R.6s
Chenal de la Helle Ldg Lts 138°
    Front Kermorvan Fl.5s20m22M Horn 60s White square tower
    Rear Lochrist DirOc(3)12s49m22M 135°-intens-140° Octagonal white tower, red top

Chenal du Four, steering S past Les Vieux Moines beacon tower and Pointe de St-Mathieu lighthouse

Chenal du Four looking SE. Grande Vinotière centre,
Kermorvan and Le Conquet far left, Pte St-Mathieu far right

Le Faix VQ.16m8M N cardinal tower
Pourceaux buoy Q N cardinal
Corsen DirQ.WRG.33m12-8M 008°-R-012°-W-015°-
 G-021° White hut
La Grande Vinotière Fl.R.10s15m5M Octagonal red
 tower
St-Mathieu auxiliary 54m bearing 291° from main
 tower Q.WRG.26m14-11M 085°-G-107°-W-116°-R-
 134° White tower
Tournant et Lochrist buoy (port) Iso.R.4s
Les Vieux Moines Fl.R.4s16m5M 280°-vis-133°
 Octagonal red tower
Southern Ldg Line 007°
 Front Kermorvan Fl.5s20m22M Horn 60s White
 square tower
 Rear Trézien DirOc(2)6s84m20M 003°-intens-011°
 Grey tower, white towards S

Communications

Ouessant Traffic on Ch 13, 16 and 79. Low visibility
 warnings on Ch 79 every H+10 and H+40. 24 hours.
Le Conquet Port Radio Ch 08, 16 0830–1200,
 1300–1800 LT.

Directions – southbound

Chenal du Four (See plan page 204)
By day Coasting southward from Le Four light a
fair offing should be given to Les Linioux and
Plateau des Fourches which are unlit and
unmarked. The Chenal du Four may then be
entered NE of La Plâtresses tower (white) with the
lighthouses of St-Mathieu (white circular tower, red
top) and Kermorvan (white square tower) in transit
bearing 158°. The remaining transits are shown on
the plan on page 204.

The area free from navigational dangers and steep
seas is considerable and in fine weather the
recommended tracks can be safely left. In heavy
weather, the recommended tracks should be kept to
as the overfalls will be worst over any irregular
bottom such as between La Grande Vinotière and
Pointe de Kermorvan.

If a vessel bound S is late on the tide she can avoid
the worst of a foul stream by standing into Anse des
Blancs Sablons and again into the bay S of Le

Conquet, but care must be taken to avoid the
dangers in the latter.

By night The transits and sectored lights are shown
on plan page 204 and chart *3345*. The channel is
excellently lit and in good weather the navigation is
easy. Navigate to the N of Les Plâtresses to bring
Kermorvan and St-Mathieu into transit bearing
158° and proceed down it. Note that in a narrow
sector each side of this St-Mathieu shows a fixed
white directional light as well as the Fl.15s light.
This will leave Les Plâtresses (Fl.RG.4s) to
starboard; La Valbelle buoy (Fl(2)R.6s), St-Paul
buoy (Oc(2)R.6s) and Taboga buoy (unlit) all to
port. When Corsen light turns white from green put
it astern on a course of about 192° and stay in this
sector to pass between Grande Vinotière
(LFl.R.10s) and Rouget buoy (Iso.G.4s). When the
St-Mathieu auxiliary light turns red make 174° and
enter the red sector of Corsen until the Tournant et
Lochrist buoy (Iso.R.4s) is abeam. The auxiliary St-
Mathieu light will then turn white and Les Vieux
Moines (Fl.R.4s) open. Steer 145° to bring
Kermorvan light in to transit with Trézien
(DirOc(2)6s) before the green sector of St-Mathieu
auxiliary is left. Steer nothing W of this transit to
clear the unlit La Fourmi buoy.

Chenal de la Helle

By day From the NW align Kermorvan lighthouse
(white square tower) with Lochrist (octagonal white
tower, red top on skyline) on 138°. If the visibility is
not clear, Luronne W cardinal buoy (unlit), Le Faix
E cardinal beacon tower and the distinctive La Helle
rock nearby will assist. Keep on this transit until
Corsen bears 012° and put it astern to pass between
Grande Vinotière and Rouget starboard-hand buoy
on 192°. This transit passes over 4·7m Basse St-
Pierre which can be avoided by leaving the St-Pierre
green buoy to starboard rather than port. Then
proceed as for the Chenal du Four.

By night Align Kermorvan light (Fl.5s) with
Lochrist (DirOc(3)12s) until the white sector of
Corsen (DirQ.WRG) bearing 012° is entered then
proceed as above. To avoid Basse St-Pierre if

necessary, leave the Kermorvan/Lochrist line when Le Stiff light on Ouessant (Fl(2)R.20s) is in transit with Le Faix light (VQ) bearing 293° and steer 113° on this stern transit to join the main Chenal du Four alignment and proceed as above.

Timing

The best time to arrive off St-Mathieu going S is at low water slack or HW Brest+6. The stream will then be fair if going up Le Goulet to Brest, but foul across L'Iroise if going on S; however, by the time Raz de Sein is reached it should be turning fair again. In strong southerly winds or heavy swell this timing, or a little later will minimise wind/swell over tide conditions off St-Mathieu.

The choice going N is not so clear cut. In heavy northerly weather the main consideration will be to minimise wind over tide conditions N of Kermorvan and it would be prudent to arrive at this latitude as the stream turns to the S at HW slack or HW Brest, and face six hours foul stream but easier seas. In good weather and no excessive swell an arrival off St-Mathieu at LW slack will give 6 hours fair stream allowing L'Aber Wrac'h at least to be reached before HW there.

Directions – northbound

The directions bound N are as for those bound S on the reciprocals and may be followed in reverse If using Chenal de la Helle at night beware of the unlit Basse St-Pierre and Luronne buoys which are close to the transit.

Anchorages

Directions for anchorages at the following are given in this book: Ile d'Ouessant, Ile Molène, Le Conquet, Anse des Blancs Sablons, L'Aber-Ildut and Melon. Charts *2694* and *3345* will show many other possibilities. *North Biscay* should be consulted for directions to Anse de Bertheaume 3M to E of St-Mathieu.

Ile de Molène

General

Molène is a small island but the largest of those between Le Conquet and Ouessant. The approach looks difficult, being beset by rocks and fierce tidal streams but in the right conditions near neaps there is a straightforward approach from the N and an anchorage sheltered from E through S to WSW. It has a character of its own, less stark than Ouessant and Sein supported by kelp gathering and fishing and with a surprising number of facilities for the visitor. There are magnificent views over the rock-strewn area surrounding it.

Warning

The tidal stream in the Passage du Fromveur to the N can attain 9 knots at springs and the flow through the islands at up to 6 knots.

The area has a higher incidence of fog and poor visibility during the summer than the nearby coast.

Data

Charts

Admiralty *2694* (ARCS)
Imray *C36*
No larger-scale plan

Tides

The times are within 5 minutes of those at Brest and the heights within 0·1m.

Tidal streams

The rising stream is to the NE and the falling stream to the SW. Tidal streams begin at the following times in relation to HW Brest:
Near Les Pierres Vertes (to the W of Molène)
−0615   NNE
HW   SSW   Maximum rates 3½ knots
In NW channel of Ile Molène
−0615   ENE   The maximum rates at the W end are 4
−0015   WSW   knots increasing to 6 knots at the E end.
In Passe de la Chimère (to the S of Molène and W of Quemenez)
−0615   N
−0015   S   Maximum rates 3½ knots

Lights

Les Trois Pierres (to the NNE) Iso.WRG.4s15m9-6M
    070°-G-147°-W-185°-R-191-G-197°-W-213°-R-070°
    White column
Molène old mole Dir 191° DirFl(3)WRG.12s6m9-7M
    183°-G-190°-W-192°-R-203°
Dir 261° DirFl(2)WRG.6s9m9-7M 253°-G-260°-W-263°-R-270°

Search and rescue, weather forecasts, communications

As for Ouessant and Le Conquet.

Approaches

From the N by day Navigate to a position ½ mile to the N of Le Faix N cardinal lighthouse and steer to make good a course of 270° to leave the distinctive solitary rock La Helle (11m) about ½

ILE DE MOLENE

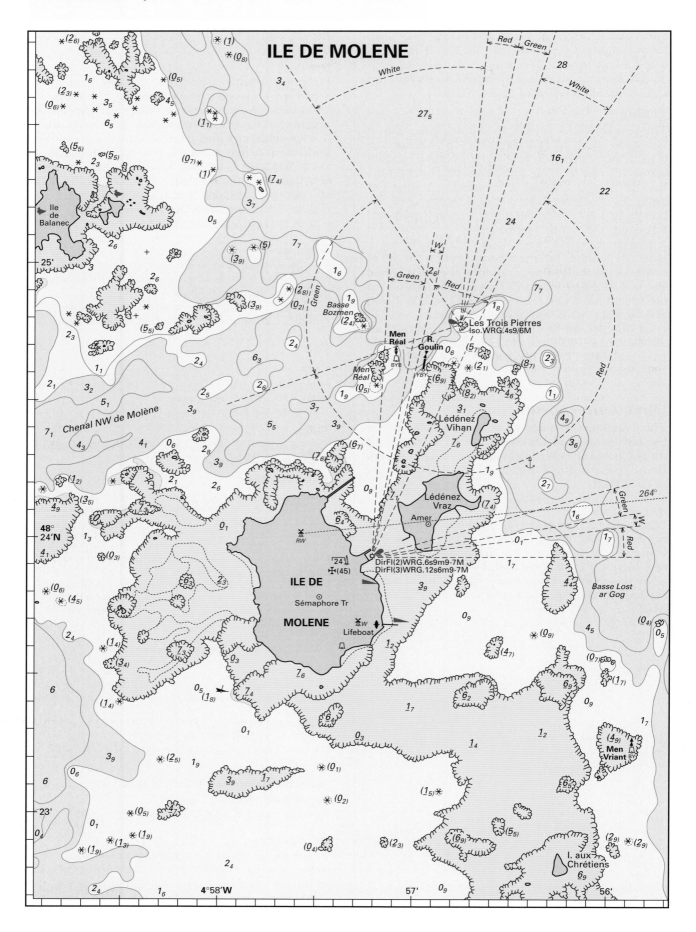

mile to port. When about ½ mile to the W of it the church spire should be well open to the right of Les Trois Pierres (white tower 15m). Turn towards Les Trois Pierres and make good a track of approximately 180° to leave it 500m to port by which time Men Réal E cardinal beacon tower and Roche Goulin W cardinal spar buoy will be identified. Put the church spire midway between the two and continue between them on a track of about 200°. To the left of the church spire will be a white framework telecommunications mast and to the right a sémaphore tower. Continue on this track leaving a line of rocks which never cover to port, and the outer breakwater to starboard. The tidal streams will be setting strongly across this approach line except at LW slack until well into the anchorage.

From the N by night Taking account of the strong cross streams mentioned above, approach Les Trois Pierres (Iso.WRG.4s) in its westerly white sector until the sectored and directional light (Fl(3)WRG.12s) on the old breakwater end is picked up. Turn down the narrow white sector on 191° and keep in it until Men Réal beacon tower and Roche Goulin buoy are past when turn to starboard to enter the green sector of the light. Stay on the W edge of this sector on a track of 183° until the anchorage is reached.

From the east The approach is via the Chenal des Laz before turning NW to round Les Trois Pierres lighthouse and then proceeding down the N approach route. Navigate to a position ½ mile to the N of Pourceaux N cardinal buoy at the S end of Chenal de la Helle. Identify the white beacon on Lédénez Vraz and turn towards it keeping it bearing 264° until the North Mill on Molène can be identified (stumpy stone tower with the top painted dayglow red) and align the two on the same bearing. At night get into the narrow white sector of the directional light on the old breakwater (Fl(2)WRG.6s) bearing 261° and continue down it until Les Trois Pierres (Iso.WRG.4s) bears 310°, or by day the W end of Quemenez bears 170°. Alter then to a northerly course to round Les Trois Pierres at least 300m off allowing for any cross set. Then join the N approach route as above.

Chenal NW de Molène and Chenal de la Chimère Both these offer narrow but deep water routes (except at LW springs) to the final approach to the island by the N channel. They are however indifferently marked and have no formal transits that may be used. See chart *2694*. They would be an interesting exercise for the skilful navigator near slack water and good visibility.

Chenal de Laz This is a direct approach from the E in the white sector of the old mole light bearing 271°. The only disadvantage to it is that is crosses the bar at the S end of the channel drying 7·3m and local knowledge is required to find the narrow channel across it which would only be negotiable at HWS in a craft of any draught.

ch spire   Telecom mast   N breakwater   Leading light   Bazou Real Bn Tr   Bar at S end channel

Ile de Molène looking N

R Goulin   *Lédénez Vraz*   *Quay*   *Church*   *Old Sémaphore*   *N Breakwater*   *Bazou Réal*

Ile de Molène north entrance looking SSW

Lifeboat slip   *Leading light*   *Anchorage*   *N breakwater end*

Ile de Molène looking S

Anchorage

In the pool about 200m NE of the N jetty there is about 1·9m. Depths decrease to the S of this but it may be possible especially at neaps to find a more sheltered and southerly anchorage still clear of moorings. The holding is patchy with rock patches and a trip line is recommended.

An anchorage is shown on chart *2694* and on the French chart ENE of the NE tip of Lédénez Vraz in sand and mud. It is exposed to the E and there will be little shelter from the W near HW.

Facilities

Water Scarce.
Fuel None.
Shops A good *huit à huit supermarché*, a post office and some chandlery from the co-operative.
Travel Occasional ferries run to Le Conquet, Ile d'Ouessant and Brest whence rail and air connections may be made with the rest of France.

Historical

The houses above the harbour are close-packed so it looks a town of substance from the approach. The principal buildings are the church and the sémaphore tower. The clock in the former was a gift from England in recognition of the services of the men of Molène when the SS *Drummond Castle* returning from South Africa was wrecked on Les Pierres Vertes. Out of the 400 on board only 3 were saved; the bodies of 29 of the passengers are buried in the cemetery and many others elsewhere around the island. A cistern for water, which the island lacked was also built and a richly jewelled chalice for the church was presented by the English in grateful memory of the kindness of the fisherfolk of Molène on this tragic occasion.

Ile d'Ouessant

General

Ile d'Ouessant (Ouessant or in Breton, Enez Eussa) is one of the major maritime turning points on the world's shipping routes. There is a Separation Zone for commercial shipping to the north and west of the island which is controlled from a centre near Le Conquet. There is no requirement for vessels under 300grt rounding Ouessant to report to Ouessant Traffic Control but they will, if asked on Ch 13 give position and navigational assistance.

Qui voit Ouessant, voit son sang may overstate the island's reputation although not in a winter storm at spring tides. Though the island is bare and windswept it has a charm of its own. Anchorages offer shelter from most quarters in settled weather and now that an airstrip has been opened it is not so isolated. There are shops to satisfy most modest needs and the island can be explored on foot or by bicycle.

Warning

The tidal streams are strong in the vicinity and can reach up to 9 knots at springs in the Passage du Fromveur where the overfalls are dangerous in any wind over tide conditions.

Fog is more prevalent, especially in July than on the neighbouring coast.

Data

Charts

Admiralty *2694* (ARCS)
Imray *C36* (plan)

Tides

The times are within 5 minutes of those at Brest and within 0·1m in heights.

Tidal streams

Tidal flows are complex especially to the SW of the island where the direction can change in a short distance and there are many overfalls and disturbances. Generally the rising stream is to the NE and falling to the SW. Tidal streams begin at the following times in relation to HW Brest:

At Baz Veur (½ mile NW of Nividic light)
NE   −0550
SW   +0045   Maximum rates 5½ knots
At La Jument
NW   +0435
S   −0045   Maximum rates 4½ knots
1½ miles SW of La Jument
NW   −0545
S   +0015   Maximum rates 3½ knots
Passage du Fromveur (between Kéréon and Ouessant)
NE   −0515   Maximum 9 knots
SW   +0045   Maximum 8 knots

There is a weak counter current close to the SE shore of Ouessant running opposite to that in the Passage du Fromveur.

Lights

Le Stiff (NE corner) Fl(2)R.20s85m24M Adjoining white towers The radar tower to the NE is 189m high
Créac'h (SW corner) Fl(2)10s70m32M Horn(2)120s 255°-vis-247° Tower with black and white bands Racon (RG)
Nividic (off SW corner) VQ(9)10s28m10M 290°-vis-225° Octagonal white tower, red bands, helo platform
La Jument (off SSW corner) Fl(3)R.15s36m22M Horn(3)60s 241°-vis-199° Octagonal grey tower with red top
Port du Stiff (mole head) DirQ.WRG.11m10-7M 251°-G-254°-W-264°-R-267°
Men-Korn (off E corner) VQ(3)WR.5s21m8/8M 145°-W-040°-R-145° 058°-obscd-119° E cardinal beacon tower
Kéréon (off SE coast) Oc(2+1)WR.24s38m17/7M Horn(2+1)120s 019°-W-248°-R-019° Grey circular tower

Search and rescue

Ouessant is in the CROSS Corsen region with radio stations at Créac'h, Le Stiff and Pointe de Sainte-Mathieu which will respond to emergency calls on Ch 16 or activation of GMDSS on Ch 70. CROSS Corsen control is situated 3M N of Le Conquet.

ILE D'OUESSANT

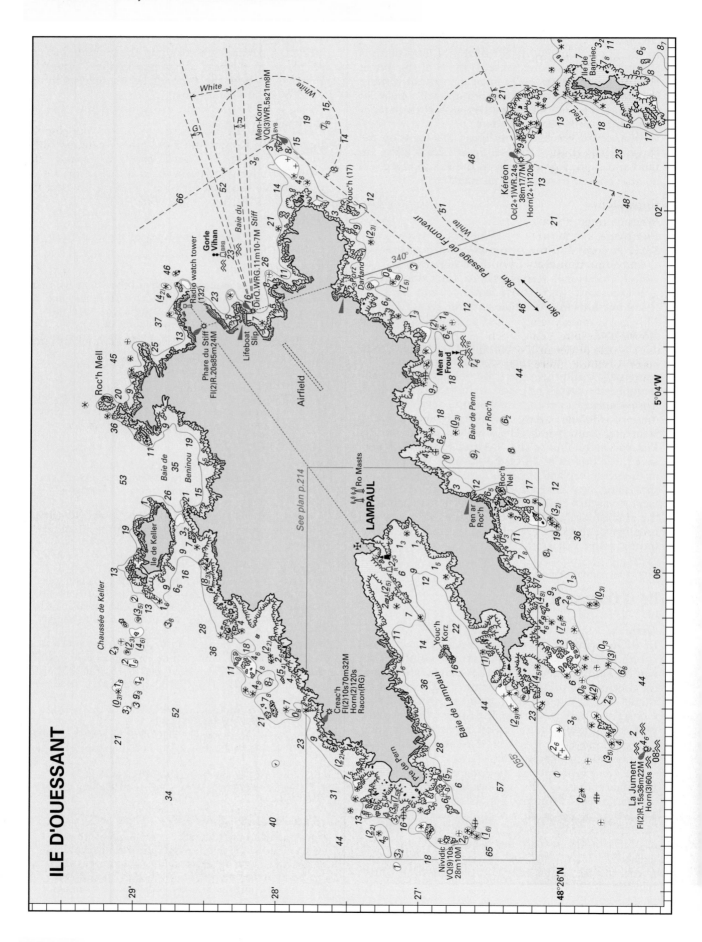

There are all-weather lifeboats at Lampaul, Le Conquet and Ile Molène.

There are hospitals at Brest.

Weather forecasts

On Ch 79 for local areas at following times: 0503, 0715, 1115, 1545, 1915 LT in French and English.

Fog warnings when required also on Ch 79.

Navtex Corsen (A) or Niton (S).

Communications

Mairie d'Ouessant ☎ 02 98 48 80 06. There is no port radio.

Approaches

Account must be taken of the strong tidal streams and overfalls in the vicinity of the island, particularly in the Passage du Fromveur and of the possibility of a deterioration in visibility.

Baie de Lampaul

This is the main yacht anchorage with a number of moorings despite being open to the SW. It is not used by the ferries unless conditions in Baie du Stiff make berthing there impossible. The lifeboat is housed here.

Approach

An approach line of either Le Stiff Lighthouse or the taller radar tower behind it open to the left of the prominent rock Youc'h Korz (34m) in the middle of Lampaul Bay bearing 055° clears all the outer dangers. The transit should be observed closely until inside the bay to counteract the strong and variable streams outside.

Entrance

Once inside the tidal streams become negligible. Pass Youc'h Korz to the S (an off-lier extends 100m to the N of it) and then approach the moorings/anchorage/harbour with Men ar Groas green beacon tower bearing 050° or less to clear the rocks in the N corner of the bay.

Berths

There is a small inner harbour (Porz Pol) 400m to the ENE inside the red and green beacon towers which dries 3·5m with an entrance less than 8m wide. It is cluttered with local boats and mooring lines and the quays, like that on the outer side are rough and uneven. Its use by deep draught yachts is not recommended but it might be possible to dry out inside after a prior recce. A number of small boat moorings obstruct the approach.

Moorings

A number of moorings have been laid for the use of visitors in the bay to the S of Men ar Groas beacon and a vacant one will nearly always be found.

Church spire   Lifeboat slip   Men ar Groas Bn Tr   Harbour entrance. Porz Pol   Mooring area

Ile d'Ouessant. Lampaul looking NE

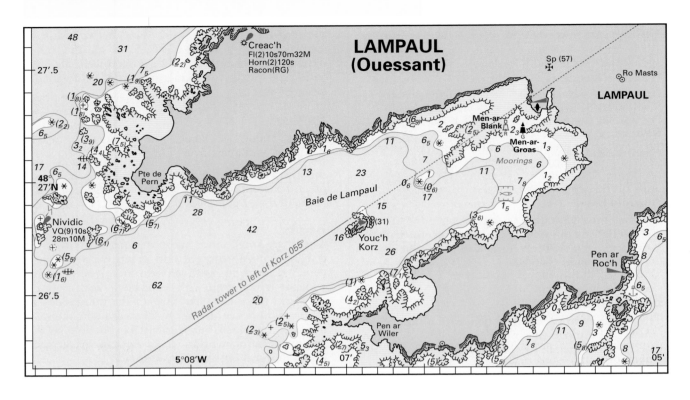

Ile d'Ouessant. Lampaul

Anchorage

There may be room and water to anchor inside the two beacon towers where some shelter from sea and swell may be found. There is 2·3m between the beacons shoaling to 0·8m near the jetty but there are many rocky patches.

Outside the beacons water may be found to the E of the moorings in up to 5m sand and mud. Otherwise anchor outside the moorings in generally good holding of sand and mud. The SE side of the bay is much encumbered with fish farms.

Facilities

Water From a tap on the quay.

Fuel From a garage 1km away.

Dinghy landing At the lifeboat slip; this dries at LW but there is a ladder to the W of it.

Shops Two small *supermachés*, also banks and a post office.

Bars and restaurants A number, also a disco in season.

Engineer At the garage.

Bicycle hire Various outlets.

Travel Ferries from Le Stiff to Le Conquet, Brest and Ile de Molène. Daily flights to Brest (Guipavas).

Leisure Apart from walks or bicycle rides round the island, the small museum at Creac'h lighthouse is worth the walk and the island's last windmill has been restored. There are a number of English graves in the churchyard from past maritime disasters.

Historical

The legends about the island are widespread since it was first mentioned by Pytheas of Marseille in 400 BC. It was long regarded as the resting place of the souls of the departed. The island was scattered with dolmens, cromlechs and other remains of Druidic or pre-Druidic worship until they were used in the construction of the first lighthouse. In the 6th century the Welsh monk St-Paul Aurelian landed in the bay that still retains his name, Lan Paul or Porz Paul, and built the first Christian church on Ouessant before continuing eastward to continue his mission in the Roscoff area. In 1388 the English landed and massacred all the inhabitants. In 1788 a French fleet beat an English squadron under Admiral Keppel nearby. At the turn of that century Châteaubriand, returning from America was wrecked off the island, one of the innumerable shipwrecks that the rocks of Ouessant have claimed over the centuries.

Baie du Stiff

General

Although apparently sheltered from the S through W to NW, heavy weather from any quarter sends in a large swell which makes the anchorage and bay untenable. The holding is poor but there are a few visitors' moorings. There are no facilities nearer than Lampaul apart from a café/bar.

Warning

Cables enter the small bay to the N of the jetty and immediately S of Le Stiff lighthouse and anchorage is prohibited here.

Approach

Straightfoward by day or night passing S of Gorle Vihan marked by an isolated danger beacon tower. At night the white sector of the pier light leads to the S of the tower.

Moorings

There is a heavy white mooring for the ferries and supply vessel in the bay to the S and W of the jetty. Some smaller moorings have been laid inshore of these for visitors and in the bay S of the jetty.

Airstrip   Yacht moorings behind breakwater   Youc'h Korz   Lampaul church

Ile d'Ouessant. Baie du Stiff looking SW

Ile d'Ouessant. Baie du Stiff looking NNW. Visitors' moorings in foreground. Semaphore and radar towers on cape

Anchorage

The holding is poor with rocky patches and the area between the ferry mooring and the jetty must be kept clear for the ferries to manoeuvre. Otherwise anchor where there is water but it would not be wise to leave the vessel unwatched except in very settled weather.

Facilities

Dinghy landing On the N side of the jetty.
Café Open in the season above the quay.
Bicycle hire From the café. 2M to the bright lights of Lampaul.

Leisure Le Stiff lighthouse is sometimes open to visitors in the summer and a climb to the top will be rewarded with a fine view. It was built by Vauban in 1695 and only has 126 steps to the top.

Wildlife In 2000 a seal showed a penchant for rubber dinghies which it boarded and could only be removed by tipping it out.

Porz Darland

A small inlet on the S side of the island to the S of Baie du Stiff. It has a breakwater with a slip inside it in the NW corner which has 3m at the outer end. It is sometimes used by the supply vessel in N winds.

Approach

Approach with Le Stiff lighthouse bearing 340° but this disappears when ½M off when continue on the same track towards the breakwater end. Avoid the rock and patches (4·8m and never covers) off the N shore.

Anchorage

Anchorage may be found in 5m, sand 100m S of the breakwater end. A mooring buoy is sometimes placed in the bay for use by the supply boat.

There is a landing slip on the N side of the jetty and a track runs from this to Baie du Stiff.

Baie du Stiff

Ile d'Ouessant. Porz Darland near LW

Ile d'Ouessant. Overfalls at NE end of Passage du Fromveur

Baie de Penn ar Roc'h

A wide bay on the S side of the island offering little shelter except from the W when it has been sometimes used by the supply boat. There is a landing slip at the W side and a track to Lampaul.

Approach and anchorage

Approach with the slip and road bearing 330° and anchor as in close as possible between the slip and Roc'h Nel to its S in 5m. See chart *2694* and plan on page 214.

The slip can be used at all states of the tide.

Appendix

Charts

I. British Admiralty and Imray charts

Chart	Title	Scale
SW England & Brittany		
1432	Le Four to Ile Vierge	25,000
	L'Aber-Wrac'h	15,000
2643	Ile D'Ouessant to Pointe de Penmarc'h	200,000
2644	Ile D' Ouessant to Ile de Batz	150,000
2668	Ile Vierge to Plateau des Roches Douvres	150,000
2669	Channel Islands & adjacent coast of France	150,000
2694	Le Four to Goulet de Brest including Ile D'Ouessant	50,000
2700	Approaches to St-Malo	15,000
3345	Chenal du Four	25,000
3656	Plateau des Minquiers & adjacent coast of France	50,000
3659	Cap Fréhel to Iles Chausey	50,000
3668	Le Four to Anse de Kernic	50,000
3669	Anse de Kernic to Les Sept Iles	50,000
3670	Les Sept Iles to L'Ost-Pic	50,000
3672	Harbours on the NW coast of France:	
	Rivière de Treguier: Granville	15,000
	Erquy: Perros Guiréc: Port Blanc	20,000
	Saint Quay-Portrieux	25,000
3673	Ile de Bréhat and Anse de Paimpol entrance to Le Triex	20,000
	Port de Lézardrieux Le Trieux: Paimpol	10,000
3674	L'Ost-Pic to Cap Fréhel	50,000
	Le Légué	
English Channel (East)		
60	Alderney and the Casquets	25,000
1136	Jersey − north coast	25,000
1137	Approaches to St Helier	25,000
1138	Jersey − east coast	25,000
807	Guernsey and Herm	25,000
	Beaucette Marina	15,000
808	East Guernsey, Herm and Sark	25,000
	Beaucette Marina	15,000
2845	Alderney Harbour	6,000
3140	St Peter Port	6,000
3278	Saint Helier	6,000
3653	Guernsey to Alderney and adjacent coast of France	50,000
3654	Guernsey, Herm and Sark	50,000
3655	Jersey and adjacent coast of France	50,000
3656	Plateau des Minquiers and adjacent coast of France	50,000

Imray charts

Chart	Title	Scale
C10	Western English Channel Passage	400,000
	Radiobeacons, lights, tides	WGS 84
C32	Le Havre to Cherbourg	155,000
	Plans Ouistreham, Cherbourg, St-Vaast-la-Hougue, Courseulles-sur-Mer, Port-en-Bessin, Trouville/Deauville, Barfleur, Baie du Grand Vey, Arromanches, Dives-sur-Mer, Le Havre Yacht Harbour, Honfleur, Grandcamp-Maisy, Cherbourg – Port Chentereyne Marina	
C33A	Channel Islands	120,000
	Plans St Peter Port, Beaucette Marina, St Sampson Harbour, Alderney Harbour, Omonville, Goury, Dielette, Carteret, Portbail, Creux Harbour Approaches, Gorey, Little Russel	WGS 84
C33B	Channel Islands and North Coast of France	120,000
	Plans St Helier Approaches, St Helier Yacht Harbours, St-Malo Approaches, St-Malo, Granville, Erquy, Dahouet, Binic, Portrieux approaches	WGS 84
C34	Cap d'Erquy to Ile de Batz	110,000
	Plans R. de Tréguier, Primel, R. de Lannion, Port de Légué, Port Clos, Port de la Corderie, Loguivy, Anse de Perros, R. de Portrieux and Anse de Paimpol, Port Blanc, Lézardrieux, Tréguier, Paimpol	ED 1950
C35	Baie de Morlaix to L'Aber-Ildut	76,600
	Plans Ile de Batz, Approaches to L'Aber Wrac'h and L'Aber-Benôit, Argenton, Pontsuval, Moguériec, Port-Sall, L'Aber-Ildut	ED 1950
C36	Ile d'Ouessant to Raz de Sein	77,300
	Plans Le Conquet, Port de Brest, Morgat, Camaret-sur-Mer, Douarnenez, Baie de Lampaul (Ouessant), Marina du Moulin Blanc, Brest	ED 1950

II. French SHOM charts

P = available folded on waterproof paper

Chart	Title	Scale
La Manche (Centre)		
4233	La Rance - De St-Malo à l'Ecluse du Châtelier	15,000
	Du Chêne vert à l'Ecluse du Châtelier	15,000
6903	Guernsey et Herm	25,000
	Marina Beaucette	15,000
6904	Guernsey Est, Herm et Sark	25,000
	Marina Beaucette	15,000
6930P	Des roches de Portsall au plateau des Roches Douvres	150,000
6934	Alderney (Aurigny) et les Casquets	25,000
6938	Abors de St Hélier	25,000
6939	Jersey − Côte Est	25,000
7124P	Baie de Lannion − De la Pointe de Primel à l'île Grande	20,000

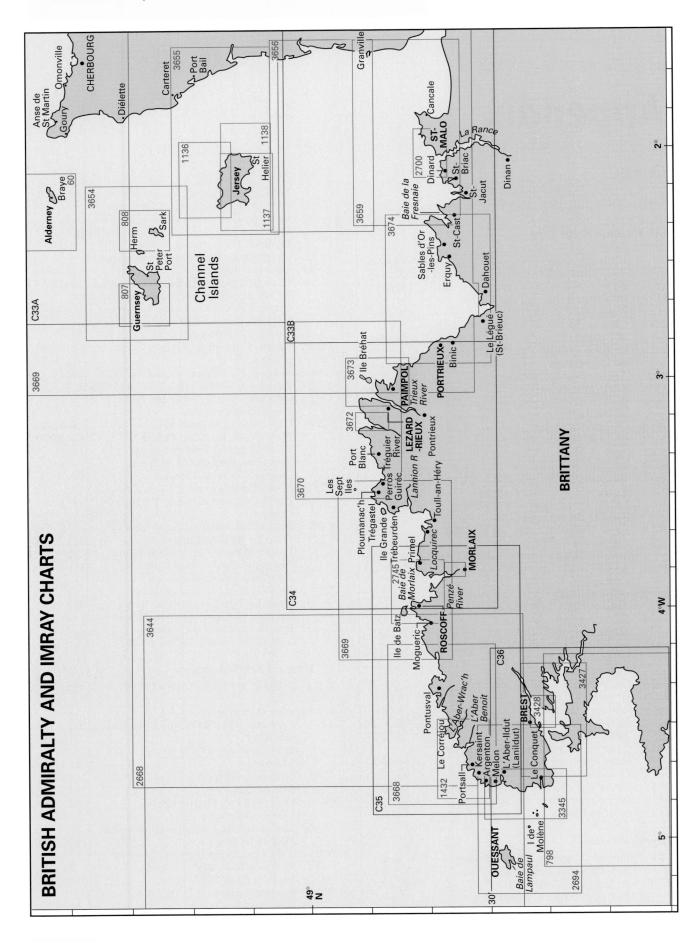

BRITISH ADMIRALTY AND IMRAY CHARTS

North Brittany & the Channel Islands

CHERBOURG

Anse de
St Martin
Goury Omonville

Diélette

Carteret

Port
Bail

3655

3656

Granville

Cancale

ST-
MALO

La Rance

Dinard

St-
Briac

St-
Jacut

Dinan

2700

Baie de la
Fresnaie

St-Cast

Sables d'Or
-les-Pins

Erquy

Dahouet

Le Légué
(St-Brieuc)

Binic

PORTRIEUX

Ile Bréhat

PAIMPOL

Trieux
River

3673

LEZARD
-RIEUX

Pontrieux

Port
Blanc

Tréguier

Guiréc.

Lannion R.

Toull-an-Héry

3672

Les
Sept
Iles

Perros

Ploumanac'h
Trégastel

Ile Grande

Trébeurden

Primel

Locquirec

2745

Baie de
Morlaix

MORLAIX

Penzé
River

Ile de Batz

Mogueric

ROSCOFF

3670

3674

3669

C33B

C34

C33A

C33B

3669

3644

2668

C35

3668

1432

Pontusval

Le Corréjou

Aber-Wrac'h

L'Aber
Benoit

Portsall

Kersaint

Argenton

Melon

L'Aber-Ildut
(Lanildut)

Le Conquet

BREST

3428

3427

C36

3345

798

2694

OUESSANT

Baie de
Lampaul

I de
Molène

BRITTANY

Alderney

Braye
60

3654

808

807

Herm

St
Peter
Port

Sark

Guernsey

Channel
Islands

Jersey

St
Helier

1136

1138

1137

3659

49°
N

30'

49°
N

5°

4°W

3°

2°

220

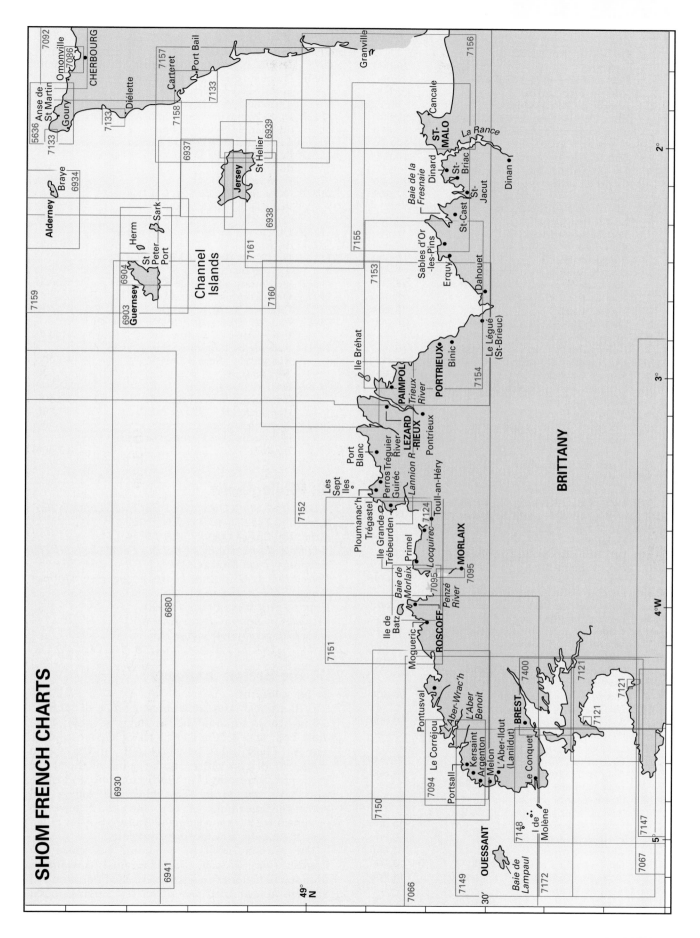

SHOM FRENCH CHARTS

Chart	Title	Scale
	Le Léguer (Rivière de Lannion)	20,000
	Port de Lannion (Le Léguer)	7,500
	Port de Trébeurden	7,500
7125P	Abords de Perros-Guirec – Les Sept Iles– De l'Ile Grande à l'Ile Balanec	20,000
	Mouillages de Trégastel	10,000
	Port de Ploumanac'h	10,000
	Port de Perros-Guirec	10,000
7126	De l'île Balanec aux Héaux-de-Bréhat – Cours du Jaudy	20,000
	Cartouche: A – Port de Tréguier	7,500
7127P	Abords de l'île Bréhat, anse de Paimpol – Entrée du Trieux	20,000
	Port de Lézardrieux – Le Trieux	10,000
	Port de Paimpol	10,000
7128P	Baie de Saint-Brieuc (Ouest) – De la Pointe de la Tour à l'Anse d'Yffiniac	25,000
	Port de Saint-Quay-Portrieux	7,500
	Port de Binic	7,500
7129	Du Cap Fréhel à Saint Briac-sur-Mer	20,000
7130P	Abords de Saint-Malo – De l'Ile des Hébihens à la Pointe de la Varde	15,000
7131P	Du Havre de Rothéneuf à Cancale	20,000
	Port de Cancale	7,500
7133	Ports de la côte Ouest du Cotentin	
	Abords de Goury	10,000
	Abords de Diélette	15,000
	Abords de Carteret et Portbail	15,000
	Carteret	10,000
	Portbail	10,000
	Havre de Regnéville	15,000
7134P	Iles Chausey	15,000
	Sound de Chausey	5,000
7151P	De l'anse de Kernic à l'île Grande	48,700
7152	De l'île Grande à l'île de Bréhat	48,700
7153P	De l'île de Bréhat au Plateau des Roches Douvres	48,600
7154	De l'île de Bréhat au Cap Fréhel – Baie de Saint-Brieuc	48,800
	Port de Légué	10,000
7155P	Du Cap Fréhel à la Pointe du Grouin – Approches de Saint-Malo	48,800
7156	De la Pointe du Grouin à la Pointe d'Agon – Baie du Mont-Saint-Michel – Iles Chausey	48,800
7157P	De la Pointe d'Agon au Cap de Carteret –Pasage de la Déroute	48,400
7158P	Du Cap de Carteret au Cap de la Hague – Raz Blanchard	50,000
7159P	De Guernsey, Herm et Sark à Alderney – Bancs de Casquets	50,000
7160	De Jersey à Guernsey	50,000
7161P	Des îles Chausey à Jersey – Plateau des Minquiers	48,500
7341	Abords de Granville	15,000
La Manche (Ouest)		
6966	Des Héaux-de-Bréhat au Cap Lévi	156,000
7095P	Baie de Morlaix – De l'île de Batz à la Pointe de Primel	20,000
	Ports de Roscoff	10,000
	Rivière de Morlaix	15,000
7150P	De Portsall à l'anse de Kernic	50,000
7151P	De l'anse de Kernic à l'île Grande	48,700
Côte Ouest de France		
5252	Raz de Sein	20,000

Chart	Title	Scale
6099P	Baie de Douarnenez	45,800
6677	Abords et port de Douarnenez	15,000
7094P	Du phare du Four à l'Ile Vierge – Port de l'Aber-Wrac'h	25,000
	Cartouche: A – Aber-Wrac'h	15,000
7122P	De la Pointe de Saint-Mathieu au phare du Four – Chenal du Four	25,000
	Cartouche: A – Port du Conquet	10,000
7123P	Ile Molène – Ile D'Ouessant – Passage du Fromveur	20,000
7147P	De la chaussée de Sein à la Pointe de Penmarc'h – Baie d'Audierne	50,000
	Cartouche: A – Port d'Audierne	12,500
7148P	Du Goulet de Brest à la Chaussée de Sein	49,300
7149	Du Goulet de Brest à Portsall – Ile d'Ouessant	49,100
7150P	De Portsall à l'anse de Kernic	50,000
7172	De la Pointe de Saint-Mathieu à la Chaussée de Sein – Iroise	49,300
7397	Rade de Brest (partie Sud) – Anse du Fret – Anse du Pulmic	10,000
7398	Rade de Brest (partie Ouest) – Baie de Roscanvel – Anse du Fret	10,000
7399	Port de Brest	7,500
7400	Rade de Brest	22,500
	Cartouche: A – Traverse de l'Hôpital	12,500
	Cartouche: B – Rivière du Faou	22,500
7401P	Accès à la Rade de Brest	22,500
	Cartouche: A – Port de Camaret-sur-Mer	10,000

III. Bibliography

Admiralty Sailing Directions – English Channel NP27
Admiralty Tide Tables Vol I NP201
Admiralty List of Lights Vol A NP74
Admiralty List of Radio Signals for Small Craft NP289
Admiralty Tidal Stream Atlases NP250, 264, 265
Votre Livre de Bord Manche/Atlantique. Bloc Marine
Rough Guide to Brittany
Brittany in a Week Frank Dawes
Mariners of Brittany Peter Anson
Naval Biography John Marshal

IV. The Breton language

By Nick Heath

It is of interest, and sometimes actually of value to the navigator, to know the meanings of some of the more common Breton words which appear in place names. Those who have cruised on the Celtic fringes of Britain will recognise some of them; the Irish *inish* corresponds to the Breton *inis*, and those who have cruised in West Highland waters will know the meanings of *glas* and *du*. I have no pretensions to a knowledge of Breton, but set down here the results of a few investigations.

The pronunciation is, or should be, more like English than French, with the final consonants sounded. The letters *c'h* represent the final sound of Scottish *loch* or Irish *lough* (but not English lock);

there is indeed a word *loc'h*, meaning a lake or pool; *ch* is pronounced as in shall. The French books and charts do not always distinguish between these, and there may be some errors in this book in consequence. In France, as in England, mobility and the radio/TV are killing regional differences and Raz is now usually pronounced Rah; Penmarc'h, pronounced Penmargh a generation ago, is now often Painmar, and Bénodet has gone from Benodette to Bainoday and collected an accent in the process. The most misleading example of this process is *porz*, which means an anchorage, possibly quite exposed and/or lacking in all shore facilities, not a port. This gets frenchified into *port*, and the French word *port* does mean a port, and not an anchorage, which is *anse* or *rade*.

A Breton glossary is hard to use because initial letters are often mutated into others, following complicated rules, depending on the preceding word. I have tried to meet this by suggesting, after the relevant letters, other(s) from which the initial might have come. Suppose that one wants to find the meaning of *I. er Gazek* (which is quite likely since The Mare seems to be the commonest name given to an islet). There is no word *gazek* in the glossary, but after G it says 'try K'; *kazek* means a mare; it mutates into *gazek* after *er*. Mutations of final letters also occur, but these do not usually cause difficulty in finding a word.

Breton	English
aber	estuary
anaon	the dead
al, an, ar	the
arvor	seaside
aven	river
B (try P)	
balan, banal	broom
bann, benn	hilltop
barr	summit, top
baz	shoal
beg	point, cape
beniget	cut, slit
benven, bosven	above-water rock
bian, bihan	small
bili, vili	shingle
bir, vir	needle, point
bran	crow
bras, braz	large
bre, brenn	small hill
breiz	Brittany
bri, brienn	cliff
C (try K)	
D (try T)	
daou	two
don, doun	deep
dour	water
du	blac k
ell	rock, shallow
enez	island

Breton	English
er a, an	the
fank	mud
froud, fred	strong current
freu	river
G (try K)	
garo, garv	rough
gavr	goat
glas	green
goban	shallow
gromell, gromilli	roaring
gwenn	white, pure
hir	long
hoc'h, houc'h	pig
iliz	church
izel	shallow
inis	island
kan(iou), kanal	channel
karn	cairn
kareg	rock
kastel	castle
kazek	mare
kein	shoal
kel(ou)	large rock
ker	house, hamlet
kern	summit, sharp peak
kleuz(iou)	hollow, deep
koad, goad	wood
kornog	shoal
koz	old
kreiz	middle
kriben	crest
lan, lann	monastery
marc'h	horse
melen	yellow
men	rock
mor, vor	sea, seawater
nevez	new
penn	head, point
plou, plo	parish
porz, porzig	anchorage
poul	pool, anchorage
raz	strait, tide race
roc'h	rock
ros	wooded knoll
ruz	red
ster	river, inlet
stiv, stiff	fountain, spring
teven, tevenneg	cliff, dune
toull	hole, deep place
trez, treaz	sand, beach
V (try B, M)	
W (try Gw)	
yoc'h	group of rocks

Index

IALA SYSTEM A BUOYAGE

Lateral marks

Port hand
All red
Topmark (if any): can
Light (if any): red

Starboard hand
All green
Topmark (if any): cone
Light (if any): green

The direction of buoyage in estuaries and port approaches is generally from seaward.

In other areas around the British Isles the general direction of buoyage runs:

Northward along the W coasts and in the Irish Sea
Eastward through the English Channel
Northward through the North Sea
Where there is doubt buoyage direction is shown thus:

Lighted buoys are marked on charts by red pear-shaped flashes

Cardinal marks

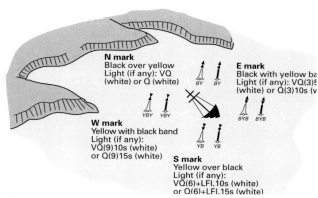

N mark
Black over yellow
Light (if any): VQ (white) or Q (white)

E mark
Black with yellow ba[nd]
Light (if any): VQ(3)5 (white) or Q(3)10s (v

W mark
Yellow with black band
Light (if any):
VQ(9)10s (white)
or Q(9)15s (white)

S mark
Yellow over black
Light (if any):
VQ(6)+LFl.10s (white)
or Q(6)+LFl.15s (white)

Isolated danger marks
(stationed over a danger with navigable water around)
Black with red band
Topmark: 2 black balls
Light (if any): Fl(2) (white)

Special Mark
Body shape optional, yellow
Topmark (if any): Yellow X
Light (if any): Fl.Y etc

Safe water marks
(mid-channel and landfall)
Red with white vertical stripes
Topmark (if any): red ball
Light (if any): Iso, Oc, LFl.10s or Mo(A) (white)

LIGHT CHARACTERISTICS

Abbreviations

Fixed	F.
Occulting	Oc.
Group-occulting	Oc(2)
Isophase	Iso.
Flashing	Fl.
Long-flashing	LFl.
Group-flashing	Fl(2)
Quick-flashing continuously	Q
Interrupted quick-flashing	Q(9)
Very Quick	VQ.
Ultra Quick	UQ.
Morse Code	Mo(F)
Alternating (colours)	Al.WR
Directional	Dir
Fixed and flashing	FFl.

SMALL CRAFT SYMBOLS

The following symbols are used on larger scale charts and plans, and are shown in magenta

- Visitors' moorings
- Visitors' berths
- Yacht marina
- Yacht berth
- Public landing
- Slipway for small craft
- Water tap
- Fuel
- Gas
- Public telephone
- Customs
- Chandlery
- Public house, inn, bar
- Restaurant
- Yacht or sailing club
- Toilets
- Public car park
- Parking for boats/trailers
- Laundrette
- Caravan site
- Camping site
- Nature reserve
- Harbour master
- Post office

ABBREVIATIONS

Bldg	building
Bn	beacon
Bu	blue
CG	coastguard station
	conspic
dest	destroyed
Dir	directional
Dk	dock
Dn	dolphin
dr	dries
ED	existence doubtful
FS	flagstaff
Ft	fort
G	green
h	hour
Ho	house
Ldg	leading
Lk	lock
LB	lifeboat station
M	sea mile(s)
m	metres
min	minutes
Obscd	obscured
Or	orange
PA	position approximate
R	red
Rk	Rock
Rep	reported
s	second(s)
SS	signal station
Stn	station
Vi	violet
vis	visible
W	white